Taking Sides:
Clashing Views in Gender,
Seventh Edition

Elizabeth Schroeder

http://create.mheducation.com

ISBN-10: 1259171035   ISBN-13: 9781259171031

Contents

Preface

As someone who has worked in sexuality education for over 20 years, I firmly believe that the most important topic we can address in sexuality education is one on which we ironically spend the least amount of time: gender. Issues relating to gender have an impact on absolutely every social interaction we have, whether parent–child, sibling-to-sibling, peer-to-peer, partner-to-partner. Knowing another person's gender informs how we approach and interact with them, how we respond when they approach and interact with us. We are taught from our earliest ages what it means to be "a real man" or "a little lady," and the accompanying lessons from parents, peers, teachers, religious leaders, and the media all work to reinforce those messages. This edition of *Taking Sides: Clashing Views in Gender* takes a leap forward in looking at gender in a far more diverse way than ever before, acknowledging the plethora of interactions and life that takes place in the world of the gender binary (male and female), while introducing readers to the unique social, emotional, and legal issues of transgender people.

Changes to This Edition

The seventh edition of *Taking Sides: Clashing Views in Gender* contains dynamic points of view, separated into challenging, often contentious questions. This book outline has changed substantially, with new questions and selections for debating some of the most interesting, contentious topics relating to gender today. Unit openers and issue introductions have been revised accordingly, along with a new *Exploring the Issue* section at the end of each issue.

Taking Sides: Clashing Views in Gender will push learners to look at gender in ways you may never have before. You will be asked to accept the reality that we are not a world of men and women, but of men, women, and transgender people. You will need to consider how you feel about the rights and responsibilities people have based on their gender, in terms of workplace, family, and social interactions. You will be encouraged to go beyond your comfort zone and examine how debating these issues makes you feel, and whether you are movable at all in your points of view.

Acknowledgments First and foremost, I would like to extend an enthusiastic "thank you" to Mary Foust, Product Developer for McGraw-Hill Create, for her flexibility, patience, and support throughout this project. More than an editor, she was a real partner in ensuring this issue had new, cutting-edge, quality content. I also want to thank Senior Product Developer, Jill Meloy, with whom I worked on *Taking Sides: Family and Personal Relationships* years ago, for saying "yes" when I reached out to see whether she needed anyone to work on TS: Gender. I also want to acknowledge my friend and colleague, Dr. Eli Green, who guided me toward some useful topics and authors relating to transgender issues and rights.

Personally, I want to thank my partner, Jennifer, and my 12-year-old son, Matthew, the latter of whom tolerates my never-ending lessons about gender equity, and who gives me hope that his generation will do better than mine has. Last, but most significantly, I need to acknowledge my best friend, Annemarie DeLuca, who, even in stage four lung cancer, cared enough about me and my work to sit and brainstorm ideas with me for interesting topics. She did not do any work relating to gender or human sexuality, yet her input significantly informed the topics that were included in this edition. I only wish she had gotten to see the final product. AM, I dedicate this book to you with gratitude and love.

Editor of This Volume

ELIZABETH SCHROEDER, EdD, MSW, is an award-winning, internationally recognized educator, trainer, and author in the areas of sexuality education pedagogy, LGBTQ issues, working with adolescent boys, using technology and social media to reach and teach young people, and helping parents and other adult caregivers talk with their children about sexuality. She has provided consultation to and direct education and training for schools, parent groups, and youth-serving organizations in countries around the world for more than 20 years.

Dr. Schroeder is the former executive director of Answer, a national sexuality education organization dedicated to providing and promoting unfettered access to comprehensive sexuality education to young people and the adults who teach them. During this time, she represented Answer on the Future of Sex Education initiative, a national partnership between Answer, Advocates for Youth, and the Sexuality Information and Education Council of the United States, which created two seminal resources for sexuality education in the United States: the *National Sexuality Education Standards: Core Content and Skills, Grades K–12* and the *National Teacher Preparation Standards for Sexuality Education*. She previously served as the associate vice president of education and training at Planned Parenthood of New York City, and, before that, as manager of education and special projects at Planned Parenthood Federation of America.

Dr. Schroeder was a cofounding editor of the *American Journal of Sexuality Education,* and has authored or edited numerous publications, including the four-part book series, *Sexuality Education: Past, Present and Future* with Dr. Judy Kuriansky, and *Sexuality Education: Theory and Practice* with Dr. Clint Bruess. She is a frequently sought-out spokesperson and guest blogger in the news media on issues relating to sexual health education and youth development, and has either contributed pieces to or been quoted by *RH Reality Check*, the *New York Times*, the Associated Press, National Public Radio, HuffPost Live, Salon.com, and others.

Dr. Schroeder provides national and international conference keynotes on sexuality and adolescent development, and has received numerous honors throughout her career, including the Healthy Teen Network Carol Mendez Cassell Award for excellence in leadership in sexuality education, the American Association of Sexuality Educators, Counselors and Therapists' Schiller Prize for her approaches to teaching Internet safety to youth, Widener University's William R. Stayton Award in recognition of outstanding contributions to the field of human sexuality, and the Planned Parenthood Mary Lee Tatum Award.

She holds a doctorate of education in human sexuality education from Widener University and a master of social work from NYU, and teaches undergraduate courses at Montclair State University and graduate courses at Widener. Her website is www .drschroe.com.

Academic Advisory Board Members

Members of the Academic Advisory Board are instrumental in the final selection of articles for *Taking Sides* books. Their review of the articles for content, level, and appropriateness provides critical direction to the editors and staff. We think that you will find their careful consideration reflected in this book.

David Chen
Rosemont College

Rose-Marie Chierici
State University of New York–Geneseo

Mirelle Cohen
Olympic College

Ellen Cole
Union Institute and University

Jennifer Cousins
University of Arizona

Keri Diggins
Scottsdale Community College

Heather Dillaway
Wayne State University

Marcia D. Dixson
Indiana University Purdue University

Helen Dosik
California State University–Northridge

April Dye
Carson-Newman College

L. M. Edmonds
Arizona State University

Bernard Frye
University of Texas, Arlington

Elizabeth Gardner
Pine Manor College

Adrienne Gillespie
Weber State University

Bethany Gizzi
Monroe Community College

Ana Maria Goldani
University of California–Los Angeles

Patrick M. Gorman
Edmonds Community College

Jacqueline Greenwood Julien
University of Minnesota–Morris

Brooke Hargreaves-Heald
University of Massachusetts, Lowell

Marissa A. Harrison
Penn State Harrisburg

Don Herrin
University of Utah

Susan Hippensteele
University of Hawaii, Manoa

Alan Hoffner
Kingsborough Community College

William Housel
Northwestern State University

John Howell
Southern Utah University

Bobby Hutchison
Modesto Junior College

Kenneth Johnson
University of South Indiana

Jessica Jones-Coggins
Madison Area Technical College

Jessica Kindred
Hunter College

Kim Kirkpatrick
Fayetteville State University

Jackie Krasas
Lehigh University

Dennis A. Lichty
Wayne State College

Mary Madden
University of Maine

M. M. Maher
Seton Hall University

Sujanet Mason
Luzerne County Community College

Chandra Massner
University of Pikeville

Rodney McDanel
Ivy Tech Community College

Maureen McGarry
Providence College

Deanna Mihaly
Eastern Michigan University

Rose Anna Mueller
Columbia College

Thalia Mulvihill
Ball State University

Mar Navarro
Valencia Community College

Jody Neathery-Castro
University of Nebraska, Omaha

Patricia E. Neff Claster
Edinboro University of Pennsylvania

Katherine Nevins
Bethel University

Nicholas Palomares
University of California Davis

Jane Emery Pather
California State University–Northridge

Jane Petrillo
Kennesaw State University

Leandra Preston
University of Central Florida

Karen Rayne
Austin Community College

Karen Clay Rhines
Northampton Community College

Doug Rice
California State University, Sacramento

Vicki Ritts
St. Louis Community College, Meramec

Louise Rosenberg
University of Hartford

Ava Rosenblum
Normandale Community College

Brittney Schrick
Southern Arkansas University

Barbara Seater
Raritan Valley Community College

Marla Selvidge
University of Central Missouri

Helena Semerjian
Worcester State University

Maya Sen
Northern Michigan University

Laura Shea Doolan
Molloy College

Deborah Sundmacher
University of San Diego

George Teschner
Christopher Newport University

Shelley Theno
University of Alaska, Anchorage

Kourtney Vaillancourt
New Mexico State University

Richard Valente
Long Island University, C. W. Post Campus

Salena Van Cleef
Prairie State College

Katherine Van Wormer
University of Northern Iowa

Glenda Warren
University of the Cumberlands

Casey Welch
Flagler College

Ellen Weller
The College of New Jersey

Rebecca Wells
Alvin Community College

Marie A. Whaley
Kent State University–Salem Campus

Nancy Williams
Wofford College

Whitney Womack Smith
Miami University–Hamilton

Sherri Zazueta
Kentucky State University

Introduction

The Taking Sides series asks readers to evaluate opposing viewpoints on specific topics, and express those views, either verbally or in writing. Regardless of how you will be using this volume, it is important to reflect on the ways in which we can express our opinions effectively. It is also important to be aware of how language is used to express these views, at times clearly revealing the politics behind an argument and at other times cleverly obscuring the political agenda. Finally, it is vital to reflect on how differences of opinion affect our lives—in particular, when these differences involve issues relating to gender.

Negotiation Versus Debate: Finding a Place on the Continuum

The most successful negotiations are between people of opposing viewpoints who are able to be flexible, compromising to the extent they believe they can while still remaining true to the goals of the particular negotiation process. We see this in the workplace when an employee is requesting a higher salary. We see this in educational settings when a student disagrees with an instructor's assessment of a paper or project. We see this globally in international peace processes. A supervisor may say, "I can't give you a 10 percent raise, but I can give you 5 percent." An instructor may not be able to raise a student's grade, but may be willing to offer the student an extra-credit assignment. A leader of one country may not be able to offer as much to the leader of another country, but may be able to expand import/export relations. If both sides have done their homework, they know how much the other has to leverage, which is also key in successful negotiation.

A debate, however, is quite different from a negotiation. The most interesting debates are between people with diametrically opposing viewpoints on a given subject and who are well-versed in the other person's views. An absolutist view, with no room for questioning one's tenets or beliefs, may be judged as inflexible in some social circles, yet is quite effective when one is involved in a debate. Political candidates emphasize this quite well during a campaign. A candidate who is clear and consistent in her viewpoints will likely be seen as a clear, consistent policymaker. A candidate who changes his mind on one or more issues will be seen as "waffling."

Desire and Reality: The "Should Be" versus the "Is"

In debate, there is an inherent concept about which we are often not even aware—the "should be" versus the "is." Simply put, the "should be" is what we would like the outcome to be in a particular situation. The "is" refers to what the current state of that situation truly is.

We express our views in terms of what we think is, or would be, best. When this reflects the reality of a given situation, it is thought to be congruent with the "is"—or what is actually happening. "Congruent," however, is not synonymous with "right." For example, if a person were to say, "I think only men should be president of the United States," his opinion would be congruent with the current reality. A viewpoint can often carry additional weight because the opposing viewpoint, that a woman should be president, has not yet happened. As a result, this opinion can be seen as less valid or lacking in strength. Do not fall into this trap! Compelling arguments that are based in sound logic can gain widespread support—and can even have the power to change a society.

Basically, in debate, the "is" should not necessarily trump the "should be"—nor should it trump the "was." You may have heard someone argue a point based solely on past experience, explaining that if something "has always been this way" it should not change. Many of us have had experiences with parents and grandparents beginning a statement with, "In my day, we. . . ." It is tempting to discount these statements as outdated or otherwise inapplicable—yet it is important to remember that our values and beliefs are based very strongly and solidly in how we were raised. Our "was," as it were.

Recognizing the Language of Political Viewpoints

Oftentimes, we will read or listen to an opinion that we believe to be mainstream, but it is actually coming from either conservative or liberal ideology. How do we sort through the language to know whose viewpoint we are actually reading? If we are reading a piece online that is representing a particular organization, we can select the "who we are" or "about us" link to reveal the ideology. Sometimes, this ideology is based in religious teachings. When this language talks explicitly about God or Christianity, for example, the bias of the group will be clear. There is, however, more subtle language that tends to express a conservative ideology. A group whose mission operates around "concern for the American family," that "champions marriage and family as the foundation of civilization," that talks about there being a "gay agenda" is most likely going to have conservative viewpoints.

A group that is more liberal will use language reflecting its views as well. If the group's mission uses language that consists of having the "right to choose," refers to protecting people's "civil rights," helping people "make informed and responsible decisions," and about empowering certain groups of people who are not in the power majority, those organizations will be more moderate to liberal.

Perhaps the greatest influencer on gender roles throughout history has been religion. Regardless of whether one belongs to an organized religious group, our country was founded on religious principles. It is ironic that one of the reasons why the original pilgrims came to America was for religious freedoms, and yet religion continues to be used as justification to influence, control, and even discriminate against others. Religion is often invoked by public officials in the United States, where the phrase "In God We Trust" appears on our money, and where every speech made by the President ends with, "God bless us, and God bless the United States of America." The assumption of religiosity is significant; a person who has strong religious values and beliefs cannot help but see the world through the lens of those values and beliefs. As you read, therefore, try to recognize where religious teaching comes in. Some religions, in particular Christian religion, use their texts and teachings to reinforce gender role stereotypes. Women and men are, they say, inherently different and their differences make them unequal by design, with men being superior to women. How do you think it must feel to be a member of one of those religious groups and believe in their religious teachings while disagreeing with their social viewpoints?

Debating Gender: Power and Privilege

The first question we ask when a baby is born is, "Is it a boy or a girl?" The answer to this question comes from a quick glance to that child's genitals. The proclamation, "it's a boy" or "it's a girl" starts a lifetime of gendered roles and interactions that play out in the classroom, on the playground, within the family, in the workplace, in adult relationships, in the media, and throughout the world in which one lives. This sex that is assigned to us at birth is, in most cases, the gender we understand ourselves to be. Most people in the world are cisgender, meaning

their biological sex matches their inner sense of who they are, or their gender identity. In some cases, however, the two do not match, and someone may identify as transgender. In other cases, a person's genitals may imply they are a boy or a girl, when in fact, their chromosomal and genital composition is more diverse, and they may be intersex (the old, now offensive term for intersex people is "hermaphrodite").

Gender is at the heart of all of our human interactions, regardless of whether we are cognizant of or intentional about this. Our interactions with other people are gendered—how we approach our work, how we parent children, how we engage in dating rituals or sexual encounters. From birth, we are actors who are given a script from the greater culture that tells us how to talk, talk, dress, and carry ourselves—whether it is acceptable to feel or show emotions; to possess or express particular character traits, such as happiness or anger, aggression or tenderness. A baby who is pronounced a girl will be given toys and clothing of one type and color; boys will be given toys and clothing of another. We use terms like "opposite" sex to imply that men and women are inherent, biological adversaries, reinforcing again that there are only men and women, rather than several sexes, several genders.

The idea of fulfilling gender role stereotypes is actually more than an idea, it is a set of requirements that is as stringent for boys as it is for girls. The rewards for following the script versus improvising from or completely changing it can be quite dramatic. In some cases, boys and girls who fulfill gender role stereotypes are praised; in other cases, they are criticized for not being more open. Girls and women who play sports, participate in activities or do work that have traditionally been reserved for boys and men are seen as strong—improving themselves, and making the world a better place for all girls and women. Other girls and women will disagree, feeling strongly about fulfilling the gender role that was dictated to them. These girls and women are sometimes ostracized or minimized. Boys and men who participate in activities or do work that have traditionally been reserved for boys and women are seen as weak—limiting themselves, not "real" boys or men. Although there has been a great deal of progress over the years, it is still not uncommon to hear high school sports coaches "motivate" their male athletes by calling those who are not performing as well as the others, "girls." Some kids, regardless of gender, will still tell a boy that he "throws like a girl" as an insult. The accompanying message for boys and men is that the worst thing one can be is a girl or a woman; for girls and women, that they will never be good enough.

Another complicating factor is that people tend to confuse gender with sexual orientation—when the two are quite different. Sexual orientation has to do with the gender(s) of people to whom we are attracted, physically and romantically. There are misconceptions that a feminine-acting man is gay; that a masculine-presenting woman is lesbian. Although sometimes this is the case, not all lesbian and gay people fulfill those stereotypes, just as not all heterosexual men are extremely masculine or heterosexual women are extremely feminine. While this edition of Taking Sides focuses exclusively on gender, it is important to reflect on how clearly our societies' needs for clear, defined, rigid gender roles is linked to homophobia—the irrational fear or hatred of or discomfort with people who are or are perceived to be lesbian, gay, or bisexual. The use of "girl" to insult a boy implies that boys who are not masculine are gay—one of the most common, feared insults that can be foisted upon or received by boys, even before they understand what sexual orientation is—or, for that matter, understand their own sexual orientation.

Add to this gender binary equation the reality check that there is NOT a gender binary—there are men, women, and intersex people; that people are male, female, transgender, or something else altogether. The human experience is extremely diverse—and as much as that diversity can serve to delight and fascinate some people, when it comes to gender, there is far greater discomfort and fear. But the idea of there being more than men and women feels threatening to many people—and the resulting transphobia (similar to homophobia, but this time applied to people who are or are perceived to be transgender) has given rise to overt discrimination and in some cases violence.

In reviewing and discussing the issues raised in this book, it is important to look at the hierarchy of power and privilege that comes up when examining and exploring gender. In the United States, the highest echelon of power has historically remained and still remains with white, heterosexual, wealthy, Christian men. This population is the majority of our representation in our federal, state, and local governments. It is the majority of business leaders throughout our country. Although being a part of this power majority does not necessarily indicate a possession of bias or disdain for others, it would be impossible for members of this group to not see the world through a privileged lens. The language of our country's founding documents reflects the morals and values of the time—as seen and dictated by men. The laws by which our public and, sometimes, private behaviors are regulated have historically been made by men, although that has begun to change. Centuries later, there is still an inherent inequality in how the country should be run. The ironic thing is that while many men believe in creating restrictive laws for women, there are many women who agree with and support them. And whenever there is social progress, there is backlash, a strong desire to put things back to the way they were.

Further, in considering the power and privilege certain groups have, it is impossible to talk about gender privilege without talking about race, ethnicity, culture, physical and mental ability, age, and the many other groups that are represented in the United States. With each additional layer of diversity in the United States, people seem to move farther and farther away from the benefits enjoyed by the power majority. To be sure, there are more women in government than ever before; more men and women of color represented in business, and at higher levels of management and leadership. But when considering American society as a whole, not just the governing bodies and businesses that steer our economy, there are still disparities—in education, in health, in education, in income, and more.

Issues in This Volume

This volume of Taking Sides is segmented into four units. We look at issues of gender in education, examining whether and how boys and girls learn differently, looking at brain research and professional experiences of those with experiences working with youth. We examine whether single-sex educational institutions and programmatic institutions should still exist, and consider the impact gendering education has on transgender and other gender-nonconforming people. We are taken into the workplace, examining disparities in earning between men and women and exploring the rights of transgender people to work in an environment free of harassment—as well as those who do not believe they should be protected. We look at some of the myriad issues affecting parents and the state of parenting, exploring the impact the gender or genders of parents and caregivers have on young people, whether parents should be able to choose the biological sex of their baby, and whether same-sex parents are as strong parents as different-sex parents. We examine the diversity of gender in the world around us, with issues raised that are as diverse as gender itself. Ranging from gender and competition to women as religious leaders to much more, this unit examines issues that many people may have never considered reflecting on before.

Conclusion

The ways in which gender has been addressed, acknowledged, treated—or blatantly ignored—over the centuries is inconsistent. Where do the lines exist around gender roles and value? Where are they blurred? Biological sex is an easy topic to discuss—it has to do with what features are a part of the human body. A person's chromosomes, body parts, and reproductive capacity are all part of designating that person's biological sex. Currently, our designations for biological sex include men, women, and intersex people.

Gender, however, is far more complex. It begins first and foremost with our inner sense of who we are—our gender identity. In most cases, biological sex will match gender identity—most people are, therefore, cisgender. In some cases, however, that is not the case—a person will have physical characteristics that result in their categorization as one sex, when on the inside, they feel quite differently. Sometimes, there will be a complete opposite across a gender binary: a person will have a vulva, XX chromosomes, and ovaries, yet feel like he is male. This person may identify as transgender and elect to have surgery to correct this incongruence. Some people may feel this way and not alter their bodies much or even at all. Being transgender is not always about men becoming women and women becoming men. There is a whole lot of gray in between these two extremes that better fits some people's concept of who they are.

This describes a person's internal experience; gender is far more complicated, however, because it has such a significant external component. Gender scripts are how we are told to behave and interact in the world. Gender roles are how we behave. Although there has been some movement toward being more flexible about these gender norms, particularly with babies and children, the need for clarity and order becomes more pronounced as a person gets older, and is far more valued in adulthood. Diversity can be seen as exciting and valuable by some; intimidating and even terrifying by others.

Regardless of the beliefs we have relating to gender, our arguments must have reason behind them. Many people can recall asking for a reason why they had to do something their parents said they had to do, and receiving the infuriating response, "Because I said so." This response only worked because of the power difference between parent and child. True debate should more thoroughly explore and express rational, sound reasoning. For some, "I think," or "I believe," will suffice. Others will justify their arguments form an experiential standpoint, as in, "I have learned from my 20 years as a public school teacher that. . . ." Some people need simply to identify themselves with a category; for example, a person who says, "As a transgender man, I know that. . . ." Still others will use religion and religious doctrine, as mentioned earlier. For some, the New Testament, Qur'an, Torah, or other religious text is brought out to "trump" any other argument, challenging one's opponents to argue with God—or at least, with the debater's sense of what or who God is and represents.

No matter what we believe, we must listen to people whose views are different from our own. We need to think before expressing ourselves. And we need to express ourselves confidently, but respectfully.

Unit 1

UNIT

Gender and Education

*T*he educational landscape in the United States has changed significantly over the past century, at the elementary, secondary, and post-secondary levels. School used to be available only to boys and men; later, it became accessible to girls and women. Single-sex schools and universities were the norm, mostly for men. These were largely—but not entirely—replaced by co-educational institutions, after which there was a resurgence of single-sex institutions—this time emphasizing the need for women to study in environments that were more nurturing and supportive of their academic needs and development. Since the dawn of formal education, teachers have been looking to find the most effective ways of teaching their students. In recent years, this has included looking at how children learn.

Beyond learning intelligences and styles, brain research has demonstrated some similarities and differences in biologically male and female brains. This includes how male and female students use technology in the classroom. Should these differences inform how we teach children? Or does doing so reinforce gender role stereotypes for students of all genders? Is there any brain research looking at how transgender students learn best? This section examines the pros and cons to gendering education—by using different teaching methods for male and female learners, and by offering single-sex schools, classrooms, and educational interventions. As you read, pay close attention to how the authors use similar research to represent quite different viewpoints. Think about your own school experiences growing up. What was the gender representation in your classes? Did you notice whether this had an impact on learning? How might it be similar or different today?

Selected, Edited, and with Issue Framing Material by:
Elizabeth Schroeder, EdD, MSW, *Elizabeth Schroeder Consulting*

ISSUE

Do Boys and Girls Learn Differently?

YES: **Madhura Ingalhalikar et al.**, from "Sex Differences in the Structural Connectome of the Human Brain." *Proceedings of the National Academy of Sciences of the United States of America* (2013)

NO: **Sara Mead**, from "The Problem with Gender-Based Education." *The Early Childhood Watch Blog,* New America Foundation (2008)

Learning Outcomes

After reading this issue, you will be able to:

- Describe at least two biological differences between how boys and girls learn, according to the brain research cited by Ingalhalikar et al.
- Explain at least two ways in which Mead refutes the use of brain-based research to explain learning differences between boys and girls.
- Identify at least two ways in which information about gender and the brain can be used while avoiding reinforcing gender role stereotypes.

ISSUE SUMMARY

YES: Dr. Madhura Ingalhalikar and colleagues found in their research that adolescent male and female brains are different, with male brains connecting perception and coordinated action more effectively than female brains, female brains connecting analytical and intuitive processing more effectively than male brains.

NO: Sara Mead works to debunk the work of Michael Gurian and Leonard Sax, both of whom are strong proponents of gender-based interventions and learning strategies, emphasizing that they are not neuroscientists themselves.

Human beings have always been intrigued by how the body works. Although we have learned a great deal thanks to the advent of technology about the organs that keep us alive and functioning, people have had a whole range of beliefs about our organs throughout time. Thousands of years ago, the brain was not seen as a particularly valuable organ—the heart was most important, and not simply because of how it keeps us alive. Some ancient societies believed the heart was where our goodness was contained, and after death, would weigh it to "know" how good or evil a person had been in life. As early as 300 B.C., however, biologists determined that the brain is where intelligence was contained. In the 1600s, scientists determined that different parts of the brain controlled different aspects of

who we are—thought, motor control, speech, personality, and so on. Beyond physical science was the development of psychiatry in the late 1890s and early 1900s. During this time, Sigmund Freud devoted most of his career to understanding the subconscious mind, and French psychologists were addressing how children learn with the first intelligence tests for children. In the 1950s, we learned that the brain did not sleep when we slept, that in fact it was extremely active throughout the sleep cycle.

For a very long time, the conventional wisdom was that the vast majority of brain development happened during childhood—that whatever and however a person developed happened intensely and completely in childhood, and then slowed down as one continued to age. With the development of the EEG in the 1920s and the

MRI, scientists have been able to learn more about brain functioning than ever before. More recent research on how the brain works and how people learn has morphed and grown, and our capacity to understand cranial functioning has improved.

Brain development is thought by some to be synonymous with the word "learning." By this definition, learning is "the process of creating, strengthening, and discarding connections among the neurons; these connections are called synapses" (Child Welfare Information Gateway, 2009). Synapses are responsible for everything we do—whether we are breathing, eating, sleeping, thinking, feeling our emotions—the brain is in charge. At birth, the synapses we possess are about survival—so we start with synapses that enable us to breathe, eat, and sleep, and for all of our vital organs to function.

These synapses develop very quickly during the first three years of life. In fact, a healthy child may create 2 million synapses per second (*Zero to Three,* 2009). By the time they reach their third year, children's brains have approximately 1,000 trillion synapses. Since this is more than a person will ever need, some are naturally eliminated by the body (Shonkoff & Phillips, 2000). By the time children reach adolescence, they have the synapses they will have for the remainder of their lives—even though the brain itself will continue to develop throughout a person's life span. This is what enables us to continue to learn from our experiences, as well as in more formal educational settings, and to adapt to new situations or surroundings as conditions change (Ackerman, 2007).

There is so much we do not know about how the human brain works. As a result, psychologists and other professionals over the years have spent a great deal of time observing, studying, and theorizing about children and the learning process. Perhaps the best known of these psychologists is Jean Piaget, who broke down the learning process into four stages, from childbirth through age 16. While at the youngest ages, learning centers around survival—how to breastfeed and eat solid food, who they can trust, how to communicate their basic needs such as a diaper change, during toddlerhood, children start to realize there is a world around them to be explored—even if at that age they are egocentric in their worldview. How does

what's going on around me have an impact on me? Children are very curious during their pre-school/elementary school years, ask a lot of questions, and are interested in exploring the world around them.

Until around late middle school age, children are primarily concrete thinkers. What this means, basically, is "what you see is what you get." They are able to consider issues and solve problem, but mostly in very basic, logic and linear ways. It is not until their brains have developed a bit more that they can think more abstractly and consider things like hypothetical situations. This is why when a child breaks a toy and a parent yells, "What were you thinking?" the child seems so confused. Quite simply, the child was not thinking about consequences—he was just thinking, in that moment, that it made sense to break the toy, perhaps to see what would happen, perhaps out of frustration, or perhaps for no reason whatsoever.

There has been a great deal of research done over the years on brain development and whether a person's brain is different based on her or his biological sex. Similarities and differences have been found relating to how men and women communicate, process various emotions, think and learn—yet what remains up to debate are the implications of that research. Some people affirm unquestionably that the brain research demonstrates that boys and girls learn differently, and therefore we should either consider single-sex schools or teach to boys and girls differently. Others argue that because of our country's history with and ongoing sexism in which boys and men typically had greater access to education and higher quality education, separating learning by gender is also sexist. This idea of schools being able to be "separate but equal" is seen by these proponents as prejudicial, and ends up doing a disservice to girls.

In these selections, Dr. Madhura Ingalhalikar and colleagues find that "male" brains connect some aspects of learning more effectively than "female" brains, and vice versa. The accompanying question as you read must be, if that is the case, what are the implications for learning? Sara Mead maintains that neuroscientists are not intending for their work to inform education, and that there is not enough in the research to merit dividing learners by gender in order to reach them more efficiently.

YES ↵

Madhura Ingalhalikar et al.

Sex Differences in the Structural Connectome of the Human Brain

Sex differences in human behavior show adaptive complementarity: Males have better motor and spatial abilities, whereas females have superior memory and social cognition skills. Studies also show sex differences in human brains but do not explain this complementarity. In this work, we modeled the structural connectome using diffusion tensor imaging in a sample of 949 youths (aged 8–22 y, 428 males and 521 females) and discovered unique sex differences in brain connectivity during the course of development. Connection-wise statistical analysis, as well as analysis of regional and global network measures, presented a comprehensive description of network characteristics. In all supratentorial regions, males had greater within-hemispheric connectivity, as well as enhanced modularity and transitivity, whereas between-hemispheric connectivity and cross-module participation predominated in females. However, this effect was reversed in the cerebellar connections. Analysis of these changes developmentally demonstrated differences in trajectory between males and females mainly in adolescence and in adulthood. Overall, the results suggest that male brains are structured to facilitate connectivity between perception and coordinated action, whereas female brains are designed to facilitate communication between analytical and intuitive processing modes.

Sex differences are of enduring scientific and societal interest because of their prominence in the behavior of humans and nonhuman species[1]. Behavioral differences may stem from complementary roles in procreation and social structure; examples include enhanced motor and spatial skills and greater proclivity for physical aggression in males and enhanced verbally mediated memory and social cognition in females[2,3]. With the advent of neuroimaging, multiple studies have found sex differences in the brain[4] that could underlie the behavioral differences. Males have larger crania, proportionate to their larger body size, and a higher percentage of white matter (WM), which contains myelinated axonal fibers, and cerebrospinal fluid[5], whereas women demonstrate a higher percentage of gray matter after correcting for intracranial volume effect[6]. Sex differences in the relative size and shape of specific brain structures have also been reported[7], including the hippocampus, amygdala[8,9], and corpus callosum (CC)[10]. Furthermore, developmental differences in tissue growth suggest that there is an anatomical sex difference during maturation[11,12], although links to observed behavioral differences have not been established.

Recent studies have used diffusion tensor imaging (DTI) to characterize WM architecture and underlying fiber tracts by exploiting the anisotropic water diffusion in WM[13–15]. Examination of DTI-based scalar measures[16] of fractional anisotropy (FA) and mean diffusivity (MD) has demonstrated diverse outcomes that include increased FA and decreased MD in males in major WM regions[17–19], higher CC-specific FA in females[20,21], and lower axial and

Significance

Sex differences are of high scientific and societal interest because of their prominence in behavior of humans and nonhuman species. This work is highly significant because it studies a very large population of 949 youths (8–22 y, 428 males and 521 females) using the diffusion-based structural connectome of the brain, identifying novel sex differences. The results establish that male brains are optimized for intrahemispheric and female brains for interhemispheric communication. The developmental trajectories of males and females separate at a young age, demonstrating wide differences during adolescence and adulthood. The observations suggest that male brains are structured to facilitate connectivity between perception and coordinated action, whereas female brains are designed to facilitate communication between analytical and intuitive processing modes.

Madhura Ingalhalikar et al., "Sex Differences in the Structural Connectome of the Human Brain," *Proceedings of the National Academy of Sciences,* vol. 11, Issue 2, November 1, 2013, Pages 823–828. Copyright © 2013 National Academy of Sciences. All rights reserved. Used with permission.

radial diffusivity measures[22] in males. Throughout the developmental period, females displayed higher FA and lower MD in the midadolescent age (12–14 y)[23], and this result was established on a larger sample size (114 subjects) as well[24]. On the other hand, sex differences on the entire age range (childhood to old age) demonstrated higher FA and lower MD in males[19,25,26]. Similar findings of higher FA in males were obtained with tractography on major WM tracts[27,28].

Rather than investigating individual regions or tracts in isolation, the brain can be analyzed on the whole as a large and complex network known as the human connectome[29]. This connectome has the capability to provide fundamental insights into the organization and integration of brain networks[30]. Advances in fiber tractography with diffusion imaging can be used to understand complex interactions among brain regions and to compute a structural connectome (SC)[31]. Similar functional connectomes (FCs) can be computed using modalities like functional MRI, magnetoencephalography, and EEG. Differences in FCs have revealed sex differences and sex-by-hemispheric interactions[32], with higher local functional connectivity in females than in males[33]. Although SCs of genders have displayed small-world architecture with broad-scale characteristics[34,35], sex differences in network efficiency have been reported[36], with women having greater overall cortical connectivity[37]. Insignificant differences between the genders were observed in a recent study on SCs of 439 subjects ranging in age from 12–30 y[38]. However, detailed analysis on a very large sample is needed to elucidate sex differences in networks reliably, as is provided in this study. Using connection-wise regional and lobar analyses of DTI-based SCs of 949 healthy young individuals, we present a comprehensive study of developmental sex differences in brain connectivity.

Results

We present results from a cohort of 949 healthy subjects aged 8–22 y (mean ± SD = 15.11 ± 3.50 y), including 428 males (mean ± SD = 14.94 ± 3.54 y) and 521 females (mean ± SD = 15.25 ± 3.47 y) (demographic details are provided in Table 1). The DTI for creating SCs was performed at a b value of 1,000 s/mm^2 with 64 gradient directions on a Siemens 3T Verio scanner. Creating the SCs involved parcellating the brain into 95 regions (68 cortical and 27 subcortical) using a high-resolution T1 image, followed by interregional probabilistic fiber tractography, which provides the connection probability between regions, leading to the construction of the 95 × 95 network matrix called the SC of the brain.

Table 1

Subject Demographics

Race	Male		Female		Total	
Caucasian, not Hispanic	212	22.3%	206	21.7%	418	44.0%
Caucasian, Hispanic	8	0.8%	6	0.6%	14	1.5%
African American, not Hispanic	150	15.8%	234	24.7%	384	40.5%
African American, Hispanic	2	0.2%	7	0.7%	9	0.9%
Asian, not Hispanic	1	0.1%	9	0.9%	10	1.0%
Mixed/other, not Hispanic	37	3.9%	35	3.7%	72	7.6%
Mixed/other, Hispanic	18	1.9%	24	2.5%	42	4.4%
Total	428	45.1%	521	54.9%	949	100.0%
Mean age, y (SD)	14.9	(3.5)	15.3	(3.5)	15.1	(3.5)

Connection-wise analysis of these SC network matrices, followed by an examination of network properties using global, lobar, and regional measures, was performed. Because the age range in this population is large, to examine developmental sex differences, the population was divided into three groups, such that they have balanced sample sizes: group 1 (8–13.3 y, 158 females and 156 males), group 2 (13.4–17 y, 180 females and 131 males), and group 3 (17.1–22 y, 183 females and 141 males). These groups correspond roughly to the developmental stages of childhood, adolescence, and young adulthood. Connection-wise and global analyses were performed in each group. Details are given in *Materials and Methods*.

Connection-Wise Analysis. Linear regression was applied to each of the connections in the SC matrix on sex, age, and age–sex interaction. Permutation testing (20,000 permutations over all the edges in the network taken together) was used to address the problem of multiple comparisons in the connection-based network analysis. This analysis revealed conspicuous and significant sex differences that suggest fundamentally different connectivity patterns in males and females. Most supratentorial connections that were stronger in males than females were intrahemispheric (permutation-tested $P < 0.05$). In contrast, most supratentorial connections that were stronger in females were interhemispheric. However, in the cerebellum, the opposite pattern prevailed, with males showing stronger connections between the left cerebellar hemisphere and the contralateral cortex.

Developmental differences were studied based on the three groups described above. Connection-based analysis revealed a progression of sex differences. The youngest group (aged 8–13.3 y) demonstrated a few increased intrahemispheric connections in males and increased interhemispheric connections in females, suggesting the beginning of a divergence in developmental trajectory. This was supported by the results from the adolescent group (aged 13.4–17 y), as well as from the young adult group, where sex differences were more pronounced, with increased interhemispheric and intrahemispheric connectivity in females and males, respectively. However, in the adolescent group, the significant interhemispheric connections displayed by the females were concentrated in the frontal lobe, whereas during adulthood, females showed fewer significant edges that were dispersed across all the lobes.

Hemispheric and Lobar Connectivity. The connection-wise analysis of the SCs can be quantified at the lobar level by the hemispheric connectivity ratio (*HCR*). The *HCR* is computed for each lobe and quantifies the dominance of intra- or interhemispheric connections in the network matrices, with a higher lobar *HCR* indicating an increased connection of that lobe within the hemisphere. We found significantly higher *HCRs* in males in the left frontal ($P < 0.0001$, $T = 4.85$), right frontal ($P < 0.0001$, $T = 5.33$), left temporal ($P < 0.0001$, $T = 4.56$), right temporal ($P < 0.0001$, $T = 4.63$), left parietal ($P < 0.0001$, $T = 4.31$), and right parietal ($P < 0.0001$, $T = 4.59$) lobes, indicating that males had stronger intrahemispheric connections bilaterally.

We also computed the magnitude of connectivity using the lobar connectivity weight (*LCW*). The *LCW* quantifies the connection weight between any two lobes. Consistent with the network differences observed and the *HCR* results, interlobar *LCW* in the same hemisphere was stronger in males, whereas left-to-right frontal lobe connectivity was higher in females (Table 2).

High Modularity and Transitivity in Males. Of the several indices of network integrity[39], two measures of segregation, modularity and transitivity, are particularly well suited for describing differences in network organization. Modularity describes how well a complex neural system can be delineated into coherent building blocks (subnetworks). Transitivity characterizes the connectivity of a given region to its neighbors. Higher transitivity indicates a greater tendency for nodes to form numerous

Table 2

LCW Differences between Genders

Connection	T statistic	P value
LF-LF	5.06	<0.000001
LF-LT	5.06	<0.000001
LF-LP	7.29	<0.000001
LT-LT	7.15	<0.000001
LT-LP	5.07	<0.000001
LT-LO	5.95	0.000001
LP-LP	6.78	<0.000001
LP-LO	4.03	0.000061
LO-LO	4.89	<0.000001
LF-RF	−4.74	0.0000024
RF-RF	5.63	<0.000001
RF-RT	5.02	<0.000001
RF-RP	7.39	<0.000001
RT-RT	5.65	<0.000001
RT-RP	4.77	0.000002
RT-RO	5.26	<0.000001
RP-RP	5.83	<0.000001
RP-RO	3.22	0.00013
RO-RO	3.78	0.00017

A positive *T* statistic indicates that the male group had higher value than the female group, and vice versa. F, frontal; L, left; O, occipital; P, parietal; R, right; T, temporal.

strongly connected communities. Both modularity and transitivity were globally higher in males (*T* statistic = 6.1 and 5.9, $P < 0.0001$, respectively), consistent with stronger intrahemispheric connectivity. Global transitivity was higher in males among all three groups (children: $T = 3.1$, $P = 0.003$; adolescents: $T = 4.9$, $P < 0.0001$; young adults: $T = 3.7$, $P = 0.0003$), whereas global modularity was significantly higher in adolescents and young adult males ($T = 5.1$, $P < 0.0001$ and $T = 2.7$, $P = 0.005$, respectively). Transitivity was also computed at the lobar level for the entire population to quantify the density of the clustered brain networks in each lobe. Local transitivity was higher in males [significant in frontal lobe, $T = $ (left) 3.97, (right) 4.13; significant in temporal lobe, $T = $ (left) 4.96, (right) 4.09; all $P < 0.0001$] suggesting stronger intralobar connectivity.

Differences in Participation Coefficients. Finally, we examined the participation coefficient (*PC*) of each individual regional node of the SC. The *PC* is close to one if

Table 3

Sex Differences in *PC*s

Node	Left	Right
	T statistic	
Frontal pole	−6.23711	−6.01209
Pars opercularis	−5.28418	−5.55390
Paracentral	−4.12355	
Superior frontal	−4.82684	−4.96510
Precentral	−3.91810	−3.89022
Supramarginal		−4.53635
Lateral orbitofrontal	−4.32909	
Inferior parietal	−5.30166	−4.52717
Rostral middle frontal		−4.05266
Superior parietal	−5.29189	−4.52765
Entorhinal	−5.54515	−4.65705
Bank of superior temporal sulcus	−5.11583	−6.70404
Pericalcarine	−4.39314	−3.62391
Temporal pole	−3.96837	
Caudate	−4.67867	−5.41545
Putamen	−3.88072	−5.51831
Pars triangularis	−3.91473	
Cerebellum	4.50010	3.69553

The t test on *PC*s revealed that many nodes have higher *PC*s in females than in males, except for the cerebellum, which has a higher *PC* in males.

its connections are uniformly distributed among all the lobes, and it is zero if all links connect within its own lobe. We found that numerous regions in the frontal, parietal, and temporal lobes had significantly higher *PC*s in females than in males (Table 3), whereas the cerebellum was the only region that displayed higher *PC*s in males.

Discussion

The study examined sex differences in a large population of 949 youths by comprehensively analyzing the diffusion-based SCs of the brain. Because the population has a large age range (8–22 y), we also examined the sex differences during the course of development. Our analysis resulted in several findings, some confirming earlier hypotheses and some providing unique insight into sex differences that were not possible with alternate modalities and forms of analysis.

The myelinated axons of WM facilitate distant signal conduction. Previous data from structural imaging showed

a higher proportion of cortical WM in the males, except in the CC[40,41]. A higher proportion of myelinated fibers within hemispheres in males compared with an equal or larger volume of WM in the callosum suggests that male brains are optimized for communicating within the hemispheres, whereas female brains are optimized for interhemispheric communication. Our analysis overwhelmingly supported this hypothesis at every level (global, lobar, and regional) and also revealed unique sex and developmental differences in the SC. Centered on connection-based analysis, we established that male brains are indeed structured to facilitate intrahemispheric cortical connectivity, although the opposite was observed in the cerebellum. In contrast, female brains displayed higher interhemispheric connectivity. The results of connection-based analysis are supported by the values of the *HCR* and *LCW* computed for the connectomes. Males had a higher *HCR* in the frontal, temporal, and parietal lobes bilaterally, indicating a higher connection within the hemisphere and within lobes. The *LCW* quantifies the relationship between lobes, with the males having higher within-hemisphere and across-lobe connections. In females, both of the values indicated across-hemispheric lobar connections.

With the aim of identifying at what stage of development these sex differences manifest themselves, we analyzed the population in three groups that align with childhood, adolescence, and young adulthood. The connectivity profiles showed an early separation between the developmental trajectories of the two genders, with adolescent and young adult males displaying higher intrahemispheric connectivity and females of the same age displaying higher interhemispheric connectivity. Although the dominance of intrahemispheric connectivity in males was established early on and preserved throughout the course of development, interhemispheric connectivity dominance in females was seen mainly in the frontal lobe during adolescence but was more dispersed across the lobes during adulthood. Also, the gradual decrease of the dominance of interhemispheric connectivity in adulthood is most likely due to the fact that the interhemispheric connections are of lower strength than the intrahemispheric connections. The lack of a significant age-by-sex interaction in the connection-based analysis suggests that although there are not statistically significant differences in the trajectory of developmental effects between males and females, analyses of age groups allows the description of the magnitude of the sex difference during the stages of development.

In addition to the connection-wise analysis, we investigated two complementary network measures, modularity and transitivity, at the global level and found these to be higher in males than in females. These measures quantify the sparsity of the connectome, that is, how easily it can be divided into subnetworks. A high lobar-level transitivity points to a region's neighbors being more strongly connected to each other within each lobe. A higher lobar transitivity showed that local clustering into subnetworks was high in males, resulting in an increased global modularity. This is indicative again of the enhanced local, short range within lobe connectivity in males compared with females. Analysis of the three age-related groups demonstrated males having a higher global transitivity at all age ranges, with the high global modularity in the later years past the age of 13.1 y. This suggests that the preadolescent male brains are potentially beginning to reorganize and optimize certain subnetworks, displaying significant enhancement in modularity only in adolescence. Dense networks are thus observed in adolescence that continue to optimize into adulthood. On the contrary, females begin to develop higher long-range connectivity (mainly interhemispheric).

Our observations of increased participation coefficients in females is consistent with global measures of modularity, transitivity, *HCR*, and *LCW* (Table 2), all of which indicated increased intrahemispheric connectivity in males and interhemispheric connectivity in females. For example, lower modularity in females was corroborated by an increased regional participation coefficient (Table 3), which indicated that certain regions (frontal, temporal, and parietal lobes) had greater across-lobe connectivity in females; notably, this was mainly between lobes in different hemispheres as shown via the *HCR*. Conversely, the cerebellum, which exerts its influence on ipsilateral motor behavior through connectivity to contralateral supratentorial areas, was the only structure with the opposite pattern. This was confirmed via connection-based analysis, which showed the left cerebellum to be connected significantly to the lobes contralaterally in males, as well as through the participation coefficient of the cerebellum, which was significantly higher in males.

Taken together, these results reveal fundamental sex differences in the structural architecture of the human brain. Male brains during development are structured to facilitate within-lobe and within-hemisphere connectivity, with networks that are transitive, modular, and discrete, whereas female brains have greater interhemispheric connectivity and greater cross-hemispheric participation. Within-hemispheric cortical processing along the posterior-anterior dimension involves the linking of perception to action, and motor action is mediated ipsilaterally by the cerebellum. Greater within-hemispheric supratentorial connectivity combined with greater cross-hemispheric

cerebellar connectivity would confer an efficient system for coordinated action in males. Greater interhemispheric connectivity in females would facilitate integration of the analytical and sequential reasoning modes of the left hemisphere with the spatial, intuitive processing of information of the right hemisphere. A behavioral study on the entire sample, of which this imaging study is a subset, demonstrated pronounced sex differences, with the females outperforming males on attention, word and face memory, and social cognition tests and males performing better on spatial processing and motor and sensorimotor speed (2). These differences were mainly observed in midadolescent age (12–14 y), where males performed significantly faster on motor tasks and more accurately on spatial memory tasks. Other behavioral studies have found similar sex differences[41,42]. These behavioral studies are carried out at a denser age sampling, which is not possible for the imaging studies because the sample size in the subgroups will be too small to identify meaningful differences.

In addition to the consistency with the behavioral tasks, our findings on anatomical connectivity obtained with diffusion imaging are consistent with previous data from T1 structural imaging, showing a higher proportion of cortical WM in males[5], except for the CC[43]. They are also consistent with activation studies using functional MRI, which have reported greater interhemispheric activation in females on a language task, in which they excelled[44], and greater focal intrahemispheric activation in males on a spatial task, in which they excelled[45]. With respect to development, DTI studies[23,24] have shown higher FA and lower MD in the CC in females during midadolescence, confirming a similar trend in our data. Although FA and MD provide measures of WM integrity, connectomic studies like ours are required to complete the picture of connection-wise systems.

Thus, the current study presents unique insights into sex differences using structural connectivity and measures defined on the connectome. Results are lent credence by supporting behavioral and functional studies. Our findings support the notion that the behavioral complementarity between the sexes has developmental neural substrates that could contribute toward improved understanding of this complementarity.

Materials and Methods

Dataset. Institutional Review Board approval was obtained from the University of Pennsylvania and the Children's Hospital of Philadelphia. The study includes 949 subjects (Table 1). For each subject, DTI [repetition time (TR)/echo time (TE) = 8,100/82 ms, resolution = $1.9 \times 1.9 \times$

2 mm, 64 diffusion directions with b = 1,000 s/mm^2 and 7 b = 0 images] and T1-weighted (TR/TE = 1,810/3.51 ms) MRI scans were acquired on the same Siemens 3T Verio scanner using a 32-channel head coil. Diffusion tensors were fitted to the DTI data (13–15), and FA maps were computed.

Creating SCs. The brain of each subject was parcellated into 95 regions of interest (ROIs; 68 cortical and 27 subcortical regions) of the Desikan atlas[46] using FreeSurfer[47] to act as node labels. The quality of the parcellation was manually checked for each subject. Each node label was treated as a seed region, and fibers were tracked probabilistically[48] from it to the other ROIs. We used the default parameters of two fibers per voxel and 5,000 sample streamlines for each tract to create a 95 × 95 matrix, P, of probability values. Each matrix entry P_{ij} represents a scaled conditional probability of a pathway between the seed ROI, i, and the target ROI, j, given by $P_{ij} = \frac{S_{i \to j}}{S_i} R_i$, where $S_{i \to j}$ denotes the number of fibers reaching the target region j from the seed region i and S_i is the number of streamlines seeded in i. We scale this ratio by the surface area R_i of the ROI, i, that accounts for different sizes of the seed region. This measure [like those found in previous studies[49–52]] quantifies connectivity such that $P_{ij} \approx P_{ji}$, which, on averaging, gives an undirected weighted connectivity measure. This now creates a 95 × 95 undirected symmetrical weighted connectivity network, W, called the SC.

Connectivity Analysis. In comparing general connectivity between groups (here, males and females), we look for significant connection-based difference in the SC W. Each connection weight P_{ij} was linearly regressed on age, sex, and age–sex interaction, and the resulting sex T statistic was used to construct the output T matrix (95 × 95). T was thresholded at positive and negative values to retain only those connections that are significantly stronger in either group. A positive T_{ij} indicates higher connectivity in the males, and a negative T_{ij} indicates higher connectivity in females.

We used a nonparametric method known as permutation testing, specifically a single-threshold test, to address the problem of multiple comparisons[53] on these high-dimensional network matrices[54]. We randomized the labels (males/females) 20,000 times to create 20,000 T matrices and found the maximum T statistic of the entire network for each of the permutations to capture differences in the network. A histogram of these maximum T statistics over the entire network for each permutation was then constructed, and a threshold value was computed at a significance level of 0.05. Finally, this threshold was applied on the regression statistics performed on age, sex,

and age–sex interaction. The connections with a higher T statistic value than the threshold were the ones that survived the correction. The three groups (children, adolescents, and young adults) were tested in a similar manner, again at $P = 0.05$ and with 10,000 permutations.

Network Measures. The structural network was analyzed at several levels of granularity, from connection-based measures as described above to measures of modularity and transitivity at macroscopic, lobar, and regional levels.

HCR. This quantifies the dominance of intra- or interhemispheric connections in the network matrices. It is the ratio of a lobe's number of intrahemispheric connections to its number of interhemispheric connections.

LCW. To assess both intra- and interlobe connectivity, we define an LCW for each pair of lobes (L_x, L_y): $LCW(L_x, L_y) = \sum_{i \in L_x, j \in L_y} w_{ij}$, where w_{ij} is the connectivity weight between regions i and j. For each $LCW (L_x, L_y)$, a T statistic was computed between males and females while covarying for age and race.

Modularity. Modularity reflects how well the network can be delineated into groups (or communities), as defined via spectral clustering that maximizes the number of intragroup connections and minimizes the number of intergroup connections. A modularity measure is then calculated from the community structure based on the proportion of links connecting regions in different groups. The weighted modularity of a network is defined as follows: $M = \frac{1}{l}\sum_{i,j \in N}\left[w_{ij} - \frac{k_i k_l}{z}\right]$, where w_{ij} is the connectivity weight between the regions i and j, k_i is the sum of the connection weights of i, and z is the sum of all connection weights in the network.

Transitivity. The transitivity of a network or subnetwork, $T = \frac{\sum_{i \in N} 2t_i}{\sum_{i \in N} k_i(k_i - 1)}$, where t_i is the weighted geometric mean of the triad of regions around the region l, quantifies the proportion of fully connected triads of regions whose neighbors are also immediate neighbors of each other, with high transitivity indicating increased local connectivity. Transitivity is also calculated by considering lobes as subnetworks, where the brain is divided into eight lobes: right and left temporal, right and left frontal, right and left parietal, and right and left occipital. Eight anatomically consistent lobe networks are constructed from the resulting submatrices of these.

PC. This is a regional measure that compares the total weight of the region's intralobar connections against the total weight of its interlobar connections. The PC of a region y_i is given by $PC(y_i) = 1 - \sum_{m \in M}\left(\frac{k_i(m)}{k_i}\right)^2$, where M is the set of subnetworks (lobes in our case) and $k_i(m)$ is the sum of the weights of all connections between *i* and regions in subnetwork *m*. A low *PC* indicates reduced connectivity to other subnetworks and/or increased connectivity within its own subnetwork.

References

1. Jazin E, Cahill L (2010) Sex differences in molecular neuroscience: From fruit flies to humans. *Nat Rev Neurosci* 11(1):9–17.
2. Gur RC, et al. (2012) Age group and sex differences in performance on a computerized neurocognitive battery in children age 8–21. *Neuropsychology* 26(2):251–265.
3. Halpern D (2007) The science of sex differences in science and mathematics. *Psychol Sci Public Interest* 8(1):1–51.
4. Allen JS, Damasio H, Grabowski TJ, Bruss J, Zhang W (2003) Sexual dimorphism and asymmetries in the gray-white composition of the human cerebrum. *Neuroimage* 18(4):880–894.
5. Gur RC, et al. (1999) Sex differences in brain gray and white matter in healthy young adults: Correlations with cognitive performance. *J Neurosci* 19(10):4065–4072.
6. Goldstein JM, et al. (2001) Normal sexual dimorphism of the adult human brain assessed by in vivo magnetic resonance imaging. *Cereb Cortex* 11(6):490–497.
7. Cosgrove KP, Mazure CM, Staley JK (2007) Evolving knowledge of sex differences in brain structure, function, and chemistry. *Biol Psychiatry* 62(8):847–855.
8. Giedd JN, et al. (1996) Quantitative MRI of the temporal lobe, amygdala, and hippocampus in normal human development: Ages 4–18 years. *J Comp Neurol* 366(2):223–230.
9. Giedd JN, Castellanos FX, Rajapakse JC, Vaituzis AC, Rapoport JL (1997) Sexual dimorphism of the developing human brain. *Prog Neuropsychopharmacol Biol Psychiatry* 21(8):1185–1201.
10. Allen LS, Richey MF, Chai YM, Gorski RA (1991) Sex differences in the corpus callosum of the living human being. *J Neurosci* 11(4):933–942.
11. Courchesne E, et al. (2000) Normal brain development and aging: Quantitative analysis at in vivo MR imaging in healthy volunteers. *Radiology* 216(3):672–682.
12. Coffey CE, et al. (1998) Sex differences in brain aging: A quantitative magnetic resonance imaging study. *Arch Neurol* 55(2):169–179.
13. Basser PJ, Jones DK (2002) Diffusion-tensor MRI: Theory, experimental design and data analysis—A technical review. *NMR Biomed* 15(7-8):456–467.
14. Basser PJ, Mattiello J, LeBihan D (1994) MR diffusion tensor spectroscopy and imaging. *Biophys J* 66(1):259–267.
15. Le Bihan D, et al. (2001) Diffusion tensor imaging: Concepts and applications. *J Magn Reson Imaging* 13(4):534–546.
16. Pierpaoli C, Basser PJ (1996) Toward a quantitative assessment of diffusion anisotropy. *Magn Reson Med* 36(6):893–906.
17. Herting MM, Maxwell EC, Irvine C, Nagel BJ (2012) The impact of sex, puberty, and hormones on white matter microstructure in adolescents. *Cereb Cortex* 22(9):1979–1992.
18. Westerhausen R, et al. (2003) The influence of handedness and gender on the microstructure of the human corpus callosum: A diffusion-tensor magnetic resonance imaging study. *Neurosci Lett* 351(2):99–102.
19. Hsu JL, et al. (2008) Gender differences and age-related white matter changes of the human brain: A diffusion tensor imaging study. *Neuroimage* 39(2):566–577.
20. Kanaan RA, et al. (2012) Gender differences in white matter microstructure. *PLoS ONE* 7(6):e38272.
21. Schmithorst VJ, Holland SK, Dardzinski BJ (2008) Developmental differences in white matter architecture between boys and girls. *Hum Brain Mapp* 29(6):696–710.
22. Kumar R, Nguyen HD, Macey PM, Woo MA, Harper RM (2012) Regional brain axial and radial diffusivity changes during development. *J Neurosci Res* 90(2):346–355.
23. Bava S, et al. (2011) Sex differences in adolescent white matter architecture. *Brain Res* 1375:41–48.
24. Asato MR, Terwilliger R, Woo J, Luna B (2010) White matter development in adolescence: A DTI study. *Cereb Cortex* 20(9):2122–2131.
25. Abe O, et al. (2010) Sex dimorphism in gray/white matter volume and diffusion tensor during normal aging. *NMR Biomed* 23(5):446–458.
26. Lebel C, Caverhill-Godkewitsch S, Beaulieu C (2010) Age-related regional variations of the corpus callosum identified by diffusion tensor tractography. *Neuroimage* 52(1):20–31.
27. Eluvathingal TJ, Hasan KM, Kramer L, Fletcher JM, Ewing-Cobbs L (2007) Quantitative diffusion tensor tractography of association and projection fibers in normally developing children and adolescents. *Cereb Cortex* 17(12):2760–2768.
28. Clayden JD, et al. (2012) Normative development of white matter tracts: Similarities and differences in relation to age, gender, and intelligence. *Cereb Cortex* 22(8): 1738–1747.

29. Sporns O (2011) The human connectome: A complex network. *Ann N Y Acad Sci* 1224: 109–125.

30. Bullmore E, Sporns O (2009) Complex brain networks: Graph theoretical analysis of structural and functional systems. *Nat Rev Neurosci* 10(3):186–198.

31. Hagmann P, et al. (2008) Mapping the structural core of human cerebral cortex. *PLoS Biol* 6(7):e159.

32. Tomasi D, Volkow ND (2012) Laterality patterns of brain functional connectivity: Gender effects. *Cereb Cortex* 22(6):1455–1462.

33. Tomasi D, Volkow ND (2012) Gender differences in brain functional connectivity density. *Hum Brain Mapp* 33(4):849–860.

34. Iturria-Medina Y, et al. (2007) Characterizing brain anatomical connections using diffusion weighted MRI and graph theory. *Neuroimage* 36(3):645–660.

35. Iturria-Medina Y, Sotero RC, Canales-Rodríguez EJ, Alemán-Gómez Y, Melie-García L (2008) Studying the human brain anatomical network via diffusion-weighted MRI and Graph Theory. *Neuroimage* 40(3):1064–1076.

36. Yan C, et al. (2011) Sex- and brain size-related small-world structural cortical networks in young adults: A DTI tractography study. *Cereb Cortex* 21(2):449–458.

37. Gong G, et al. (2009) Age- and gender-related differences in the cortical anatomical network. *J Neurosci* 29(50):15684–15693.

38. Dennis EL, et al. (2013) Development of brain structural connectivity between ages 12 and 30: A 4-Tesla diffusion imaging study in 439 adolescents and adults. *Neuroimage* 64:671–684.

39. Rubinov M, Sporns O (2010) Complex network measures of brain connectivity: Uses and interpretations. *Neuroimage* 52(3):1059–1069.

40. Steinmetz H, Staiger JF, Schlaug G, Huang Y, Jäncke L (1995) Corpus callosum and brain volume in women and men. *Neuroreport* 6(7):1002–1004.

41. Cherney ID, Brabec CM, Runco DV (2008) Mapping out spatial ability: Sex differences in way-finding navigation. *Percept Mot Skills* 107(3):747–760.

42. Hamilton C (2008) Cognition and Sex Differences (Palgrave Macmillan).

43. Dubb A, Gur R, Avants B, Gee J (2003) Characterization of sexual dimorphism in the human corpus callosum. *Neuroimage* 20(1):512–519.

44. Shaywitz BA, et al. (1995) Sex differences in the functional organization of the brain for language. *Nature* 373(6515):607–609.

45. Gur RC, et al. (2000) An fMRI study of sex differences in regional activation to a verbal and a spatial task. *Brain Lang* 74(2):157–170.

46. Desikan RS, et al. (2006) An automated labeling system for subdividing the human cerebral cortex on MRI scans into gyral based regions of interest. *Neuroimage* 31(3): 968–980.

47. Fischl B, Sereno MI, Dale AM (1999) Cortical surface-based analysis. II: Inflation, flattening, and a surface-based coordinate system. *Neuroimage* 9(2): 195–207.

48. Behrens TE, et al. (2003) Characterization and propagation of uncertainty in diffusion-weighted MR imaging. *Magn Reson Med* 50(5):1077–1088.

49. Hagmann P, et al. (2010) White matter maturation reshapes structural connectivity in the late developing human brain. *Proc Natl Acad Sci USA* 107(44):19067–19072.

50. Bassett DS, et al. (2008) Hierarchical organization of human cortical networks in health and schizophrenia. *J Neurosci* 28(37):9239–9248.

51. Gong G, et al. (2009) Mapping anatomical connectivity patterns of human cerebral cortex using in vivo diffusion tensor imaging tractography. *Cereb Cortex* 19(3): 524–536.

52. Sporns O, Honey CJ, Kötter R (2007) Identification and classification of hubs in brain networks. *PLoS ONE* 2(10):e1049.

53. Holmes AP, Blair RC, Watson JD, Ford I (1996) Nonparametric analysis of statistic images from functional mapping experiments. *J Cereb Blood Flow Metab* 16(1):7–22.

54. Nichols TE, Holmes AP (2002) Nonparametric permutation tests for functional neuroimaging: A primer with examples. *Hum Brain Mapp* 15(1):1–25.

MADHURA INGALHALIKAR, ALEX SMITH, DREW PARKER, AND RAGINI VERMA are affiliated with the Section of Biomedical Image Analysis at the University of Pennsylvania. THEODORE D. SATTERTHWAITE, KOSHA RUPAREL, RAQUEL E. GURB, AND RUBEN C. GURB are all in the Department of Neuropsychiatry, Perelman School of Medicine, University of Pennsylvania. HAKON HAKONARSON is from the Center for Applied Genomics, Children's Hospital of Philadelphia. MARK A. ELLIOTT is affiliated with the Center for Magnetic Resonance and Optical Imaging, Department of Radiology, University of Pennsylvania.

Sara Mead

The Problem with Gender-Based Education

Yesterday's *New York Times* Magazine featured a very long article that's purportedly about single-sex public schooling, but is really about a narrower—and much more problematic—concept of gender-based education. Gender-based education is the notion that "Boys and Girls Learn Differently"—that's even the title of a book by Michael Gurian, one of the leaders of a cottage industry that's grown up to promote the idea. Specifically, it's the idea that recent neuroscience research shows significant difference in male and female brains and that as a result educators must employ different approaches in teaching male and female students. Unfortunately, many of the arguments for gender based education are bunk—and often have more to do with outdated gender stereotypes than the cutting edge research proponents claim they're based on.

In the NYT magazine piece, author Elizabeth Weil profiles Dr. Leonard Sax, a family doctor from Washington, D.C.'s Maryland suburbs and a leading advocate of gender-based schooling. She also describes 3 different public schools implementing single-sex education—an all-male and an all-female New York City charter school, as well as a coed district school in Alabama teaching children in sex-segregated classrooms. And she does a decent job in laying out some of the key critiques of Sax's work. Sax and Gurian exaggerate the neuroscience and get some of it flat-out wrong. Much of the science they do cite is primarily descriptive—it's not adequate to serve as a guide to making decisions about teaching or policy. And they ignore the fact that variation among both males and females often far exceeds average differences between the genders. But, since the critiques don't appear until roughly halfway through a very long article—the first part of which reads like a puff piece on Dr. Sax—many readers may miss them. Moreover, while Weil's airing of critiques gives the article an appearance of balance, she glosses over a bigger issue: There wouldn't be a "controversy" over gender-based public education at all if Sax and Gurian weren't aggressively marketing their idiosyncratic—and flawed—notion of gender-based education.

Actual neuroscientists—whose work Sax and Gurian claim to base their arguments on, though neither are themselves neuroscientists—aren't the ones banging the drum on gender-based education. In fact, many caution against trying to draw practical implications for schooling from their work. Much of what Gurian and Sax call "brain research" is still in its infancy, a long way from being able to support practical applications in education. Jay Geidd, one of the preeminent neuroscientists studying brain development in children (including gender differences) cautions that gender is much too crude a tool to differentiate educational approaches: the variation within each gender is often larger than the average difference between genders, and there's substantial overlap in the distributions.

Geidd's caution is well worth heeding even in areas where science—not just neuroscience but also other less flashy but often more relevant fields of child development research—does show real differences in boys' and girls' development. There is pretty strong evidence that preschool-aged boys develop gross motor skills faster than girls do, while preschool-aged girls tend to have an advantage in language development. As a result, boys and girls are, on average, at different levels of language and motor development when they enter school. Sax and Gurian see this as one argument for separate sex, gender-based schooling. That might be reasonable if gender were the only source of variance in young children's learning. But it's not: Young children's development is highly variable. Some 5-year-old girls might lag many boys in language skills, and some boys' motor skills might lag those of their female peers. If one is really concerned about adjusting education to variations in children's development, increased customization and multi-age groupings in early elementary school, which allow teachers to group children who are developmentally similar, regardless of age, and children to progress at their own paces, are a far better solution than simply separating children by sex.

The appetite for single-sex and gender-based educational approaches is understandable—and it's not just a manifestation of sexism. While this country does a lousy job of educating low-income and minority students generally, we do a particularly poor job of educating poor and minority boys—and there's a desperation for approaches to correct the high rates of disciplinary problems and school dropout among these young men. When folks like Gurian and Sax come along promoting single sex education as a silver bullet approach, it's no wonder some educators seize on the idea.

Unfortunately, there's no evidence that the gender-based approaches work in improving student achievement. Even if Sax and Gurian's didn't have such a weak basis in neuroscience, a basis in neuroscience isn't enough to make an educational approach effective. Lots of educational strategies based in "cutting edge" evidence about "how students learn" have proved to be failures. What's needed are rigorous evaluations showing the approach produces positive results in practice. But Sax and Gurian's theories have never been subject to a rigorous, independent evaluation of their effectiveness. There are no randomized controlled trials of gender-based educational approaches. There's even evidence that some of their recommendations are wrong: For instance, Sax argues boys will do better in school if parents wait until they're 6 to enroll them in kindergarten—a practice known as kindergarten redshirting. But researchers have studied the effects of kindergarten redshirting and found no evidence it make[s] a significant difference for long-term educational outcomes. And, while there has been research on single sex education, a recent Department of Education meta-analysis of that research found mixed results.

Two of the schools' Weil profiles—The Young Women's Leadership School (which, while single-sex, does not employ a gender-based education approach) and Excellence Charter School—do seem to be having a positive impact for the predominantly low-income, minority students they serve. But that impact has at least as much to do with their rigorous academic approach, commitment to high-quality teaching, and shared culture of excellence as it has to do with the fact that they're single sex. No one disputes that single sex schooling can have benefits for some students—particularly for girls in math and science.

And a single sex approach may also help educators to create the strong, shared culture and values we know highly effective schools have. But there are plenty examples of schools doing this in coed settings as well—which is good, because for the foreseeable future the vast majority of students will be attending coed schools. (Sax claims that 360 public schools nationally are single sex—but in a nation with more than 14,000 school districts and 4,000 charter schools, that's not even a drop in the bucket). Wouldn't it be nice if the *New York Times* devoted at least as much attention to the strategies we know are working to educate students in these settings, as it has on a faux controversy about marginal gender-based educational approaches?

One incident described in the article deserves particular attention. Weil writes:

> In his second book, "Boys Adrift: The Five Factors Driving the Growing Epidemic of Unmotivated Boys and Underachieving Young Men," Sax credits Bender for helping focus a boy who was given a wrong diagnosis of attention-deficit disorder by telling him that his father, who had left the family, would be even less likely to return if all his mother had to report was the boy misbehaving in school.

This is shocking. Suggesting, to a child, that he in any way bears responsibility for the success or failure of his parents' marriage is despicable behavior, bordering on emotional abuse. The fact that Sax would praise an educator for doing so should cause anyone who's thinking of heeding his arguments to have serious second thoughts.

Sara Mead is a principal with Bellwether Education Partners in the Policy and Thought Leadership practice. In this role, she writes and conducts policy analysis on issues related to early childhood education and K–12 education reform and provides strategic advising support to clients serving high-need students. Before joining Bellwether in 2010, she directed the New America Foundation's Early Education Initiative.

EXPLORING THE ISSUE

Do Boys and Girls Learn Differently?

Critical Thinking and Reflection

1. Think about your own experience at school. Was there any way you noticed you or your friends playing or participating in class that you feel could be linked to gender?
2. Did you ever notice any of your teachers favoring one gender over another?
3. What about the propositions made in Ingalhalikar's article resonated with you? What of it seemed to reinforce gender role stereotypes?

Is There Common Ground?

Dr. Ingalhalikar and colleagues and Sara Mead agree that brain research should not be used to reinforce stereotypes. Dr. Ingalhalikar's research could be extrapolated for use in educational settings to inform teachers and administrators in fine-tuning how to best reach male and female students. Mead believes single-sex interventions are, by definition, sexist.

Would those who oppose single-sex classrooms and schools support the interventions if there were conclusive evidence that they were better for students? Or would there always be opposition? And what should be done for students who are transgender—who were born biologically one sex, but identify on the inside as a different sex? Single-sex interventions would need to be flexible enough to ensure transgender students are not left out, or forced to go against their gender identity and be forced to be grouped by the sex they were assigned at birth.

Additional Resources

Hines, M. (2011). Gender development and the human brain. *Annual Review of Neuroscience, 34,* 69–88.

Sadker, D. and Zittleman, K.R. (2009). Still failing at fairness: How gender bias cheats girls and boys in school and what we can do about it. New York: Simon & Schuster.

The Secret Life of the Brain: PBS. http://www.pbs.org /wnet/brain/history/450bc.html?position=208?button=4

Internet References . . .

American Council for Co-Educational Schooling

https://thesanfordschool.asu.edu/acces

The Gurian Institute

http://gurianinstitute.com/

National Association of Single-Sex Public Education

http://www.singlesexschools.org/home-introduction .htm

Selected, Edited, and with Issue Framing Material by:
Elizabeth Schroeder, EdD, MSW, *Elizabeth Schroeder Consulting*

ISSUE

Are Single-Gender Classes Necessary to Create Equal Opportunities for Boys and Girls?

YES: Frances R. Spielhagen, from "How Tweens View Single-Sex Classes," *Educational Leadership* (April 2006)

NO: Kelley King and Michael Gurian, from "Teaching to the Minds of Boys," *Educational Leadership* (September 2006)

Learning Outcomes

After reading this issue, you will be able to:

- Summarize the achievement differences between male and female students.
- Discuss the views of students who have participated in both single- and mixed-gender classrooms.
- Describe the strategies used to support student learning in single- and mixed-gender classrooms.

ISSUE SUMMARY

YES: Frances R. Spielhagen, a postdoctoral research fellow at the Center for Gifted Education at the College of William and Mary, argues that single-gender classes are viewed as more conducive to learning than are coeducational classes by students, especially younger students.

NO: Kelley King and Michael Gurian argue that coeducational classrooms can be made to be more accommodating to the learning profiles of both boys and girls, and they illustrate this approach through the example of classrooms that became more "boy friendly" through the inclusion of experiential and kinesthetic activities around literacy.

Despite changing attitudes and the enactment of laws designed to ensure that males and females are afforded equal educational opportunities, gender-related differences in academic achievement still exist. In reading and language arts, girls score higher on achievement tests and are less likely to be referred for remedial programs than are boys. In math and science, boys maintain an advantage. Although gender differences in academic achievement are relatively small, and certainly less than the differences observed among males or among females, they are important because of their influence on the career paths available to men and women.

Gender-related differences in academic achievement are due, in part, to the beliefs that children bring to school and to their behavior in the classroom. Importantly, there is considerable evidence that differences in academic preparation and behavior are largely the result of the environment rather than of direct biological influences on development.

Parents are an important part of the environment that serves to push boys and girls down different academic paths. The role of the media has also been much debated. Unfortunately, teachers and the culture of most U.S. schools are at fault as well. Consider the following:

1. In preschool and early elementary school years, the physical arrangement of the classroom often segregates boys and girls and reinforces the differences between them. For example, a pretend kitchen and associated role-playing materials are

typically used in a different location than are blocks and other building materials.

2. Teachers attend more to boys than to girls, are more likely to ask boys questions (especially open-ended, thought-provoking questions), and give boys more constructive criticism. Such behaviors are especially evident in traditionally male domains, such as science.

3. Teachers are more tolerant of interruptions from boys than from girls and encourage the latter to wait their turn.

4. Teachers are more likely to provide help to girls during difficult academic tasks, including during experiments and other hands-on science activities, while encouraging boys to resolve difficulties on their own.

5. Teachers spend more time with girls during reading and language arts classes but more time with boys during math classes.

6. Teachers are less likely to assign girls than similarly achieving boys to high-math-ability groups. In general, girls are less likely than boys to be identified for inclusion in programs for gifted students.

How can schools be reformed to ensure that they help children to break free of gender stereotypes rather than maintain and even exacerbate achievement differences between boys and girls? Much of the debate surrounding the question of reform has focused on the achievement gaps in math and science, which appear to have the greatest potential for limiting career options. Two approaches to reform have been advocated. In the first, and certainly more popular, approach, scholars and policymakers, assuming that coeducational classrooms are a fact of life, have made suggestions for changing the culture and practices of these classrooms. Proponents of the second, more controversial, approach argue that gender-segregated classes are necessary to allow girls or boys the opportunity to learn in a climate that is suited to their characteristics and needs.

The following two selections weigh in on this issue of gender-segregated classes. In the first, Frances R. Spielhagen presents excerpts from interviews with middle-school students. In general, the students support single-gender classes, seeing them as containing fewer distractions and more supports for learning, although an interest in romantic relationships leads older students to "overlook" the shortcomings of coeducational classrooms. In the second selection, Kelly King and Michael Gurian argue that gender-equitable education is possible within the context of a coeducational classroom provided that the curriculum and pedagogical activities are adapted to meet the unique needs and challenges of students of both genders.

YES

Frances R. Spielhagen

How Tweens View Single-Sex Classes

Have you ever heard that saying, 'Time flies when you're having fun?' All-boy classes are fun! James, a 6th grader, cheerfully offered this opinion of the single-sex academic classes at Hudson Valley Middle School.[1] He quickly added, "I will probably want to be with girls when I am in high school."

Melissa, 13, expressed an older adolescent's point of view: "You can say what you want in all-girl classes and not be afraid of being teased, but sometimes we just want to be with the guys."

James and Melissa are part of the majority of students at this middle school in the rural Hudson Valley of upstate New York who have chosen to attend single-sex classes in language arts, math, science, and social studies. Hudson Valley Middle School, a public school whose 600 students come mostly from low-income backgrounds, has offered voluntary single-sex academic classes to its 6th, 7th, and 8th grade students for the last three years. Students remain in mixed groups for nonacademic classes and at lunchtime so they are not isolated from opposite-gender peers. In the first year of this reform, approximately 75 percent of the school's students chose to take single-sex classes; during the last two years, the majority of those students continued with that choice.

As part of my research into single-sex education (Spielhagen, 2005), I interviewed 24 Hudson Valley students a combination of 6th, 7th, and 8th graders who had attended single-sex classes for at least one academic year. Their comments offer insights into the minds of tweens who have sampled single-sex learning. Their perspectives indicate that voluntary single-sex classes can be a viable option for middle school students, but that such arrangements are most effective when classes are designed to address students' developmental needs. The younger students were more likely to find being in a single-sex class a positive experience; as students got older, they expressed more desire to be in mixed classes, even when that choice entailed potential problems.

Why Try Single-Sex Learning?

Concern over state standardized test scores prompted Hudson Valley Middle School to create voluntary single-sex classes. The school hoped that providing an environment free of the distraction caused by mixed-gender social interaction would lead to higher scores.

In the 19th century, single-sex schools were common, especially in grades 7 through 12. However, because classes for girls did not include academic subjects that would lead to higher education, early feminists urged that schools give *all* students access to the entire academic curriculum. Coeducational schools soon became the preferred model of public education, opening the doors to college enrollment for substantial numbers of girls.

Even then, secondary schools continued to maintain single-sex physical education classes until 1975. In that year, the provisions of Title IX (Tyack & Hansot, 2002) specifically forbade separate-gender physical education classes. According to Salomone (2003), many school districts misunderstood Title IX as a ban on all single-sex classes. Either way, emphasis on coeducational physical education classes quickly led to coeducation as the norm for public schools.

Meanwhile, over the last 20 years, education policymakers have noted the need to reverse declines in achievement among both boys and girls. Researchers agree that the middle school years are crucial to forming sound study habits (Clewell, 2002), but they have mixed opinions as to whether a return to single-sex classes would enhance the achievement of young adolescents.

For example, in 1995, Sadker and Sadker claimed that coeducational schools shortchange girls. At the same time, the American Association of University Women (AAUW) endorsed single-sex arrangements as a means of promoting female achievement, particularly in mathematics and science. Within a few years, however, the AAUW (1998) reversed its stance and concluded that single-sex classes could lead to programming decisions that discriminated against girls. In terms of boys, Sommers (2002) believes that single-sex arrangements are advantageous for boys who lag in academic areas, particularly reading and writing.

Listening to Student Voices

From ages 9 through 13, young adolescents experience tremendous physical, emotional, and cognitive development, so it is not surprising that the responses of students with whom I talked varied according to their ages. I asked students about their classroom choices, their perceptions of the classroom environment in single-sex as compared with mixed-gender groups, and their satisfaction level. The majority of the students had positive feelings about single-sex classes, with 62 percent stating that they could focus better without the opposite sex present. In general, the younger the student, the more enthusiastic the praise of the single-sex arrangement.

The 6th Grade Perspective

Sixth grade students' comments revealed a pre-adolescent viewpoint that the behavior of the other sex was a problem. Both boys and girls in 6th grade referred to their opposite-gender peers as "noisy" and "annoying."

James, a slightly built 11-year-old, responded energetically to questions about being in all-boy classes. He admitted that his favorite class was gym "because you get to play games using your skills," but noted that he didn't pay much attention to the girls in the mixed gym classes because he and his friends (all boys) liked to be on teams together. James also said that he felt "more challenged" in his all-boy classes because he enjoyed the competition with other boys:

> I want to try to beat them. I didn't try to beat the girls [when I was in mixed classes] because I didn't think I could beat the top girls, so why bother?

The comments of 6th grade girls reinforced the conventional wisdom that girls experience more freedom in single-sex academic classes, particularly math and science. Alison, 11, said she "loves all-girl classes," especially math classes, because she's "good at math." She emphasized that in all-girl classes, "you don't have to worry about boys making fun of you." Twelve-year-old Becky echoed Alison's concerns about intellectual safety in mixed classes. When asked why she chose all-girl classes, she replied,

> The boys always picked on me because I am smarter than they are. In all-girl classes, the teachers word things better and say them differently. In mixed classes, they say things more simply for the boys.

She added that all-girl classes are fun and the students get more accomplished, even though the girls "get loud and ask too many questions."

7th and 8th Grade Perspectives

Although by 7th grade many students' attitudes had begun to shift toward typically adolescent emotional and social concerns, 7th graders consistently remarked on their ability to focus better in their single-sex classes. Mary, a 13-year-old 7th grader, reported that she had meant to try all-girl classes for just a year but had decided to stay with the arrangement. She reported a definite improvement in her grades, noting that "I can concentrate better. I am not afraid to raise my hand."

Another 7th grader, Nancy, reported that

> In mixed classes, you are too nervous to ask a question and be wrong and the boys might laugh at you. We get higher grades because we pay attention more and don't get distracted.

On the other hand, Heather, 13, complained that she was in an all-girl class because "my mom decided to torture me." Heather went along with her mother's choice because she was curious. She conceded that she liked the all-girl classes because they made it easier to relate to her girlfriends but added that the situation allowed girls to "help each other with guy problems." Heather was clearly becoming more interested in mixed-gender social pairing. She offered another adolescent insight, noting,

> In some ways it's really nice to be with your friends, but sometimes the girls get catty, and it is hard to get space away from them.

The 7th and 8th grade boys were less enthusiastic than the girls about single-sex classes. Bullying seemed to become more of a problem with only boys present. Danny, 13, noted that he had been curious about all-boy classes, but that after two years in such classes, he planned to choose mixed-gender classes for 8th grade. In the all-boy classes, Danny reported, he could talk more about sports with his friends and "just hang out," but that "boys try to act tougher" in that environment. Eighth grader Jim, also 13, admitted that he had been picked on by other boys in mixed classes in 7th grade, but that mistreatment was worse in the all-boy classes. He explained, "The guys who pick on us would be more interested in impressing the girls" in a mixed-gender group. Jim added that he missed being with his female friends.

What Are the Students Telling Us?

From these tweens' perspective, single-sex classes can clearly contribute to a comfortable yet intellectually challenging middle school experience. Such arrangements work as long as students can choose whether or not to participate.

Students in all grades reinforced the importance of emotional, intellectual, and physical safety perennial concerns in the middle grades. The problem of bullying reared its head among the 7th and 8th grade boys, but the students did not agree on which arrangement might be less bully-prone. However, caution dictates that schools take measures to ensure that a *Lord of the Flies* scenario does not emerge from a policy that keeps boys in the same single-sex grouping during all three years of middle school. Sorting students into different all-male configurations for different years might address this problem.

The overwhelmingly positive responses from the girls in this study suggest that single-sex classes are particularly beneficial to middle school girls. Even 8th grade girls supported the notion that greater concentration is possible in all-girl classes. As the girls grew older, they became more assertive about their interest in boys. Unlike the boys, however, they expressed a feeling of bonding with their female classmates and enjoyed discussing issues about boys together.

Students experienced the distraction presented by the opposite gender in different ways as they grew older. Younger kids complained about the noisiness of their opposite-sex peers, whereas older students simply referred to the social distractions of having the opposite sex in their classrooms. However, older students loudly and clearly stated their preference for facing those distractions.

Offering Multiple Options

Turning Points 2000 (Jackson & Davis, 2000), a landmark document on middle school reform, recommended that middle schools organize learning climates that promote intellectual development and shared academic purpose. According to the students in my study, single-sex classes in public middle schools support these goals. *Turning Points 2000* also called for middle schools to offer multiple options to students. Hudson Valley Middle School displays innovative programming by restricting single-sex classes to the academic core courses so that students can experience the benefits of both single-sex classes and day-to-day interaction with students of the other sex. Offering subject-specific single-sex classes in each grade might provide even more flexibility, as long as the curriculum remains identical for both genders.

Providing optional single-sex environments for young adolescents with the existing public middle school framework would offer cost-effective school choice for parents, involving them as stakeholders in the education of their children. For many tweens, single-sex classes provide an enviable situation in which learning time flies because students are having fun.

Note

1. All names in this article are pseudonyms.

References

American Association of University Women. (1998). *Separated by sex: A critical look at single-sex education for girls*. Washington, DC: Author.

Clewell, B. (2002). Breaking the barriers: The critical middle school years. In E. Rassen, L. Iura, & P. Berkman (Eds.), *Gender in education* (pp. 301–313). San Francisco: Jossey-Bass.

Jackson, A., & Davis, G. (2000). *Turning points 2000: Educating adolescents in the 21st century*. New York: Carnegie Corporation.

Sadker, M., & Sadker, D. (1995). *Failing at fairness: How our schools cheat girls*. New York: Simon & Schuster.

Salomone, R. (2003). *Same, different, equal: Rethinking single-sex schooling*. New Haven, CT: Yale University Press.

Sommers, C. (2002). Why Johnny can't, like, read and write. In E. Rassen, L. Iura, & P. Berkman (Eds.), *Gender in education* (pp. 700–721). San Francisco: Jossey-Bass.

Spielhagen, F. (2005). *Separate by choice: Single-sex classes in a public middle school*. Unpublished manuscript.

Tyack, D., & Hansot, E. (2002). Feminists discover the hidden injuries of coeducation. In E. Rassen, L. Iura, & P. Berkman (Eds.), *Gender in education* (pp. 12–50). San Francisco: Jossey-Bass.

Frances R. Spielhagen is an associate professor of education at Mount Saint Mary College.

Kelley King and Michael Gurian

 **NO**

Teaching to the Minds of Boys

Boys who don't read or write as well as we'd like come in all kinds. There's Garrett, who's perpetually in motion, his fingers drumming the desk. He's not focusing on his reading and pokes the student in front of him. He's becoming a discipline problem. There's Jared, who stares into space, failing to fill more than a few short lines with words. There's Dan, who turns in rushed and sloppy work and receives failing grades. When it comes to fulfilling the kinds of assignments that we call "literacy," boys are often out of their chairs rather than in them.

At Douglass Elementary School, in Boulder, Colorado, a significant literacy gap existed among the 470 students. On the 2005 Colorado State Assessment Program (CSAP), boys attending Douglass underperformed the girls in grades 3–5 (the boys' scores ranged from 6–21 points lower, with a 13-point gap overall). Because boys represented at least half the student population at every grade level—and 75 percent of the special education population—it was clear that the gender gap had powerful implications for the school as a whole and for the futures of the students.

In looking closely at these statistics, the staff suspected that Douglass was not alone in facing classrooms full of boys who were not learning to read and write as well as the girls were. In fact, all over the world boys are struggling in school, with lower grades, more discipline problems, more learning disabilities, and more behavior disorders than girls (Gurian & Stevens, 2005). As experienced teachers of boys, as parents of sons, and as professionals charged with solving a specific and compelling problem, the educators at Douglass went to work. They discovered that recent brain research backed up many of their intuitions about gender and learning styles (see Gurian, Henley, & Trueman, 2001).

By introducing more boy-friendly teaching strategies in the classroom, the school was able to close the gender gap in just one year. At the same time, girls' reading and writing performance improved.

On the Colorado State Assessment Program, Douglass Elementary students experienced an overall net percentage gain of 21.9, which was the highest achievement gain of any school in the Boulder Valley School District. Moreover, Douglass reversed the typical trend of girls outperforming boys: The boys experienced a 24.4 percentage point gain in reading and writing; the girls a 19 percentage point gain, which constituted three times the gain of girls in other district elementary schools. Most remarkably, Douglass special education students achieved 7.5 times the average gain for this population of students in the district, coming in with a 50-point gain.

A Look Into Boy-Friendly Classrooms

How did Douglass manage these successes? Using a theory developed by one of the authors (Gurian et al., 2001; Gurian & Stevens, 2005), the school analyzed the natural assets that both girls and boys bring to learning (see "The Brain: His and Hers," p. 59). Douglass realized that its classrooms were generally a better fit for the verbal-emotive, sit-still, take-notes, listen-carefully, multitasking girl. Teachers tended to view the natural assets that boys bring to learning—impulsivity, single-task focus, spatial-kinesthetic learning, and physical aggression—as problems. By altering strategies to accommodate these more typically male assets, Douglass helped its students succeed, as the following vignettes illustrate.

Increasing Experiential and Kinesthetic Learning Opportunities

Today's assignment in Mrs. Hill's 4th grade class is to arrange words and punctuation marks into a sentence that makes sense and is grammatically correct. Instead of relying on worksheets or the overhead, which might have bored students like Alexander, the teacher directs the students to arrange cards representing the sentence parts across the classroom floor. The task-oriented discussion and interaction, the physical movement, and the orientation in space access the boys' neurological strengths, keeping them energized and attentive. Alexander and his

King, Kelley; Gurian, Michael. From *Educational Leadership*, September 2006, pp. 56–61. Copyright © 2006 by ASCD. Reprinted by permission. The Association for Supervision and Curriculum Development is a worldwide community of educators advocating sound policies and sharing best practices to achieve the success of each learner. To learn more, visit ASCD at www.ascd.org.

group are working hard to complete their grammatical challenge before the other groups do.

These male-friendly elements have also energized the girls. Many of them like a good debate, competition, and moving around.

Supporting Literacy Through Spatial-Visual Representations

Across the hall in Mrs. Johnston's 3rd grade classroom, the students are writing. Timothy has great ideas and is always trying to please, but at the beginning of the year, he had great difficulty writing even a single paragraph. Formulating his ideas into well-organized thoughts, coupled with sitting still and the fine-motor task of writing, often overwhelmed him. His mother testified to his frequent meltdowns at home.

Realizing the need for nonverbal planning tools, especially in males, to help bridge the gap between what students are thinking and what they're able to put down on paper, Mrs. Johnston now asks Timothy and his classmates to create storyboards, a series of pictures with or without words that graphically depict a story line. The pictures on the storyboard prompt the brain to remember relevant words, functioning for these learners as first-stage brainstorming. Now when Timothy writes, he describes what he has previously drawn and then adds to that foundation. His spatial-visual assets are helping him to write.

Letting Boys Choose Topics That Appeal to Them

Although parents and educators are quick to point out to students the more practical relevance of reading—you need to read to get through high school and college so you can get a job—this kind of reasoning works more readily for girls than for boys. Said one 6th grade boy, "The only reading that's a *must* is reading what's on the computer or in a football manual. There's no point to reading a book for pleasure."

Many teachers are familiar with this kind of response. Boys often seem to think that what they read in language arts class is irrelevant. Mrs. Vanee decided to innovate in this area. In her 2nd grade classroom, most of the boys read and write about such topics as NASCAR racing, atomic bombs, and football or about such situations as a parrot biting a dad through the lip. Many of the girls write about best friends, books, mermaids, and unicorns.

When asked why he thought he was writing about superheroes whereas Brittany was writing about her best friend, 8-year-old Luke replied, "Because boys have more R-rated minds than girls do," with "R-rated" referring to a preference for aggression scenarios, competition, action, and superhero journeys. Brittany concurred as she rolled her eyes in a "Yes."

Although Mrs. Vanee is aware of the potential for excess here, she now understands how relevant this focus on action and heroism is to males, and she sees that letting boys write on these topics has improved their papers. It has also provided her with numerous opportunities to teach lessons on character, nonviolence, and civility. Moreover, giving students greater choice in what they read and write has improved writing among both boys and girls.

Helping Boys with Homework

One of the primary reasons that some boys get *D*s and *F*s in school is their inattention to homework. This was true for 5th grader Todd, who generally did his homework in a shoddy way—or not at all.

Douglass teachers now request that parents sign homework assignments. Homework with no signature requires an explanation. This way, the school gets parents involved, encouraging them to supervise homework and cut out distractions that their children may be experiencing, such as TV and video games, until the homework is completed. This policy also keeps parents apprised of the quality of the homework that their child is turning in.

Todd's grades have improved since this policy was started. He's now getting *B*s instead of *D*s on his language arts assignments. His teacher, Mrs. Steposki, is especially vigilant, meeting with him regularly to see whether he's gotten his homework signed and supporting his parents in keeping him focused. Although Todd still doesn't enjoy a lot of his homework—much of it feels like busywork to him—he does feel pride in getting a *B*. "Things are better now," he says.

Offering Single-Gender Learning Environments

One of the innovations that teachers can use in targeted ways in coeducational classes is single-gender grouping. Mrs. Holsted has decided to divide her 2nd grade class today to give the students a choice in reading material. The girls choose several *American Girls* doll books; the boys choose Lynne Reid Banks's *The Indian in the Cupboard* (HarperTrophy, 1999).

Soon the girls are on the floor with a giant piece of chart paper and markers. They label each of three circles of a Venn diagram with the name of a female book character and then they write down adjectives to describe that character.

Meanwhile, in the boys' group, Ryan and David are writing lines for a play about the novel they've chosen, happy to be able to act out the battle scene. A lot of what these students need to learn "sticks" because of this approach. Tomorrow, the students will return to their coed groupings, and some will note that they like being back together.

Making Reading and Writing Purposeful

Quite often, boys do their best work when teachers establish authentic purpose and meaningful, real-life connections. In his 4th grade classroom, Mr. Hoyt talks to 10-year-old Clayton about his narrative fiction piece. Clayton doesn't feel the need to do any more work on his D+ paper. When Mr. Hoyt asks who his audience is, Clayton replies, "Just the class and you." "What if you were reading this to someone else?" asks Mr. Hoyt. "Say, a high school basketball player you like?" Clayton ponders this. "Think about an older guy you respect," Mr. Hoyt suggests. "Write this for him to read." Clayton thinks of just the right person—his older brother—and starts the paper over again.

Garrett sits across the room. His real-life project is to draw to scale a map of the school and playground and then annotate it. From there, he'll develop a proposal for a new playground layout and present it to the school's landscape design architect and the playground revitalization committee.

Meanwhile, Greg is designing a Web site on which students can post their writing projects for others to read. In fact, to create a greater sense of the importance of writing, Mr. Hoyt suggested that Douglass Elementary start providing opportunities for all students to share their writing in front of large audiences—at monthly school assemblies, for example. Competition and the opportunity to earn public respect have helped motivate many under-motivated students—especially the boys.

Seeking Out Male Role Models

Douglass Elementary recognizes the special insight and impact of teachers like Mr. Hoyt, who serve as valuable role models for boys. The school actively encourages men to visit classrooms to share their own writing and speak about their favorite books. This is an area in which the school successfully partnered with parents. Several of the students' fathers write professionally as journalists, screenwriters, authors, or lyricists. Appealing to fathers to be role models for literacy has yielded many special guest speakers and several weekly "regulars" in the classroom.

Getting Serious About Gender Learning

There's nothing revolutionary about the strategies that we have suggested. Teachers have already used many of them in their classrooms, but perhaps they haven't used them in an organized and scientific way. Teacher training at Douglass, which focused on the gender learning work conducted by the Gurian Institute, connected brain science to classroom practice. Teachers learned that good science supported many of their personal observations about how boys and girls learn.

By incorporating new theories from gender science into classroom practice, teachers *can* close gender gaps and significantly improve learning. Douglass Elementary school provided the action research that proves just that. But to bring about these improvements, teachers need to ask themselves some key questions:

- As teachers, do we fully understand the challenges that boys face in education today?
- Do we realize that there is a scientific basis for innovating on behalf of both girls and boys as disaggregated groups?
- Does my school incorporate boy-friendly and girl-friendly learning innovations in full knowledge of how essential they are in accommodating the structural and chemical gender differences built into the human brain?
- Do the educators in my school realize that many behaviors typical of either boys or girls are neurologically based?

Although tackling these questions is challenging, acting on what we have learned can lead to rewards for everyone—for teachers, parents, communities, and especially our students.

References

Blum, D. (1997). *Sex on the brain: The biological differences between men and women*. New York: Viking.

Havers, F. (1995, March 2). Rhyming tasks male and female brains differently. *The Yale Herald*.

Gurian, M. (1996). *The wonder of boys*. New York: Tarcher/Putnam.

Gurian, M., Henley, P., & Trueman, T. (2001). *Boys and girls learn differently: A guide for teachers and parents*. San Francisco: Jossey–Bass.

Gurian, M., & Stevens, K. (2005). *The minds of boys: Saving our sons from falling behind in school and life.* San Francisco: Jossey-Bass.

Rich, B. (Ed.). (2000). *The Dana brain daybook.* New York: The Charles A. Dana Foundation.

Sax, L. (2005). *Why gender matters.* New York: Doubleday.

Taylor, S. (2002). *The tending instinct.* New York: Times Books.

KELLEY KING is the former principal of Douglass Elementary School in the Boulder Valley School District, Boulder, Colorado.

MICHAEL GURIAN is a marriage and family counselor in private practice, author, and cofounder of the Gurian Institute, which is nonprofit foundation supporting educational research and training.

EXPLORING THE ISSUE

Are Single-Gender Classes Necessary to Create Equal Opportunities for Boys and Girls?

Critical Thinking and Reflection

1. Summarize the findings from Spielhagen's study of same-sex middle-school classrooms. What are the strengths of the study? What are its weaknesses or limitations?
2. Briefly summarize King and Gurian's suggestions for ensuring a boy-friendly classroom. Do you think that the accommodations suggested for boys may put girls at a disadvantage? Why?
3. Imagine that you are the teacher for an all-boys math class. How would you organize and conduct the class? How would it be similar to and different from the class described by King and Gurian? Why?

Is There Common Ground?

Can we rely on empirical research to decide whether or not single-gender classes ensure that boys and girls have equal chances to succeed in all academic fields? In principle, the answer is yes. It should be possible, for example, to compare the math or science achievement of girls enrolled in girls-only classes to that of girls enrolled in coeducational classes. Do the former have higher achievement than the latter? Does their achievement equal that of boys? In fact, several studies suggest that achievement is higher for girls in single-gender classes than in coeducational classes. See "The Effects of Sex-Grouped Schooling on Achievement: The Role of National Context," by David P. Baker, Cornelius Riordan, and Maryellen Schaub, *Comparative Education Review* (November 1995).

Unfortunately, interpreting such comparisons is often not a straightforward matter because researchers have been content largely with comparisons of "naturally occurring" classes, that is, classes over which they had little or no control in terms of the assignment of students and teachers to classes or the curriculum. As a result, the classes that were compared may have differed in many ways, including in parental beliefs about innate differences between boys and girls, the motivation of the students to master the subject in question, the intensity and content of the instruction, and the extent to which single-gender classes are perceived to have high status or prestige by the community. This makes it difficult to determine whether differences in achievement between girls in girls-only classes and girls in coeducational classes are due to the gender composition of the classes (and the associated differences in climate) or to one or more of these "confounding" factors. Controlled experiments are needed to show the full impact of single-gender classes on the achievement of girls and boys.

Additional Resources

Dara E. Babinski, Margaret H. Sibley, J. Megan Ross & William E. Pelham, "The Effects of Single Versus Mixed Gender Treatment for Adolescent Girls with ADHD," *Journal of Clinical Child & Adolescent Psychology* (2013, 42:2, 243–250, DOI: 10.1080/15374416.2012.756814).

Christy Belcher, Andy Frey, and Pamela Yankeelov, "The Effects of Single-Sex Classrooms on Classroom Environment, Self-Esteem, and Standardized Test Scores," *School Social Work Journal* (Fall 2006).

Deborah A. Garrahy, "Three Third-Grade Teachers' Gender-Related Beliefs and Behavior," *The Elementary School Journal* (vol. 102, 2001).

Marlon C. James., "Never Quit: The Complexities of Promoting Social and Academic Excellence at a Single-Gender School for Urban African American Males," *Journal of African American Males in Education* (vol. 1, no. 3, 2010).

Internet References . . .

The Gurian Institute

http://gurianinstitute.com/

American Association of University Women

http://www.aauw.org/

The Myra Sadker Foundation

http://www.sadker.org/

Selected, Edited, and with Issue Framing Material by:
Elizabeth Schroeder, EdD, MSW, *Elizabeth Schroeder Consulting*

ISSUE

Is Gender Related to the Use of Computers?

YES: Tim Olds et al., from "How Do School-Day Activity Patterns Differ with Age and Gender Across Adolescence?" *Journal of Adolescent Health* (vol. 44, no. 1, 2009)

NO: Susan McKenney and Joke Voogt, from "Technology and Young Children: How 4–7 Year Olds Perceive Their Own Use of Computers," *Computers in Human Behavior* (vol. 26, no. 4, 2010)

Learning Outcomes

After reading this issue, you will be able to:

- Identify the relation between age and interest in, and use of, computers. Does the age of the youth studied affect the conclusions drawn by the researchers?
- Determine how factors such as immigration status as well as socioeconomic status affect children's attitudes toward, and use of, computers.
- Understand the relation between children's attitudes toward, and perceptions of, computers and their goals for the future.
- Decide whether the country affects the results and would the results be generalizable to the United States, given the fact that the studies reported here were conducted in the Netherlands and in Australia.

ISSUE SUMMARY

YES: Tim Olds and his colleagues examined how much time adolescents spent in different activities during the school day and found that boys had higher levels of screen time, which included television, video games, and computer use, which peaked in the peripubertal years.

NO: Susan McKenney and Joke Voogt studied children's use of technology both within and outside school settings and found no gender differences in young children's perceptions of their own use of computers or in ability level.

Computers, and other technologies, are ubiquitous. More and more computer applications games, for educational and recreational purposes, are being developed for children. It has been claimed that children ages 8–18 are exposed to eight-and-a-half hours of digital and video sensory stimulation a day. In fact, people in their 20s and younger are now called "digital natives." They have never known a world without computers, the Internet, and cell phones. Two questions seem to dominate discussions about computers and kids. Are they good for them? Are girls at a disadvantage? As one digs to find answers to

these questions, opinions and evidence abound on both the yes and no side. In general, it appears to depend on the context. On the one hand, there is concern that too much time on computers will undermine children's development of social skills. There is an amusing commercial on TV for an automobile that shows a teenager, sitting alone at her computer, bemoaning the fact that she read (online) that adults become more antisocial as they get older. So she insisted that her parents join Facebook but noted what a pathetically low number of friends they have compared to the hundreds she has. All the while in the background is an image of her parents with other adults having lots of fun that involves the car being advertised. What cultural ideas does this commercial reflect about online social networks, having fun, and age? It suggests that it is the teen with the socialization problem. On the other hand, evidence says that computers are really good for children. One study of Head Start children found that 15–20 minutes a day working on a computer with educational software substantially improved their cognitive development and school readiness, as well as visual and gross motor skills. Adding to these findings was the observation that children who used the computer at home and school showed greater improvement than the children who used the computer only at school.

Gary Small and Gigi Vorgan recently said, "Even using a computer for Web searches for just an hour a day changes the way the brain processes information." This seems to be confirmed by studies that have shown that just an hour a day on the computer affects the way the brain functions. In their 2008 article entitled "Meet your iBrain" in *Scientific American Mind*, Small and Vorgan present several findings about the "brain on technology":

- Daily exposure to high technology, including computers and video games, creates changes in the brain.
- Playing video games and other technological experiences can sharpen some cognitive abilities by altering neural networks and synaptic connections.
- Playing video games and other technological experiences can increase reactions to visual stimuli and improve many forms of attention, particularly the ability to notice images in our peripheral vision.
- The brain's plasticity allows for technology-related alterations in neural processing.
- A constant barrage of e-contacts is both stimulating and draining.
- Increased focus on technology skills shifts brain functioning away from social skills, such as reading facial expressions during a conversation.
- Frequent digital connectivity can create strain and may increase fatigue, irritability, and distraction.
- Constant monitoring of social information can lead to "continuous partial attention," a form of mental distraction (i.e., keeping tabs on lots of things but focusing on none of them).

They also described a study by cognitive psychologist Pam Briggs of Northumbria University in England, who found that Web surfers spent two seconds or less on any particular site before moving on to the next one when looking for facts about health. She suggested that many

of us develop neural circuitry that is suitable for rapid spurts of directed concentration, a sort of "digital ADD."

If the "digital natives" have arrived, what does this mean for male and female natives? Are the opportunities and advantages available equally for all? Many would say no, that there is still evidence of a serious gender gap in computer use. The American Association of University Women reports that girls make up only a small percentage of students who take high-level computer courses in high school. This report also noted that girls' use of computers is more likely to be limited to activities such as word processing rather than problem solving or actually writing programs, activities boys are more likely to do. They also made the observation that girls see themselves as less competent with computers than boys and see the high-tech domain as a masculine world. Of course, such attitudes and a lack of training reduce considerably the likelihood of pursuing technology careers. In fact, girls are five times less likely to consider taking technology courses in college or pursuing a technology-related career. The seriousness of this problem is compounded by the fact that the proportion of girls considering majoring in computer and information sciences has steadily decreased relative to the proportion of boys, from 20 percent in 2001 to 12 percent in 2006. Program developers and marketers may be contributing to this problem by developing educational software that has more male than female characters and then marketing products more vigorously to boys than to girls. The situation is complicated even more by some scholars who argue that the female and male brains are actually different and therefore the impact of technology will be different. Thus, if we want to close the gender gap, we need to transform schools in gender-specific ways. This is the recommendation of Michael Gurian and Kathy Stevens of the Gurian Institute, which trains education professionals in gender difference and brain-based learning, which they call the nature-based approach. In a 2004 article they wrote for the Association for Supervision and Curriculum Development's journal *Educational Leadership*, they claim that the brains of girls and boys are different, affecting the way they learn. They suggest that PET and MRI technologies show both structural and functional differences between girls and boys that affect the way they learn. What they do not establish is which came first, the brain differences that cause the learning style differences or gender-related experiences that helped shape the brain differences. Relevant to the current discussion on gender and computer, they describe the InterCept program in Colorado Springs. This is a female-specific program for girls at risk for school failure.

They argue that by helping these girls appreciate the importance of being "tech-savvy," they can reduce school failure, juvenile delinquency, and teen pregnancy. The curriculum involves a computer-based program the girls use to explore future careers. The program allows them to see what kind of education is necessary, as well as provide income projections, for various occupations. The project did not include high-risk boys, so it is not known how they would respond to similar mentoring.

YES

Tim Olds et al.

How Do School-Day Activity Patterns Differ with Age and Gender Across Adolescence?

An understanding of how young people use their time is important to developers of social policy, parents, and healthcare providers. For social policy issues, such knowledge should inform the development of interventions designed to target health issues, modeling consumer behavior, forward planning for services such as transport and sporting facilities, and the design of school curricula. Parents may find it of interest to have a sense of how much time children of various ages typically devote to activities such as sport, play, sleep, videogames, and television viewing. Intervention research with anything more than short-term follow-up needs to take into account typical age-related differences to interpret any incremental impacts of intervention over and above these normal age-related differences.

Activities can only be understood in the context of broader patterns of time use, taking into account interactions with peers, adults, and the media, and normal age-related differences. Between early childhood and young adulthood, it is known that sleep time and physical activity decrease. There has been a great deal of recent concern regarding the association between poor sleep and the risk of overweight and a range of psychosocial disorders. Screen time (television, videogames, computers) appears to peak around puberty. These changes probably reflect mutually reinforcing biological (maturational) and social influences. A sudden decline in play and exploratory behavior around the time of sexual maturation in mammals coincides with reductions in the dopaminergic system's activity. The evolutionary rationale for this is easy to understand. Play brings benefits (in the development of one's own skills, strength, motor abilities, and knowledge of the environment), but also risks (e.g., accidental injury and exposure to predators). As animals get older and more experienced, there is a diminishing benefit, so it is possible that the risk:benefit ratio is tilted in favor of less play. The arrival of puberty, however, also coincides with major life transitions, as the child moves from primary to secondary school. As the young person's focus is redirected toward the extrafamilial world, for example, into part-time work, biological drivers are likely to be reinforced by social and cultural changes.

Although there is general agreement on age-related differences in broad use-of-time classes (e.g., sleep and physical activity), there are fewer data on more specific classes of activities, such as passive and active transport (e.g., cars vs. bicycles), chores, phone use, and specific sports. Children's use of time is highly variable, and shows consistent variation related to geography, day of the week, type of day (school day, weekend, holiday), season, and gender.

Purpose

This study aimed primarily to describe age- and gender-related patterns in the self-reported use of time on school days in a large sample of Australian children and adolescents aged between 10 and 18 years.

Methods

Dataset and Subjects

This study analyzed 6,024 use-of-time diaries recorded by children aged 10–18 from several state and regional surveys conducted in the states of South Australia (SA) and Victoria between 2001 and 2006. . . .

Instrument

Use-of-time data were collected using a computerized activity diary, the Multimedia Activity Recall for Children and Adolescents (MARCA). The software asks young people to recall everything they did on the previous day from wake-up to bedtime. It uses a segmented day format with self-determined anchor points (e.g., meals, school bells) and multimedia cues to aid recall. Young people choose from a list of about 250 activities grouped under seven main categories (inactivity, transport, sport and play, school, self-care, chores, and other). They can recall activities in time slices as fine as 5 minutes. Each activity is associated with an energy expenditure (EE) so that an overall estimate of daily energy expenditure can be determined by multiplying the duration of each activity by the associated energy cost. Energy costs were assigned using a compendium of energy costs that contains metabolic equivalent total (MET) scores calculated from studies conducted in youth, where available. The compendium comprises 40% MET scores from studies conducted in children and 60% adult MET scores from Ainsworth and colleagues' adult compendium. However, studies . . . have concluded that the ratio of activity EE and resting EE (i.e., a MET score) appears to be similar in adults and youth. The MARCA has a same-day test–retest reliability of $r = .84-.92$ for major outcome variables (moderate to vigorous physical activity [MVPA]; physical activity level [PAL], and screen time), and a convergent validity against accelerometry of $r = .57$ in a similar age range as the current sample.

The MARCA was administered in small groups in school computer laboratories during school time, overseen by a trained research assistant. Young people recalled between 1 and 7 days according to the needs of the survey; in studies requiring more days, there was an option for young people to take CDs home and e-mail subsequent completed profiles to researchers. Where more than 1 day was recalled, 1 day only was randomly chosen so that no child was overrepresented.

Sampling Frame

Because high-resolution use-of-time data on children require more time to collect, and surveys with very large sample sizes are very expensive, it was necessary to combine data from various surveys to get an adequate coverage of children from across the age range. Although these surveys used the same instrument, the MARCA, they drew from different geographical areas (South Australia and Victoria) and used different sampling frames. The South Australian data were collected across a series of independent surveys over a 5-year period between 2000 and 2005. In most surveys (encompassing 4,676 children), schools were randomly selected from a list of all schools in the state, and all children from a particular age group were invited to participate. In these surveys, the average response rate was 69% for schools, and 92% for children within the chosen age group within each school. In a small number of

cases (427 children), data were collected from students at individual schools at the invitation of the schools themselves, or as part of pilot projects. In Victoria (921 children), MARCA profiles (a "profile" is a recall of 1 day by one child) were collected as part of the third wave of a longitudinal survey, the Health of Young Victorians Study.

Because the MARCA was usually administered during school time, there were fewer recalls of nonschool days (mainly weekends, and some holidays), especially by younger children. In addition, there were scarcely any recalls of Saturdays, because the MARCA is a previous day recall. Therefore, this paper will deal only with school day recalls. Furthermore, only 5% of all profiles recalled a Friday, as opposed to 19% to 27% for each of the other weekdays. However, there were no significant differences between age-related waking time, screen time, physical activity level (or overall daily energy expenditure), or moderate to vigorous physical activity between Fridays and the other weekdays in this dataset. Because of examinations and school holidays, few data were collected in January and December, although profiles were fairly evenly distributed across the remaining months. The dataset initially consisted of 16,250 profiles, of which 474 were excluded as yielding improbably high- or low-energy expenditures (PAL <1.1 or >3.0). This was reduced to a total of 6204 profiles when only recalls of school days, and just one profile for each child, were selected.

Data Analysis

The main response variables in this study were the following activity sets.

Activity Related

PAL (the average daily rate of energy expenditure in multiples of resting metabolic rate); minutes of MVPA (participation in any activity eliciting at least three METs); organized sport and play (formal or informal structured games and school physical education classes); free play (playground games, "mucking around," unstructured activity); and active transport (walking, cycling, skateboarding etc.).

Sedentarism Related

Minutes of waking time (i.e., 1,440 minutes per 24-hour day, minus minutes spent sleeping), small screen time (i.e., time spent watching television, playing videogames, using the computer for the internet, etc.), and passive transport (riding in cars, buses, trains, etc.). Time awake rather than sleep time was used because the MARCA profiles record activities from wake-up to bedtime. The predictor variables were age at last birthday (10–17+ in 1-year increments), and gender.

Profiles were therefore divided into 16 subsets (8 ages [10–17+ years] × 2 genders). Data analysis consisted of both descriptive and comparative components. Average (mean and median) values are reported by age–gender slices for the main response variables. . . .

The time distribution of activities across the day was described by calculating the percentage of children who were engaged in each of the specified activity sets at 15-minute intervals from midnight to midnight. A 15-minute interval was chosen to minimize the time required for this computing-intensive task, and because it gives sufficient resolution to capture time-related patterns.

Results

. . . *Components of screen time and MVPA.* Overall, TV constituted about 69% of total screen time for boys, and 75% for girls; videogames made up 17% for boys and 8% for girls; and computer use made up 13% for boys and 16% for girls. On average, 70% of nonvideogame computer time was accumulated during school hours. However, the relative contribution of these different components varied with age, with the contribution of television declining from 78 (95% confidence interval [CI]: 75%–82%) at age 10 to 71 (67%–76%) at age 17, and the contribution of nonvideo-game computer time increasing from 7 (5%–9%) to 16 (11%–21%).

Organized sport/play made up close to 50% of all MVPA (51% for boys, 45% for girls), and free play about 20%. The rest consisted mainly of active transport and chores. The mix differed with age, with free play in particular decreasing rapidly with increasing age. At age 10, 50 (95% CI 46%–53%) of MVPA was organized sport/play and 26 (23%–29%) free play. By age 17, these figures were 37 (31%–43%) and 8 (5%–12%), respectively.

Time distribution of activities. The time distribution of activities across the day was largely governed by the school regimen. Physical activity spiked before school, at recess, lunch, and after school. . . . Overall patterns of MVPA were fairly similar, older adolescents were less active than younger adolescents, particularly at lunch and recess, and had less MVPA during in-school hours. Older adolescents also accumulated less screen time. There was a very large spike in screen time before school in the younger adolescents, particularly boys, and somewhat higher levels during school hours and after dinner. Peak screen time was later for older adolescents than for younger children.

Comparisons Between Genders and Across Age Groups

. . . *Activity-related variables. Age-related patterns:* PAL, MVPA, organized sport/play, and free play all declined linearly with age. PAL declined at the rate of about 2.5% per year of age. MVPA declined at the rate of 13–17 min $\cdot$ day^{-1} per year of age. Average daily organized sport/play declined at the rate of about 9 min $\cdot$ day^{-1} per year of age in both boys and girls. Free play showed a similar trend, with declines of 6–7 min $\cdot$ day^{-1} per year of age in both boys and girls. Active transport showed a different pattern, peaking at around age 14, before falling in later adolescence.

Gender-related patterns: Boys reported higher levels of PAL, MVPA, and organized sport/play across the age span, but similar levels of free play. The rate of age-related decline in PAL was not different between boys and girls. At every age, boys had higher levels of both MVPA (by about 30–60 min $\cdot$ day^{-1}) and organized play/sport (by about 15–50 min $\cdot$ day^{-1}). In contrast, girls had higher levels of active transport than boys, but the differences were slight (about 5 min $\cdot$ day^{-1}).

Sedentarism-related variables. Age-related patterns: Sedentary behavior also declined with age, particularly in late adolescence. Time awake increased (and, hence, overall sleep time decreased) approximately linearly with age, at a rate of about 13 min $\cdot$ day^{-1} per year of age. Screen time, television time, and computer time tended to peak at around 12–14 years, declining fairly rapidly thereafter. Daily screen time peaked at age 12, declining thereafter at the rate of 14–18 min $\cdot$ day^{-1} per year of age. Television time decreased between the ages of 12 and 17. Videogame time decreased across the age span in boys, but there were no trends in girls. Passive transport increased throughout the age span, with a rapid rise around age 13.

The time devoted to most activities (screen time, sleep, physical activity) decreased in late adolescence. So what do older adolescents do with their time? Their time budget is mainly filled with nonscreen sedentary activities. Homework increases from 14 min $\cdot$ day^{-1} at age 10 to 33 min $\cdot$ day^{-1} at age 17. The time spent sitting or standing and talking, including talking on the phone, increased from 38 min $\cdot$ day^{-1} at age 10 to 80 min $\cdot$ day^{-1} at age 17.

Gender-related patterns: In most sedentarism-related variables, boys had higher values than girls. There were small gender differences in time awake, with girls sleeping on average 5 min $\cdot$ day^{-1} longer, whereas the rates of increase with age were similar. At every age, boys exceeded girls in screen time (by 35–75 min $\cdot$ day^{-1}) and videogame time (by 14–32 min · day^{-1}). Boys watched somewhat more television (by 5–47 min · day^{-1}), but there were no differences in computer time. The age-related differences in total screen time were similar for boys and girls. Girls had higher levels of passive transport than boys by 5–10 min · day^{-1}.

Discussion

The data presented here provide "baseline" patterns of age- and gender-related differences in young people's time use. They may assist when making comparisons among studies on children of different ages. They may also be useful, when interventions are tracked over time, in distinguishing intervention effects from "normal" underlying age-related differences. For example, a 2-year intervention to reduce screen time in 12-year-olds might be considered "successful" if it manages to halt the age-related increase in screen time across those years of adolescence.

One striking pattern to emerge from these data is how components of various activity categories vary with age. It would be unwise, for example, to consider MVPA as a unitary concept. As children get older, a much smaller proportion of MVPA is derived from free play. Similar considerations apply when construing screen time as a single item: as children get older, television plays a lesser role, and computer time a greater role. These shifts are important when planning and monitoring interventions.

The broad patterns of age- and gender-related differences found in this study have also been found in other recent Australian and international studies [that have] found that MVPA increased and screen time decreased with age, and that boys had higher levels of both MVPA and screen time than girls. . . .

Age-Related Differences

Physical activity, as indexed by PAL, MVPA, organized sport/play, and free play, decreased with age. This has been a consistent finding in the literature. Our data suggest that much of this decrease results from lower participation in MVPA during school hours. This may reflect increasing interest in the more social aspects of school life (while fewer than 10% of 17-year-old girls were active at lunch time, almost 80% of 10-year-old boys were). Participation also declined during class hours, perhaps as a result of the crowded school curriculum in the upper years and because of the reduction in compulsory physical education classes in the upper secondary years. In Australia, physical education is compulsory in primary and lower secondary school, but often not in upper secondary school. Sport is not compulsory in government schools after Year 10.

There was no clear evidence in these data that puberty represented a watershed in physical activity patterns. The pattern of decline was generally linear from age 10 to age 17. However, pubertal stage was not assessed in this study across the relevant years, so discontinuities may be obscured by puberty occurring at different times. There were clear patterns in both active transport and screen time roughly contemporaneous with puberty, with the amount of time devoted to these activities peaking around ages 12–14. Similar patterns have been found in studies of U.S. children's media use. It is unclear whether these patterns reflect biological (puberty) or social (transition to high school) changes. . . .

Active transport plateaued at age 14, when most young people have access to bicycles and may be given road autonomy by their parents, but before they have their own driver's licences or can rely on those of their older friends. Total transport (passive plus active) increased with age. This perhaps reflects (a) the greater average distance from home to secondary school versus primary school (and, hence, the greater likelihood that the child will not walk to school), and (b) the greater social and sporting commitments of the older child, to which they may be chauffeured by their parents. The rapid increase in passive transport above the age of 15 may reflect the number of young people who get their own driver's licences around age 16. Alternatively, they may have older friends with driver's licences, and hence, have reduced reliance on walking and cycling. However, driving age varied in the different jurisdictions in this sample. Most of the age-related increase in passive transport time seems to occur before and after school, suggesting either that trips to school are longer, or that older adolescents arrive at and leave school across a wider range of times, perhaps for early classes or extracurricular commitments.

As children get older, sleep, MVPA, and screen time decline. However, other kinds of sedentary behaviors fill the time void left by these declines. Nonscreen sedentary behaviors (less active school classes, talking with friends, "hanging out," reading) rise from about 2 hours per day at age 12 to over 9 hours per day at age 17. Consequently, the age-related decline in screen time is more than compensated by increases in other kinds of sedentarism. This has implications for monitoring interventions, as screen time has often been used as a surrogate for all sedentary behaviors. Older adolescents may be sedentary in different ways, sitting and talking, for example, rather than using the videogame console.

Gender Differences

Boys had both higher MVPA and higher screen time than girls, a finding that replicates those of other studies. However, there were no differences between boys and girls in the total time committed to activities eliciting 1.0–1.5 METs (data not shown). Girls, therefore, compensated for their lower screen times with other types of sedentary behaviors (e.g., phone use, talking to friends). This, again, suggests that screen time may not be an ideal surrogate for all sedentary behaviors.

Time use showed rather stereotypical gender differences, with girls spending less time in organized sport/play and MVPA and screen time, and showing lower overall PALs. Girls also spent more time shopping, doing chores, playing with pets, and talking on the phone or texting (data not shown). The higher levels of both active and passive transport in girls may reflect either the greater willingness of parents to drive daughters to social events, or girls having older boyfriends or girlfriends who have their driver's licence, and therefore have the opportunity to travel to more distant events.

Strengths and Limitations

This dataset represents the largest and most detailed analysis of use-of-time in this group of young Australians yet conducted. The instrument used to collect data, the MARCA, uses a diary format, and therefore obliges the user to account for each minute of the day. Furthermore, the high-resolution nature of the data makes it possible to cluster activities into different activity sets. Each activity is linked to an energy cost, so that activity sets can be defined in terms of energy requirements as well as by thematic clustering.

However, this sample is not nationally representative. There will be some degree of clustering by school, and a degree of self-selection because of schools and individuals opting in or out of the various surveys, and because of drop-out of heavier and older students in the longitudinal sample. Sampling across ages in this study was not geographically homogeneous, with most of the younger children being interviewed in South Australia, and most of the older children in Victoria. These are, however, neighboring states in southeastern Australia with a similar socioeconomic and ethnic mix, including similar percentages of overseas-born residents (SA = 21.2%; Victoria = 24.6%; national = 23.1%). South Australia has a somewhat lower socioeconomic profile than Victoria (the mean census-based Socioeconomic Indexes for Areas value is 973 for SA, 1,011 for Victoria, and 1,000 [SD 100] nationally). The sample described here also resembles young people of this age across Australia in height, mass, and prevalence of overweight and obesity.

A further limitation is that the data are not sampled evenly across days of the week and months of the year. Apart from January and February, the percentage of days sampled varies from 7.6% in May to 13.5% in September. Twenty-six percent of the data were collected in autumn, 32% in winter, and 31% in spring. It is likely that school-day behaviors are different in the summer. However, the months of December and January are largely holiday months in Australia, and the error introduced in relation to school day activity patterns in likely to be modest.

The data presented here are in the form of averages. Often it is the extreme values that are of greater interest in formulating public policy (e.g., targeting "extreme users" of screen technologies). Moreover, many of these extreme behaviors (long periods of screen time, catch-up sleeping, weekend sport) occur on nonschool days, which have not been covered in this study. Furthermore, it is likely that use of time during school holidays will be quite different from both school and weekend days. An analysis of the distributional characteristics of children's use of time, stratified by day type, would complement this study.

Tim Olds is a professor in the School of Health Sciences, Physical Education, Exercise and Sport Studies at the University of South Australia, Adelaide, Australia. His research has covered the mathematical modeling of cycling performance, anthropometry, and secular and geographic trends in fitness, fatness, physical activity, and food intake. Professor Olds developed the Multimedia Activity Recall for Children and Adolescents (MARCA), a computerized 24-hour use-of-time recall which permits the study of how people use their time, especially when undertaking behavioral change programs.

Susan McKenney and Joke Voogt

Technology and Young Children: How 4–7 Year Olds Perceive Their Own Use of Computers

Introduction

In the past century, the introduction of new media such as films, radio and television, has spawned debate and research concerning the (educational) benefits for children versus the fears related to (over)exposure. In this millennium, the opportunities and concerns regarding widely accessible Information and Communications Technologies (ICTs) are no different. Society's perceptions of technology and expectations for its use are important. Those notions impact the use of computers at home, as well as shape the course of implementation in educational settings. While many assert that computers do not have a place at the hands of young children, others contend that those who do not embrace new media may be in danger of losing touch with the popular culture of young children and their families.

While the debate in favor of and against young children's computer use rages on, there is little dispute that today, children are using computers even before they know how to read and write. However, research is lacking on how young children use computers and what the (intentional and unintentional) effects are. This is especially true in the Netherlands. Current literature is dominated by investigations conducted in the United States. Studies involving young children and computers have increased in recent years, with greater emphasis on exploring innovative applications for this age range and only a few examining usage patterns. Of those studies that look at how children are using computers, most rely on parent and caregiver reports; and very few involve asking children directly about how they perceive their own use of computers. In analyzing the 60 structured interviews and 1852 questionnaire responses from parents and caregivers in the England, [it was] found:

- *Frequency:* 53% of the children in the 0–6 age range use computers on a typical day, usually for less than 1 hour.
- *Type:* Children's favorite type of application was playing games, either on websites (especially those associated with BBC television programs) or on CD/DVD.
- *Gender:* When listing website favorites, boys' and girls' preferences were the same for the first three rankings (CBeebies, CBBC, and Nickolodeon Junior, respectively), but differed in the fourth and fifth rankings. Boys preferred Bob the Builder and Thomas the Tank Engine, while girls liked Barbie and the Tweenies.
- *Parental attitude:* Parents were overwhelmingly positive about their children using computers, noting their acquisition of computing skills as well as software-specific knowledge and skills as beneficial. Concerns about the children using computers were not expressed.

Perhaps even more problematic is the prevalence of "few facts and many opinions" about the use of computers by young children. The need for increased research into young children's computer use has been expressed by researchers and practitioners. Though early, this call is garnering response, as exemplified by programs and projects undertaken on both sides of the Atlantic such as:

- Technology and Young Children Special Interest Forum within the [American] National Association for the Education of Young Children (NAEYC); and
- Children's Awareness of Technology (CHAT) and Developmentally Appropriate Technology in Early Childhood (DATEC), sponsored by the European Union. . . .

As early as the 1990s, young children's attitudes towards computers [have been studied]. Data were collected from 1990 to 1994 and examined the impact of computer use on children in grade 1–3 (6–9 year olds) from Japan, the USA and Mexico. The results showed that computer exposure in school had a positive impact on children's attitudes towards computers and that children's perceptions of computers were not related to their home country. Studies such as this have not been conducted in the Netherlands. Therefore, the research reported in this paper focuses on computer attitudes, computer use and computer skills of pre-K–grade 2 children (4–7 year olds), an age range slightly younger than the children who were involved in the study reported above. Better insight in computer use and attitudes of young children informs the debate of the desirability of young children's exposure to computers at home as well as in educational settings.

As with an educational resource, equitable use is worthy of consideration. . . . Gender differences in attitudes towards computers for children in grade 1–3 [were not found], girls' participation in technology-related activities has been a serious concern in the last decade. Perhaps even more disquieting is the 'digital divide,' now generally defined as "situations in which there is a marked gap in access to or use of ICT devices". The digital divide usually exists when a group's access to ICT differs along one or more dimensions of social, economic, cultural, or national identity. In this study, we explore whether indications can be found for a digital divide in this age range with respect to gender, socio-economic status and (ethnic) minority versus (ethnic) majority groups in the Dutch society. Studies with older children have shown that lower-income students have less access to computers in the home, and use computers at school more often for repetitive practice; whereas higher-income students have far greater access to computers in the home and use computers at school more often for more sophisticated, intellectually complex applications. . . . Very few of the already scarce studies looking at computer use in this age range, examine the access to ICT with regard to gender and ethnic minorities. What we do know . . . [from one] study:

- Considerable inequality of access to ICT in the home: In this study, 28 children were from English families, 17 from Bangladeshi families, and 3 from another ethnic origin (African and Kosovan). 26 of the 48 households contained a computer, but only 3 of these were in Bangladeshi homes.
- Young girls are as likely as young boys to be using a home computer.
- Middle-class parents tend to be more involved in their children's computer use than lower class parents.
- No evidence that home advantages in terms of technology access directly influenced computer use at school.

The finding that girls and boys are equally likely to be using a home computer is consistent with the findings of a previous study. However, the finding that home advan-

tages do not influence computer use at school is especially interesting, as it is contradicted by the beliefs of early years educators who responded to an earlier . . . survey.

The study reported in this article took place in the Netherlands, and speaks to the need for better insight into how children are using computers, how they experience computers, and differences associated with gender and ethnicity. With the ultimate aim of understanding how Dutch 4–7 year olds perceive their own use of computers, the following four research questions were formulated:

1. Is access to computers outside school associated with gender, age, socio-economic status or ethnic group?
2. What activities do young children do on the computer, in and out of school?
3. To what extent are they able to conduct these activities independently or with help?
4. What attitudes do young children have?
5. Are differences in the use, skills or attitudes associated with gender, age, socio-economic status and ethnic group?

Methods

Participants

Children in pre-kindergarten (pre-K) through second grade (Dutch groups 1–4) from two schools participated. In total, 167 children (82 boys and 85 girls) were involved in the study. The age range varied between 4 and 8 years. The Dutch school system starts at the age of 4 when children start in pre-K, and is compulsory from kindergarten (K) starting at age 5. In the Netherlands, 98% of all 4-year olds attend pre-K. In this study we explored in and out of school use of computers. For this reason we prefer not to use age level, but to use grade level as an indicator of age. In the Dutch school system most four year olds attend pre-K, most 5 year old attend K, the 6 year olds are in grade 1 and the most 7 year olds are in grade 2. Learning to read and to write, as well as basic arithmetic starts in grade 1, but preparatory activities are carried out in pre-K and K.

Regardless of nationality, children were classified as native Dutch or Dutch immigrants. In accordance with national guidelines, native Dutch children were defined as those whose parents were both born in the Netherlands; children of one or more parents born in another country were categorized as Dutch immigrants. Both schools were located in the same city of 150,000. One school, hereafter referred to as "Southside," is located on the outskirts of town, in an area of lower socio-economic status and many second and third generation immigrant families from Morocco or Turkey with Arab-Berber or

Turkish ethnic backgrounds, respectively. Teachers in this school openly share their ongoing concerns about pupil welfare and regularly conduct home visits. 81 children from this school participated in the study. 36 were classified as Dutch natives, and can be considered as belonging to the ethnic majority; while 45 were classified as immigrants and belonging to the ethnic minorities present in this part of town. In this study, we consider the immigrants of Southside to represent ethnic minorities and compare them with the Dutch natives from Southside as a representation of an ethnic majority group.

The other school, hereafter referred to as, "Central," is located in the city center, with primarily middle class children attending. Pupil welfare issues are less common in this school, and home visits by teachers are rarely made. This school is the only school in the region that offers instruction in English for long-term visiting children whose parents work in international companies or at the local university. Children attend the English language class a few hours each day, but spend the majority of their time in their home class with the Dutch children. In addition, the school prides itself on their Early English program, teaching English as a second language to Dutch-speaking children from pre-K onwards, which is exceptional in the Dutch education system. From this school, 86 children participated, with 58 classified as Dutch natives (ethnic majority) and 33 as immigrants. It should be noted, however, that this group of immigrants is much more mixed than those from Southside, and cannot be classified as an ethnic minority group.

. . . [W]e view the Southside population to represent low socio-economic status and the Central population to represent middle socio-economic status.

Both schools had similar technology facilities: one or two computers in each classroom and computer clusters in one or more hallways. Southside has a technology coordinator who manages the infrastructure and also worked with the children on a weekly basis. This school prides itself on their approach to technology integration, which begins with the pre-K groups. In contrast, Central assigns the role of technology coordinator to a regular classroom teacher, whose main task is to manage the infrastructure including, when necessary coordination with the service provider. Both schools used the same third-party provider for technology services.

Data Collection

In a preliminary study conducted in 2003, experience was acquired in collecting data with children of this age level. The data for this study were collected through one-on-one interviews with the children. The interviews contained closed questions and were designed to take less than 15 min each. They addressed five areas: demographics, computer availability/access, computer activities use, attitudes and abilities. . . .

Demographics. The demographics section included name, class, school, grade, age, gender, land of birth (of self and parents) and language spoken at home.

Computer availability, access and activity types. . . . For school and at home, the computer activities section included the following categories of activities: practicing words/math; drawing; writing letters/stories; playing games; searching for information on Internet; reading/writing e-mail; and chatting (this last one was only asked for at home, as schools do not allow this practice). . . .

Attitudes. The attitude section was based on the computer importance and computer enjoyment subscales . . . designed for first through third graders. . . .

Skills to use the computer independently. . . . Children indicated how they used each computer activity: independently, with help, or neither (meaning, not at all). . . .

Except for the demographic information, black and white icons on colored cards were used to help the learners understand and stay focused on the interview questions. For example, children were shown the school icon card and then asked, "While at school, do you use the computer?" If they said yes, then a yellow set of cards was shown. . . . Children were then told what each one meant, then asked to turn face-down the ones that represent activities they did not do. For the remaining activities, children were asked if they did this often (daily or weekly) or sometimes (less than once a week). Children were first given practice questions on how often they watch television or go to the movies. . . .

The interviews were conducted with two trained interviewers. They used the icon cards when asking each question to a child and based on the child's answer completed the questionnaire. . . .

Results

Access to Computers Outside School

While both schools have computer facilities for use by the children, we were more interested in the availability of computers for children at home. The results . . . show that the penetration of computers at home is very high. It is notable that there is a relatively low presence of computers (computers with Internet access in particular) in the homes of Dutch native children in Southside. However, the overall picture is that most children do have access to a computer, often with Internet access, in their homes.

If you ask the children where, outside school, they mainly use the computer, most of them report that they use the computer at home. A few also use the computer mainly at a friend's house or at school (after school hours). Almost 10% of children in pre-K report not using the computer outside of school. Also, (relatively few) girls report more often than boys that they do not use the computer outside school.

In and Out of School Computer Use: Activities

. . . The findings show that only a few children report never playing a computer game, but that many at this age level never search the Internet or read or write e-mail.

. . . Boys and girls do not differ a lot in the kind of use of the computer. Both boys and girls report that in school and outside the school they use the computer most often for 'playing a game.' This is followed by 'practicing words/math' (in school use) and 'searching the Internet' (out of school use). 'Reading and writing e-mail' is the least often mentioned use of the computer in this age range both in school and outside school. Although the majority of the children (both boys and girls) never chat on the computer, 'chatting' is fairly often mentioned by about 40% of the children as an activity they do on the computer.

Medium–medium effect sizes in favor of boys were found for 'drawing' 'writing a letter/story', 'playing a game', indicating that boys use the computer in school for these activities more often than girls. With regard to out of school use, a medium+ effect size was found in favor of boys for 'searching the internet' and a medium effect size for 'drawing' in favor of girls.

. . . With regard to in school use, children report that 'playing games' is most often used in the lower grades (4–5 year olds), but in the middle grades (6–7 year olds) 'playing games' and 'practicing words/math' is about equally reported. The other activities are mentioned considerably less. A large effect size between pre-K and grade 2, in favor of the latter, is found for 'practicing words/math', it indicates that in the middle grades compared to the lower grades the computer is more often used for school-based activities. Also 'writing a letter/story' is mentioned considerably more in grade 2 compared to pre-K, which makes sense, because pre-K students usually do not have formal writing skills. A medium+ effect size of 'playing a game' in favor of pre-K indicates that games are more often used in the lower grades.

. . . [O]utside school, an increase in use is found for all distinguished computer activities for grade 2 children compared to children in pre-K. 'Playing games' clearly is the most frequent use of the computer across grade levels. Followed by 'searching the Internet' (pre-K, grade 1 and grade 2) and 'drawing' (K).

. . . The overall picture is the same: both groups use the computer most often for playing games, both in school and outside school. Concerning the use of computers in school, differences between the two groups with medium to large effect sizes for writing letter/story and playing a game, suggesting that Dutch natives at Southside use the computer in school for these activities more often than their immigrant peers. For the other activities, no differences were found between the two groups. However, out of school computer use provides a very different picture. Immigrant children seem to use the computer more often for quite a number of activities. . . . The only activity for which Dutch native children report more frequent use than their immigrant peers, is 'writing a letter/story'.

. . . The picture that emerges throughout is the use of the computer for playing games, which seems the most favorite use for children from both schools. With regard to in school use, children attending Southside use the computer more, compared to Central children, for 'drawing', while children at Central use the computer more for searching the Internet, and reading/writing e-mail. It should be noted however that e-mail use does not happen very often in both schools. The picture for computer use outside school is different. Southside children use the computer more for chatting; drawing, writing letter/story and reading/writing email compared to their peers from Central, while Central children use the computer, more for playing games.

Skills to Operate the Computer Independently

. . . The results . . . show that the majority of both boys and girls in this age range are able to play a computer game, start a computer game, make a drawing and search on the Internet alone or with some help. Differences in skills between boys and girls, with small+ effect sizes, were found for starting a computer game (in favor of boys), writing a letter/story (in favor of girls) and searching for information (in favor of boys).

With respect to grade level, the results show that the majority of the youngest children in pre-K are already able to start and play a game (with help or alone). However, it is striking that already at this age level (most pre-K children are 4 years old) so many children report being able—often with help—to handle the computer. It far less surprising that this has changed by grade 2 (most children are then 7 years old). In grade 2, the majority is able to use the computer (with help or alone) for all the different skills that were distinguished. . . .

. . . The results show that the majority of children in both ethnic groups (Dutch natives and immigrants) are able to start and play a computer game and to make a drawing. The majority of the immigrants at Southside are also able to search for information on the Internet. . . .

With regard to socio-economic status, we did find differences . . . in favor of Southside with regard to making a drawing, reading/writing e-mail and chatting. But, Central children report being more able to write a letter/story compared to their Southside peers.

Attitudes

Overall, children express positive attitudes towards computers. Significant differences in attitudes towards computers were found for gender (in favor of boys), grade level (in favor of the older children in grade 2) and socio-economic status (in favor of the children from a lower socio-economic neighborhood, Southside).

Discussion and Conclusions

Examining how young children perceive their use of computers provides information for educators and parents, many of whom are struggling to find practical, developmentally appropriate applications of technology in classrooms and at home. This study set out to explore young children's access to computers, their perceptions of what they do on the computer (in school and outside school), their abilities to operate the computer for specific activities, and their attitudes towards computers. . . .

The findings of this study showed that most young children had access to computers, regardless of gender, socio-economic background or ethic group. . . . The findings of this study suggest that the digital divide with regard to computer access is not so much an issue anymore in the Netherlands, but more large scale studies are needed to confirm this conclusion.

Regardless of gender, age, socio-economic status and ethic group, playing games is the computer activity young children most frequently do, both at home and at school. As playing games is the most common way for children of all ages to spend their free time, it is not surprising that children report playing games as the most frequent computer activity at home both in this study and in research with older children. Next to playing games, searching the Internet is the second most-frequently reported activity for out of school computer use. The other activities are carried out less often.

It is notable that children report that they also use the computer most for playing games while at school. Children in pre-K (4 year olds) play games in school more often than their peers from grade 2 (7 year olds). These results may imply that the computer in school is used as a bonus for children who are finished with their school tasks and are allowed to play a game on the computer. However, it is also possible that especially the younger children experience their activity as a game, even though their teachers might differently describe the same software, due to its affordances with regard to, for example, learning or practice in the area of (preparatory) literacy or numeracy. Further research is necessary to better understand this finding. Next to playing games, practicing words/math is the second reported use of the computer in school. This computer activity increases with grade level. Except for drawing on the computer, the other activities are carried out less often across grade levels. For in school computer use, not many differences were found between boys and girls, nor between Dutch natives and immigrants. However, at Southside the computer is used considerably more for drawing and at Central for searching the Internet. It is not clear whether this is due to the socio-economic background of the school population or if this has more to do with other factors, such as the educational view of the school team.

It is no surprise that outside school, older children (grade 2) use the computer more often and also are more able to operate the computer for a variety of activities than younger ones (pre-K). Literature has long suggested that pupil attitudes toward computers are favorable; this is consistent with the findings from this study. In addition, this study found that older children have a more positive attitude towards computers than younger children have.

Concern about girls' lack of interest in technology has been growing in the last decade. No big differences between boys and girls out of school computer use were found. Also no gender differences were found in the ability level of using various computer activities. These findings concur with those from a recent study in which young girls and young boys were equally likely to be using a home computer as well as another in which young girls now report using home computers as often, and with as much confidence as boys. While the findings of this study revealed that boys have a comparably more positive attitude towards computers than girls have, both groups remain generally positive. . . . Children's perceptions of computers are also influenced by the software they use.

[A] gender-bias content analysis of educational software for preschoolers found significantly more male characters than female characters in preschool educational software, which . . . makes it difficult for teachers to address gender diversity and suggests that girls are not as valued as boys are. Subsequent research on gender differences in computing would benefit from a deeper look at the software being used.

Literature suggests that ethnic minority children may be disadvantaged by a lack of home experience with computers. The findings of this study suggest that immigrant children have more exposure to computers out of school than Dutch children from a low socio-economic background. In addition, immigrant children seem to be better able to operate the computer for a number of different activities, searching information on the Internet in particular. An explanation put forth by Southside teachers is that, often, computer use in immigrant families is focused on communication with family members still living in the country of origin. However, more research is necessary to fully understand this finding. No differences between immigrant children and Dutch children were found in attitude towards computers. The findings of this study also suggest that children from a lower socio-economic background use the computer slightly more often outside school compared to middle class children, and have a more positive attitude towards computers. . . . Further research is necessary to understand how crucial it is that schools take it upon themselves to ensure equal opportunity for less-advantaged children to access the benefits of the more intellectually powerful uses of computer technology. . . .

It is known that the benefits of using technology with young children vary with the kind of experiences offered and how frequently the children have access to computers. . . . As our picture of how children are spending their computer time sharpens, further research should be conducted into the quality and appropriateness of those experiences. . . . Understanding children's practices and attitudes can inform educators and parents in the search for developmentally appropriate uses of technology, as well as a healthy balance between computer use and other means for children to learn and explore the world around them.

SUSAN MCKENNEY is a professor at the University of Twente and the Open Universiteit in the Netherlands, specializing in curriculum design and educational innovation. Her work has emphasized the supportive role of technology in curriculum and teacher development, with a recent focus on early childhood literacy. She has consulted broadly in the Netherlands, India, and southern Africa, offering research expertise in the design, evaluation, and revision of educational improvement initiatives.

JOKE VOOGT is an associate professor in the Department of Curriculum Design and Educational Innovation at the University of Twente, in the Netherlands. The primary focus of her research is on innovative uses of information and communication technologies in the curriculum, with a special interest in the demands on teachers when integrating technology into the classroom. She also serves as editor-in-chief of the *International Handbook of Information Technology in Primary and Secondary Education*.

EXPLORING THE ISSUE

Is Gender Related to the Use of Computers?

Critical Thinking and Reflection

1. What might be the gender implications of looking broadly at the use of a variety of technologies, such as television, video games, smart phones, and computers? In what ways are these technologies and their purposes similar and different?
2. Might there be relevant questions about gender and technology use when the various applications of the technologies are used, such as for communication (i.e., social network sites), knowledge exchange (i.e., blogging), learning (i.e., online courses), or gaming?
3. If there are meaningful gender differences in the use of computers and various technology-related skills, what are the intervention implications? Should schools have gender-specific programs?
4. Do developers and marketers of various technologies and their applications have a responsibility to address any gender-relevant consequences of their products and activities?

Is There Common Ground?

Tips for Monitoring Computer Use by Young Children

The National Association for the Education of Young Children (NAEYC) is an organization that sets standards of excellence for programs designed for children from birth through age 8. The organization bases these standards on current research in child development and on the professional opinions of early childhood educators.

NAEYC has issued the following specific recommendations regarding computer use by young children. In addition to helping your child have the best educational experience when working on a computer, these strategies may also decrease your young child's risk of fatigue-related eye strain, computer vision syndrome, and computer ergonomics problems:

- Computers should supplement, not replace, educational activities such as art, books, music, outdoor exploration, dramatic play, and socializing with other children.
- Parents should guide children's use of computers. Be on hand to help your child, answer questions, and interact with him as he works on the computer.
- Take the time to observe your child at the computer and participate in computer activities with him. Observing children working at a computer can reveal a lot about the way they think and solve problems.
- Encourage your child to work with a sibling or friend at the computer whenever possible. Using computers with others encourages important social skills, such as turn-taking and cooperation, and helps build your child's ability to speak and listen.
- Learn more about software for young children and carefully preview the software your child uses. While many high-quality products are available, some software is not appropriate for young children because it is difficult to use, highlights violent themes, or does not foster language or learning.

Additional Resources

Gary Heiting, *Kids, Computers and Computer Vision*, All About Vision. http://www.allaboutvision.com/parents/children-computer-vision-syndrome.htm

Girls and Computers. http://schoolcomputing.wikia.com/wiki/Girls_and_Computers

Girls and Computers, *New York Times* Opinion page. http://www.nytimes.com/1998/10/19/opinion/girls-and-computers.html

Michael Gurian and Kathy Stevens, "With Boys and Girls in Mind," *Educational Leadership*. Retrieved November 2004, from http://www.ascd.org/publications/educational-leadership/nov04/vol62/num03/With-Boys-and-Girls-in-Mind.aspx

Internet References . . .

Gender Differences in Computer Technology Achievement

http://www.ncsu.edu/meridian/sum2002/gender/

Gender-Related Differences in Exposure to and Use of Computers: Results of a Survey of Secondary School Students

http://link.springer.com/article/10.1007/BF03172940#page-1

The Internet and Computer Games Reinforce the Gender Gap

http://www.apa.org/monitor/oct00/games.aspx

Unit 2

UNIT

He Said, She Said, They Said

No matter how much social progress has been made when it comes to promoting equality between men and women in the workplace, disparities remain. Certain jobs are still gendered as being more "appropriate" for men or women, or, further, that they only can be done by a man or a woman. Further, there is greater understanding and acceptance that there are not only "men" and "women"—openly transgender people in the workplace have unique social, legal, and healthcare needs that are new human resource terrains for many businesses and organizations. These disparities are more pronounced when additional demographics are added in—white women experience sexism; women of color experience racism and sexism; women with disabilities experience sexism and ableism, and so on.

The role men play in fighting sexism is important—yet complicated. As part of the power majority, many men—in particular, heterosexual white men—have been and continue to be true partners and allies to women in leveling the professional playing field. At the same time, however, many men are threatened by the idea of women being seen as equal to them. Their backlash against women's equality has resulted in a "men's movement" of sorts, which has ranged anywhere from progressive, pro-feminist men to more religious groups like the Promise Keepers, which uses the Bible to justify men's and women's roles, and men's superiority. As you read the selections, think about the idea of inequality—why do you think there is resistance to true equality among genders? Are the resistance and any other accompanying concerns justified? What would need to happen, do you think, to help allay those concerns? Think, too, about the question relating to the Employment Non-Discrimination Act. For the longest time, gender equality focused exclusively on men's and women's rights. Introducing a third gender confuses many, and has an impact on how they regard the idea of equal rights. As you come to understand what "transgender" means and who transgender people are, try to reflect on where your comfort and discomfort lie in the idea of equality for all genders.

Selected, Edited, and with Issue Framing Material by:
Elizabeth Schroeder, EdD, MSW, *Elizabeth Schroeder Consulting*

ISSUE

Does a Wage Gap Exist Between Women and Men?

YES: U.S. Department of Commerce, Economics and Statistics Administration and the Executive Office of the President, Office of Management and Budget, from "Women in America: Indicators of Social and Economic Well-Being," White House Council on Women and Girls (2011)

NO: Andrew Syrios, from "Lies, Damned Lies, and Statistics: The Wage Gap," Swifteconomics.com (2009)

Learning Outcomes

After reading this issue, you will be able to:

- Describe at least three statistics according to the U.S. government relating to wage differences between men and women.

- Explain at least two ways in which these statistics could be interpreted to support the argument that there is no wage difference between men and women.

- Identify at least one argument why men and women should be paid equally, and one argument why they should not be, according to the selections.

ISSUE SUMMARY

YES: Data from the U.S. Department of Commerce demonstrates that while what women earn as compared to what men earn has grown over time, the gap in earning between men and women remains.

NO: Real estate investor and blogger Andrew Syrios presents four reasons why a wage gap based on gender does not exist, explaining that a comparison of people of different genders doing the same work is an inappropriate comparison when it comes to the business of work.

Men and women have always had to work to survive, going back to our earliest history as human beings. When the first settlers came to the United States, everyone was expected to work hard, including children. The type of work an adult (or child) did was based on gender, with boys and men typically doing work in the fields, building homes, and more. Women's work was also physically demanding, including differing tasks in the fields, taking care of the home, and both bearing and raising children.

Not until societies began growing did a more formal commerce of work for pay as we understand it in current terms begin. The expectation for women, however, was to get married, have children, and take care of them and the home. Women worked if they were single or otherwise had to; women who were married were occupied with the work of maintaining their homes and raising the children. Unless a woman was living in wealth, this status represented an enormous amount of (unpaid) work in which the home was expected to be clean, meals prepared, children well-behaved and their non-home needs managed, and more. Women who were not married had to work, but they typically did so in a limited number of professions. Since our country was founded on a capitalist system that values money above all, by definition "women's work," typically lower paid if outside of the home and unpaid if inside the home, was devalued. Professional fields that have traditionally been dominated by women—schoolteacher, nurse, caregiver—do not generate income, and are therefore valued lower on a socioeconomic level, even though the actual work is invaluable to the continuation and health of society. All of this also reflects the history of sexism that has pervaded the world, in which women were seen, in most but not all cultures, as inferior to men.

Today, women and men are both in the workforce—thanks in no small part, ironically, to our involvement in the two world wars. Although World War II is heralded as the most significant event to have an impact on women in the workforce, it all began with World War I. Women had to work, although predominantly their work was done to support the male soldiers—cooking for them, sewing for them, caring for them when they were injured, and so on. But women also worked for the Red Cross, operated switchboards, translated documents if they were multilingual—and, for the first time, were allowed to actually serve in the armed forces. There was not a large representation of women in World War I, and their contributions receive very little attention to this day.

While World War I opened the door for women to work outside of the home, World War II approximately 30 years later would require far more women doing far more difficult and intensive work to replace the male soldiers who were being sent overseas to fight. And the pay disparity was apparent; even though the National War Labor Board urged employers to adjust what they paid women versus men for greater equity, the average salary for a woman during that time was $31.21 a week, but the men who were not sent to war made $54.65.[1] This does not take into account the harassment women experienced from the men who remained at home on a daily basis. Factories were unsafe places where women wanted or had to work to support the war effort, feed their children, and survive themselves.

When the war was over, women were expected to return home and take care of their families and husbands again, although many did not want to do that. They enjoyed working; they enjoyed earning their own money and having the independence to spend it as they wished. Women continued working, although in jobs that were not of equal status to men and for less pay. In fact, until the early 1960s, job listings in the newspapers were separated by gender. Women who did have the same jobs as men made somewhere between $.59 and $.64 for every

dollar men earned. In 1964, the Equal Pay Act was put into effect, which made it illegal for women to be paid less than men for the same job; merit, expertise, performance, and other work-related factors could be taken into consideration, but gender could no longer be the determining factor in setting salary levels.

While the work environment changed, especially with the advent of the women's, civil, and gay rights movements of the 1960s and 1970s, what continues to straggle is pay equity. And the inequity is far worse in the United States for women of color than for white women. In 2009, President Barack Obama signed the Lily Ledbetter Fair Pay Act, which made it illegal to base pay levels on "sex, race, national origin, age, religion and disability.[2]" This law enables people to file complaints against an employer if they believed they were being discriminated against with regards to pay due to being a member of any of the groups listed above. Under the Act, claims of unfair pay can be filed within 180 days of receiving a discriminatory paycheck and the 180-day limit is reset with each new discriminatory paycheck, and employers must make reparations if decisions are ruled against them.

If there is so much historical documentation and actual current laws working to end wage discrimination based in gender, why is this even an issue? Doesn't everyone agree that women are being paid less than men for equal work? The answer is that there is not universal agreement on this issue. The U.S. Department of Commerce has done extensive analysis of data to show that widespread disparities remain—yet other economists argue that the data is being misinterpreted and misrepresented for political gain; that pay rates by gender have actually improved dramatically. Andrew Syrios, however, contends that data can be interpreted—and in the case of the U.S. Department of Commerce, it has been interpreted incorrectly. Which is fact, and which is opinion?

References

1. Bryant, J. (2009). *How war changed the role of women in the United States.* Yale-New Haven Teachers' Unit, http://www.yale.edu/ynhti/curriculum/units/2002/3/02.03.09.x.html.
2. National Women's Law Center (2009). Fact Sheet: The Lilly Ledbetter Fair Pay Act of 2009. http://www.nwlc.org/sites/default/files/pdfs/lilly_ledbetter_fair_pay_act_of_2009_01.07.2013.pdf.

U.S. Department of Commerce, Economics and Statistics Administration and the Executive Office of the President, Office of Management and Budget

Women in America: Indicators of Social and Economic Well-Being

Employment

Over the past several decades, women have dramatically reshaped their role in the nation's labor force. They have become much more likely to work or seek work outside the home. They are also employed in more varied occupations and are more likely to work year-round. In addition, women have attained higher levels of education. Reflecting their greater work activity and education, women's earnings as a proportion of men's earnings have grown over time and women are contributing increasingly important shares of family incomes, but the earnings gap between men and women remains. As more women have entered the labor force, interest has risen in how they divide their time between their jobs and other activities.

Labor Force Participation

The labor force participation rate for women—the percentage of all adult women who are working or looking for work—rose steadily during the latter half of the 20th century.[1] This rate increased from about 33 percent in 1950 to 61 percent in 1999. During the first decade of this century, it has held steady at around 61 percent. In contrast, men's labor force participation rate has declined steadily since the 1950s.

Despite the trends of recent decades, women remain less active in the labor market than men. The labor force participation rate of adult women (age 20 and older) was still significantly lower than that of adult men, 61 percent versus 75 percent in 2009. Moreover, on average, women at every educational level and at every age spend fewer weeks in the labor force than do men. The differences between men and women in labor force attachment are much smaller among those with a college degree or more education.[2]

As part of the overall growth of women's presence in the labor force, the participation rate of mothers also increased. From 1975 to 2000, the labor force participation rate of mothers with children under age 18 rose from 47 percent to a peak of 73 percent. This rate receded to about 71 percent in 2004, where it has remained through 2009. Unmarried mothers had a higher labor force participation rate than their married counterparts, 76 percent compared to 70 percent in 2009.

Occupations

The jobs working women perform also have changed as their market activity has increased. A larger share of women now works in management, professional, and related occupations.[3] In 2009, women accounted for 51 percent of all persons employed in these occupations, somewhat more than their share of total employment (47 percent).

One reason for the shift in occupations is women's greater educational attainment. Among women age 25–64 in the labor force, 36 percent held college degrees in 2009, compared to 11 percent in 1970. Over the same period, the proportion of women workers with less than a high school diploma fell from 34 percent to 7 percent. Individuals with higher levels of education generally have better access to higher paying jobs than do individuals with less education. The earnings of both women and men age 25 and older without a high school diploma were less than half of those with a college degree, respectively.

Earnings and Contributions

The earnings gap between women and men has narrowed over time, but it remains. Among full-time wage and salary workers, women's weekly earnings as a percent of men's have increased from 62 percent in 1979 to 80 percent in 2009.[4,5] This comparison of earnings is on a broad level and does not control for many factors that can be significant in explaining or further highlighting earnings differences.

U.S. Department of Commerce Economics and Statistics Administration and Executive Office of the President Office of Management and Budget, 2011.

As women's earnings have risen, working wives' contributions to their family incomes also have risen. In 2008, working wives contributed 29 percent of their families' incomes, up by 5 percentage points from 1988, when wives' earnings accounted for 24 percent of their families' total incomes. The proportion of wives earning more than their husbands also has grown. In 1988, 18 percent of working wives whose husbands also worked earned more than their spouses; in 2008, the proportion was 27 percent.[6] Dual-earner couples made up 57 percent of all married-couple families in 2008, compared to 46 percent in 1970.[7]

Working women spend their days somewhat differently than do working men. In 2009, on the days that they worked, employed married women age 25–54 spent less time in labor market work and work-related activities than did employed married men in the same age group—7 hours and 40 minutes, compared to about 8 hours and 50 minutes. However, these employed wives spent about 40 minutes more time than did their male counterparts doing household activities such as cooking, housework, and household management.

1. After Decades of Significant Increases, the Labor Force Participation Rate for Women Has Held Steady in Recent Years

- The labor force participation rate for women (age 20 and older) nearly doubled between 1948 (32 percent) and 1997 (61 percent). Since 1997, it has held steady (61 percent in 2009). The labor force participation rate for men (age 20 and older) has fallen from about 89 percent in 1948 to 75 percent in 2009.
- At all levels of educational attainment, the labor force participation rate of men was higher than that of their female counterparts. In 2009, the participation rate of women with less than a high school diploma was only 34 percent, compared to 59 percent for men. Among those with college degrees or higher, the participation rate of women was 73 percent, compared to 82 percent for men.
- Between 2005 and 2009, the labor force participation rate increased for White women (59.7 percent to 60.4 percent) and Hispanic women (57.4 percent to 59.2 percent). By comparison, the rate for Black women, who have the highest labor force participation among women, has edged down (64.4 percent to 63.4 percent). For men, labor force participation continued to fall across all racial and ethnic groups.
- Among mothers age 16 and over, those with older children (age 6 to 17 only) were more likely to be

in the labor force (77 percent) in 2009 than those with children age 5 or younger (64 percent).
- The labor force participation rate of persons age 55 and older began to rise in 1996 for both women and men, but the pace of the increase has slowed in recent years.

2. Unemployment Rates for Women Have Risen Less Than for Men in Recent Recessions

- During the past four recessions, the unemployment rate among women rose less than the rate for men. During the most recent recession, the unemployment rate among women (age 20 and older) rose from 4.4 percent to 7.7 percent; by comparison, the rate for men (age 20 and older) more than doubled, from 4.4 percent to 9.9 percent.
- Prior to the 1980s, the unemployment rate for women tended to be higher than the rate for men. Since the early 1980s, the jobless rates for both men and women have tracked one another quite closely during economic expansions.
- During the past four recessions, the relatively large increases in the jobless rates among men can be attributed to their concentration in more cyclically sensitive occupations, such as manufacturing production and construction.
- In contrast, women are more concentrated in less cyclically sensitive and more rapidly growing occupations, such as health care, which has dampened the impact of recent recessions on their unemployment rates.

3. More Women Than Men Work Part Time, and Women and Men Have Roughly Equal Access to Flexible Work Schedules

- Historically, women have been more likely than men to work part time (less than 35 hours per week). In 2009, 24 percent of employed women (age 20 and older) worked part time, compared to 11 percent of men.
- Women are considerably more likely to work year round than they were in past decades. In 2009, 75 percent of women worked year round, up from 51 percent in 1968. The proportion of men who worked year round changed little over this same time period (from 74 percent to 76 percent).
- In May 2004, about 30 percent of wage and salary workers reported having flexible schedules that allowed them to vary their work hours to some degree. Between 1985 and 2004, the proportions

of employed men and women able to vary their work hours were about equal; the same was true of both mothers and fathers who work.

- Due to the nature of the work required for each particular job, the prevalence of flexible schedules varies by occupation. In May 2004, the proportion of White and Asian workers in occupations in which they could vary their schedules exceeded that of other groups. About 30 percent of employed Whites and Asians could vary their work hours, while the proportion was closer to 21 percent among Black workers and those of Hispanic ethnicity.

4. Education Pays for Both Women and Men, but the Pay Gap Persists

- Earnings for both women and men typically increase with higher levels of education. However, the male-female pay gap persists at all levels of education for full-time workers (35 or more hours per week).
- Earnings of full-time female workers have risen by 31 percent since 1979, compared to a 2 percent rise in male earnings. In addition, earnings for women with college degrees rose by 33 percent since 1979 while those of their male counterparts rose by 22 percent.
- At all levels of education, women earned about 75 percent as much as their male counterparts in 2009. Although both women and men with less than a high school diploma have experienced declines in earnings since 1979, the drop for women (9 percent) was significantly less than that for men (28 percent).
- The earnings gap between women and men narrowed for most age groups from 1979 to 2009. The women's-to-men's earnings ratio among 25- to 34-year-olds, rose from 68 percent in 1979 to 89 percent in 2009, and the ratio for 45- to 54-year-olds increased from 57 percent to 74 percent.
- Compared to the earnings of all men (of all race and ethnic groups), Black women earned 71 percent and Hispanic women earned 62 percent as much in 2009. White and Asian women earned 82 percent and 95 percent as much as all men, respectively.
- Compared to their direct male counterparts, however, White women earned 79 percent as much as White men in 2009, while Asian women earned 82 percent as much as Asian men. For Blacks and Hispanics, the figures were 94 percent and 90 percent, respectively.

5. Women and Men Continue to Work in Different Occupations

- While women are three times more likely to work in administrative support jobs than men, relatively few women have construction, production, or transportation jobs.
- While women are more likely than men to work in professional and related occupations, they are more highly represented in the lower-paying jobs within this category. For example, in 2009, professional women were more likely (nearly 70 percent) to work in the relatively low-paying education (with $887 median weekly earnings) and health care ($970 median weekly earnings) occupations, compared to 32 percent of male professionals.
- In 2009, only 7 percent of female professionals were employed in the relatively high paying computer ($1,253 median weekly earnings) and engineering fields ($1,266 median weekly earnings), compared to 38 percent of male professionals.
- The proportion of women working in management, business, and finance jobs has increased from 9 percent to 14 percent since 1983.
- Women continue to be concentrated in a small number of traditionally female occupations. In 2009, nearly one-fifth of all women were employed in just five occupations: secretaries, registered nurses, elementary school teachers, cashiers, and nursing aides.

6. Female-Headed Families Have the Lowest Family Earnings Among All Family Types

- Family earnings levels among female-headed families were the lowest among all family types in both 1988 and 2008, despite increasing by 27 percent over this timeframe. A family is a group of two or more people living together and related by birth, marriage, or adoption.
- In 2008, female-headed families with children earned 30 percent less than their counterparts without children, although their earnings grew faster (43 percent) than the other family types between 1988 and 2008.
- Over the past two decades, women's earnings have constituted a growing share of family income in all family types.
- Married couples had the highest family incomes. Incomes for married-couple families with children increased by 28 percent from 1988 to 2008, while incomes for married-couple families without children increased by 16 percent over the same period.

- In female-headed families with children, non-earned income as a share of total family income has declined sharply, from 24 percent in 1988 to 16 percent in 2008. About 63 percent of nonearned income for female-headed families with children in poverty is government cash transfer income.

7. In Families Where Both Husband and Wife Are Employed, Employed Wives Spend More Time in Household Activities Than Do Employed Husbands

- On an average workday in 2009, employed married women spent 1.6 hours in household activities and an additional hour caring for household members. In contrast, employed married men spent nearly one hour in household activities and about 40 minutes caring for household members.
- On average in 2009, employed husbands spent about 3.2 hours engaged in leisure and sports activities on workdays, and employed wives spent about 2.7 hours. For both employed husbands and wives, watching television accounted for just over half of this time (1.8 hours and 1.4 hours, respectively).
- Employed married men spent more time in labor market work and related activities (including commuting) on an average workday in 2009 than did employed married women—8.8 hours and 7.6 hours, respectively.
- On days that they worked, 87 percent of married women also engaged in household activities in 2009, compared to 65 percent of married men.

Wives were more likely to do housework and prepare food, while husbands were more likely to care for the lawn and do home maintenance.
- On an average workday in 2009, employed single mothers spent 37 minutes more in labor market work and related activities than did employed married mothers.

8. Women Are More Likely Than Men to Do Volunteer Work

- In 2009, 30 percent of women volunteered, compared to 23 percent of men. Women most frequently volunteered with religious organizations (34 percent of all female volunteers), followed by educational or youth service related organizations (28 percent).
- Female volunteers were most likely to fundraise (13 percent); collect, prepare, distribute, or serve food (12 percent); or tutor or teach (11 percent). Male volunteers were most likely to engage in general labor (12 percent); coach, referee, or supervise sports teams (9 percent); provide professional or management assistance (9 percent); or fundraise (9 percent).

THE U.S. DEPARTMENT OF COMMERCE promotes job creation, economic growth, sustainable development, and improved standards of living for all Americans by working in partnership with businesses, universities, communities, and our country's workers.

 **NO**

Andrew Syrios

Lies, Damned Lies, and Statistics: The Wage Gap

Now we turn from the mostly meaningless college gap to the mostly nonexistent wage gap. It is quoted ad-nauseum that a woman makes 75 cents for each dollar a man makes for the exact same work (it used to be 59 cents, now it ranges from 75 to 80). In response to this, Nancy Pelosi helped push through Congress the Fair Pay Act. Furthermore, April 20th, 2010 not only represents a day we should all get stoned out of our gourds, it's "Equal Pay Day." This holiday (of sorts) symbolizes how far into 2010 a woman would have to work to make what a man makes in 2009 alone. Obviously this is a sign of discrimination; as Jessica Valenti, founder of Feministing.com, states rather bluntly, "the wage gap is like a big f*ck you to women."

Unfortunately (for Jessica, fortunately for every other woman in the country), even a faint knowledge of business or economics should immediately raise a degree of skepticism about this dubious claim. I'll let John Stossel ask what should be the obvious question:

"Suppose you're an employer doing the hiring. If a woman does equal work for 25 percent less money, businesses would get rich just by hiring women. Why would any employer ever hire a man?"

Of course, by itself, this means nothing.

Many people seem to believe that businessmen, (I mean businesspeople, sorry), care about nothing other than making money. However these same people also seem to believe businesspeople discriminate against everyone but white, Protestant, straight men with no handicap and well parted hair. So apparently, businesspeople do have values other than making money: they are racist, sexist, xenophobic, homophobic, Islamophobic, Christian fundamentalists. Well, at least they have some principles, right?

The truth is that businesspeople discriminate in favor of the color green; money. Market economies discriminate mightily against those who discriminate. If it were true that men make approximately 33% more for the same work, companies that predominantly hired women

would crush companies that predominantly hired men. Ask any business owner what would happen if he or she could decrease his or her labor expenses 25% and he or she would tell you he or she would soon be hiring his or her competitor's employees (as his or her competitor's employees would be unemployed, because his or her competitors got crushed).

Discrimination assuredly exists, but for such a large wage gap to be present, there are really only four options for someone to believe: (1) There is an all-encompassing agreement among business owners throughout the entire country, both male and female, to discriminate against women, thereby preventing any one business from undercutting another by hiring only women at 75 cents on the dollar. To believe this puts you in the company of the wildest conspiracy theorists. (2) Profits are not particularly

Figure 1

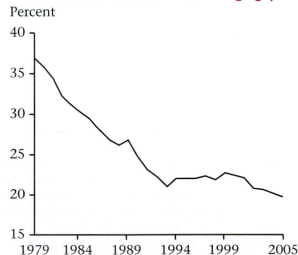

An estimated male-female wage gap.

Source: Authors' calculations using the CPS for full-time workers and controlling for education and age.

important to a business, so business-humans can hire based on just about anything they want. This would make you one of the dumbest people on the planet. (3) Women aren't as productive as men and therefore, while doing the same job, women provide less output (approximately 25% less) than men do. This would make you a pretty run-of-the-mill sexist. (4) This statistic is wrong.

Before continuing on, I should note that this discussion will not deal with discrimination that may occur with regards to hiring or promoting. Glass ceilings and pink ghettos will not be discussed. The fallacy here is that men and women are paid vastly different amounts for doing the exact same work. As you will soon see, the "same work" has a very flexible definition indeed.

What we need to recognize is that having the same job, (or the same type of job, as these statistics are often based on), does not infer that one does the "same work" and should be paid equally. For example, there is a much greater demand for business professors than history professors, so business professors will be paid more. Furthermore, the longer someone's had a job, the more they will usually get paid. And obviously, the more hours they put in, the more they will get paid. And when the position is paid by commission, any discrimination that occurs would be by the consumer, not the business-homosapiens who employ them.

Once we recognize these things, we can start to come to grips with what is actually happening. First, we cannot assume that men and women have the same career aspirations in the aggregate. Second, we have to look at what happens when men and women get married, namely, we must investigate the marital asymmetry hypothesis.

Let's start with the types of jobs men and women seek. As mentioned with regards to the college gap, men and women tend to seek different professional aims and career goals. Men are much more likely to take on dangerous positions, as evidenced by the fact that 93% of workplace fatalities are men. Hazardous conditions usually come with hazard pay. Men are also more likely to take jobs in uncomfortable conditions, which brings a premium as well (if you ever watch an episode of Dirty Jobs, you'll quickly notice there aren't a lot of women on the show).

Professor James T. Bennett compiled 20 major reasons for the wage gap, which include some of the following:

- Men go into technology and hard sciences more than women.
- Men tend to take more stressful jobs that are not "nine-to-five."
- Men are more likely to work longer hours, and the pay gap widens for every hour past 40 per week.
- Women are nine times more likely than men to drop out of work for "family reasons." Less seniority leads to lower pay.
- Men work more weeks per year than women.
- Women place greater value on flexibility, a humane work environment, and having time for children and family than men do.

None of these things are either right or wrong, they just represent different choices. What it does mean, though, is that we cannot say women are paid less for doing the same work when men typically work longer, less flexible hours in more dangerous and uncomfortable positions. Warren Farrell's calculations highlight the difference between the average hours worked, concluding that men who work full time work an average of 44 hours per week, while women who work full time average 41 hours per week. This represents a bigger difference than you'd immediately think, as a person who works 44 hours a week makes approximately 100% more than someone who works 34 hours a week. Warren Farrell concludes that this accounts for 70% of the wage gap in and of itself.

Furthermore, some of the explanations Professor Bennett discusses represent the single biggest difference between the genders when it comes to wages: marital asymmetry. In other words, marriage tends to increase a man's earning potential and reduce a woman's earning potential. Regardless of whether it's right or wrong, women typically take up more responsibilities at home than men do. Since women usually spend more time at home, they have less time to work, and thereby their earning potential is reduced. Since men have many of their domestic responsibilities taken care of for them, they have more time to work and thereby their earning potential increases. Economist Thomas Sowell elaborates:

"Not all domestic responsibilities can be shared equally, such as having babies, which is not an inconsequential thing since the existence of the human race depends on it. What it means is that women make choices that make a lot of sense for them. For example, the choice of occupations . . . women tend not to go into occupations in which there's a very high rate of obsolescence. If you're a computer engineer and you take five years out to have a child and [raise him] until the age you can put him in daycare, well my gosh, the world has changed. You'd have to start way, way back. On the other hand, if you become a librarian, a teacher or other occupations like that, you can take your five years off and then come back pretty much where you left off."

While more women go to college than men, women typically go into fields that have less earning potential. In 2005, women received more than 60% of the doctorates in education, but less than 20% of the doctorates in engineering. Men are over-represented, proportionally, in business, finance, accounting, engineering, computer science and medicine, the fields with the highest earning potential. Denise Venable, of the National Center for Policy Analysis, further proves this point showing that, "in general, married women would prefer part-time work at a rate of 5 to 1 over married men." Additionally, women over 25 years of age have held their current job for an average of 4.4 years vs. 5 years for men and pay raises come with seniority. This makes sense when we look at it in terms of the marital asymmetry hypothesis. And again, a higher earning potential doesn't mean better, it's simply means different. A career in education is likely more interesting, fulfilling and flexible than a career in finance, but it comes with less money. It's all about the trade-offs folks.

The marital asymmetry hypothesis and specifically, child rearing, seems to be of huge importance here. And luckily, there is an easy way to test the importance of it; namely compare the wages of never-married women to that of never-married men. In 1982, never-married women earned 91% of what never-married men did. In 1971, never-married-women in their thirties earned slightly more than never-married men. Today, among men and women living alone from the age of 21–35, there is no wage gap. Among college-educated men and women between 40 and 64 who have never married, men made an average of $40,000 a year and women made an average of $47,000!

This should pretty much end any question about whether or not the wage gap exists. Certainly there is discrimination, but it's not as simple as comparing gross wages. If we do that, we'd have to come to some very strange conclusions. For example, Asian Americans make more money than white Americans do on average; do business-mammals-with-the capacity-for-higher-cognitive-abilities discriminate against white people in favor of Asians? Since 1960, and continuing through today, black women with a college degree earn more than white women with a college degree. In 1970, black women who had graduated college earned 125% of what white women who had graduated college earned. Would anyone like to stand-up and make the argument that employers discriminate against white women in favor of black women? I didn't think so.

So let's just go one step further and get all controversial: should men and women be paid equally across the board? The answer is more complex than one would expect. People, in general, should be paid as individuals, so however productive an individual is should determine his or her pay. Therefore, in jobs where men typically have an advantage, say jobs requiring physical strength, odds are the average man will be more productive in that profession than the average women, and therefore should typically get paid more regardless of the other factors mentioned above. In jobs where women have a natural advantage, say jobs requiring an excellent memory (yes, much to the chagrin of every straight man in the history of the world, the ladies typically have a better memory, if this bothers any guys out there, worry not, you'll probably forget about it fairly soon), women will typically be more productive and should therefore get paid more. However, this only applies when discussing aggregates. The differences within each gender are far greater than the differences between the genders. Everyone should be paid based on their individual productivity. It simply means we have to be very careful when we are interpreting wage data.

Finally, let's get one last thing straight, which should be completely obvious, but apparently isn't: being a stay-at-home mother, or father for that matter, is morally neutral. It all depends on what the individual wants. If a woman gains fulfillment from raising her kids, taking care of the home and perhaps having a part-time job or being involved in her community in another way, then staying at home is what she should do. If, on the other hand, she would prefer a career, then there is a problem. Same goes for career woman who would prefer to stay at home with the kids. And the same thing applies for men as well.

Certainly there are other issues that come into play, mostly financial, and every relationship requires some give and take, but the general principle holds throughout. I find it ironic that liberals, who often decry materialism, tend to judge equality based solely upon materialism (in this case, wages). Take your standard family unit: father, mother and 2.3 kids. There are a host of tasks that need to be completed, some family members bring in an income and others do not. This in no way infers that one type of work is superior to the other, since both types need to be completed. Now, I'm not a big fan of strict gender roles because it's collectivist thinking; it's gender socialism. But still, however these tasks are delved up is morally neutral (assuming it's a similar amount of work), it all depends on the individuals involved. And we shouldn't be denigrating the work that doesn't come with a dollar sign attached to it.

Unfortunately, that's what we're implicitly doing when we see the wage gap for what it is: a comparison of apples and oranges. Certainly discrimination exists, but the market grinds away at it with ruthless tenacity. The concept that women earn 75 cents on the dollar is simply a bogus statistic that simultaneously denigrates work done at home and implies the need for some very nonsensical policies.

ANDREW SYRIOS is a Kansas City–based real estate investor and partner with Stewardship Properties who blogs for swifteconomics.com and the Ludwig von Mises Institute for economics.

EXPLORING THE ISSUE

Does a Wage Gap Exist Between Women and Men?

Critical Thinking and Reflection

1. Are there inherent differences between people of different genders that would ever merit different pay for the same work? Under what circumstances?
2. Why do you think it has taken so long for there to be greater attention and response to equal pay for equal work?
3. Can you think of any examples, whether related to pay or job description, where you believe men are discriminated against rather than women?

Is There Common Ground?

Whenever a population or group of people claim discrimination by another group, the group that has the power will often become defensive and bend over backwards to demonstrate how their practices are not discriminatory and how good the members of that group actually have it. This is referred to as "backlash," and we see it in response to accusations of racism, sexism, homophobia, ableism, ageism, and any other possible "ism" one can imagine. This is perhaps the greatest challenge to remedying any of these injustices—the people who have the power need to acknowledge that a wrong has been done and be willing to take the necessary steps to remedy those injustices if they can.

This is where, for some people, we have not yet reached common ground on pay inequity. There is a strong feeling that in order for people to be treated equally, others have to give up their rights or benefits. The common ground is that everyone wants to work hard, be paid for that hard work, and not be paid less than someone else who is equally qualified or able. The reality, however, is that our "isms" exist—and there remain plenty of men who absolutely feel justified in being paid more than women; people of particular races or ethnicities who believe they should be paid more than people of other races or ethnicities; younger people who believe they deserve to be paid more than older people, and vice versa.

Additional Resources

Elborgh-Woytek, K., Newiak, M. et al. (2013). Women, work, and the economy: Macroeconomic gains from gender equity. Washington, DC: International Monetary Fund.

Gottfried, H. (2013). Gender, work, and economy: Unpacking the global economy. Edison, NJ: John Wiley & Sons.

Lips, H.M. (2013). The gender pay gap: Challenging the rationalizations. Perceived equity, discrimination, and the limits of human capital models. *Sex Roles,* 68(3–4), 169–185.

Internet References . . .

The Centre for Gender Economics and Innovation

http://centreforgendereconomics.org/

American Association of University Women: Economic Justice

http://www.aauw.org/issues/economic-justice/

National Committee on Pay Equity

http://www.pay-equity.org/

Selected, Edited, and with Issue Framing Material by:
Elizabeth Schroeder, EdD, MSW, *Elizabeth Schroeder Consulting*

ISSUE

Should the Employment Non-Discrimination Act (ENDA) Be Passed?

YES: Jaime M. Grant et al., from "Injustice at Every Turn: A Report of the National Transgender Discrimination Survey," Thetaskforce.org (2011)

NO: Family Research Council, from "The Employment Non-Discrimination Act (ENDA): A Threat to Free Markets and Freedom of Conscience and Religion," Family Research Council (2011)

Learning Outcomes
After reading this issue, you will be able to:
• Differentiate between sexual orientation and gender identity while explaining the rationale behind promoting each as a protected class of people.
• Explain what the Employment Non-Discrimination Act (ENDA) is, including a brief history of the bill from the 1970s.
• Describe at least two reasons to support and two reasons to oppose ENDA.
• Define "religious exemption" and its applicability to ENDA and other federal legislation.

ISSUE SUMMARY

YES: Jaime Grant, director of the Global Transgender Research and Advocacy Project of the Arcus Foundation, and her colleagues promote the need for ENDA based on data showing transgender and gender nonconforming people face discrimination and violence in the workplace.

NO: The Family Research Council asserts that transgender people are not a protected population under federal civil rights legislation, and that ENDA would therefore contradict the provisions of that law.

Lesbian, gay, bisexual, and/or transgender (LGBT) people have long experienced discrimination and even violence in the workplace. As more and more social activism relating to LGBT individuals took place in the 1960s and 1970s, most notably the Stonewall Riots of 1969 in New York City, national attention was brought to the violence and harassment LGBT people were experiencing nationwide on a daily basis. In 1974, congressional Representatives Bella Abzug and Ed Koch, both Democrats from New York, introduced the Equality Act, the first federal legislation that had the goal of ending discrimination against lesbian and gay individuals in housing or employment, or at any public place where people who were or perceived to be lesbian or gay could be refused admittance. This bill, which did not pass, did not include transgender people.

Similar bills have been introduced into Congress over the past 40 years. According to the National LGBTQ Task Force (formerly the National Lesbian and Gay Task Force), there are three reasons why they think this law has not yet been passed:

1. Publicly endorsed homophobia and transphobia, mostly orchestrated by large, well-funded socially conservative people and organizations (such as Anita Bryant and Pat Buchanan beginning in the 1970s).

2. The emergence of HIV and AIDS, the laws relating to which LGBTQ activists focused most of their time and energy on in the 1980s and 1990s.
3. The increased power exerted in the federal government from 1994 on by strongly socially conservative lawmakers who, to please their equally conservative constituents, continue to oppose equal rights for women, people of color, immigrants, and LGBTQ people.[1]

In 1994, the Employment Non-Discrimination Act was introduced as an offshoot of the Equality Act, homing in on the workplace, not all the other public spaces the first bill tried to address. It was not passed in 1996, but continued to be reintroduced every year. There was some controversy among advocates for this bill because it originally focused on sexual orientation only, then was expanded to include gender identity for transgender individuals. In 2007, after failing to be brought to a vote, the bill's sponsor removed the language relating to gender identity and the House passed the bill. That is, however, as far as it got—it was never brought to a vote in the Senate. All sponsors of the bills and advocates pushing for its passage agreed that, even if not having gender identity included made it more "palatable" to legislators who were skittish about supporting the bill, all subsequent versions needed to include both gender identity and sexual orientation.

In early 2014, ENDA passed in the Senate this time, but stalled in the House. Then something happened that had nothing to do with ENDA, but that has had a significant impact on ENDA and other bills. In June 2014, the U.S. Supreme Court issued a ruling in *Burwell v. Hobby Lobby Stores*, in which they said that Hobby Lobby, a family-owned, religious-based company could be exempted from the Affordable Care Act requirements that all companies provide health insurance to its employees that covers contraceptive methods. Hobby Lobby argued that, due to their religious beliefs that contraception is wrong and tantamount to an abortion, they should be exempt from the requirement to pay for those types of contraceptive methods, just as more traditional religious organizations (churches, synagogues, mosques, etc.) had been exempt from that and various other requirements over the years that would require them to go against their religious beliefs.

The Supreme Court ruled for Hobby Lobby, and quickly religious-based organizations, colleges, and universities around the United States jumped on the ruling. Some colleges and universities maintained they did not need to take protective measures for LGBTQ students or to provide contraceptive services on campus because doing so went against their beliefs. Some supporters of ENDA are concerned that the same thing could happen with

this bill—that if it is passed and made law, companies and educational institutions will claim a religious exemption, thereby effectively using ENDA to give them proactive permission to discriminate against LGBTQ people in the workplace. For this reason, the American Civil Liberties Union, Gay & Lesbian Advocates & Defenders, Lambda Legal, the National Center for Lesbian Rights, the National LGBTQ Task Force, and the Transgender Law Center all pulled their support of the bill—while the National Center for Transgender Equity and Human Rights Campaign continue to push for its passage.

Socially conservative groups have opposed ENDA from its inception for some of the reasons listed above. In addition, the strongest argument that is repeated against ENDA is that LGBTQ people "choose" their sexual orientation or gender identity, and therefore giving LGBTQ individuals the same protections that people of different races have is offensive to the original intentions of the civil rights movement. Race, they argue, is immutable—sexual orientation can be changed through therapy or prayer. Focusing more on same-sex sexual behaviors than orientations or identities, ENDA opponents also believe that including gender and sexual orientation infringes on the religious freedoms of employers who believe it is immoral to be anything other than heterosexual and cisgender. In addition, opponents believe that ENDA will be harmful to business, in particular, small business because they think that passing this law will encourage frivolous lawsuits by LGBT individuals seeking compensatory damages against organizations, whether they were discriminated against or not. In response to that concern, proponents of ENDA argue that organizations not previously known for being religion-based will claim they are in order to receive the exemption. There are, clearly, a lot of "what ifs?" on both sides of the debate—and neither side is willing to give the other the benefit of the doubt that, regardless of the outcome, people might not actually engage in frivolous lawsuits. In states that have had state-level ENDA-like legislation passed, there have been very few lawsuits instigated, valid or frivolous.

In the following selections, Jaime Grant and colleagues couch their arguments for the passage of ENDA under the umbrella of employment and the need to be safe at work without discrimination as basic human rights that should be guaranteed under the Universal Declaration of Human Rights. The Family Research Council maintains that acknowledging transgender individuals in the workplace would only serve to "sexualize" the workplace, thereby making it an unsafe place for cisgender men and women who may not feel comfortable having a transgender coworker.

YES

Jaime M. Grant et al.

Injustice at Every Turn:
A Report of the National Transgender
Discrimination Survey

Employment

Employment is fundamental to people's ability to support themselves and their families. Paid work is not only essential to livelihood; it also contributes greatly to a sense of dignity and accomplishment over a lifetime. The Universal Declaration of Human Rights asserts the rights of individuals to work at the job of their choice, receiving equal pay for equal work, without discrimination. Yet far too often, transgender people are denied these basic human rights.

There are also serious social consequences associated with unemployment and under-employment. The loss of a job and unemployment are linked to depression and other mental health challenges.[1] Given the high rates of unemployment seen in our sample and the high rates of suicide attempts noted in the Health chapter of this document, employment issues are of particular concern to transgender and gender non-conforming people.

Field work for this study was done from September 2008 through February 2009, with a large majority completing questionnaires during September. Accordingly, the employment statistics here largely precede the widespread layoffs and double digit unemployment that the nation as a whole experienced as the economy moved into a major recession. The data that follow show that due to discrimination, study participants were experiencing very high rates of unemployment and extremely poor employment conditions. Given that respondents were faring worse than the nation as a whole before the recession led to large-scale layoffs, the data suggests that in the current crisis, transgender and gender non-conforming people are likely facing even higher unemployment than their gender-conforming peers.

The data show not only the rampant discrimination against transgender and gender non-conforming people, but also show that large numbers have turned to the underground economy for income, such as sex work or drug sales, in order to survive. Throughout this chapter, we refer to this as "underground employment."

Key Findings in Employment

- **Double the rate of unemployment:** Survey respondents experienced unemployment at twice the rate of the general population, with rates for people of color up to four times the national unemployment rate.
- **Near universal harassment on the job:** Ninety percent (90%) of those surveyed reported experiencing harassment or mistreatment on the job or took actions to avoid it.
- **Considerable loss of jobs and careers:** Forty-seven percent (47%) said they had experienced an adverse job outcome, such as being fired, not hired or denied a promotion because of being transgender/gender non-conforming; 26% of respondents said that they had lost a job due to being transgender or gender non-conforming.
- **Race multiplies the effect of discrimination:** For Black, Latino/a, American Indian and multiracial respondents, discrimination in the workplace was even more pervasive, sometimes resulting in up to twice or three times the rates of various negative outcomes.
- **Living in dire poverty:** Fifteen percent (15%) of our respondents reported a household income under $10,000/year, nearly four times the rate of this category for the general population. **Those who lost a job due to bias lived at this level of poverty at six times the rate of the general population.** More information about income can be found in the Portrait and Education chapters.
- **Rampant under-employment:** Forty-four percent (44%) reported experiencing under-employment.
- **Large majorities attempted to avoid discrimination** by hiding their gender or gender transition (71%) or delaying their gender transition (57%).
- **The vast majority (78%) of those who transitioned from one gender to the other**

reported that they felt more comfortable at work and **their job performance improved.**

- **Eighty-six percent (86%)** of those who have not lost a job due to bias reported that they **were able to access restrooms at work** appropriate for their gender identity, meaning that 14% of those who kept their jobs were denied access.

- **People who had lost a job due to bias or were currently unemployed reported much higher involvement in underground employment such as sex work or drug sales,** had much higher levels of incarceration and homelessness, and negative health outcomes.

- Sixteen percent (16%) said they had been compelled to engage in underground employment for income. **Eleven percent (11%) turned to sex work.**

- **Many respondents demonstrated resilience:** Of the 26% who reported losing a job due to bias, 58% reported being currently employed.

Outness at Work

We asked about outness at work in two different ways, only examining those who were currently employed. First, we asked respondents whether they tell work colleagues they are transgender or gender non-conforming. Second, we asked whether or not people at work knew that the respondent was transgender or gender non-conforming.

In the first measure, 38% reported that they tell work colleagues that they are transgender or gender non-conforming.[2]

In the second measure, whether or not people at work knew that the respondent was transgender or gender non-conforming, we found that over one third (35%) reported that "most" or "all" coworkers knew they were transgender or gender non-conforming. Another third (37%) said "some" or "a few" coworkers knew, and 28% said no one knew.

Among those who had transitioned, we see slightly elevated rates of coworkers being aware of their transgender or gender non-conforming status. Half (50%) reported "most" or "all" coworkers knew, 34% said "some" or "a few" knew, and 16% said no one knew.

Employment Discrimination

Forty-seven percent (47%) of survey respondents said they had experienced an adverse job action—they did not get a job, were denied a promotion or were fired—because they are transgender or gender non-conforming.

Job Loss Due to Discrimination

An alarming number of the people surveyed, 26%, reported losing their jobs directly due to their gender identity/ expression. Particularly hard hit were those who were Black (32%), multiracial (36%), and American Indian (36%).

Male-to-female transgender respondents reported job loss due to bias at a frequency of 36% while female-to-male transgender respondents reported 19%. Twenty-nine percent (29%) of transgender respondents experienced job loss due to bias while gender non-conforming participants reported 15%.

Respondents who reported having lost a job due to bias reported being currently unemployed (26%), many times the general population rate at the time of the survey (7%), which suggests that they have been unable to find new employment after a discriminatory termination. Twenty-eight percent (28%) of those who have lost a job due to bias have also reported work in the underground economy. Those who were living in the South were more likely to have lost a job due to bias (30%) than those living in other regions of the country. Undocumented non-citizens (39%) reported lost jobs due to bias more often than U.S. citizens (26%). Those with no high school diploma (37%) and those with only a high school diploma (33%) also experienced particularly high rates of job loss due to bias.

Discrimination in Hiring

Forty-four percent (44%) of survey respondents reported they did not get a job they applied for because of being transgender or gender non-conforming. Eighty-one percent (81%) of those who had lost their job due to bias also reported discrimination in hiring as did 71% of those currently unemployed. Also particularly hard hit were multiracial respondents (56%), American Indians (55%) and those making under $10,000/year (60%).

Sixty-one percent (61%) of those who reported doing sex work, drug sales or other underground work also say that they had experienced discrimination in hiring in the traditional workforce.

Male-to-female respondents experienced discrimination in hiring at 55%, compared to 40% of female-to-male respondents. Gender non-conforming respondents experienced this form of discrimination at 32%.

Denied Promotion

Twenty-three percent (23%) of respondents reported that they were denied a promotion because of being transgender or gender non-conforming. Thirty-three percent (33%)

of those with no high school diploma reported denial of a promotion due to bias along with 31% of those who made under $10,000/year. Also hard hit were Latino/a (29%), multiracial (31%) and American Indian (31%) respondents.

Twenty-nine percent (29%) of male-to-female respondents reported denial of promotion due to bias, while female-to- male respondents reported an 18% rate. Twenty percent (20%) of gender non-conforming respondents reported denial of promotions due to bias.

Unemployment

Transgender and gender non-conforming people are unemployed at alarming rates. Overall, the unemployment rate for respondents was 14%; double the weighted national average at the time of the survey.[3] Nineteen percent (19%) of respondents were out of the workforce and "not looking." Black, American Indian, Latino/a and multiracial respondents experienced unemployment at considerably higher rates than their white counterparts. Black respondents were unemployed at 28%, four times the rate among the general population; American Indian/Alaska Native respondents were unemployed at over three times the general population rate at 24%, Latino/a and multiracial respondents were unemployed over twice the general population rate at 18%

Under-Employment

We asked respondents whether they were currently or previously under-employed due to their gender identity/ expression; that is "working in the field I should not be in or a position for which I am over-qualified."

Forty-four percent (44%) of our respondents reported that they considered themselves under-employed. Seventy-seven percent (77%) of those who lost a job due to bias also reported experiencing under-employment at some point as well. Sixty-four percent (64%) of those currently unemployed also reported under-employment. Those who made less than $10,000/year reported current or previous under-employment at a rate of 56%. Also highly impacted were multiracial respondents (56%).

Workplace Abuse—A Near-Universal Experience

Harassment and mistreatment at work is a near universal experience for transgender and gender non-conforming people and its manifestations and consequences are many. Not only do many face mistreatment and discrimination directly from coworkers and supervisors; others feel distressed and intimidated when they see others discriminated against, and decide they must hide who they are or give up certain career aspirations in order to stay protected.

Ninety percent (90%) of respondents said they had directly experienced harassment or mistreatment at work or felt forced to take protective actions that negatively impacted their careers or their well-being, such as hiding who they were, in order to avoid workplace repercussions.

Mistreatment ranged from verbal harassment and breaches of confidentiality to physical and sexual assault, while bias-avoidant behaviors included hiding one's gender, delaying transition, or staying in a job one would have preferred to leave. Given the broad spectrum of workplace abuse experienced by our study participants, their persistent engagement in the workforce speaks to a determination and resilience that goes largely unheralded in statistics and discourse about transgender and gender non- conforming people in the workplace.

Direct Mistreatment and Discrimination

Respondents reported on a wide range of workplace abuses, including direct discrimination and mistreatment by coworkers and supervisors. Seventy-eight (78%) of respondents said they experienced some type of direct mistreatment or discrimination.

In answering each negative work experience question, transgender respondents reported higher levels of abuse than their gender non-conforming counterparts, often with a gap of 10 percentage points or more. Male-to-female respondents experienced harassment and mistreatment slightly more often than female-to-male respondents, though MTF experience of job loss, denial of promotion and discrimination in hiring was much higher than for FTM respondents.

People of color in the sample generally reported higher levels of abuse than the sample as a whole. Other respondents reporting higher vulnerability to mistreatment at work were those who had lost jobs due to discrimination; the unemployed; respondents who had done sex work, drug sales, or other underground work for income; and those earning under $10,000 annually.

Harassment

Fifty percent (50%) of respondents reported experiencing harassment in the workplace. This was the most common negative experience at work. Risk of harassment was higher for those earning lower incomes. High numbers of those who were currently unemployed also reported that they had been harassed when they were working. Similarly, a large number of those who reported having lost jobs due to bias also reported having been harassed at work. Last, those that had done underground work such as sex work, drug sales, or other underground activities for income also frequently reported that they had been harassed at work.

Physical Assault at Work

Seven percent (7%) of our sample reported being physically assaulted at work because of being transgender or gender non-conforming. Undocumented noncitizens in our sample reported the highest rates of physical assault at 25%, over three times the rate of the overall sample.

Sexual Assault at Work

Six percent (6%) of respondents reported being sexually assaulted by someone at work because of being transgender or gender non-conforming. Undocumented noncitizens reported the particularly high rates of sexual assault at 19%, over three times the rate of the overall sample.

Forced to Present in the Wrong Gender

Thirty-two percent (32%) of respondents reported being forced to present in the wrong gender to keep their jobs. Our question did not specify whether they were required to do so by their employer, or they felt forced to because of fear of discrimination. Undocumented noncitizens reported this experience at a particularly high rate (45%).

Restrooms at Work

Eighty-six percent (86%) of those who have not lost a job due to bias reported that they were able to access restrooms at work appropriate for their gender identity, meaning that 14% of those who kept their jobs were denied access. Looking at the full sample, regardless of whether they were able to keep or they had lost a job, 78% were given access to restrooms appropriate for their gender identity and 22% were denied access.

Inappropriate Questions

Forty-one percent (41%) of respondents reported having been asked inappropriate questions about their transgender or surgical status.

Deliberate Misuse of Pronouns

Forty-five (45%) of our sample reported having been referred to by the wrong pronouns "repeatedly and on purpose" at work.

Breaches of Confidentiality

Forty-eight percent (48%) reported that supervisors or coworkers shared information about the respondent that they should not have had.

Attempts to Avoid Discrimination

In order to avoid discriminatory actions and workplace abuse, many study respondents reported having "delayed my gender transition" (57%) or "hid my gender or gender transition" (71%). Given the importance of transition for many people, it is striking that well over half of our respondents delayed this life-affirming, and often live-saving step. Even more alarming is that nearly three-quarters of respondents reported they felt they had to hide who they are on a daily basis for job security.

Many respondents stayed in jobs they would have preferred to leave (45%) or didn't seek promotions or raises (30%) in order to avoid discrimination. Others (42%) said they had changed jobs to escape discrimination.

The discrimination avoidant behaviors described in this section all have implications for career achievement and secure livelihood. Those who have lost a job due to discrimination display the highest levels of discrimination avoidant behavior.

Employment Bias by Association

We asked respondents whether their spouses/partners or children experienced job discrimination due to the respondent being transgender or gender non-conforming.[4] Fourteen percent (14%) of respondents reported that due to their gender identity, their spouse or partner experienced job discrimination. Respondents who reported having lost a job due to bias reported discrimination against their partners at twice that rate (28%).

Respondents also reported that their children were subject to job discrimination due to associational bias at 11%. For those who lost jobs due to bias, discrimination against their children was reported at 25%.

Undocumented non-citizens reported high levels of associational discrimination for both spouses/partners (20%) and children (20%).

Improved Job Situation for Those Who Transition

Of respondents who are living full-time in accordance with their gender identity, 78% said they felt more comfortable and their performance improved at work. Respondents in the higher income categories more often reported an increase in feeling comfortable and performing better after transitioning. Transgender men (78%) and transgender women (79%) who have transitioned reported nearly identical rates of improved job situation.

These respondents who felt their performance improved experienced similar rates of harassment and other forms of mistreatment in the workplace as other transgender and gender non-conforming people. For example, of those who transitioned who said their job performance improved, 51% also reported being harassed at work, compared 50% of the overall sample.

Sex Work, Drug Sales, and Other Underground Work for Income

Given that transgender and gender non-conforming people are often denied access to, forced out of or grossly mistreated in traditional employment markets, it follows that underground work can be an essential survival strategy.

Sixteen percent (16%) of our sample has had some experience in sex work, drug sales, and other underground work. Those at high risk for underground work were those who had lost jobs due to bias (28%), compared to those who had not lost a job (13%), and the unemployed (29%), compared to 14% of those who were employed.

Black (53%) and Latino/a (34%) respondents had extremely high rates of underground work, likely related in part to barriers and abuse within educational systems and dramatically higher rates of employment discrimination.

Male-to-female (19%) respondents had slightly higher rates of underground work than female-to-male (15%) respondents, and transgender (18%) and gender non-conforming (16%) respondents were involved at almost equal frequency.

Sex Work

Eleven percent (11%) of respondents did sex work for income. Here we take a closer look at the demographics of sex workers in our sample and then examine their rates of incarceration, homelessness, and health outcomes.

MTF respondents were more likely to report sex work (15%) than FTM respondents (7%); these data unearths the reality that some transgender men have also done sex work at some point in their lives. Transgender respondents, overall, reported sex work at 12%, only slightly higher than gender non-conforming respondents (10%).

Respondents of color were more likely to have reported having done sex work; African-American respondents reporting the highest rate at 44%. Latino/a respondents had the next highest rate at 28%. These data aligns

with extremely high rates of unemployment and workplace abuse experienced by respondents of color in the study.

Those with higher educational attainment were less likely to report sex work. Those with no high school diploma reported a 33% rate of sex work, compared to those with college degrees at 7%. However, sex work among those with high levels of attainment remained elevated, including 6% of those with graduate degrees.

Homelessness

Respondents reporting sex work were far more likely to also report experiencing homelessness due to bias than the full sample; anecdotal evidence indicates that many who face homelessness do sex work to pay rent or to stay in a hotel. Forty-eight percent (48%) of those who had done sex work also reported experiencing homelessness due to bias. This compares to 19% of the sample overall and 7.4% for the general population overall.[5]

Incarceration

Participants who did sex work were almost four times as likely to have been incarcerated for any reason (48%) than the overall sample (16%).

HIV

Those who had did sex work were over 25 times more likely to be HIV-positive (15.32%) than the general population (0.6%).[6]

Smoking

The rate of smoking among those who had done sex work was much higher (49%) than the overall sample (30%).

Drinking and Drugs

Respondents who had done sex work were twice as likely to misuse drugs or alcohol to cope with the mistreatment (18%) as the overall sample (8%).

Suicide Attempts

The rate of attempted suicide among those who had done sex work was much higher (60%) than the overall sample (41%) and more than 37 times higher than the general population (1.6%).

Making the Connections: Employment Discrimination, Economic Security, and Health

In this section, we examine the connections between employment discrimination and present income, incarceration, homelessness and health outcomes.

Respondents Who Have Lost Jobs Due to Discrimination

We looked at present household income of the more than one quarter (26%) of our sample who said they had lost jobs because they were transgender or gender non-conforming and found the apparent effects to be severe. Respondents who had lost a job due to bias were six times as likely to be living on a household income under $10,000/year (24%) as the general U.S. population (4%).[7] They were nearly twice as likely to be living on between $10,000 and $20,000/year (17%) as the general population (9%).

Homelessness

Respondents who had lost a job due to bias were four times more likely to have experienced homelessness due to bias (40%) than those who did not lose a job due to bias (10%).

Incarceration

Respondents who had lost a job due to bias were 85% more likely to have been incarcerated for any reason (24%) than those who did not lose a job (13%).

HIV

Respondents who had lost a job due to bias reported an HIV rate (4.59%) over seven times higher than the general population (.6%),[8] and more than double the rate of those who did not lose a job (2.06%).

Smoking

Respondents who had lost a job due to bias were more likely to be smokers (38%) than the overall sample (30%).

Drinking & Drugs

Respondents who had lost a job due to bias were 70% more likely to misuse drugs or alcohol to cope with the mistreatment they face (12%) than those who had not lost a job (7%).

Suicide Attempts

Respondents who had lost a job due to bias were much more likely to have attempted suicide (55%) than those respondents who had not lost a job due to bias (38%), and both figures are striking in contrast to the general population figure of 1.6%.

Unemployed Respondents

Here we take a closer look at those respondents who reported being currently unemployed and describe the higher incidence of negative outcomes they experienced.

These respondents may be unemployed because they lost a job due to bias, because they experienced discrimination in hiring, or for other reasons.

Homelessness

Respondents who were unemployed were more than twice as likely to have experienced homelessness due to bias (38%) than those who were employed (14%).

Incarceration

Respondents who were unemployed were 85% more likely to have been incarcerated for any reason (24%) than those who were employed (13%).

HIV

Respondents who were unemployed reported an HIV rate (4.67%) over seven times higher than the general population (.6%),[9] and more than double the rate of those who were employed (1.81%).

Smoking

Respondents who were unemployed were more likely to be smokers (38%) than the overall sample (30%), and almost twice as likely to be smokers than those who were working (20%).

Drinking & Drugs

Respondents who were unemployed were almost two times as likely to misuse drugs or alcohol to cope with the mistreatment they face (13%) than those who were working (7%).

Suicide Attempts

Respondents who were unemployed were much more likely to have attempted suicide (51%) than those respondents who were working (37%), and both figures are striking in contrast to the general population figure of 1.6%.

"I was fired from a good job because I tried to transition on the job. I then lived on menial employment for over 3 years before finally landing another good one that was full-time job and had benefits. At one point, I had an offer of employment withdrawn after the would-be employer found out I was transgender."

Conclusions for Employment

Transgender and gender non-conforming people face staggering rates of harassment mistreatment, and discrimination at work. In this chapter we have shown that many of those who faced this discrimination also experienced multiple, devastating outcomes across many areas of life.

The most obvious sign of this discrimination was the extremely high unemployment figure: double the rate of the general population at the time of study. Underemployment and low household income were also widely reported.

Encouragingly, most of those who have transitioned reported feeling more comfortable at work and that their job performance had improved. However, many of our respondents are unable to reap that benefit because they delayed their gender transition in order to avoid discrimination. The data appears to indicate that transition is not only pivotal to the individual's well-being, but also that employers would be wise to support and facilitate gender transition of their employees to increase productivity.

Many report changing jobs to avoid discrimination or the risk of discrimination. Again, employers should be aware how environments hostile to transgender workers negatively affect their bottom line, as they lose experienced employees and face the added expense of hiring and training replacements.

High rates of workplace abuse and unemployment among respondents, and resulting poverty, indicate that anti-transgender discrimination has left many in a position where sex work and drug sales are necessary for survival. Respondents of color were particularly vulnerable to being pushed into underground work, with a combination of discrimination based on gender, race and citizenship forcing them farthest to the margins.

The data show that there is a high price to pay for those who must do sex work and other underground work, including homelessness, incarceration and catastrophic health outcomes.

This survey is a call to action; employment discrimination has devastating effects on transgender and gender non-conforming people and must be confronted and eradicated. Not only must individual employers be held accountable, but society as a whole must be held accountable for widespread violations of a basic human right.

Recommendations for Employment

Respondents in this study faced overwhelming bias and mistreatment in the workplace due to gender identity and expression. In the absence of workplace protections, employers and coworkers are free to engage in a broad range of abuses from arbitrary firings to demeaning and even violent treatment. The solution to this problem requires the attention of the legislative and executive branches of government, corporations and other employers, labor organizations and non-profit organizations.

- Federal, state, and local laws should be enacted to prohibit discrimination on the basis of gender identity or expression.
  - Federal employment non-discrimination legislation should be enacted with transgender/gender non-conforming protections intact.
  - States and local governments should prioritize enactment of non-discrimination laws.
- Government agencies should implement laws through regulations, compliance guidelines, training, and publicized decisions by enforcement agencies.
  - Only a handful of the states/localities that currently have legal protections have written regulations or guidelines showing employers how to properly treat transgender and gender non-conforming employees. Without these specifics, employers are not sure what the law requires of them and employees cannot engage in effective self-advocacy when being mistreated or discriminated against.
  - Enforcement agency staff should undergo training to better understand the specific issues that transgender and gender non-conforming employees experience in the workplace and should learn how to respectfully deal with transgender and gender non-conforming complainants.
  - Decisions, investigations, and settlements related to discrimination on the basis of gender identity/expression should be publicized as much as possible to increase awareness of what constitutes illegal discriminatory actions.
  - Enforcement agencies should develop and offer trainings for employers on how to comply with the law. If this is not done, non-profit organizations should develop and provide these trainings.
  - Enforcement agencies and non-profit groups should develop "Know Your Rights" materials and trainings for transgender and gender non-conforming people.
- Corporations should enact and enforce their own gender identity/expression non-discrimination policies.
  - All employees should be trained on how to comply with the policy. Hiring officers must be instructed to ensure they are not consciously or unconsciously discriminating in hiring and should also be educated about how to recognize when an applicant has a poor work record due to discrimination.
  - Written policies should be developed concerning gender transition in the workplace so that all employees understand proper, respectful

protocol. This policy should address confidentiality, access to gender-segregated facilities, dress standards (if relevant), medical leave policies, pronouns and forms of address, harassment, change of employee records and badges, and any other topic necessary for a smooth gender transition in the workplace.

- Companies should actively recruit transgender and gender non-conforming applicants.
- Government agencies at all levels should develop transgender-specific workforce development programs, or modify existing programs, to train and match transgender and gender non-conforming people to the best jobs available.
  - Staff running these programs should be properly trained to address and work with transgender and gender non-conforming participants respectfully.
  - Special attention in such programs should be paid to devising ways to expunge criminal records of persons who have been incarcerated for survival behaviors, and/or find employers who are willing to hire applicants with criminal records.
  - These programs should train cooperating employers on how to avoid discrimination in hiring transgender and gender non-conforming employees and require that staff of cooperating employers have received training on how to respectfully treat these coworkers.
  - Government agencies should work with transgender organizations to develop such programs, ideally providing grants to these organizations for their assistance.
- Labor organizations should ensure that contracts include gender identity/expression nondiscrimination clauses, train union officers and rank-and-file on the importance of nondiscrimination in the workplace, and how to process grievances related to discriminatory treatment.
- Governments should focus their resources on providing meaningful pathways out of poverty, such as by increasing employment opportunities for transgender and gender non-conforming people, rather than expending significant resources on arresting, prosecuting, and incarcerating those doing sex work.

Notes

1. U.S. National Library of Health and the National Institutes of Health, Medline Plus, "Out of Work May Mean Out of Sorts: Mental health takes a beating with economic downturn, http://www.nlm.nih.gov/medlineplus/news/fullstory_102374.html

2. This includes people who said they tell "everyone."
3. Seven percent (7%) was the rounded weighted average unemployment rate for the general population during the six months the survey was in the field, based on which month questionnaires were completed. See seasonally unadjusted monthly unemployment rates for September 2008 through February 2009. For information on how we calculated the unemployment rate for respondents, see the Portrait chapter. U.S. Department of Labor, Bureau of Labor Statistics, "The Employment Situation: September 2008," (2008): http://www.bls.gov/news.release/archives/empsit_10032008.htm
4. See Appendix B: Survey Instrument—Issues and Analysis for more discussion of this question.
5. Bruce G. Link, PhD, et al., "Lifetime and Five-Year Prevalence of Homelessness in the United States," *American Journal of Public Health* 84, (December 1994): http://ajph.aphapublications.org/cgi/reprint/84/12/1907.
6. HIV rates are reported without rounding in order to make a more precise comparison with general population data.
7. 4.15% of the population had a household income below $10,000 per year. U.S. Department of Commerce, U.S. Census Bureau and U.S. Department of Labor, Bureau of Labor Statistics, "Current Population Survey: Annual Social and Economic Supplement" (2008).
8. HIV rates reported without rounding in order to make a more precise comparison with general population data.
9. HIV rates reported without rounding in order to make a more precise comparison with general population data.

JAIME M. GRANT, director of the Global Transgender Research and Advocacy Project, was the Policy Institute Director at the National Gay and Lesbian Task Force and the founding executive director of the Arcus Center for Social Justice Leadership.

LISA A. MOTTET is the deputy director for the Center for Lesbian and Gay Studies in Religion and Ministry, is the former community education and outreach manager at the National Center for Transgender Equality and former director of communications for Out & Equal Workplace Advocates, based in San Francisco, which advocates for equal employment rights for LGBT people.

JACK HARRISON is an LGBTQ activist and researcher who is the e-learning manager at the National LGBTQ Task Force.

JODY L. HERMAN is the manager of transgender research and Peter J. Cooper Public Policy Fellow at the Williams Institute.

MARA KEISLING is the founding executive director of the National Center for Transgender Equality.

Family Research Council

The Employment Non-Discrimination Act (ENDA): A Threat to Free Markets and Freedom of Conscience and Religion

The Employment Non-Discrimination Act (ENDA) was re-introduced in the 113th Congress in April 2013 as H.R. 1755 and S. 815. ENDA would prohibit employers from making employment decisions on the basis of actual or perceived sexual orientation or gender identity. It is misleadingly labeled as a logical extension of Title VII of the Civil Rights Act. While the Civil Rights Act was enacted primarily to protect the rights of racial minorities, ENDA is aimed at providing special protections for "sexual orientation" (which includes voluntary homosexual conduct) and "gender identity" (referring not to one's biological sex, but to "the gender-related identity, appearance, or mannerisms or other gender-related characteristics of an individual, with or without regard to the individual's designated sex at birth").

The "gender identity" provision would protect anyone who is "transgendered," a broad umbrella term that includes transsexuals (people who have had sex-change surgery), anyone who has changed or is changing their public "gender identity" (regardless of whether they have had surgery or hormone treatments), transvestites (people who dress as the opposite sex on an occasional basis for emotional or sexual gratification), and drag queens and drag kings (people who dress as the opposite sex for the purpose of entertaining others).

ENDA should be opposed by anyone who believes in freedom of speech, freedom of association, freedom of conscience and religion, and a free market economy. Here are some reasons why:

- **ENDA would increase federal government interference in the free market.** It would substitute the judgment of the federal government for that of the employer regarding what qualities or characteristics are most relevant to a particular job.
- **"Sexual orientation" and "gender identity" are unlike most other characteristics protected in civil rights laws.** The Civil Rights Act of 1964 bars discrimination based on "race, color, national origin, sex, and religion." The first four of these are included largely because they are inborn, involuntary and immutable. (Religion, while voluntary, is explicitly protected by the First Amendment to the U.S. Constitution.) While sexual attractions may be involuntary, neither sexual conduct nor transgender behavior meets any of these criteria. Ten federal circuit courts and the U.S. Supreme Court have declined to subject classifications based on "sexual orientation" to the "strict scrutiny" that applies to race.[1]
- **ENDA would lead to costly lawsuits against employers.** It would invite disgruntled employees to sue for "discrimination" over a characteristic (in the case of sexual orientation) which is not even visible and of which the employer may have been unaware. In the case of public employers (which are explicitly covered by ENDA), such laws at the local and state level have led to large settlements being paid at taxpayers' expense.[2]
- **ENDA would increase sexualization of the workplace.** There is an inherent contradiction in the arguments of the advocates of ENDA, who contend that what they do in private has nothing to do with their work, but then also argue for the right to be "out of the closet" while at work.
- **ENDA's "gender identity" provisions would undermine the ability of employers to impose reasonable dress and grooming standards.** The bill professes to protect such standards. However, it requires that such standards be consistent with the employee's chosen and variable "gender identity." This effectively forbids employers from using the most fundamental standard of all—that people be dressed and groomed in a way that is culturally appropriate for their biological sex.
- **ENDA's "gender identity" provisions would violate the privacy of others.** Because

transgender status is not dependent on having "sex-change surgery," ENDA would allow some biological males (who claim to be female) to appear nude before females (and vice versa) in bathrooms, locker rooms, and showers. (Previous versions of ENDA included an exemption for "shared shower and dressing facilities in which being seen unclothed is unavoidable." This exemption has been *removed* from the current version of the bill.)

- **ENDA would mandate the employment of homosexual, bisexual, and "transgendered" individuals in inappropriate occupations.** ENDA disregards the fact that sexual conduct may in fact be relevant to employment. For example, under ENDA, employers in the area of education and childcare would be denied the right to refuse to hire homosexuals or transgendered individuals, even if they consider such persons to be inappropriate role models for children and young people.

- **ENDA would force some employers to violate their moral and religious convictions.** This includes those which provide products, services, or catering for weddings, or groups and businesses providing dating services, which would be forced under penalty of law to hire homosexuals, even though homosexual behavior and same-sex "marriage" are expressly contrary to their religious convictions.

- **ENDA's "religious exemption" is inadequate to protect people of faith.** ENDA contains an exemption for certain "religious organizations," such as houses of worship or religious schools. However, the exemption fails to protect individual Christians, Jews, Muslims and others who have objections to certain sexual behaviors from making employment decisions consistent with their faith. In fact, it is questionable whether any profit-making corporations would qualify for the exemption, meaning that Christian bookstores, religious publishing houses, and religious television and radio stations could all be forced to compromise their principles in mandated hiring practices.

- **ENDA prepares the way for reverse discrimination.** The more open homosexuals become the more people who hold traditional values will be forced to conceal their views. This can happen even if the employee's views are expressed outside of work,[3] and when no reference is made to sexual orientation.[4]

- **ENDA would "legislate morality"—the "morality" of the sexual revolution.** Often, social conservatives are accused of trying to "legislate morality." Yet ENDA itself is fraught with moral significance. From time immemorial human societies have used legal and cultural means to encourage the traditional family because of its unique and far reaching benefits to society.[5] ENDA, on the other hand, would be an official government declaration that homosexual behavior is the equivalent of heterosexual behavior in every way, and that those who believe otherwise are simply bigoted. A majority of Americans reject this view.[6]

- **ENDA would pave the way for further redefinition of marriage.** State courts which have redefined "marriage" to include homosexual couples in Massachusetts, California, Iowa, and Connecticut cited the existence of "non-discrimination" laws like ENDA at the state level as establishing a principle regarding the legal irrelevance of "sexual orientation," which they have then applied to the institution of marriage.[7] Passage of ENDA at the national level could give fuel for a similar decision by the U.S. Supreme Court, forcing the redefinition of marriage in every state in the union, at some time in the future.

Notes

1. Paul McHugh and Gerard V. Bradley, "Sexual Orientation, Gender Identity, and Employment Law," *Public Discourse* (July 25, 2013) ; online at: http://www.thepublicdiscourse.com/2013/07/10636/.

2. For examples from Portland, Oregon; Bay City, Michigan; Pacific Grove, California; Santa Barbara, California; and the State of New York, see: Tony Perkins, *Testimony in opposition to H.R. 3017,* "Employment Non-Discrimination Act" (September 29, 2009); online at: http://www.frc.org/testimony/testimony-in-opposition-to-hr-3017-employment-non-discrimination-act.

3. This happened to Allstate's Matt Barber, who was fired: Ron Strom, "Allstate Terminates Manager over Homosexuality Column," *WorldNetDaily* (June 24, 2005); http://www.wnd.com/2005/06/30993/.

4. This happened to the City of Oakland's Good News Employee Association, which was forbidden to speak about "family values:" "US Court Rules it's OK to Censor the Terms 'Natural Family,' 'Marriage' and 'Family Values,'" *LifeSiteNews* (March 8, 2007); online at: http://www.lifesitenews.com/news/archive/ldn/2007/mar/07030805.

5. Patrick Fagan, Henry Potrykus and Anna Shafer, "Family Intactness: Influence on Major State Policy Outcomes," Marriage and Religion

Research Institute (July 2012); http://marri.us/get.cfm?i=OR12G01.

6. A poll taken in September 2012 showed that 52% of Americans believe that "sex between two adults of the same gender" is "morally wrong," and only 42% say it is "morally acceptable." See *American Values Survey 2012,* Public Religion Research Institute (September 13–30, 2012); online at http://publicreligion.org/site/wp-content/uploads/2012/10/AVS-2012-Topline-FINAL.pdf.

7. Iowa Code §216.6 "Unfair Employment Practices" is cited by the Iowa Supreme Court in *Varnum v. Brien* (763 N.W. 2d 862) to justify redefining marriage; online at http://www.iowacourts.gov/wfData/files/Varnum/07-1499(1).pdf.

The **FAMILY RESEARCH COUNCIL'S** mission is to advance faith, family, and freedom in public policy and the culture from a Christian worldview.

EXPLORING THE ISSUE

Should the Employment Non-Discrimination Act (ENDA) Be Passed?

Critical Thinking and Reflection

1. Are sexual orientation and gender identity categories that you think should be included in federal laws relating to discrimination alongside other civil rights laws?
2. If ENDA could only be passed with sexual orientation language in it but not gender identity language, should transgender rights activists support it?
3. ENDA opponents believe religious organizations should receive exemptions from particular laws. If a religion encourages a particular practice—like female genital mutilation, which is illegal in the United States—should they be allowed to practice it under the religious exemption clause?

Is There Common Ground?

Whether there is common ground on this topic truly depends on who you ask. There is a lot of misinformation about what sexual orientation and gender identity are, which can lead to discomfort, fear, and biases. There are very strong religious beliefs that put a moralistic lens on this discussion, where various teachings dictate how followers are to feel about and behave toward those who are different from them.

There are equally strong feelings from those who identify as LGB and/or T, as well as their allies, that absolute equality is necessary regardless of sexual orientation or gender identity. They point to science and research to demonstrate that sexual orientation and gender identity are not chosen, but rather innate—and feel that the research trumps religious belief.

As with any topic, when people are at the extremes, middle ground is challenging if not impossible to obtain. The most important middle ground here is that everyone, regardless of sexual orientation or gender identity, regardless of religious affiliation, deserves to work in an environment that is free from violence and harassment.

Additional Resources

Anderson, R.T. (2013). ENDA threatens fundamental civil liberties. The Heritage Foundation, Backgrounder Report #2857. http://www.heritage.org/

research/reports/2013/11/enda-threatens-fundamental-civil-liberties.

King, E.B. and Cortine, J.M. (2010). The social and economic imperative of lesbian, gay, bisexual, and transgendered [sic.] supportive organizational policies. *Industrial and Organizational Psychology*, 3, 69–78.

Weinberg, J. (2010). Gender nonconformity: An analysis of perceived sexual orientation and gender identity protection under the Employment Non-Discrimination Act. 44 U.S.F. L. Rev. 1 (2009–2010).

Reference

1. Hunt, J. (2011). A history of the Employment Non-Discrimination Act. Center for American Progress: July 19, 2011. http://www.americanprogress.org/issues/lgbt/news/2011/07/19/10006/a-history-of-the-employment-non-discrimination-act.

Internet References . . .

Family Research Council

www.frc.org

Human Rights Campaign

http://www.hrc.org/topics/workplace

National Center for Transgender Equality

http://transequality.org/

United States Conference of Catholic Bishops

http://www.usccb.org/

Selected, Edited, and with Issue Framing Material by:
Elizabeth Schroeder, EdD, MSW, *Elizabeth Schroeder Consulting*

ISSUE

Has the Economic Recession Been Harder on Women's Employment Than Men's Employment?

YES: Government Equalities Office, from "The Economic Downturn—The Concerns and Experiences of Women and Families" (2009)

NO: Teri Fritsma, from "Minnesota's He-Cession: Are Men Bearing the Brunt of the Economic Downturn?" *Minnesota Economic TRENDS* (2009)

Learning Outcomes

After reading this issue, you will be able to:

- Determine if the recession been equally harmful for women and men.
- Determine if the effects of recession been similar across all ages, races, ethnicities, and social classes.
- Identify the indicators of being affected by the economic downturn.
- Identify the role of regional and national differences in understanding the effect of the economy on families.

ISSUE SUMMARY

YES: The Government Equalities Office presents data suggesting that women are experiencing more challenges than men due to the economic recession.

NO: Teri Fritsma, in an analysis of data based on employment patterns in Minnesota, suggests that men are being more negatively affected by the recession than are women.

Historically, poor women have always worked, perhaps as a housekeeper or a nanny or a seamstress in a sweatshop. In recent U.S. history, women were most likely to enter the workforce in masses during times of war. Their presence was needed to compensate for the lack of male laborers. Rosie the Riveter became the patriotic role model. However, after each of the two major world wars, women were encouraged to return to their rightful place in the home with as much enthusiasm as they had been encouraged to leave the home. Suzi Homemaker became the new cultural icon for women. Issues of women's equal treatment in the workplace did not really come to the forefront for debate until large numbers of women entered higher education and participated in the civil rights movement and the antiwar movement of the 1960s. The second wave of the women's movement was the result. Many believed that as more women obtained more education and began to climb the career ladder, gender inequities would begin to dissipate. However, although in 40 years there has been progress at the entry level for women, women at the top find themselves in a minority. Ironically, during the 2008–2009 recession, men held 78 percent of the jobs lost. As a result, women may actually be faring better by comparison. But are they? Women now hold almost 50 percent of all jobs today (compared to 36 percent 40 years ago). But once again, in the words of Lisa Belkin, "The history of women in the workplace (both their leaps forward and then slips back) is a reaction to what was happening to men." Women currently are returning to the workforce because they have to and they are cheaper to hire than are men. The glass ceiling has not been broken. Some have suggested that women no longer "want it all"—career and family; rather, women are willingly choosing to opt out of the fast-paced, competitive rat race to be stay-at-home moms. There is evidence that some women with advanced degrees from some of the most prestigious institutions in the United States have done this. However, these women are married to highly successful men who generate enough income to maintain an upper-middle-class lifestyle. Other women have opted out of the corporate race to the top because they realized they were not going to break through the glass ceiling. Women are a fast-growing group to start their own businesses. However, such examples ignore the fact that the vast majority of people (women and men) do not have the resources to begin their own businesses, nor can they maintain a comfortable lifestyle without two incomes; and for single mothers, it is not a question of lifestyle but a matter of survival. Economists have evaluated the notions of the mommy track and the fast track. The mommy track had originally been proposed as a career path that recognized women's role as child-bearers; the idea was that a woman's career trajectory would be adjusted to allow for this reality without jeopardizing her chances of advancement. It did not work. Such a choice by women has resulted in subtle discrimination. A self-fulfilling prophecy occurred. An employer is more likely to put a male than a female employee on the fast track, believing that he will not be distracted by child-care responsibilities like a female employee. As a result, effort rather than talent is being rewarded. The man is expected to be on the fast track and to put forth more effort than his partner who is on the mommy track. Only permanent changes in public policy will remove the discrimination.

In the current economic climate, it is necessary to consider a host of factors that likely interact with gender to understand fully the impact of the downturn. For example, one recent analysis suggested that both older employed women and men who have an employed spouse have more financial capability (i.e., making ends meet and managing money) than other groups of individuals; young, currently unemployed adults have the least capability. Furthermore, the economic climate affects factors other than financial capability. For example, in a recent 2008 *Journal of Men's Health* article, Siegfried Meryn of the International Society of Men's Health reported that the economic downturn is taking a serious toll on men's health, especially men of color. He noted that men's mortality is higher than women's and that decreases in

health budgets will only exacerbate the health problems that are emerging.

Because we are currently in the middle of an economic crisis, it is difficult to assess its full long-term impact. However, scholars have studied the impact of past economic downturns and have findings that may offer insights into the current situation. Sociologists have suggested that there is typically social and political mobilization in the face of economic restructuring and the household is often the site of the day-to-day coping with economic stress. One study of farm families in the Midwest during the 1980s observed that women exerted a more radicalizing influence on their spouses than did men, at least among women who joined political organizations. The study looked at the family as a source of adaptive strategy and found that women were more likely than men to join political activist groups and when they did, it affected their husbands' activism. They stated that "women's distinct roles in farming, household reproduction, and as mediators between household and community suggest that farm women . . . may have a 'moral framework of public life'. . . that differs from men." In a recent *Washington Post* article, Ezra Klein raised the question of women in the current Tea Party movement. Does the study of women, political mobilization, and the economic crisis among Midwestern farmers in the 1980s offer any insight into the extent to which women are welcomed and comfortable in the newest political movement? Only time will tell.

Of importance in the discussion of who is suffering the most as the result of the recession is the question of who is the focus of discussion and what are the criteria for determining a negative impact. For example, the Institute for Women's Policy Research reported that women, and single mothers in particular, have been experiencing the highest rates of financial strain and are having the most difficulties on a day-to-day basis. They noted that these women are recovering from a "mancession." In contrast the Women's Enterprise Task Force, set up in the United Kingdom by the government, found that women were losing their jobs at a slower pace than men. They also found that female entrepreneurs in particular were faring fairly well, did not see themselves as victims, and were not having difficulty accessing financing. Such contrasting reports underscore the importance of paying close attention to which segments of the population and where in the world they are located are being studied before sweeping conclusions can be made. For example, the report in the YES selection suggesting greater hardships on women and families is based on data from Great Britain, whereas the data in the report in the NO selection suggesting a greater negative impact on men is from the state of Minnesota.

YES ⬅

The Economic Downturn—The Concerns and Experiences of Women and Families

Background

The Government Equalities Office (GEO) commissioned Ipsos MORI to undertake qualitative and quantitative research on the impact of the economic downturn on women and families. In particular, the research examines how the downturn has influenced women's fears, their finances, working and caring arrangements, family life, future plans and wellbeing. Comparative research was undertaken among men as well, to look for similarities and differences.

The research comprised both qualitative and quantitative elements. The qualitative work consisted of 10 discussion groups (seven among women and three among men) in three locations in England (London, Northampton and Newcastle) in January and February 2009. In addition, two quantitative telephone surveys were administered to representative samples of British adults to test the extent to which the views of participants in the qualitative research were indicative of wider public opinion.

The survey research, or quantitative work, was designed to provide robust data that is representative of the views of the British population as a whole. The focus group work, or qualitative research, is not statistically robust or representative, but rather was designed to illustrate and explore participants' understanding of and reasoning about the issues at hand.

Key Concerns About the Impact of the Downturn

Three-quarters (75%) of British adults were concerned about the impact of the economic downturn on their family life, with 80% of women concerned compared with 70% of men. This is a trend felt throughout this research project, which finds women more concerned than men on a range of subjects, especially those that centre around family and caring. Many women in the discussion groups expressed deep-seated concerns about job prospects, the threat of redundancy for themselves and/or for their

partners, and the pressure both on the individual and [on the] household.

Men in the discussion groups tended to focus primarily on concern about job loss per se, as opposed to overall effect on their family, and were much more expressive on the *causes* of the downturn than on the effects. The discussion groups with men tended to focus more on who to blame for the downturn rather than dealing with the aftermath.

It is important to note, however, that opinions were not universal across group participants, and also that there were notable differences in attitudes between women (and men) of different ages and social grades. It may also be the case that the type of industry an individual works in affects their level of concern about job loss; the group discussions found that people in industries they perceived to be less stable showed more concern about losing their jobs (for example, the service industries).

From the survey, and mirrored by the opinions of discussion group participants, one of the most immediate concerns for the public was losing their jobs, or someone in their household losing their job. A third (33%) of men were worried about unemployment, compared with four in 10 (40%) women. In addition, Ipsos MORI's monthly Issues Index which asks an open-ended question about the most important issues facing the country, shows that in January 2009 public levels of concern about unemployment reached a 10-year high, with 24% of Britons naming unemployment as one of the main issues facing Britain today, an increase of 9 percentage points since December 2008. There was no difference in concern between men and women on this measure.

Participants' other concerns centred around bills and family worries, although these often differed depending on the individual's life stage and socio-demographic profile. Mid-life participants (middle-aged, and often with children), for example, were more concerned with paying their mortgages and the welfare of their children. Many older participants seemed resigned to the recession—some had lived through rationing—and, though they were upset

From *Impact of the Economic Downturn on Women*, March 2009.

about their (often) reduced income and certainly felt pessimistic about the future, they did not demonstrate the same levels of anxiety and confusion as younger participants who had not lived through a recession before.

Younger participants under age 30 tend to have fewer commitments and thus fewer concerns, but where there was anxiety about their finances, it was associated more with "lifestyle" costs (clothes, the cost of a night out, etc.) rather than concerns about job loss or family members. This group also displayed more confusion and uncertainty about the future, especially when contrasted with the more "resigned" attitudes of the older group participants.

The oldest and youngest participants in the discussion groups seemed to be concerned about each other, but less about themselves. Younger participants often expressed concern for older individuals who lived with fixed incomes, worrying that savings and/or pensions losses would impact adversely on older people's lives. Participants over age 65, while they did feel concern about issues such as loss of personal savings, were also less worried for themselves because they felt that they had previous experience of living with a limited income (living through past recessions), or at least felt themselves more able to adjust to a more limited income. They expressed concern both for people struggling to raise children, as well as for younger generations in general who they felt would experience a real "shock" at the limitations a recession would impose on them (never having experienced one before).

Concerns About Finances

From the quantitative research, the age group most likely to think that their personal financial circumstances would worsen over the coming years were those over age 65, almost half (46%) of whom felt that their circumstances would get worse—compared with a quarter (27%) of those age 16–34 who said the same. This finding was strongly reflected in the qualitative research, where the groups that unanimously and immediately mentioned feeling real effects due to the economic downturn (though not necessarily worrying as much about them) were the older (65+) individuals. These men and women stated that they had felt the effects of the downturn already, in their savings and pensions accounts—and also, as a result, in their ability to pay bills.

When asked about general experiences and worries, concerns such as the price of food and utilities were more frequently mentioned by the female group participants (particularly those over age 25) than the male ones. Participants' concern levels were high enough that they were

genuinely cutting back on their spending—some because they needed to financially, while others were doing so preemptively because they felt they needed to start saving or cutting back now.

Women with children and/or families, as well as those with caring responsibilities of any kind were among the most worried groups of women. Those who felt more at risk of job losses within the family were especially anxious about issues such as arrears and repossession (although very few were at risk of it at the time the groups were conducted).

Concerns About Working and Caring

Just under half (48%) of men and women said that the downturn has had no effect on their working hours. However, many women—especially those with children or those in part-time work—expressed concern about their jobs and balancing their work lives and home lives.

People with mortgages and/or children to support said that they felt the impacts of the downturn on their family life most strongly. Worries about job security, income and problems at work due to the downturn were all cited as reasons by some people for tension in their family relationships, especially in relationships with partners. Some group participants said their family life had been made more difficult by the need to live within a tighter budget, due to either a decrease in income or an increase in the amount spent on bills.

Many women in the groups felt that the loss of men's jobs would affect their lives deeply, as they and their families were, in many cases, partly or fully dependent on the more significant incomes of their partners. This view was widely held across the groups, although least strongly in the youngest groups and most strongly in the middle-aged groups of women of lower social grades (C2DE).

A number of mothers in the groups noted that their childcare costs were rising. This affected all types of care, both formal and informal, with parents finding nursery and childminders' fees rising, and increasing costs related to informal care, such as the cost of groceries and simple medical supplies. Women whose working hours had increased in the last few months reconsidered care provision in the family, with greater reliance on informal care, such as grandparents and elder siblings.

The **Government Equalities Office** is part of the Department for Culture, Media and Sports of Her Majesty's Government. It was created in 2007 when the Women and Equality Unit became an independent department.

Teri Fritsma

 **NO**

Minnesota's He-Cession: Are Men Bearing the Brunt of the Economic Downturn?

Several recent articles in the popular press have suggested that men are taking it on the chin during this economic downturn. A recent *New York Times* article reported that more than four out of five jobs lost since 2007 were held by men. The executive editor of *The Nation* is blogging about the new gender gap in unemployment, and the *Los Angeles Times* dubbed this a "he-cession."

The current economic slump isn't unique in this regard. Men's job losses have dramatically outpaced women's in each of the last five recessions. What's behind this phenomenon? And do Minnesota patterns parallel the national trends?

The unemployment rate for men and women shows a clear disparity and suggests that men are far more vulnerable to layoffs these days both nationally and in Minnesota. The male and female unemployment rates have both increased over the past year, but while female unemployment rose fairly modestly, male unemployment nearly doubled. Sex differences in unemployment are even more pronounced in Minnesota than they are nationally. Male unemployment in Minnesota rose by 5 percent, while female unemployment edged up by less than 0.5 percent over the past year.

Why is the risk of unemployment so much greater for men? There are probably a combination of reasons, but most analysts and commentators point to one major factor: the employment patterns of men and women. While many men are employed in the hard-hit construction and manufacturing industries, women are more likely to work in the relatively stable government, health care and education services industries. How accurate is this claim and how much can these differences account for the sex gap in unemployment?

No Hard Hats for Women?

A large body of research is devoted to studying sex differences in industry or occupational employment. What this research makes clear is that women and men generally occupy different space in the labor market. And while men frequently benefit from these differences in the form of higher average pay, they also appear to be far more exposed to layoffs during economic downturns.

[In] Minnesota, . . . we see . . . that two male-dominated industries—construction and manufacturing—were responsible for about half of all unemployment claims in March 2009. Meanwhile, the two most female-dominated industries in Minnesota—health care and education services—together made up less than 5 percent of all UI claims. It's worth noting that there were many industries that didn't fit this pattern. Three heavily male-dominated industries—agriculture, mining, and transportation and utilities—were each responsible for less than 3 percent of unemployment claims, and two industries that are almost 50 percent female (wholesale and retail trade, and information) each accounted for more than 10 percent of UI claims.

The Role of Industry Sex Composition

Suppose you could take all people in the labor market and randomly assign them to industries so that women were just as likely as men to be employed in the hard-hit construction and manufacturing industries. Then imagine you computed a new, hypothetical unemployment rate for women. The difference between that hypothetical rate and the true rate is the share of unemployment that can be attributed to the different industry employment patterns. For example, suppose the true unemployment rate for women and men is 6.5 and 9 percent, respectively. Then suppose the hypothetical rate for women is 8.5 percent. This means that the different employment patterns can account for 2 percentage points, or about 80 percent (2/2.5) of the total gap in unemployment.

As it turns out, this type of "what if" analysis is possible with specialized statistical techniques developed by sociologists studying the labor market. We used this methodological approach for the following analyses to better understand the relationship between men's and women's industry composition and the risk of unemployment. . . .

From *Minnesota Economic Trends*, September 2009.

[Comparing] the true U.S. unemployment rate for men and women from March 2008 through April 2009 [with] the hypothetical unemployment rate for women that would result if they were as likely as men to be employed in the male-dominated sectors of the economy, [we] document, again, that the true unemployment rates for men and women have both risen, with the male rate rising more dramatically than the female rate. However, the hypothetical rate for women from March through September 2008 actually exceeds the true male rate—meaning that if women and men were equally likely to be employed in the hard-hat industries like construction and manufacturing, women's unemployment would actually have been higher than men's by a few percentage points during those months.

Beginning in December 2008, and continuing through April 2009, the true male and hypothetical female unemployment rates merge—meaning that men['s] and women's different employment patterns currently account for the entire gap in unemployment. That is, if we could rearrange people so that women and men were employed in the same industries at the same rate, their unemployment rates would be almost identical.

[A]t the state level, . . . we see that while the male rate has jumped to 10.4 percent since September 2008, the female unemployment rate has barely moved. Furthermore, the hypothetical female rate is consistently about 1 to 2 percent higher than the true female rate. In April 2009, the different employment patterns of men and women in Minnesota accounted for 2.2 percentage points, or just over 40 percent, of the total gap in unemployment. That is, if we rearranged men and women in the labor market so that women's concentration in construction and manufacturing was the same as men's, the male/female unemployment gap would be 40 percent smaller in Minnesota.

Conclusion: Stay Tuned

The analysis above suggests that there are some substantial differences between Minnesota and U.S. patterns. The first difference is the female unemployment rate: While the national female unemployment rate has risen (albeit modestly, compared to men's) the Minnesota female unemployment rate has stayed more or less constant over the last 12 months.

Secondly, the industry employment concentration accounts for essentially the entire unemployment gap at the national level, but it explains only 40 percent of the unemployment gap at the state level.

What can account for these differences? What is unique about Minnesota? Time and space limitations preclude us from answering these questions in this article. . . .

Who Has It Better?

What's clear from this study is that Minnesota men are indeed taking the lion's share of job losses in the recession, primarily because men and women are concentrated in different industries.

What the analysis can't answer, however, is the more subjective question of which sex has it "better" or "easier" these days. It might be tempting to assume from the patterns of job loss that men alone are affected by this recession. Before jumping to that conclusion, however, consider the following:

First, when any member of a household is laid off, the whole household is impacted—and the impact may be greater when the salary lost is the man's. Working women still earn less than men. According to the U.S. Bureau of Labor Statistics, men out-earned women in every age, race, major occupational group and state in 2007. (In Minnesota, the average woman's earnings were 76.9 percent of the average man's.) This means that making ends meet on one woman's salary is likely to prove more challenging for a household or family accustomed to relying on both a male and female salary.

Second, nonworking men and women tend to spend their time in different ways. According to data from the 2003–2006 American Time Use Survey, married fathers who were not employed spent an average of 2.32 hours on housework and 1.26 hours on child care each day. Married mothers who were not employed spent nearly double the time on these same activities: 3.64 hours on housework and 2.48 hours on child care. And full-time working moms? They spent almost as much time as nonemployed dads on household and child care activities (2.05 and 1.22 hours, respectively).

One can always find exceptions to these broad trends—and it's likely that men's and women's salaries and time-use will continue to edge toward parity. Still, it's worth keeping in mind that the women who remain in the labor market during this recession are, on average, working for less money and putting in nearly the same hours at home as their unemployed male counterparts.

TERI FRITSMA is a senior project consultant for the Minnesota State Colleges and Universities System, curating several career exploration websites and developing Web-based tools for individuals exploring their career options. Her background is in employment research and labor market information, and her recent work has focused on skills assessments, green careers, and union membership among women.

EXPLORING THE ISSUE

Has the Economic Recession Been Harder on Women's Employment Than Men's Employment?

Critical Thinking and Reflections

1. Are there some indicators that suggest a greater impact of the economic downturn on women and some that suggest a greater impact on men?
2. Is it wise to consider factors other than employment status and income in assessing the impact of the economic climate, dimensions such as mental and physical health, educational opportunities, and crime rates?
3. Regardless of whether it is women or men who are more affected, what about the impact on families, and on society?
4. How might gender roles contribute to the effect of the economic downturn?
5. What are the implications of the economic downturn for women breaking the glass ceiling? Will it be easier or more difficult?

Is There Common Ground?

It seems that if one looks hard enough it is possible to find evidence that supports contradictory claims that the economic downturn is harder on women than men and vice versa. However, in reality the sum total of evidence suggests that just about everyone is suffering by some measure, be it economic, psychological, or societal. Overall, according to the Bureau of Labor Statistics, as of September 2011, unemployment was just over 9 percent, with real earnings dropping, although there is great variability across region and various demographic categories. Some analysts say these numbers are too low because they do not take into account the huge numbers of people who are underemployed and who are no longer even looking for work because they have just given up. This last point is one of great concern. To the extent that one gives up, the consequences can have cascading negative effects. For example, there is an increased risk of depression, with all the other serious problems that are often associated with this and other serious mental health problems. It has been estimated that the rate of suicide is two to three times higher among the unemployed than the employed. Furthermore, according to the National Institute for Justice, unemployment has been associated with increases

in violence, including domestic violence. It has been estimated that the rate of domestic violence is 12.3 percent for men who have been unemployed two or more periods, but only 4.7 percent when employed. The problem is compounded by the finding that lack of money is one of the major reasons a female victim does not leave an abusive partner.

Additional Resources

Cown, T. (2014). Why the economic gender gap will eventually close. *The New York Times*, September 13, 2014. http://www.nytimes.com/2014/09/14/upshot/gauging-the-gender-gap-present-and-future.html?_r=0&abt=0002&abg=1.

Elborgh-Woytek, K., Newiak, M., Kochhar, K. et al. (2013). Women, work, and the economy: Macroeconomic gains from gender equity. Strategy, Policy, and Review Department and Fiscal Affairs Department, International Monetary Fund. https://www.imf.org/external/pubs/ft/sdn/2013/sdn1310.pdf.

Gottfried, H. (2012). Gender, Work, and Economy: Unpacking the Global Economy. Hoboken, NJ: John Wiley & Sons.

Internet References . . .

The Economist

http://www.economist.com/

UN Women: Economic Empowerment

http://www.unwomen.org/en/what-we-do/economic
-empowerment

Women, Business, and the Law

http://wbl.worldbank.org/

Unit 3

UNIT

Parental Presence, Parental Choices

Societies around the world have traditionally invested a great deal of thought into who should be raising children. The so-called "nuclear family" is defined as two parents and a dependent child or children. While most definitions refer to "two parents" without gendering those parents, it is safe to assume that, historically, these two parents were only socially acceptable if they were a male-female couple. Today, family constellations have become far more diverse—and in some cases, larger. A child might be raised by a mother and a father, by two mothers or two fathers, by one parent alone, by a grandparent, aunt, or uncle, by an older sibling, by a foster or adoptive parent—or by someone else altogether. The accompanying question that is asked about each of these situations is, what is the impact? What other social factors come into play aside from the number of parents or parent figures, other than gender? For example, is it better for there to be a mother and a father even if there is domestic abuse happening in that relationship rather than having a child raised by a single mother? Or two mothers or two fathers?

Alongside the issues of who makes up the parenting/caregiving unit is the question of what roles and what kind of power should these adults have? Advances in technology have made it possible to know more about a fetus growing inside a woman than ever before. Parents who have genetic disorders in their families can find out in advance whether their fetus has the markers for the same anomaly; the genitals of the fetus can be discerned through ultrasound, and so on. To what extent can and should parents be able to manipulate the fetus as it grows? If parents have two boys and really want a girl and are certain they can only afford to have a third child, should they be able to do what they can through assisted technology to try to make that happen? Or should they leave it to fate and accept a child of any gender?

What happens if parents are in disagreement about what to do about the fetus? Currently, laws relating to reproductive health protect the right of a woman to make her own decisions about whether to keep or terminate a pregnancy (unless she is a minor, in which case some state laws require her to notify or obtain permission from her parent(s) to terminate the pregnancy). What if the biological father disagrees with her choice? If she wants to terminate the pregnancy, but he does not want her to, or vice versa? As you read, you will notice that issues relating to parenting and children can be particularly emotionally charged. Pay attention to the reasoning each side in a particular debate takes, who relies on research vs. religious doctrine, and how you feel about both.

Selected, Edited, and with Issue Framing Material by:
Elizabeth Schroeder, EdD, MSW, *Elizabeth Schroeder Consulting*

ISSUE

Are Fathers Necessary for Children's Well-Being?

YES: William Scott and Amy De La Hunt, from "The Important Role of Fathers in the Lives of Young Children," *parentsasteachers.org* (2011)

NO: Jane Waldfogel, Terry-Ann Craigie, and Jeanne Brooks-Gunn, from "Fragile Families and Child Well-Being," *The Future of Children* (vol. 20, pp. 87–112, 2010)

Learning Outcomes

After reading this issue, you will be able to:

- Identify the difference between family structure and family stability.
- Determine whether certain family structures affect some child outcomes but not others.
- Determine if one sex naturally better at parenting than the other. Are there essential characteristics of fathering versus mothering?
- Decide if having a parent of each sex is necessary for the well-being of children.

ISSUE SUMMARY

YES: William Scott and Amy De La Hunt highlight research demonstrating the impact, positive and negative, that having or not having a father in a child's life, particularly around that child's emotional and cognitive development.

NO: Jane Waldfogel, Terry-Ann Craigie, and Jeanne Brooks-Gunn, in a detailed analysis of various family structures, find that family instability has a negative effect on children's cognitive and health outcomes, regardless of structure, meaning that children with single or cohabiting parents are not necessarily at risk.

On Father's Day, June 21, 2009, President Obama gave a speech in which he said, "We need fathers to step up." He used his own experiences as a child growing up without a father, as well as his observations as a community organizer and legislator as a basis for his plea. His concerns reflect long-standing assumptions that fathers are necessary for children's well-being. But are they? For decades there has been active debate about parenting roles and responsibilities. Traditionalists assume that there is a maternal instinct and that children will just naturally fare better if there is a mother in the home and a father who fulfills the role of breadwinner. Myths abound about single mothers. These include: Today's family problems are due

to the increase in single parenthood; the increase in unwed motherhood was due to the sexual revolution; children of unwed or divorced mothers are doomed to fail; and the male-breadwinner family is the best model. Another myth is reflected in the claim that so many young, poor urban males are involved with gangs, drugs, and guns because they lack a father figure.

The twentieth century saw significant changes in the American family. Well over half of mothers are currently in the paid workforce. More than half of all new marriages end in divorce. One-third of all births are to single women. The traditional family ideal in which fathers work and mothers care for children and the household characterizes less than 10 percent of American families with children under the age of 18. Mothers' increased labor force participation has been a central catalyst of change in the culture of fatherhood. Mothers began to spend less time with children, and fathers began to spend more time. Thus, the cultural interest in fatherhood increased, and it was assumed that fathers were becoming more nurturing and more essential. The history of the ideals of fatherhood reveals that fathers have progressed from distant breadwinner to masculine sex-role model to equal co-parent. Despite changes in the *ideals* of fatherhood, some family scholars observe that fathers' behavior has not changed. Rather, it appears that mothers' behavioral change may be responsible for the change in the culture of fatherhood. A recent review of comparisons of fathers' and mothers' involvement with their children (in "intact" two-parent families) reveals a gap: fathers' engagement with their children is about 40 percent that of mothers'; fathers' accessibility is about two-thirds that of mothers. Fathers' lesser involvement is even more characteristic of divorced and never-married families. Nearly 90 percent of all children of divorced families live with their mothers. Most single-parent fathers are "occasional" fathers. More than one-third of children in divorced families will not see their fathers at all after the first year of separation. Only 10 percent of children will have contact with fathers 10 years after divorce. Yet, at the same time, research has documented the important ways in which fathers influence their children. But does this mean that fathers are essential? Some contend that fathers are not mothers; fathers are essential and unique. Many reject a gender-neutral model of parenting, arguing that mothers and fathers have specific roles that are complementary; both parents are essential to meet children's needs. Proponents of this model assert that fatherhood is an essential role for men and pivotal to society. They maintain that fathers offer unique contributions to their children as male role models, thereby privileging their children. Moreover, fathers' unique abilities are necessary for children's successful development. However, some scholars have shown that boys raised without fathers, even when their mothers are of low income, can turn out remarkably well. Such findings challenge traditional views of fathering, that is,

boys can thrive without fathers. Responsible parenting can occur in a variety of family structures, including single parents and same-sex parents.

At least four contextual forces challenge a redefinition of fathering: (1) Legal notions of fatherhood disregard nurturing. Adequate fathering is primarily equated with financial responsibility. (2) Concepts of masculinity conflict with nurturant parenting. Nurturant fathers risk condemnation as being "unmanly." How can nurturant fatherhood fit into notions of maleness and masculinity? (3) Homophobic attitudes further obstruct nurturant fatherhood. Ironically, active legal debate about sexual orientation and parenting might be influential in reconstructing fatherhood. Is there a model of shared parenting within the gay community? (4) Whether with a two-parent marriage or with parents living in separate households, one parent usually does most, if not all, of the nurturing. Interestingly, it is the case that nurturance is a better predictor of effective parenting than is sex.

Gender neutrality and equality in parenting is undefined. How would you conceptualize a model of shared parenting (taking care not to discriminate against single-parent families)? What would parental equality look like in practice? Is it essential that children be exposed to both female and male role models? If so, why? If women and men were not expected to conform to a specific set of expectations associated with their sex, would the sex of the people raising children matter? Which benefits the child more, a heterosexual set of parents who are bound by strict gender-related conventions, which results in an overbearing, abusive father, or a loving single father or loving, nurturing gay parents?

The following selections advance two models. In the YES selection, William Scott and Amy De La Hunt point to research that emphasizes the positive impact fathers can have on a child's life, providing specific suggestions on what that research means in practical terms. In contrast, in the NO selection, Jane Waldfogel and her colleagues show that it is the stability within a family structure that is more important than the structure itself.

YES

William Scott and Amy De La Hunt

The Important Role of Fathers in the Lives of Young Children

Fathers play a significant role in fostering social-emotional, cognitive, language, and motor development in the lives of their young children. Research shows that fathers strengthen development when they take an active role early and often in the lives of their children, even before they are born.

Child development is part of a complex social system that varies widely from family to family (Lamb, 2010). There is no single "right" way for fathers to be involved. Instead, there are many types of father involvement in all aspects of raising a child. These include playing together, being nearby while a child explores, and taking a child for health checkups (Marsiglio, Day, Braver, Evans, Lamb, & Peters, 1998). Research has found that the value of father involvement is determined by the quality of the interaction between fathers and their children—for example, a father's responsiveness to the needs of his child—rather than the amount of time fathers spend with their children (Palkovitz, 2002).

To better understand the unique and specific ways that fathers impact the lives of their children, researchers study the many roles fathers play in child development. The following findings provide insights into how children benefit developmentally from their fathers' involvement.

Social-Emotional Development

- Early involvement by fathers in the primary care of their child is a source of emotional security for the child (U.S. Department of Health and Human Services, 2011).
- Fathers' affectionate treatment of their infants contributes to high levels of secure attachment (Rosenberg & Wilcox, 2006).
- When fathers acknowledge their child's emotional response and help them address it with a problem-solving approach, the children score higher on tests of emotional intelligence (Civitas, 2001).

- Quality father-and-child time increases self-esteem, confidence, social competence, and life skills (Amato, 1994).
- Children who have close relationships with their fathers have higher self-esteem and are less likely to be depressed (Dubowitz et al., 2001).
- Mothers may use more parenting techniques of gentleness and security, while fathers may favor independence and confidence-building. These approaches help children understand the world in different ways; they balance each other (U.S. Department of Health and Human Services, 2004).
- Rough-and-tumble play with fathers can help children manage aggressive impulses and learn to control their emotions during physical activity (Goldman, Salus, Wolcott, & Kennedy, 2003).
- Fathers' involvement in their children's lives before age 7 may protect against psychological maladjustment during the teen years (Flouri & Buchanan, 2002).

Intellectual Development

- "A number of studies suggest that fathers who are involved, nurturing, and playful with their infants have children with higher IQs, as well as better linguistic and cognitive capacities" (Pruett, 2000, as cited in Rosenberg & Wilcox, 2006, Section I.2.2, para. 1).
- Early, positive involvement of fathers in intellectually stimulating activities, physical care, and general caregiving activities is associated with lower levels of cognitive delay as measured by children's babbling and their exploration of objects with a purpose (Bronte-Tinkew, Carrano, Horowitz, & Kinukawa, 2008).
- Mothers and fathers may have very different styles of play, and their children can benefit from both of them. For example, a father may hold his child's attention with vigorous types of play, including roughhousing that allows the child to take risks and solve problems by using his body, while the

child's mother typically may play cooing games and use more toys and books in her play (Parke & Tinsley, 1987).

- Fathers tend to do more than mothers to promote their child's independence and exploration of the outside world (Rosenberg & Wilcox, 2006).
- Fathers are more likely to find new and unexpected ways to play with familiar toys, which expands their child's creative horizons (Ladd, 2000).

Language Development

- While both mothers and fathers tend to use the higher-pitched, slowed-down variation of speaking called "parentese," fathers are more likely to speak in ways that challenge their child's developing language abilities and teach them about social communication exchanges (Lamb, 2010).
- Fathers tend to use more "wh-" questions and more requests for clarification than mothers, both of which encourage conversation (Rowe, Cocker, & Pan, 2004).
- Two-year-olds whose fathers use a more varied vocabulary have greater language skills a year later (Pancsofar & Vernon-Feagans, 2006).
- Girls whose fathers read to them are likely to have better verbal skills (Bing, 1963).

Motor Development

- Six-month-olds whose fathers are involved in their care score higher on tests of motor development (Gestwicki, 2010).
- Fathers tend to play more one-on-one, rough and tumble games with their children, which encourages large motor development, lets children explore what their bodies can do, and helps them learn to regulate their emotions when engaging in impulsive physical contact (Rosenberg & Wilcox, 2006).

When parent educators share information about how impactful father involvement is, it can help both mothers and fathers become aware of fathers' important role in their children's lives. In addition, parent educators can encourage fathers to practice the behaviors that are most beneficial to positive child development outcomes. For example, by lifting up fathers' strengths in observations of parent-child interaction, parent educators can encourage moms to acknowledge and be supportive of those parental strengths.

Tip from the Field

Absent dads and positive male figures

Unfortunately, there are a number of reasons a father might be separated from his child. If this should happen, positive male figures can serve as role models and mentors for the child. A competent, caring male figure can nurture and guide a young child effectively and contribute to all areas of the child's development.

Parent educators can encourage the child's mother to consider looking to male role models among immediate and extended family members, colleagues in her workplace, teachers at school, and leaders in places of worship.

They can also encourage absent dads to remain involved even if they are not able to be physically present. For example, a father could record himself reading books for his child.

And, although a father involved early and often is considered best practice, it's never too late for fathers to re-connect and engage with their child.

By William Scott

References

Amato, P. R. (1994). Father-child relations, mother-child relations, and offspring psychological well-being in early adulthood. *Journal of Marriage and Family, 56*(4). 1031–1042. Retrieved from www.jstor.org/stable/353611.

Bing, E. (1963). The effect of child-rearing practices on the development of differential cognitive abilities. *Child Development 34,* 631–648.

Bronte-Tinkew, J., Carrano, J., Horowitz, A., & Kinukawa, A. (2008). Involvement among resident fathers and links to infant cognitive outcomes. *Journal of Family Issues, 29*(9), 1211–1244. doi: 10.1177/0192513X08318145.

Civitas. (2001, December). *How do fathers fit in?* [Factsheet.] Retrieved from www.civitas.org.uk/hwu/FatherFactsheet.pdf.

Dubowitz, H., Black, M. M., Cox, C. E., Kerr, M. A., Litrownik, A. J., Radhakrishna, A., English, D. J., Schneider, M. W., Runyan, D. K. (2001). Father involvement and children's functioning at age 6 years: A multisite study. *Child Maltreatment: Journal of the American Professional Society on the Abuse of Children, 6*(4), 300–309. Retrieved from www.corwin.com/upmdata/2850_11cmt01.pdf#page=24.

Flouri, E., & Buchanan, A. (2002). The role of father involvement in children's later mental health. *Journal of Adolescence, 26*(1), 63–78. doi: 10.1016/S0140-1971(02)00116-1.

Gestwicki, C. (2010). *Home, school, and community relations* (7th ed.). Belmont, CA: Wadsworth.

Goldman, J., Salus, M.K., Wolcott, D., & Kennedy, K.Y. (2003). A coordinated response to child abuse and neglect: The foundation for practice. U.S. Department of Health and Human Services, Administration for Children and Families, Administration on Children, Youth and Families, Children's Bureau, Office on Child Abuse and Neglect. Retrieved from http://secure.psychoanalyticce-credit.com/articles/100843/foundation_Practice_child_abuse.pdf.

Ladd, L.D. (2000). *What fathers contribute*

Lamb, M. E. (2010). *The role of the father in child development* (5th ed.). Hoboken, NJ: John Wiley & Sons.

Marsiglio, W., Day, R., Braver, S., Evans, V.J., Lamb, M., & Peters, E. (1998, June). Chapter four: Social fatherhood and paternal involvement: Conceptual, data and policymaking issues. In *Nurturing fatherhood: Improving data and research on male fertility, family formation, and fatherhood.* Washington, DC: Federal Interagency Forum on Child and Family Statistics. Retrieved from http://fatherhood.hhs.gov/CFSForum/front.htm#toc.

Palkovitz, R. (2002). Involved fathering and child development: Advancing our understanding of good fathering, in C.S. Tamis-LeMonda & N. Cabrera (Eds.), *Handbook of father involvement: Multidisciplinary perspectives.* Erlbaum, N.J.: Routledge Academic.

Pancsofar, N., & Vernon-Feagans, L. (2006). Mother and father language input to young children: Contributions to later language development? *Journal of Applied Developmental Psychology, 27*(6), 571–587.

Parke, R.D. (1996). *Fatherhood.* Cambridge, MA: Harvard University Press.

Parke, R.D., & Tinsley, B.J. (1987). Parent-Infant Interaction. In J. Osofsky (Ed.), *Handbook of Infancy.* New York: Wiley.

Pruett, K. (2000). *Father-need.* New York: Broadway, as cited in J. Rosenberg & W. B. Wilcox. (2006).

The importance of fathers in the healthy development of children: Fathers and their impact on children's well-being. U.S. Children's Bureau, Office on Child Abuse and Neglect. Retrieved Oct. 17, 2011, from www.childwelfare.gov/pubs/usermanuals/fatherhood/chaptertwo.cfm#fnh9.

Rosenberg, J., & Wilcox, W. B. (2006). *The importance of fathers in the healthy development of children: Fathers and their impact on children's well-being.* U.S. Children's Bureau, Office on Child Abuse and Neglect. Retrieved Oct. 17, 2011, from www.childwelfare.gov/pubs/usermanuals/fatherhood/chaptertwo.cfm#fnh9.

Rowe, M.L., Cocker, D., & Pan, B.A. (2004.) A comparison of fathers' and mothers' talk to toddlers in low-income families. *Social Development, 13*(2), 278–291. doi: 10.1111/j.1467-9507.2004.000267.x.

U.S. Department of Health and Human Services, Administration for Children and Families, National Child Care Information and Technical Assistance Center. (2011, June). *Father involvement in children's education, care and support.* Retrieved Oct. 17, 2011, from http://nccic.acf.hhs.gov/poptopics/fatherinvolvement.html.

U.S. Department of Health and Human Services, Administration for Children and Families, Administration on Children, Youth and Families, Head Start Bureau (2004, June). Building blocks for father involvement: *Building block 1: Appreciating how fathers give children a head start.* Retrieved from www.headstartresourcecenter.org/fatherhood/Resources/root/data/Building%20Blocks/HSBCombo4.1.pdf.

WILLIAM SCOTT's background is in family and consumer science. He currently works for the National Center for Parents as Teachers as a national trainer and program coordinator, with a special emphasis in working with fathers and Head Start programs.

AMY DE LA HUNT is the curriculum developer for Parents as Teachers, a St. Louis-based nonprofit.

Jane Waldfogel, Terry-Ann Craigie, and Jeanne Brooks-Gunn

Fragile Families and Child Well-Being

For much of the nation's history, the vast majority of American children were born into and spent their childhood in intact married-couple families. Almost the only exceptions were children whose families suffered a parental death. Over the course of the twentieth century, however, as divorce became more common, an increasing share of children experienced a breakup in their families of origin and went on to spend at least some portion of their childhood or adolescence living with just one parent or with a parent and stepparent. A large research literature developed examining the effects of such living situations on child outcomes.

More recently, as unwed births have risen as a share of all births, family structure in the United States has increasingly featured "fragile families" in which the mother is unmarried at the time of the birth. Children born into fragile families spend at least the first portion of their lives living with a single mother or with a mother who is residing with a partner to whom she is not married. For simplicity, we will refer to the first of these types of fragile family as single-mother families and the second as cohabiting-couple families.

An astonishing 40 percent of all children born in the United States in 2007 were born to unwed parents and thus began life in fragile families. That share was more than twice the rate in 1980 (18 percent) and an eight-fold increase from the rate in 1960 (5 percent). Half of the children born to unwed mothers live, at least initially, with a single mother who is not residing with the child's biological father (although about 60 percent of this group say they are romantically involved with the father), while half live with an unwed mother who is cohabiting with the child's father. These estimates imply that today one-fifth of all children are born into single-mother families, while another fifth are born into cohabiting-couple families. Therefore, in examining the effects of unwed parenthood on child outcomes, it is important to consider both children living with single mothers and those living in cohabiting-couple families.

Single parenthood and cohabitation have lost much of their stigma as their prevalence has increased. But there

are still many reasons to be concerned about the well-being of children in fragile families, and, indeed, research overwhelmingly concludes that they fare worse than children born into married-couple households. What remains unclear is how large the effects of single parenthood and cohabitation are in early childhood and what specific aspects of life in fragile families explain those effects.

In this article, we review what researchers know about the effects of fragile families on early child development and health outcomes, as well as what they know about the reasons for those effects. Many underlying pathways or mechanisms might help explain the links between fragile families and children's cognitive, behavioral, and health outcomes. Identifying these mechanisms is important to efforts by social scientists to understand how family structure affects child outcomes and to develop policies to remedy negative effects. A challenge that must be addressed is the role of "selection." The characteristics of young women and men who enter into single parenthood or cohabiting relationships differ from those of men and women in married-couple families, and those pre-existing characteristics might lead to poorer outcomes for children regardless of family structure. Parents in fragile families, for example, tend to be younger and less educated than those in married-couple families, and they may also differ in ways that cannot readily be observed even using detailed survey data. A final question is the degree to which the stability of the family setting affects how well children fare. In fact, recent research holds that it is in large part the stability of the traditional family structure that gives it its advantage.

We highlight new answers to these questions from studies using data from the Fragile Families and Child Wellbeing Study (FFCWS)—a data set designed specifically to shed new light on the outcomes of children born into single-mother and cohabiting families and how they compare with those of children in married-couple families. The study follows children from birth and collects data on a rich array of child health and developmental outcomes, thus providing evidence on how children's outcomes differ depending on whether they grow up in single

From *The Future of Children*, vol. 20, 2010, pp. 87–112, a collaboration of the Woodrow Wilson School of Public and International Affairs at Princeton University and the Brookings Institution.

and cohabiting versus married-couple families and on the factors that might underlie those differences.

We review the evidence on the effects of fragile families on child well-being by comparing outcomes for three types of families. The first type is families where children live with two married parents (for simplicity, we refer to these as traditional families). In this category are children living with their married biological parents as well as children living with married stepparents. (Research has documented differences in outcomes between these two subgroups of children, but those differences are not our focus here.) Rather, we are interested in two other types of families—both fragile families—that have become increasingly prevalent in recent years. One is single-mother families in which the mother was not married at the time of the birth and in which she is not currently living with a boyfriend or partner. The other is cohabiting-couple families in which the mother was not married at the time of the birth but is currently cohabiting with a boyfriend or partner, who might be either the child's biological parent or a social parent (someone who is not biologically related to the child but who functions at least partially in a parental role). We do not distinguish between families that share and do not share households with extended family members or with other families or friends. We also do not distinguish between single mothers who are in a dating or visiting relationship and those who are not. Such distinctions likely matter, but our focus is on the three more general family types: traditional married-couple family, single-mother family, and cohabiting-couple family.

Explaining the Links between Fragile Families and Poorer Child Well-Being

Many studies, reviewed below, concur that traditional families with two married parents tend to yield the best outcomes for children. But the specific pathways by which growing up in traditional families lead to this advantage are still being debated. The key pathways, or mechanisms, that likely underlie the links between family structure and child well-being include: parental resources, parental mental health, parental relationship quality, parenting quality, and father involvement. As noted, the selection of different types of men and women into the three different family types also likely plays a role, as does family stability and instability. We discuss each of these mechanisms in turn. . . .

Past Research on the Links between Family Structure and Child Outcomes

An extensive body of work has examined the effects of parental divorce on child outcomes. As noted, however, most of this work was published before the massive increase in unwed parenthood that now characterizes American families. Thus, informative as it was about the effects of divorce, this early wave of research lacked data to explain how unwed parenthood might affect child outcomes.

The classic study by Sara McLanahan and Gary Sandefur, published in 1994, bridged the gap by bringing together an array of evidence on how growing up in various types of nontraditional families—including both divorced families and unwed-mother families—affected child well-being. Even after controlling for the selection of different types of individuals into different types of family structure, the authors concluded that children who spent time in divorced- or unwed-mother households fared considerably worse than those remaining in intact two-parent families throughout their childhood and adolescence. While they were still in high school, they had lower test scores, college expectations, grade-point averages, and school attendance, and as they made the transition to young adulthood, they were less likely to graduate from high school and college, more likely to become teen mothers, and somewhat more likely to be "idle" (a term that refers to those who are disengaged from both school and work). . . .

With regard to mechanisms, McLanahan and Sandefur found that income was an important explanatory factor for the poorer outcomes of children in single-parent families (but not for children in stepparent families). On average, single-parent families had only half the income of two-parent families, and this difference accounted for about half the gap between the two sets of children in high school dropout and nonmarital teen birth rates (in regression models that also controlled for race, sex, mother's and father's education, number of siblings, and residence). The other important mechanism was parenting. When McLanahan and Sandefur entered parenting into the regressions (instead of income), they found that the poorer parenting skills and behaviors in single-parent families explained about half the gap in high school dropout rates, but only a fifth of the gap in teen birth rates (again controlling for race, sex, mother's and father's education, number of siblings, and residence). Because the authors did not control for income and parenting in the same models, the question of how much overlap there was in their effects remains.

Although child health was not a focus in the McLanahan and Sandefur analysis, other analysts have consistently found effects of family structure on children's health outcomes. Janet Currie and Joseph Hotz found that children of single mothers are at higher risk of accidents than children of married mothers, even after controlling for a host of other demographic characteristics. Anne Case and Christina Paxson showed that children living with stepmothers receive less optimal care and have worse health outcomes than otherwise similar children living with their biological mothers (whether married or single). An extensive body of research also links single-parent and cohabiting-family structures with higher risk of child abuse and neglect.

As McLanahan and Sandefur noted at the time, their findings were worrisome given the burgeoning growth in unwed parenthood in the United States at the time. Although an earlier generation of researchers had debated whether or not divorce affected children's well-being, McLanahan and Sandefur's findings left little doubt that children of unwed parents were worse off than other groups. Concern about how children would fare in unwed families ultimately led to the Fragile Families and Child Wellbeing Study.

The Fragile Families and Child Wellbeing Study

The Fragile Families and Child Wellbeing Study is a new data set that follows a cohort of approximately 5,000 children born between 1998 and 2000 in medium to large U.S. cities.

Approximately 3,700 of the children were born to unmarried mothers and 1,200 to married mothers. The study initiated interviews with parents at a time when both were in the hospital for the birth of their child and therefore available for interviews. As a consequence, FFCWS is able to comprehensively detail the characteristics of both parents and the nature of their relationship at the time of the child's birth.

The study also contains extensive information on early child developmental and health outcomes. . . .

Interviewers gather data on children's behavior problems by asking mothers questions from the Child Behavior Checklist about both externalizing and internalizing behaviors—that is, both outward displays of emotion, including violence and aggression, and introverted behavioral tendencies, including anxiety, withdrawal, and

depression. The study assesses prosocial behavior (which includes the child's ability to get along in social situations with adults and peers). . . .

Finally, FFCWS includes several measures of child health. The initial survey records whether a child had a low birth weight. In addition, at the age-three and age-five in-home assessment, the interviewer records physical measurements of the child's height and weight to make it possible to calculate the child's BMI and to determine whether the child is overweight or obese. At the same interviews, the mother is asked about four other health outcomes: whether the child has ever been diagnosed with asthma; the child's overall health, from the mother's perspective; whether the child was hospitalized in the past year; and whether the child had any accidents or injuries in the past year. The study also includes fairly extensive information on child abuse and neglect, which captures another aspect of child health and well-being. The primary caregiver's use of discipline strategies is measured by the Conflicts Tactics Scale (including the child neglect supplement). Parents are also asked whether their family has ever been reported to child protective services for child abuse or neglect.

Studies using data from FFCWS have found that in general, children in traditional married-couple families fare better than children living in single-mother or cohabiting families. We summarize separately below the evidence on cognitive development, child behavior, and child health.

Fragile Families and Child Cognitive Development

. . . [A]mong couples unmarried at the time of the child's birth, marriage improved cognitive scores for children whose parents later married. . . . [However, there is] no difference in children's vocabulary scores at age three between stable two-parent families (whether cohabiting or married) and stable single-mother families, but . . . scores are lower in unstable families (whether cohabiting or married) than in stable families. . . .

Fragile Families and Child Behavior Problems

. . . [C]hildren living with cohabiting parents have more externalizing and internalizing behavioral problems than children living with married parents, even at age three. One explanation may be the pre-existing risks that accompany nontraditional families. . . . [W]hen single mothers have more material and instrumental support, children have fewer behavior problems and more prosocial behavior. . . . [R]elationship conflict exacerbates externalized behavioral problems in children regardless of past family structure transitions.

. . . [B]ehavioral problems are intensified with each additional change in family structure the child experiences (changing from single to cohabiting parent, or cohabiting to single, for example), with this association mediated at least in part by differences in maternal stress and parenting quality. . . . [B]oth cohabiting and dating mothers confirm that mothers experiencing instability in their relationships go on to report more stress and to engage in harsher parenting.

It appears, however, that there is an important interaction between family structure and stability. . . . [S]tability seems to matter in cohabiting families, but not in single-mother families, where the risk of behavior problems is elevated even if that family structure is stable. . . . [H]aving a social father involved in a child's life can lower behavioral problems just as having an involved biological father can. . . .

Fragile Families and Child Health

. . . [C]hildren born to unwed mothers have worse health across a range of outcomes, even after controlling for other differences in characteristics such as maternal age, race and ethnicity, and education. Children living with single mothers have worse outcomes on all five health measures than children living with married parents, while children in cohabiting-couple families tend to have worse outcomes on some but not all measures. . . . [I]nstability for the most part does not affect children's health outcomes (the exception is hospitalizations, where they find, unexpectedly, that children who experienced more instability are less likely to have been hospitalized). These findings suggest that what negatively affects health among children in fragile families has to do with living with single or cohabiting parents (rather than experiencing changes in family structure). . . .

[S]ome of the mechanisms that link unwed parenthood with greater risk of low birth weight [include smoking cigarettes and using] illicit drugs during pregnancy, and less [receipt of] prenatal care in the first trimester of their pregnancy. . . . [However,] unwed mothers who received support from the baby's father are less likely to have a low-birth-weight baby, as are those who cohabited with the father.

Studies based on FFCWS also confirm earlier research finding that children living with single mothers are at higher risk of asthma. . . .

A few studies have taken advantage of the data in FFCWS to examine the effects of family structure on child abuse and neglect. . . . [A]lthough marriage appears to be protective in the raw data, that effect disappears in models that control for parental and family characteristics. . . . [B]oth single-mother families and cohabiting families where the mother is living with a man who is not the biological father of all her children are at higher risk of having been reported than are families where the mother is living with the biological father of all her children. . . . [The] presence of a social father in the home is associated with increased risk of abuse or neglect.

Our Own Analyses of FFCWS

The many studies in this area, including the recent ones using FFCWS data, do not always define family structure or stability in a consistent way. Studies also vary in the extensiveness of other controls that are included in the analyses. These differences across studies can make it difficult to generalize across studies and to summarize their results.

Accordingly, we carried out our own analyses of FFCWS data, estimating the effect of a consistently defined set of family structure and stability categories on a set of child cognitive, behavioral, and health outcomes at age five. The family categories we defined account for both family structure at birth and stability since birth. We divide families into the following six categories: stable cohabitation, stable single, cohabitation to marriage, married at birth (unstable), cohabiting at birth (unstable), and single at birth (unstable). We then contrast them with the traditional family reference group (that is, families in which parents were married at the child's birth and have remained so). . . .

Cognitive Outcomes

[A]ll types of nontraditional or unstable families are associated with lower scores, with the exception of the cohabitation to marriage category, which is [not] significantly different from the stable married category. The possible mediators explain some, but not all, of these negative effects.

Aggressive Behavior Outcomes

[A]ll types of nontraditional or unstable families are associated with worse scores. . . . However, in contrast to the results for cognitive outcomes, it appears that for aggressive behavioral problems, growing up with a single mother (stable or unstable) is worse than growing up with a cohabiting mother. The effects of growing up with a single mother . . . remain significant after controlling for demographic differences . . . plus possible mediators.

Health Outcomes

Results for the health outcomes reveal a different pattern. [F]or obesity, the worst outcomes are associated with growing up with a single parent (whether stable or unstable) or an unstable cohabiting parent. This pattern is true as well for asthma, although after controlling for demographic differences (or demographic differences plus the possible mediators), instability appears to be most important (with the worst outcomes found for children of unstable single or unstable cohabiting mothers).

These results suggest that the relative importance of family structure versus family instability matters differently for behavior problems than it does for cognitive or health outcomes. That is, instability seems to matter more than family structure for cognitive and health outcomes, whereas growing up with a single mother (whether that family structure is stable or unstable over time) seems to matter more than instability for behavior problems.

Summary and Conclusions

In this article we summarize the findings from prior research, as well as our own new analyses, that address the question of how well children in fragile families fare compared with those living in traditional married-parent families, as well as what mechanisms might explain any differences. . . .

Until recently, most . . . research focused on divorced parents. The sharp rise over the past few decades in births to unwed mothers, however, has shifted the focus to unmarried single and cohabiting parents. These demographic changes make it difficult to compare research done even ten or fifteen years ago with research on cohorts from the beginning of this century. Rapid changes in the characteristics of parents over time also could result in different selection biases in terms of which parents (both mothers and fathers) have children when married or when unmarried (for example, as the pool of parents having unwed births grows, the characteristics of unwed parents may become more similar to those of married parents, which would result in smaller estimated associations between fragile families and child outcomes). And given that recent cohorts of children born to single and cohabiting parents are relatively young, an additional complication involves comparing outcomes across studies (that is, analysts cannot yet estimate effects of family structure on adolescent and adult outcomes for

cohorts such as FFCWS). Therefore, although growing up with single or cohabiting parents rather than with married parents is linked with less desirable outcomes for children and youth, comparisons of the size of such effects, across outcomes, ages, and cohorts, is not possible. In addition, analysts have used vastly different controls to estimate family structure effects, again complicating the quest for integration across studies. We addressed this latter problem by carrying out our own analyses using a consistent set of controls across outcomes. . . .

As noted, past research focused mainly on children whose parents were married when they were born but then separated or divorced (and subsequently lived on their own or remarried). Today, an increasing share of American children is being born to unwed mothers and thus the children are spending the early years of their lives in fragile families, with either a single mother or a cohabiting mother.

That worrisome change informed the launch of the Fragile Families and Child Wellbeing Study a decade ago. Today FFCWS provides a wealth of policy-relevant data on the characteristics and nature of relationships among unwed parents. . . .

Studies using the FFCWS data have shed new light on how family structure affects child well-being in early childhood. The findings to date confirm some of the findings in earlier research, but also provide some new insights. In terms of child cognitive development, the FFCWS studies are consistent with past research in suggesting that children in fragile families are likely at risk of poorer school achievement. Of particular interest are analyses suggesting that some of these effects may be due to family instability as much as, or more than, family structure. That is, some studies find that being raised by stable single or cohabiting parents seems to entail less risk than being raised by single or cohabiting parents when these family types are unstable. Because findings are just emerging, the relative risks of unmarried status and turnover in couple relationships cannot be specified yet. . . .

With regard to child behavior problems, evidence is consistent that children in fragile families are at risk for poorer social and emotional development starting in early childhood. In contrast to the results for cognitive outcomes, it appears that behavioral development is compromised in stable single-mother families, but, in common with the results for cognitive outcomes, such problems are aggravated by family instability for children in cohabiting families. The research also sheds a good deal of light on mechanisms, such as maternal stress and mental health as well as parenting, that might help explain why behavior problems are more prevalent in fragile families.

FFCWS is also providing some new insights on the effects of family structure on child health. Across a range of outcomes, findings suggest that children of single mothers are at elevated risk of poor health; evidence of health risks associated with living with cohabiting parents is less consistent. Findings for child abuse and neglect are also intriguing and suggest that children of single mothers and cohabiting mothers are at elevated risk of maltreatment, although marital status per se may be less consequential than whether a man who is not the child's biological father is present in the home. . . .

To the extent that children in fragile families do have poorer outcomes than children born into and growing up in more stable two-parent married-couple families, what are the policy implications? In principle, the findings summarized here point to three routes by which outcomes for children might be improved. The first is to reduce the share of children growing up in fragile families (for example, through policies that reduce the rate of unwed births or that promote family stability among unwed parents). The second is to address the mediating factors that place such children at risk (for example, through policies that boost resources in single-parent homes or that foster father involvement in fragile families). The third is to address directly the risks these children face (for example, through high-quality early childhood education policies or home-visiting policies).

JANE WALDFOGEL is a professor of social work and public affairs at Columbia University School of Social Work and a visiting professor at the Centre for Analysis of Social Exclusion at the London School of Economics. Her research is centered around children, youth, and families, with a focus on the effect of children on women's pay and the influence of maternal employment on child outcomes. Current projects investigating the impact of public policy on child and family well-being, especially work–family related policies and child well-being in families at risk of breaking up or living in poverty.

TERRY-ANN CRAIGIE is a professor of economics at Connecticut College, New London, Connecticut. Her research covers the economics of the family, labor and urban economics, and applied microeconomics, and has recently focused on the causes and consequences of family formation on early child outcomes, as well as child support of complex family structures in large urban areas.

JEANNE BROOKS-GUNN is the Virginia and Leonard Marx Professor of Child Development at Teachers College and the College of Physicians and Surgeons at Columbia University. Her research focuses on designing and evaluating interventions and policies to enhance the well-being of children in poverty. Her scholarly interests include child and family policy, early childhood interventions and education, adolescent transitions and development, and neighborhoods and poverty.

EXPLORING THE ISSUE

Are Fathers Necessary for Children's Well-Being?

Critical Thinking and Reflection

1. Do you think there is such a thing as "maternal" or "paternal" instinct? How would you differentiate between the two? Are there any similarities?
2. Are fathers essential? Are male role models essential? If so, for whom—boys or girls or both?
3. If fathers play such a key role in raising children, does this make the case that children raised by two fathers who are in a same-sex relationship would do much better than children raised by two parents of different sexes?
4. Many children are raised by single mothers, and although there are struggles, many grow up to be more independent and successful. How would you explain their success if there was not a father figure present?
5. Do you think the gender(s) of parent(s) matter? Is it better for a child to be in a home that has a mother and a father in which there is domestic violence and/or child abuse or in a household that didn't have a father in it at all? What are the priorities in terms of a child's overall health and well-being?

Is There Common Ground?

In the NO selection, Jane Waldfogel, Terry-Ann Craigie, and Jeanne Brooks-Gunn suggested that there are five pathways related to family structure that affect child outcomes: parental resources, parental mental health, parental relationship quality, parenting quality, and father involvement. Their analyses suggest that the presence of a father can often be a plus, at least in the context of a stable family structure. However, given these multiple pathways, one could conclude that fathers are good for children but not essential. Likewise, one could argue the opposite. Mothers are good for families but not necessary. Unfortunately, much less research has been conducted on father-only families.

Researchers have explored under what conditions optimal father involvement is possible. Some state that the three necessary conditions are (1) when a father is highly motivated to parent, (2) when a father has adequate parenting skills and receives social support for parenting, and (3) when a father is not undermined by work and other institutional settings. The reconstruction of fathering, whatever the redefinition, has proven to be very difficult and contested by many cultural forces. At issue is the assumption that there is something natural and thus rooted in the basic nature of women and men that makes a two-parent family, with a mother and father, essential and ideal for

children's well-being. The fundamental assumption of different parenting styles and roles of men and women has led to debates about whether "fathers can mother." That is, can men, and should they, begin to fill the role of nurturer? The result is that men's "job description" as fathers is less clear than expectations of women as mothers. Therefore, fathering is very sensitive to context (including the marital or co-parental relationship, children, extended family, and cultural institutions). The role of mother is especially delimiting. Mothers often serve as gatekeepers in the father–child relationship. Father involvement is often contingent on mothers' attitudes toward, expectations of, and support for the father. Many mothers are ambivalent about active father involvement with their children. The mothering role has been a central feature of adult women's identity, so it is no wonder that some women feel threatened by paternal involvement in their domain, which affects their identity and sense of control. In the absence of social consensus on fathering and counterarguments about the deficits of many fathers, many mothers are restrictive of father involvement. However, some maintain that responsible mothering will have to evolve to include support of the father–child bond. In addition, with increasing latitude for commitment to and identification with their parental role, men are increasingly confused about how to exercise their roles as fathers. This also makes them sensitive to contextual factors such as others' attitudes and expectations. Worse yet, they frequently encounter disagreement among different individuals and institutions in their surrounding context, further complicating their role choices and enactment.

Additional Resources

Cabrera, N.J., and Tamis-LeMonda, C.S. (2013). Handbook of father involvement: Multidisciplinary perspectives, 2nd edition. London: Routledge.

Castillo, J., Welch, G., and Sarver, C. (2011). Fathering: The relationship between fathers' residence, fathers' sociodemographic characteristics, and father involvement. *Maternal and Child Health Journal*, 15(8), 1342–1349.

Flynn, C. (2012). Caring for the children of imprisoned mothers: Exploring the role of fathers. *Child Abuse Review*, 21(4), 285–298.

Internet References . . .

National Fatherhood Initiative

www.fatherhood.org

Fatherhood First

http://www.fatherhoodfirst.org/

National Center on Fathers and Families

https://workfamily.sas.upenn.edu/archive/links /national-center-fathers-and-families%20

Selected, Edited, and with Issue Framing Material by:
Elizabeth Schroeder, EdD, MSW, *Elizabeth Schroeder Consulting*

ISSUE

Should Parents Be Allowed to Choose the Sex of Their Children?

YES: Z. O. Merhi and L. Pal, from "Gender 'Tailored' Conceptions: Should the Option of Embryo Gender Selection Be Available to Infertile Couples Undergoing Assisted Reproductive Technology?" *Journal of Medical Ethics* (2008)

NO: Jasmeet Sidhu, from "How to Buy a Daughter: Choosing the Sex of Your Baby Has Become a Multimillion-Dollar Industry." *Slate.com* (2012)

Learning Outcomes

After reading this issue, you will be able to:

- Describe at least two reasons why parents would want to be able to choose the sex of their child(ren).
- List at least two reasons why parents should not be allowed to choose the sex of their child(ren) from an ethics standpoint.
- Explain at least one potentially positive and one potentially negative outcome of child sex selection on the child's future.

ISSUE SUMMARY

YES: Physicians Z. O. Merhi and L. Pal discuss the conditions under which selection of the sex of a child does not breach any ethical considerations in family planning among infertile couples.

NO: Writer/filmmaker Jasmeet Sidhu believes that the process of sex selection is problematic due to its lack of regulation and potential to earn significant profits for companies providing this service.

The potency of sex and gender as explanations for differences between males and females escalates early in life. By early childhood, a host of differences are observed between boys and girls as children internalize a sense of themselves and others as gendered. Concern has been raised about inequities and deficits resulting from the effects of sex and gender. All of these concerns are compounded by issues of preference for, and ability to select prenatally, a particular sex. Even before conception many people think about the sex of their child—which sex they want. For some, the decision even to carry a fetus to term can be influenced by gender. Research has consistently documented the preference and desire for sons in America and in other cultures. In many cultures, such as India and

China, maleness means social, political, and economic entitlement. Men are expected to support their parents in their old age. Moreover, men remain with their family throughout life; women, upon marriage, become part of the husband's family. Thus, women are traditionally seen as a continuing economic burden on the family—particularly in the custom of large dowry payments at weddings. In some cultures, if a bride's family cannot pay the demanded dowry, the brides are often killed (usually by burning). Although dowries and dowry deaths are illegal, the laws are rarely enforced. In such cultures, there is an expressed desire for male children and an urgency to select fetal sex. In contrast to this pattern, a recent 2010 study based on data from several health and demographic surveys, by Kana Fuse, published in *Demographic Research*, suggests that in some developing countries there has been a shift in attitudes toward a preference for balance (i.e., sons and daughters), with some countries showing a preference for daughters. In general, Fuse found that the preference for daughters is strongest in Latin America and the Caribbean (with the exception of Bolivia) and in some Southeast Asian countries. Southern Asia, western Asia, and northern Africa show a preference for sons, which was also the pattern in 16 of the 28 countries of sub-Saharan Africa studied with the remaining countries showing a daughter preference. Thus, it appears that there may be much more heterogeneity currently in preferences for sex of children than in the past.

Recently, sex-determination technology is most commonly used to assay the sex of fetuses, although in many cultures the use of such technology has been banned. When the fetus is determined to be female, abortion often follows because of cultural pressures to have sons. Such sex-determination practices have led to many more male than female infants being born. The gap grows even wider because of a high childhood death rate of girls, often from neglect or killing by strangulation, suffocation, or poisoning. Furthermore, women are blamed for the birth of a female child and are often punished for it (even though, biologically, it is the male's sperm, carrying either X or Y chromosomes, that determines sex). Research shows that in contemporary America, 78 percent of adults prefer their firstborn to be a boy. Moreover, parents are more likely to continue having children if they have all girls versus if they have all boys. Faced with having only one child, many Americans prefer a boy.

The issue of prenatal sex selection can be considered within the larger context of the "sexual revolution" and the burgeoning expansion in reproductive technologies. As a child, my peers and I would taunt each other with the saying, "First comes love, then comes marriage, then comes [name] with a baby carriage." Such childhood teasing reflected the cultural understanding that the order of things was love, marriage, and then children (with heterosexuality assumed). This is no longer the case. Sexual activity, without a reproductive goal, at earlier ages, parenthood without marriage, and the increase in the number of same-sex parents challenge much of what we understand about relationships and parenting. Additionally, discussions of the desired sex of one's child, along with the possibility of prenatal fetal sex selection, become even more real given all the reproductive technologies that are readily available. These include the use of sperm donors, *in vitro* fertilization, artificial insemination, and surrogate mothers, to the more controversial techniques of artificial wombs and cloning.

The availability of sex-selection technology in the last quarter of the twentieth century has been met with growing interest and widespread willingness to make use of the technology. Available technologies for sex selection include preconception, preimplantation, and postconception techniques. Preconception selection techniques include folkloric approaches like intercourse timing, administering an acid or alkaline douche, and enriching maternal diets with potassium or calcium/magnesium, all thought to create a uterine environment conducive to producing male or female fetuses. There are also sperm-separating technologies whereby X- and Y-bearing sperm are separated, and the desired sperm are artificially inseminated into the woman, increasing the chance of having a child of the chosen sex. Preimplantation technologies identify the sex of embryos as early as 3 days after fertilization. For sex-selection purposes, the choice of an embryo for implantation is based on sex. Postconception approaches use prenatal diagnostic technologies to determine the sex of the fetus. The three most common technologies are amniocentesis (available after the 20th week of pregnancy), chorionic villus sampling (available earlier but riskier), and ultrasound (which can determine sex as early as 12 weeks but is not 100 percent accurate). The American demand for social acceptance of sex-selection technologies has increased in the past decade. Preconception selection techniques are becoming quite popular in the United States, and preimplantation technologies (though more expensive) are also more frequently used. It has become more and more socially accepted to use prenatal diagnostic technologies to determine fetal sex. But incidence rates for sex-selective abortions are difficult to obtain. There is mixed opinion about the frequency of sex-selective abortions, tinged by political controversy.

In the following selections, Physicians Merhi and Pal argue that a desire for gender balance in the family is ethical. Conversely, Jasmeet Sidhu asserts that because the process of sex selection is a multimillion-dollar business, by definition it cannot be ethical or neutral in supporting parents to make an impartial decision about whether to test for their child's sex.

YES ⬅

Z. O. Merhi and L. Pal

Gender "Tailored" Conceptions: Should the Option of Embryo Gender Selection Be Available to Infertile Couples Undergoing Assisted Reproductive Technology?

Preimplantation genetic diagnosis (PGD) was introduced at the beginning of the 1990s as an adjunct to the prenatal diagnostic armamentarium, allowing for genetic diagnoses earlier in the gestational period. This diagnostic option allows couples the opportunity of reaching decisions regarding terminating a genetically compromised fetus earlier in the course of the pregnancy, thus minimising the psychological stress as well as medical risks associated with terminations performed at more advanced gestations. Since its inception, PGD testing has been utilised for evaluation of a spectrum of inherited diseases (e.g., cystic fibrosis, sickle cell disease, hemophilia A and B, Lesch-Nyhan syndrome, thalassemia, Duchenne muscular dystrophy, and recently, Marfan's syndrome) allowing parents to avoid the lengthy, fearful wait for results of traditional testing (e.g., amniocentesis, chorionic villous sampling) while their pregnancy continues to progress. However, the application of PGD has raised multiple ethical issues, many of which were addressed by the President's Council on Bioethics in a recent paper in which the council sought to improve the application of PGD. One of the thorniest issues currently being confronted is the use of PGD for gender selection.

The methods used for preconception gender selection have evolved over time. An influence of coital timing on the gender of the conceptus was proposed by Shettles, who described an exaggerated motility by the smaller Y-bearing sperm in the mid cycle cervical mucus, and hypothesised that there would be male offspring dominance if the timing of coitus was proximate to ovulation. The length of the follicular phase of the menstrual cycle (i.e., period of maturation of the ovarian follicle and the contained egg therein), risk modifications by changing vaginal pH, possible effects of ionic concentrations in the woman's body, susceptible to dietary modifications and pre-fertilisation separation of X-bearing from Y-bearing spermatozoa, have all been stated to demonstrate varying degrees of success in gender determination. However, while some of these methodologies offer successes greater than predicted by the "toss of a coin," the results remain far from "guaranteed."

Among the prominent motivations driving a demand for preconception gender selection is the desire for children of the culturally preferred gender, and to achieve gender balance within a given family. Recently, an interest in PGD testing for the purpose of "gender selection" for social reasons seems to be escalating, although no concrete data are available. This use of PGD for "family tailoring" has engendered debate and controversy. While the acceptability of PGD for traditional medical indications is generally condoned, utilisation of this modality for non-medical purpose has generated ethical concerns. The American College of Obstetricians and Gynecologists has taken a clear stance on this issue as reflected in the following committee opinion, "The committee rejects the position that gender selection should be performed on demand. . . ." Additionally, the American Society of Reproductive Medicine states that "in patients undergoing IVF, PGD used for gender selection for non medical reasons holds some risk of gender bias, harm to individuals and society, and inappropriateness in the use and allocation of limited medical resources." An introspective assessment of the published literature on clinical practices suggests that, while the stance of the principal governing bodies on the issue of PGD for gender selection is unambiguous, the actual practice of the technology of "gender tailoring on demand" is not uncommon. In fact, a recent survey of IVF clinics in the United States, an access to and provision of PDG services for sex selection was acknowledged by as many as 42% of the providers of assisted reproductive technique (ART) services; furthermore, beyond these geographical

From *Journal of Medical Ethics*, vol. 34, 2008, pp. 590–593. Copyright © 2008 by Institute of Medical Ethics. Reprinted by permission of BMJ Publishing Group via Rightslink.

boundaries, the literature is replete with documentation of couples undergoing ART specifically wishing for family completion and/or balancing requesting that embryo(s) of a preferred gender be utilised for transfer.

Acknowledging the contrasting stance of the licensing and governing bodies on ethical concerns related to a wider availability and access to gender selection option versus the prevalent practices (as mentioned above), the authors herein attempt to explore whether the explicit utilisation of PGD for the purpose of gender selection by the infertile couple already undergoing a medically indicated ART procedure encroaches on breach of basic dictates of medical ethics.

It is currently not the "standard of care" (an individualised paradigm of diagnostic and treatment plan that an appropriately trained clinician is expected to pursue in the care of an individual patient) to perform PGD in the absence of a medical indication. However, "standards of care" should remain receptive to evolving scientific data, both that which supports and that which stands in opposition to changes in the standard. Accordingly, the opportunity to explore ethical arguments for and against the utilisation of PGD for gender selection by infertile couples undergoing ART is undertaken in this paper. This process might enable the patient and the provider to make informed and rational decisions when considering PGD utilisation for such a non-medical indication.

Beneficence and Non-Maleficence

Within the context of beneficence-based clinical judgment, a physician's inherent obligation towards his/her patient (i.e., the potential benefits of PGD) *must* be balanced against the risks of the proposed technique. For the infertile patients undergoing ART, and therefore already anticipating a procedure with some treatment related inherent risks, that is, minimal and yet real risks of anaesthesia, infection, bleeding, and ovarian hyperstimulation syndrome (a potentially lethal complication of attempts at inducing multiple ovulation), PGD for targeted genetic anomalies has been shown to improve ART outcomes (i.e., successful pregnancy following treatment), and to significantly reduce the risk of aneuploidy and miscarriage rates in a high-risk population. We believe, that in this patient population, use of additional gene probes per request, that is, for sex chromosomes, would not in any way jeopardise the principle of beneficence.

The limiting factor within this prototype of allowing PGD for gender selection "on request" will be the availability of an adequate number of cleaving embryos. A small yet real

possibility does exist for a failure to achieve an embryo transfer either because of evidence of aneuploidy in the entire cohort of the tested embryos, a scenario that can be easily conjured for an older woman, or because of a procedure-related embryo loss due to the mechanisms used to create an opening in the zona pellucida (a membrane surrounding the egg) for the explicit purpose of removing a cell from the dividing embryo for PGD. The proposed benefits of PGD for the sole intention of gender selection in a patient undergoing ART must be thus balanced against the small yet real risks of embryo loss, and even failure to achieve an embryo transfer, as well as the incremental costs incurred (approximately \$2500 per cycle above the costs of approximately \$7500–\$10000 for the IVF cycle and related procedures). To date, there are no reports of increased identifiable problems (fetal malformations or others) attributable to the embryo biopsy itself. On the contrary, data suggest that PGD for aneuploidy screening may significantly reduce the risk of spontaneous abortions and of aneuploidies in the offspring of women undergoing IVF, particularly so in the reproductively aging patient population.

The principle of beneficence is maintained in offering PGD to couples undergoing ART (the analysis of risks and benefits being based on the physician's assessment, and the risks being primarily confined to the embryo, and not to the patient). However, the same may not hold for otherwise fertile couples. In that case, the female partner would be subjected to medically unindicated risks as well as substantial financial costs (\$10000–\$15000), driven solely by a desire for a child of the preferred gender. Such couples may represent a "vulnerable population" whose vulnerability lies within a potential, enticed by a promise of a child of the preferred gender, for making impetuous decisions regarding an expensive and medically non-indicated intervention that has an uncommon, yet real potential for health hazard. For the fertile population, this desire may lead them to "medicalise" the spontaneous procreative process, transforming it into a controlled and expensive process.

While the authors believe that the principles of beneficence and non-maleficence are upheld within the context of allowing couples anticipating undergoing ART for the management of infertility, we believe that the medical community needs to pause and ponder on any potential for generation of *unwanted surplus embryos* of the undesired sex prior to declaring this as an "acceptable practice." Aspects for further "beneficence" may be appreciated within the folds of this latter concern as couples may consider donation of discard embryos of the non-desired gender to the less fortunate infertile patients. These plausible scenarios must be discussed at length with any couple wishing to discuss the possibility of embryo gender selection while undergoing a medically indicated IVF.

In contrast to an infertile patient anticipating undergoing medically indicated IVF and requesting embryo gender selection, a similar request from an otherwise fertile couple merits additional consideration. A decision to discard embryos of an undesired gender may be less onerous to a reproductively competent individual, although data in support of such a conjecture are lacking. Whether or not this concern regarding abandonment of the "unwanted" embryos is legitimate depends on the perception of the status accorded to the embryos. Although debatable, some would agree that since embryos are too rudimentary in the developmental paradigm to have "interests," there is simply no basis upon which to grant the embryos "rights." Additionally, the ethical principle of non-maleficence is not violated since this principle is directed to "people" rather than "tissues." Future debates on this particular concern might be needed to settle this issue.

To summarise, the performance of PGD per request specifically for gender selection in an infertile couple already planning to undergo ART for medical indications may not breach the principle of beneficence nor hold undue harm for the patient. However, the principles of justice and autonomy must also be considered.

Justice

The principle of justice requires an equitable distribution of the benefits as well as the burdens associated with an intervention. While at one end of the spectrum, this concept addresses the concern of societal gender imbalance resulting from utilisation of PGD for gender selection, at the other extreme, there may be concerns of gender imbalance in relation to socioeconomic strata, as an economic differential in the utilisation of ART services is well recognised.

Concerns are voiced regarding a potential of PGD, if deemed acceptable for the explicit purpose of sex selection, for disrupting the societal gender balance. Indeed, examples of gender preferences abound in existing communities and societies. For example, in certain regions of China, termination of pregnancies, infanticide, and inferior medical care for baby girls have created a shift in the population to a ratio of approximately 1.5 to 1 favouring males. Gender preference for the firstborn can thus overwhelmingly favour male gender, particularly if "one child per family" population policies continue to be implemented. Similarly, a preference for male offspring is recognised in other regions across the globe including India and the Middle East. In contrast, in Nigeria, anecdotal

tradition suggests that although a son is beneficial for propagating the family's name, a female infant is preferentially hoped for, as a daughter holds promise for eventual financial gains at the time of marriage. Similarly, in Haiti, a female firstborn is welcomed as a potential caregiver to the future siblings (personal communication).

It is important to appreciate that concerns voiced by the community regarding a potential for creating a gender differential across global regions if PGD for sex selection while undergoing a medically indicated IVF indeed achieves wider acceptability, while not unreasonable, appear based on "snap shot" views of cultural preferences. One is reassured by results of a recent cross-sectional web-based survey of 1197 men and women aged 18–45 years in the United States which revealed that the majority of those surveyed were unlikely to utilise "sperm sorting," an already existing, cheaper and less invasive technology, as a means for preferential preconception gender selection (sperm sorting employs flow cytometric separation of the 2.8% heavier "X chromosome" from the relatively lighter "Y chromosome" bearing sperm, thus providing an "X" [destined to contribute to a female fetus] or "Y" [destined to create a male fetus] enriched sperm sample for subsequent utilisation for artificial insemination or ART). Given the lack of enthusiasm for this simpler modality for preconception gender selection (an intervention that involves no risks to the patient or the embryos), at the population level, individuals are even less likely to opt for a more aggressive approach, that is, proceeding with ART and PGD, just for gender selection reasons. Similarly, a study from England on 809 couples revealed that gender selection is unlikely to lead to a serious distortion of the sex ratio in Britain and other Western societies. Yet another survey performed on a sample of German population (1094 men and women aged 18–45 years were asked about their gender preferences and about selecting the sex of their children through flow cytometric separation of X- and Y-bearing sperm followed by intrauterine insemination), revealed that the majority did not seem to care about the sex of their offspring and only a minority expressed a desire for gender selection. These authors concluded that preconception gender selection is unlikely to cause a severe gender imbalance in Germany. Similar conclusions, that is, the lack of an overwhelming interest in preconception gender selection were deduced in a survey of infertile Hungarian couples with regard to utilisation of sperm sorting for gender selection. These data are thus reassuring and suggest that, at least in the developed world, even if given access to technology facilitating preferential gender selection, and subsequently while undergoing a medically indicated IVF, use of such methods is not likely to significantly impact on the natural sex ratio within the communities. It needs to be appreciated, however, that surveys generated within the industrialised nations are not representative of global perceptions regarding access to and utilisation of similar technology for ensuring conception of progeny of a preferred gender.

Another concern regarding the possibility of breaching the principle of justice is the ART-related cost as well as the additional expenditure related to the use of PGD. The financial burden is likely to preclude a section of the infertile population from using this service, hence holding the potential for a breach in the principle of justice. However, given that utilisation of PGD for gender selection may be limited secondary to financial constraints, such a differential would render significant shifts in population gender distribution very unlikely (like in ART, the issue of social and economic differences pose a distributive bias here that is beyond the scope of our paper).

Given the lack of information regarding the magnitude of utilisation of technologies for gender selection (PGD or sperm sorting) within societies, it may not be unreasonable to suppose that PGD would not be accessible to large enough numbers of people to make a real difference in the population gender balance. A potential donation of the undesired embryos by couples who opt to utilise PGD for gender selection is likely to negate any concerns regarding eventual disturbance of the sex ratio, enhance the balance towards "beneficence" by offering a possibility of parenthood to those who would otherwise not be able to afford the cost associated with ART and thus address some concerns regarding the principle of "justice" voiced earlier.

To summarise, although the existing literature touches upon aspects of preferential and differential biases in terms of gender preferences in the various communities around the world, data specifically addressing this aspect in infertile couples undergoing medically indicated ART are nonexistent, and voice a need to more formally assess the use of preconception gender selection technologies globally, so as to fully evaluate the impact of these practices on the principle of justice. It follows that performing PGD for gender selection might be consistent with substantive justice–based considerations until more thorough analysis for societal disruptive imbalance of the sexes has been performed.

Patient Autonomy

The freedom to make reproductive decisions is recognised as a fundamental moral and legal right that should not be denied to any couple, unless an exercise of that right would cause harm to them or to others. Access to and use of contraceptive choices, recognition of a woman's right to request for a termination of an unplanned and/ or undesired pregnancy, and an emerging acceptance of an individual's right to determine his or her sexual orientation reflect evolving social and societal perceptions as relates to "reproductive autonomy, the authors believe that utilisation of PGD for the purpose of gender selection by infertile couples already undergoing ART may be incorporated within this paradigm of "reproductive autonomy." Across the societies, while parental autonomy in shaping the social identity of their progeny (behaviour, education, attire, . . . etc.) is an acceptable norm, this debate proposes that, in defined clinical situations, allowing parents to shape the genetic identity of a much-desired child will be within the purview of patient autonomy.

It is of interest that most of the ethical debates around use of PGD for gender selection stem from concerns regarding termination of pregnancies. Opponents to use of PGD for gender selection project that acceptability of such a practice will add yet another indication to justifying pregnancy termination, namely termination of a conceptus of an undesired gender. This latter concern however pales against the escalating requests for "selective reduction" of fetuses (a procedure in which one or more fetuses in a multiple pregnancy is/are destroyed in an attempt to allow the remaining embryo/s a better chance to achieve viability as well as minimise health risks to the mother) resulting from ART, driven by patients' "demands" for transfer of surplus embryos so as to ensure "success," albeit at escalating health risks for the mother and the fetus(es). If indeed a request for "selective reduction" of fetuses by an infertile couple is an acceptable exercise of parental autonomy, the authors put forth that compliance with a request for "gender selection" by an infertile couple undergoing ART be viewed in a similar vein.

By the same token of parental autonomy, the couple has to assume all responsibility of consequences resulting from such a decision, including a possibility of not achieving an embryo transfer secondary to failure of embryos to demonstrate ongoing development following the biopsy, a possibility of all embryos being of the less desired gender, as well as of the child of the desired gender failing to conform to their expectations! Extensive counselling of the couple must therefore be an integral part of the consenting process, if couples and practitioners are considering utilisation of such procedure.

Conclusion

While concerns regarding a potential for breach of ethical principals related to a generalised acceptance of such a practice are real, this paper attempts to evaluate the integrity of principles of ethics within the context of acceptability and use of PGD for the purpose of gender selection, exclusively in patients undergoing ART for the management of infertility. The authors believe that given the current prevalence of such practices despite a stance to the contrary taken by the licensing bodies, the needs and desires of an individual seeking care within the context of the overall society's perspective be considered; this extrapolation seems not to breach the basic four principles of ethics, nor does it hold harm for the patient/embryos. Accessibility of PGD for gender selection to couples undergoing ART for management of infertility is unlikely to influence the gender balance within this society and is very distant from being in the "bright-line" areas described by the President's Council on Bioethics.

Z. O. Merhi is on the staff of Maimondes Medical Center, Brooklyn, New York, specializing in gynecology and obstetrics.

Jasmeet Sidhu  **NO**

How to Buy a Daughter: Choosing the Sex of Your Baby Has Become a Multimillion-Dollar Industry

The conventional wisdom has always been that, given a choice, couples would prefer sons. In the United States, families are using expensive reproductive procedures so they can select girls instead.

Megan Simpson always expected that she would be a mother to a daughter.

She had grown up in a family of four sisters. She liked sewing, baking, and doing hair and makeup. She hoped one day to share these interests with a little girl whom she could dress in pink.

Simpson, a labor and delivery nurse at a hospital north of Toronto, was surprised when her first child, born in 2002, was a boy. That's okay, she thought. The next one will be a girl.

Except it wasn't. Two years later, she gave birth to another boy.

Desperate for a baby girl, Simpson and her husband drove four hours to a fertility clinic in Michigan. Gender selection is illegal in Canada, which is why the couple turned to the United States. They paid $800 for a procedure that sorts sperm based on the assumption that sperm carrying a Y chromosome swim faster in a protein solution than sperm with an X chromosome do.

Simpson was inseminated with the slower sperm that same day. Fifteen weeks later, she asked a colleague at the hospital to sneak in an after-hours ultrasound. The results felt like a brick landing on her stomach: another boy.

"I lay in bed and cried for weeks," said Simpson, now 36, whose name has been changed to protect her privacy. She took a job in the operating room so she would no longer have to work with women who were giving birth to girls.

Simpson and her husband talked about getting an abortion, but she decided to continue with the pregnancy. In the meantime, she looked for a way to absolutely guarantee that her next child would be the daughter she had always dreamed about. She discovered an online community of women just like her, confiding deep-seated feelings of depression over giving birth to boys. The Web forums mentioned a technique offered in the United States that would guarantee her next baby would be a girl. It would cost tens of thousands of dollars, money Simpson and her husband did not have. Simpson waited until her third son was born. Then she began to make some phone calls.

The conventional wisdom has always been this: Given a choice, couples would prefer sons. That has certainly been the case in places like China and India, where couples have used pregnancy screening to abort female fetuses. But in the United States, a different kind of sex selection is taking place: Mothers like Simpson are using expensive reproductive procedures so they can select girls.

Just over a decade ago, some doctors saw the potential profits that could be made from women like Simpson—an untapped market of young, fertile mothers. These doctors trolled online forums, offering counseling and services. They coined the phrase "family balancing" to make sex selection more palatable. They marketed their clinics by giving away free promotional DVDs and setting up slick websites.

These fertility doctors have turned a procedure originally designed to prevent genetic diseases into a luxury purchase akin to plastic surgery. Gender selection now rakes in revenues of at least $100 million every year. The average cost of a gender selection procedure at high-profile clinics is about $18,000, and an estimated 4,000 to 6,000 procedures are performed every year. Fertility doctors foresee an explosion in sex-selection procedures on the horizon, as couples become accustomed to the idea that they can pay to beget children of the gender they prefer.

Inside a fourth-floor office suite off a palm-tree-lined street in Encino, Calif., in an embryology lab, two men wearing maroon scrubs peer into high-tech microscopes. The men are fertilizing human eggs with sperm samples collected earlier that day. After fertilization and three days of incubation, an embryologist uses a laser to cut a hole through an embryo's protective membrane and then picks out one of the eight cells. Fluorescent dyes allow the embryologist to see the chromosomes and determine whether the embryo is carrying the larger XX pair of chromosomes or the tinier XY. The remaining seven cells will go on to develop normally if the embryo is chosen and implanted in a client's uterus.

The lab is part of the Fertility Institutes, a clinic set up by Jeffrey Steinberg, one of the most prominent gender selection doctors in the United States. In his spacious, oak-paneled office down the hall, Steinberg is surrounded by photos of his own naturally conceived children. His clinic is the world leader for this gender selection technique, known as preimplantation genetic diagnosis (PGD). "We're by far number one. Number two is not even a close second," he said.

The United States is one of the few countries in the world that still legally allows PGD for prenatal sex selection. The procedure was designed in the early 1990s to screen embryos for chromosome-linked diseases. It is illegal for use for nonmedical reasons in Canada, the U.K., and Australia.

Steinberg's gender-selection patients are typically around 30 years old, educated, married, middle to upper class. They also typically have a couple of children already, unlike the women in his waiting room undergoing in vitro fertilization and hoping to conceive any child at all.

Statistics on gender selection are sparse. A 2006 survey by Johns Hopkins University found that 42 percent of fertility clinics offered PGD for gender selection. But that was half a decade ago, before many clinics undertook aggressive online marketing campaigns to drive the demand.

Gender selection is the primary business at Steinberg's Fertility Institutes, with nurses casually asking couples in the waiting room whether they, too, are interested in selecting the gender of their baby. Business quadrupled when Steinberg started advertising PGD for gender selection.

Steinberg said he never intended to make gender selection his niche. But then the ethics committee of the American Society for Reproductive Medicine, a non-profit organization that attempts to set standards in the industry, came out against prenatal sex selection for non-medical reasons in 1994. The group said the practice would promote gender discrimination and was an inappropriate use of medical resources. That made Steinberg angry.

"I took it on as a challenge," he said. "The fact that they didn't like it, and the fact that I saw nothing wrong with it, made me more aggressive."

He advertised in Indian-American and Chinese-American newspapers. Local groups accused him of stoking cultural biases for boys in those communities, and his ads were pulled by the publishers.

In 2009, Steinberg came under a worldwide media firestorm when he announced on his website that couples could also choose their baby's eye and hair color, in addition to gender. He revoked the offer after receiving a letter from the Vatican. Steinberg seems to enjoy the attention, whether good or bad. After all, the publicity only helps bring in more patients to his clinics.

Many women who undergo PGD for gender selection discovered the procedure in online forums. Reading the posts on these forums is like entering another world. Users adorn their avatars with pink and princess imagery. They talk about their desperation to have daughters. They share notes on the process of going through PGD, recounting in detail their own experiences: blood-test results, drug effects, in vitro cycles.

Daniel Potter, the medical director of the Huntington Reproductive Center, has written more than 1,000 posts for in-gender.com and answered forum members' questions about the procedure and its costs. He arranged in-person and phone consultations with forum members, including Megan Simpson. In 2011, he even started a personal website where he calls himself the "gender selection expert."

From posting on message boards to using Twitter, Facebook, and YouTube, fertility doctors have appropriated 21st-century marketing methods to bring a 21st-century technology to the masses. Competition is stiff for search-friendly domain names for clinic websites and sponsored Google search ads. For example, there's genderselection.com, not to be confused with gender-selection.com. There's also gender-select.com and genderselectioncenter.com, all websites maintained by fertility clinics promoting PGD. These sites are filled with glossy stock photos of happy families, polished YouTube videos of doctors making their pitch, and patient testimonials in numerous languages.

In May 2008, Simpson and her husband traveled to California to undergo PGD at the Laguna Hills branch of the Huntington Reproductive Center. There, she met up with some of the women she had made friends with online. "We went shopping and picked out girly clothes and dreamed of the day we could have a baby to wear them," Simpson recalled.

Three days after arriving in California, Simpson underwent egg retrieval surgery. Eighteen eggs were retrieved; of these, 11 were mature and were fertilized.

Her husband left after the surgery to return home and take care of their three boys. After resting for five days, Simpson returned to the clinic for her embryo transfer.

She was met with devastating news: all of her embryos were found to be chromosomally abnormal. None were useable.

"I cried. And cried some more," recalled Simpson. "All that money, the drugs, the travel, time off work. The *money*."

Despite the financial and emotional setbacks, she wanted to try again, soon. Three months later, she was back in Laguna Hills, this time to try a more sophisticated sperm-sorting method plus in-vitro fertilization. She had taken out $15,000 on a line of credit to pay for the second attempt.

This time, the embryos were good to go. An ultrasound was used to guide a catheter containing the embryos into her uterus. Six days later, Simpson took a pregnancy test. It was positive.

When she was 15 weeks pregnant, she asked a friend at work to once again sneak her into an after-hours ultrasound. Simpson was anxious, haunted by the memory of her last ultrasound.

But this time, it was different. She was pregnant with a girl.

After nearly four years and $40,000, Simpson's dreams of being a "girl-mommy" were finally going to come true.

Simpson gave birth to her daughter during a home delivery in her bathtub in 2009. "The moment she was born, I asked if it was still a girl," she recalled.

Simpson had to work six days a week right up until the delivery and months afterward to repay the loan she took.

"My husband and I stared at our daughter for that first year. She was worth every cent. Better than a new car, or a kitchen reno."

Much of the evidence that Americans preferentially choose girls is anecdotal, as no larger body tracks gender selection procedures. But data from Google show that "how to have a girl" is searched three times as often in the United States as "how to have a boy." Many fertility doctors say that girls are the goal for 80 percent of gender selection patients. A study published in 2009 by the online journal Reproductive Biomedicine Online found Caucasian-Americans preferentially select females through PGD 70 percent of the time. Those of Indian or Chinese descent largely chose boys.

So where does this preference come from? And with the sex-selection rhetoric in the United States centered around "family balancing," a feel-good term that implies couples are rationally planning their families, is it still sexist to choose for girls?

For Jennifer Merrill Thompson, the reasons were simple. "I'm not into sports. I'm not into violent games. I'm not into a lot of things boys represent and boys do," she said. Thompson is the author of *Chasing the Gender Dream*, a self-published book that documents her use of gender-selection technology to conceive her daughter.

Interviews with several women from the forums at in-gender.com and genderdreaming.com yielded the same stories: a yearning for female bonding. Relationships with their own mothers that defined what kind of mother they wanted to be to a daughter. A desire to engage in stereotypical female activities that they thought would be impossible with a baby boy.

The American Society for Reproductive Medicine says it's concerned that gender selection is leading otherwise healthy women to undergo unnecessary medical procedures, and that fertility doctors might turn their attention away from treating infertility to pursue a more lucrative specialty. And the group points out the possible psychological harm to children born through gender selection. They fear these children would be pressured to live up to the stereotypes of the gender that was picked out and paid for by their parents.

"It's high-tech eugenics," said Marcy Darnovsky, director of the Center for Genetics and Society, a Berkeley, Calif. nonprofit focused on reproductive technologies. "If you're going through the trouble and expense to select a child of a certain sex, you're encouraging gender stereotypes that are damaging to women and girls. . . . What if you get a girl who wants to play basketball? You can't send her back."

Despite the objections from some medical ethicists, it seems that gender selection, like many aspects of fertility medicine, will remain legal and unregulated in the United States.

Correction, Sept. 17, 2012: *This article originally stated that Megan Simpson underwent PGD twice, the second time successfully conceiving a girl. She used PGD once and then used a sperm-sorting technique plus in-vitro fertilization to conceive a girl.*

Jasmeet Sidhu is an award-winning journalist, television and music video producer, and activist whose investigative pieces and columns have focused on a wide array of topics, including on the for-profit sex selection industry in the United States.

EXPLORING THE ISSUE

Should Parents Be Allowed to Choose the Sex of Their Children?

Critical Thinking and Reflection

1. What assumptions about sex and gender underlie the desire to have boy or girl children?
2. Is fetal sex selection ever ethical? Does the method used to make the selection affect your answer to this question?
3. Is using sex-selection as a "small family planning tool" an acceptable use of sex-selection technologies?
4. Are sex differences located in biology and/or culture?
5. Can children's gender roles be redefined?

Is There Common Ground?

A primary focus of critics' concern about sex-selection technologies (and cultural biases toward males) is their impact on population sex ratios. A skewed sex ratio, they fear, will cause dire consequences for a society, particularly for heterosexual mating (although it is ironic that the same class of reproductive technological advances not only facilitates sex selection but also makes reproduction less reliant on conventional heterosexual mating). But what about social concerns about sex-selection? How will the increasing frequency of the use of sex-selection technologies impact families? How will it affect gender assumptions and sex discrimination? Is the acceptability of sex selection conditional? If Americans were not as biased toward having just boys or just girls, and therefore the population sex ratio would not be threatened, would sex selection be acceptable to control the birth order of the sexes, to ensure a mixture of boys and girls, or to have an only child of a certain desired sex? Sex selection technology might reduce overpopulation by helping families who already have a child of one sex "balance" their family with a second child of the other sex, rather than continue to have children "naturally" until they get the sex they want. Is using sex-selection as a "small family planning tool" an acceptable use of sex-selection technologies? Many feel that using sex selection to balance a family is not sexist. But others argue that it is sexist because it promotes gender stereotyping, which undermines equality between the sexes. Some feminists argue that sex selection for any reason, even family balancing, perpetuates gender roles and thus the devaluation of women. Some people in the disabilities rights movement have joined with this perspective, suggesting that if it is permissible to select against female embryos (is sex per se a genetic "abnormality"?), then so it is permissible to select against embryos with genetic abnormalities of all types; and who is to define what is "abnormal"—height, IQ? Then the door is open to increasing discrimination against people with disabilities. Should abortions solely for the purpose of sex selection be allowed? This is a profound dilemma for many pro-choice feminists for whom a woman's right to choose an abortion for any reason is opposed to gross sex discrimination in the form of sex-selective abortions (usually of female fetuses). It is interesting to note that when parents choose to abort based on fetal sex in an effort to "balance" their family, sex selection is regarded as more acceptable than when only female fetuses are aborted because of a preference for males.

Additional Resources

Chen, Y, Li, H. and Meng, L. (2013). Prenatal sex selection and missing girls in China: Evidence from the diffusion of diagnostic ultrasound. *Journal of Human Resources*, 48(1), 36–70.

Egan, J.F.X., Campbell, W.A., Chapman, A., Shamshirsaz, A.A., Gurram, P. and Benn, P.A. (2011). Distortions of sex ratios at birth in the United States; Evidence for prenatal gender selection. *Prenatal Diagnosis*, 31(6), 560–565.

Hu, L. and Schlosser, A. (2012). Trends in prenatal sex selection and girls' nutritional status in India. *Economic Studies*, 58(2), 348–372.

Internet References . . .

Center for Human Reproduction

http://www.centerforhumanreprod.com/gender
_selection.html

The Future of Children

http://futureofchildren.org/

World Health Organization: Gender and Genetics

http://www.who.int/genomics/gender/en/index4.html

Selected, Edited, and with Issue Framing Material by:
Elizabeth Schroeder, EdD, MSW, Elizabeth Schroeder Consulting

ISSUE

Should Men Have a Say in Whether Their Partner Has an Abortion?

YES: Catherine T. Coyle, from "An Online Pilot Study to Investigate the Effects of Abortion on Men," Menandabortion.com (2006)

NO: Crystal M. Hayes, from "My Abortion Story, and My Right to Choose," Thegrio.com (2013)

Learning Outcomes

After reading this issue, you will be able to:

- Describe at least two possible emotional impacts abortion can have on men whose female partners terminate a pregnancy they wanted to keep.
- Identify at least two arguments why women should retain control over their own reproductive decision making.
- Explain at least two impacts giving men the right to have equal say in reproductive decision making could have on other laws not related to sexual or reproductive health.

ISSUE SUMMARY

YES: Catherine Coyle, author of the book, *Men and Abortion: A Path to Healing*, discusses research relating to the impact a woman's abortion has on her male partner to justify his right to be involved in the decision whether to have or abort a pregnancy.

NO: Crystal Hayes' first-person description of her experience with choosing to have an abortion focuses on a woman's right to choose.

Since our earliest recorded history, girls and women have found ways to terminate pregnancies through a range of methods. These include drinking concoctions made of different herbs and having the pregnant girl or woman over-exert herself physically, practices that are continued in some cultures today. But some of these herbs when combined, especially when they were combined in ancient history and less was known about them, can be toxic or even deadly—and extreme physical exertion can cause other medical problems or even death. Other attempts to terminate pregnancies before the establishment of safe medical procedures included using a sharp object of some kind—in more recent decades, an unwound metal coat hanger—to pierce the mucosal cap so that the amniotic fluid would leave the uterus and the body would expel the pregnancy. Equally barbaric and unsafe was the practice of putting extreme pressure on the abdomen, or striking it repeatedly to cause a spontaneous abortion or miscarriage. This practice still exists today, particularly among younger women who may discover they are pregnant, do not want to become parents, and do not wish to or cannot tell their own parents they are pregnant. In any of these examples, if the body does not expel the contents of the uterus completely, the remaining tissue can cause serious infection which can put the woman's health or life at risk. In addition, non-sterilized implements inserted into the body can also cause infection, and repeated beating of the uterus can cause damage to or rupture other organs around the uterus.

In the 19th and 20th centuries, seeing a financial gain, a variety of companies produced and sold abortifacients—pills that were designed to terminate a pregnancy. They could never be marketed as such, because the predominant view of the time was that abortion was wrong. Yet money was still money—so the pills were still produced and sold, with varying levels of success. Laws relating to surgical abortion were extremely restrictive, and the consequences on a doctor or midwife performing such a procedure were severe. As with all health issues, however, rich women could secure an abortion if they needed one, quietly and relatively safely for the time.

At the same time, however, abortion as a procedure had to exist; in many countries, abortion was allowed if it was determined that it was necessary to save the life of the pregnant woman. The first surgical procedure involved dilating the cervix (opening to the uterus) and gently removing the contents of the uterus with a tool called a "curette." This, along with a later procedure called manual vacuum aspiration, was designed to be performed earlier in the pregnancy. In the early 1990s, medication abortion—a combination of mifepristone and misoprostol or methotrexate and misoprostol—was approved by the U.S. FDA for use in women up to 7 weeks of pregnancy. A woman was given the first dose of the medication or injection, then could take the second medication in the privacy of her own home.

As all these medical techniques were being created and tested, the topic of abortion itself was being argued in the popular culture. Various religious groups spoke out in vehement opposition to its practice, while others maintained abortion was a private matter, something for a woman to decide on her own and with her doctor or clinician. With the social rights movements of the 1970s, what also changed was a greater acceptance of women's autonomy and self-determination relating to her body. As a result, the pro-choice battle cry has always been that a woman has the right to choose what happens to her body. There was support for discussing her options if she were to become pregnant with her male partner, but that in the end, the decision whether to keep or terminate a pregnancy is hers alone. The rationale behind this was more than supporting women's self-determination, it was also to protect women who had been raped or were in abusive relationships or marriages from the trauma of having to carry a pregnancy and give birth to a baby that had been conceived by force or that would then make it far less likely she could leave her abusive situation.

Sexual and reproductive health issues have always focused first and foremost on women's needs, with boys and men being seen as an afterthought or even as adversaries. An unfair assumption has been made on male-female relationships in which the female partner gets pregnant—particularly when it is a teen relationship—that the male partner will not wish to be involved, that if she chooses to carry the pregnancy to term he will not help support the baby. Such sexism does not serve the male or female partner, yet it pervades. As a result, many men step back and do not advocate for themselves in having some input into what happens with a pregnancy into which they contributed half of the DNA. Others do not wish to step back, and have very strong feelings about a pregnancy. What happens when men and women disagree? What if a woman wants to terminate the pregnancy, but her male partner wants her to carry the pregnancy to term and have a baby? What if a woman wants to become a parent, but her male partner does not want to? These questions are particularly loaded if a man's cultural or religious background has strong messages about abortion.

In the United States, more socially conservative groups have tried to have an impact on abortion access in states around the country, with significant successes over the past 8 years in particular. What they have not been successful on, however, is setting a legal precedent for a man having equal say in his female partner's reproductive decision making. As recently as 2009, state-level legislation has been introduced that would require a man's written consent in an abortion or other reproductive procedure that involves his sperm (such as the outcome of fertilized embryos for future insemination); these bills have not yet been brought to a vote or passed. But with very strong feelings on both sides of the debate, efforts will continue into the future.

YES

Catherine T. Coyle

An Online Pilot Study to Investigate the Effects of Abortion on Men

Introduction

The internet has changed many aspects of modern culture. It has provided a rapid means of communication to and from almost anywhere in the world. The internet has also proven to be a source of vast amounts of information on a multitude of topics including health, the sciences, current events, weather, and even humor. Recently, the internet has been used as a tool by social scientists to engage in online research.

While still relatively new, the use of the internet for research purposes is rapidly expanding. This avenue of research offers considerable benefits including the following: cost efficiency, access to large and diverse samples, the ability to draw from self-selected samples, complete anonymity of participants, and findings that are similar to those obtained using more traditional methods of research.

Given these potential benefits, a pilot study was conducted to determine the usefulness of an online survey to collect data concerning the effects of abortion on men. Data obtained through this pilot study are summarized following a review of research pertaining to post abortion men. It should be noted that current U.S. laws allow women to have an abortion for any reason at any time during pregnancy. Men have no legal power in the abortion decision even if they are married to women who choose abortion. Furthermore, there is no legal requirement to inform the father of the child being aborted.

Men and Abortion

Rothstein (1978) published one of the first studies concerning men and abortion. The author interviewed sixty males in the waiting room of an abortion clinic. During analysis of their answers to open ended questions, two prominent themes emerged. These themes were related to caretaking and nurturing, as well as to issues of autonomy.

The autonomy theme was particularly apparent among the adolescent males who were concerned about making autonomous decisions independently of their parents. These adolescent males expressed a desire to be caring husbands and fathers but, at the same time, struggled with dependency needs.

Only two intervention studies involving men and abortion have been published (Gordon and Kilpatrick, 1977; Coyle, 1997). In the first of these, Gordon & Kilpatrick (1977) implemented a program of group counseling for males accompanying their female partners to an abortion clinic. They noted the following emotions experienced by the men: anxiety, helplessness, guilt, regret, and confusion regarding responsibility. The defense mechanisms of denial, projection, intellectualization, and withdrawal were also in evidence among males who participated. In addition, "many clients said they did not express their feelings to their partners and instead felt the need to be a source of support by presenting a strong front" (p. 293).

In the second intervention study, Coyle (1997) utilized a forgiveness therapy program with men who identified themselves as having been hurt by their partner's decision to abort. The men were observed to have high anxiety, anger, and grief levels prior to intervention and significantly decreased levels of these variables after treatment as compared to control participants. At a three month follow up, participants continued to demonstrate these psychological improvements. Similar significant findings were observed among the control participants after they completed the intervention program. The men participating in this study reported, in varying degrees, the following as a consequence of their abortion experience: frequent thoughts about the lost child, difficulty concentrating, anger, anxiety, grief, guilt, helplessness, relationship problems, and confusion about the man's role in society. Role confusion was expressed as a direct result of the seemingly contradictory demands of a society that wants men to care for and support their offspring but simultaneously denies them the ability to care for their children before birth. A majority of men also discussed their perceived need to put aside their own discomfort as they attempted to support their partners.

This tendency of males to repress their emotions was also observed by Shostak and McLouth (1984) who note that "the typical man rushes to placate his partner, repress his emotions, and take his cues from an environment that others structure for him" (p. 22). Similarly, Patterson (1982) reports that a survey of men in an abortion clinic revealed that 77% of the men believed that the most valuable way they could help their partners was by maintaining control over their own emotions. Thus, many men are prone to passively accept a woman's suggestion that she have an abortion. Since he feels his role is to suppress his own emotions and as she has the legal right to obtain abortion, he is not likely to debate the abortion decision with his partner. Unfortunately then, he is also not likely to have the kind of discussion with his partner that would lead her to keep their child. Rue (1996) also notes that the suppression of negative emotions may make their resolution considerably more difficult. In other words, the denial and repression of a man's emotions makes him disinclined to seek the help he needs. He is, in effect, twice injured, first, by not actively attempting to participate in the abortion decision and second, by denying the psychological effects of the abortion after its occurrence.

Buchanan and Robbins (1990) investigated the consequences of adolescent pregnancy and its resolution as evidenced in adulthood. As hypothesized, the psychological distress scores were lowest among those adult males who had never experienced an adolescent pregnancy. However, an unexpected finding was that men whose partners had abortions during adolescence were more distressed in adulthood than the men who became fathers during adolescence.

Coleman and Nelson (1998) surveyed college students and found that of those with a prior history of abortion, 51.6% of the male students reported feeling regret following abortion. These authors suggested that men may "be more inclined to experience pronounced post abortive effects than women, because the decision to abort is ultimately the female's and the final decision opted for may not be congruent with the male's choice" (p. 428).

Still other researchers have investigated the effects of abortion on relationships and all report that relationships frequently do not survive after abortion. Failure rates ranged from 25% (Shostak & McLouth, 1984) to 70% (Milling, 1975). Mattinson (1985) observed the following effects of abortion within the marriage relationship:

inability to conceive, emotional withdrawal, sexual and interpersonal conflicts, and a loss of trust.

The most comprehensive work pertaining to men and abortion was published by Shostak and McLouth (1984). These authors surveyed 1,000 men in 30 abortion clinics across the United States and followed up with postabortion interviews involving 75 of those men. The persistence of occasional thoughts about the fetus was evident among the majority of post abortion men interviewed. Less than one third of the men reported having no thoughts about the fetus and 9% reported having frequent thoughts.

In addition, the men were observed to suffer from ambivalence as evidenced by the fact that while "39% believed the fetus was a human life, and 26% felt that abortion was the killing of a child, 83% did not want abortion outlawed" (p. 38). In fact, "only 15% believed the fetus was not human until birth and . . . as many as 60% were troubled by the irrevocable ending of the life they had helped set in motion" (p. 162). Of those men surveyed, 11% stated that they were opposed to their partners' decision to abort and were described as experiencing a very profound sense of personal loss.

If Shostak and McLouth's (1984) sample is representative of males in the United States, we may extrapolate in terms of current abortion statistics. Given that over 50 million abortions have been performed since its legalization in 1973, there may be as many as 5 million men who have been negatively affected by abortion. This inference may be too conservative since it is based only on the 11% of men who were opposed to abortion in the Shostak and McLouth (1984) study and does not account for many other men who may not experience or even be aware of negative effects until quite some time after the abortion.

A recent study by Lauzon et al. (2000) compared women and their male partners involved in first trimester abortions with a control group of men and women who had participated in a previous public health survey. Participants were given self administered questionnaires at the first consultation appointment prior to abortion at which time 56.9% of the women and 39.6% of the men evidenced significantly higher levels of psychological distress than the respective controls. After the abortion, participants were given a follow up questionnaire and "three weeks after the abortion, 41.7% of women and 30.9% of the men were still highly distressed" (p. 2033). The authors concluded that "being involved in a first trimester abortion can be highly distressing for both women and men" (p. 2033). Kero et al. (1999) administered pre abortion questionnaires to 75 men whose female partners had applied for abortion. The topics covered in the questionnaire included: psychosocial history, current living conditions, relationship with partner, contraception use, abortion motivation and decision making process, and questions related to pregnancy, current abortion, and previous abortions. Authors note the ambivalence experienced by participants stating that they saw abortion as bringing "relief, release, and responsibility but simultaneously the consequences of the choice were expressed in such words as anxiety, anguish, grief, and guilt" (p. 2674). A follow up study with 26 of the men (Kero & Lalos, 2004) involved interviews at 4 and 12 months post abortion. At the four-month interview, a majority of men (16) expressed both positive and negative feelings and at 12 months, 11 of the men did so. At the latter interview, the men were asked if they ever thought about the abortion and 12 stated that they did so once or more each month while one man stated he did so once or more each week. Thus, half of the men still had frequent thoughts about the abortion. In still another publication (Kero & Lalos, 2000), using the same sample referred to in Kero et al. (1999), these authors argued that the ambivalence experienced by both men and women prior to and following abortion is a positive response "indicating openness to the complexity of the abortion issue" (p. 90).

A recent case study (Holmes, 2004) highlighted the effects of abortion on a young man who learned that his partner had obtained an abortion nearly six months after the abortion occurred. Holmes describes the effects of worthlessness, emasculation, voicelessness, and the threat to the young man's belief system as a result of the abortion.

To summarize, those few who have researched the effects of abortion on men have found that such effects may include grief (Raphael, 1983), anxiety, guilt, helplessness (Gordon & Kilpatrick, 1977), and anger (Shostak & McLouth, 1984). The unequal power distribution concerning abortion may intensify those emotions and contribute to relationship failure (Milling, 1975; Shostak & McLouth, 1984). The fact that men tend to repress their emotions may also make their resolution more difficult (Rue, 1996). One may reasonably conclude from both the available research and clinical reports that, for some men, abortion poses significant psychological risk.

Summary of Results

Over a period of approximately 24 months, 142 men responded to an online survey concerning their abortion experience. **Because all respondents did not answer all questions, the sample size (n) for each question is indicated in parentheses.**

Table 1

Demographic Information

Age (n = 140)	Average age = 31 1/2 years Age Range = 18–67 years The majority of respondents (67%) were between the ages of 20 and 39 years.
Current Marital Status (n = 118)	Married = 24 (20%) Single/Never-Married = 67 (57%) Single/Divorced = 13 (11%) Widowed = 3 (2.5%) Separated = 11 (9.5%)
Education (n = 117)	Less than 12 years = 8 (7%) High School Diploma = 25 (21%) Technical Training/Associate Degree = 35 (30%) Bachelor's Degree = 28 (24%) Graduate Degree = 21 (18%)
Race (n = 120)	Caucasian = (79%) Afro-American = 5 (4%) Hispanic = 5 (4%) American Indian = 1 (1%) Asian = 4 (3%) Other= 10 (8%)
Religion (n = 118)	Christian = 76 (64%) Jewish = 2 (2%) Islam = 4 (3.5%) Other = 16 (13.5%) None = 20 (17%)

Table 2

Significance

The average "meaning" respondents ascribed to their religion was 3.5 on a five-point Likert scale. Of the 115 respondents who answered this question, 27% claimed their religion was "somewhat important" while 36% stated their religion was "very important" to them.

Table 3

Responses, Prior Events

Responses to questions pertaining to events prior to the abortion decision

Marital Status	Thirty (21%) of 142 respondents said they were married to their partners at the time the abortion occurred.
Contraception	Forty-four (31%) of 141 respondents claimed to have been using birth control prior to pregnancy.
Time (n = 140)	The average time between abortion occurrence and completion of the survey was five years. However, the majority of abortions (73%) occurred five years or less prior to survey completion. The range of responses was from 1 month to 32 years thus skewing the mean. Thirteen (9%) of the abortions occurred between 15 to 32 years ago.

Continued

Continued

Responses to questions pertaining to events prior to the abortion decision

Decision-Making (n = 142)*	Both partners agreed to obtain abortion = 40 (28%) Man pressured partner to abort = 18 (12%) Other pressured partner to abort = 35 (25%) Man left relationship prior to abortion = 8 (6%) Partner chose to abort against man's wishes = 64 (45%) Man passively left decision to partner = 38 (27%) Man unaware of abortion until after it occurred = 25 (18%)
Reasons for Choosing Abortion (n = 139)*	Mental Health/Emotional Distress = 59 (42%) Physical Health = 23 (16%) Financial Concerns = 85 (61%) School/Educational Plans = 67 (48%) Career Plans = 86 (62%) Family Size = 18 (13%) Social Reasons (i.e. embarrassment) = 63 (45%)

*Note: Respondents were instructed to choose all that apply when responding to the questions concerning abortion decision-making and reasons for choosing abortion. Therefore, the percent values indicated for responses to those questions do not add up to 100.

Table 4

Responses to questions pertaining to effects of the abortion decision

(n = 140)

Relationship Status	The number of men who indicated that their relationships failed following the abortion = 93 (66%) Seventy-seven (83%) of these men stated that their relationships ended within five years or less following the abortion. Number of men still in a relationship with partners who aborted = 47 (33%) Of these 47 men, 39 experienced abortion less than five years ago. Therefore, one may reasonably expect more of their relationships to eventually fail. In fact, the average time for relationship failure following abortion was 1.41 years. This average is skewed given that a small number of relationships lasted for many years after the abortions occurred. Most of those that failed did so within the first year after abortion.
Looking Back Men who would choose abortion again if they could go back to the time the decision to abort was made	Of the forty men who agreed with their partners to obtain an abortion. 18 stated "yes", 20 stated "no" and 2 did not respond. Of the 18 men who pressured their partners into choosing abortion, 2 stated "yes" and 16 stated "no". Of the 8 men who left before the decision to abort was made, 2 stated "yes", 6 stated "no". Of the 38 men who passively left the decision to their partners, 11 stated "yes", 25 stated "no", and 2 did not respond.

Continued

Continued

Looking Forward

Men who would choose abortion in the future if faced with another unplanned pregnancy (n = 130)	Seventeen of 130 respondents stated that they would choose abortion in the future if faced with another unplanned pregnancy.
Communicating Who the men shared their experience with (n = 136; respondents could choose all that applied)	Friend = 93 (68%) Parent = 50 (37%) Sibling = 49 (36%) Counselor = 40 (29%) Clergy = 22 (16%) Other = 28 (20%) Note that clergy was the least likely confidant chosen by the men who responded to the survey question asking whom they had confided in about their abortion experience. Furthermore, 24 (18%) of the men stated that they hadn't spoken with anyone about the abortion.
Incidence of Post-Abortion Problems	Grief/Sadness = 128 Persistent thoughts about the baby = 128 Helplessness = 116 Relationship Problems = 115 Anger = 113 Guilt = 112 Isolation = 103 Difficulty Concentrating = 102 Anxiety = 102 Difficulty Sleeping = 91 Sadness at Certain Times of Year = 89 (time of abortion, time of potential birth) Confusion about the male role = 87 Sexual Problems = 79 Disturbing Dreams/Nightmares = 77 Increased Risk-taking = 73 Alcohol/Drug Abuse = 68 Only five respondents did not report any of the problems listed above. Each of these five indicated that they and their partners had agreed to abort. However, 35 of the 40 men who agreed with their partners to abort *did* report experiencing one or more of these problems.

The data reported here indicate that the majority of men experienced relationship failure, regret, and numerous other psychological problems following abortion. Given that this is a relatively small, self selected sample, generalizations cannot be made concerning post abortion men overall. Nonetheless, the data confirm observations by other researchers and clinicians.

Conclusion

An online pilot study was implemented to explore the usefulness of the internet for conducting abortion research. Such a method offers efficiency, anonymity, and the

Continued

potential to reach a large and diverse sample. In addition, the exploratory nature of this research may help to more clearly define future studies and to direct clinical practice involving those affected by abortion.

References

1. Buchanan, M. & Robbins, C. (1990). Early adult psychological consequences for males of adolescent pregnancy and its resolution. Journal of Youth and Adolescence, 19 (4), 413–424.
2. Coleman, R.K. & Nelson, E.S. (1998). The quality of abortion decisions and college students' reports of post abortion emotional sequelae and abortion attitudes. Journal of Social and Clinical Psychology, 17 (4), 425–442.
3. Coleman, P. K., Reardon, D.C., Strahan, T. & Cougle, J.R. (2005). The psychology of abortion: A review and suggestions for future research. Psychology and Health, 20 (2), 237–271.
4. Coyle, C.T. (1997). Forgiveness intervention with postabortion men. Journal of Consulting and Clinical Psychology, 65 (6), 1042–1046.
5. Gordon, R.A. & Kilpatrick, C. (1977). A program of group counseling for men who accompany women seeking legal abortions. Community Mental Health Journal, 13, 291–295.
6. Holmes, M.C. (2004). Reconsidering a "woman's issue:" Psychotherapy and one man's postabortion experiences. American Journal of Psychotherapy, 58 (1), 103–115.
7. Kero, A., Lalos, A., Hogberg, U. & Jacobsson, L. (1999). The male partner involved in legal abortion. Human Reproduction, 14 (10), 2669–2675.
8. Kero, A. & Lalos, A. (2000). Ambivalence—a logical response to legal abortion: A prospective study among women and men. Journal of Psychosomatic Obstetrics and Cynecology, 21, 81–91.
9. Kero, A. & Lalos, A. (2004). Reactions and reflections in men, 4 and 12 months post abortion. Journal of Psychosomatic Obstetrics and Gynecology, 25, 135–143.
10. Lauzon, R, Roger Achim, D., Achim, A. & Boyer, R. (2000). Emotional distress among couples involved in first trimester induced abortions. Canadian Family Physician, 46, 2033–2040.
11. Mattinson, J. (1985). The effects of abortion on a marriage. Abortion: Medical progress and social implications, Ciba Foundation Symposium, 115, 165–177.
12. Milling, E. (1975, April). The men who wait. Woman's Life, 48-89, 69–71.
13. Patterson, J. (1982). Whose freedom of choice? Sometimes it takes two to untangle. The Progressive, 46 (1), 42–45.
14. Raphael, B. (1983). The Anatomy of Bereavement. New York: Basic Books.
15. Rothstein, A.A. (1978). Adolescent males: fatherhood and abortion. Journal of Youth and Adolescence, 7 (2), 203–204.
16. Rue, V.M. (1996). His abortion experience. Ethics and Medics, 21, 3–4.
17. Shostak, A. & McLouth, G (1984). Men and abortion: Lessons, Losses, and Love. New York: Praeger

CATHERINE T. COYLE is a registered nurse with a master's degree in clinical psychiatric nursing and a doctorate in developmental psychology. She has developed a "healing program for men who have been hurt by abortion."

Crystal M. Hayes    **NO**

My Abortion Story, and My Right to Choose

I had two abortions years ago in the first trimesters, and today the only regret I have, is that I didn't speak up sooner about what the right to choose means to me.

For years, I felt so much shame and guilt. I felt silenced by the stigma of a culture preoccupied with using women's bodies for the purposes of power and control, and where "pro-life" advocates use violent language like "baby killers" to describe anyone who believes in a women's right to choose.

For the most part, I lived in secrecy—both times.

"It Was My Choice"

At the time of my first abortion, I was 19 years old. The second time, I was in my mid-20s, a single mother, and in an abusive relationship with someone I thought I wanted to marry. It took me years to figure out my life and to make sense of everything that happened to me, but I was fortunate.

As pro-choice advocate, Texas Democratic State Senator Wendy Davis recently said, I had "the privilege of making the choice." I had access to safe, affordable, and legal abortion care that allowed me autonomy over my body and my decisions.

I don't know what would have happened to me if I had been forced to continue the unintended pregnancies during those very painful and difficult times in my life. I will never forget the loneliness, fear and desperation I felt in those difficult moments, but I was lucky that I didn't let it define me.

Even when I did decide to become a mother, life was still difficult and complicated. I was an unwed 21-year-old college student with little to no family support. And yet, that too was my choice. This basic right to decide my own fate made all the difference in the world. It shaped how I felt about, and approached, motherhood. I felt empowered to choose to have a child, and equally emboldened to live my life on my terms. I have lived my life that way ever since.

Women Are Not Domesticated Animals

"Choice" is a critically important element of a fully actualized and meaningful life, and our very basic human right to make decisions about our reproductive health and bodies is essential to what it means to be a whole human being.

It's what distinguishes us from domesticated and farm animals, whose reproduction we humans control every day. Think of the dairy cows and hens who are kept continually pregnant, even painfully, so that people can satisfy their insatiable appetites for milk, cheese and eggs; or the dogs and cats we spay and neuter to keep their populations under control. When lawmakers legislate and regulate women's bodies and restrict abortion-related healthcare, it's a form of violence that's not much different from the way our culture brutalizes and controls animals for our own pleasure and benefit. I, for one, am sick of it.

I didn't realize it at the time, but I know now, that when I made the choice to become a mother, I also made the choice that as a black woman, a woman, and a sexual human being, I would live as a whole integrated person and not as parts of myself. Ever since, I've rejected and resisted the narrative that I was told about myself as a poor, working class black girl and single mother. I started writing my own story.

It's taken me years to get here, but I have learned to embrace all of my imperfect human messiness. This changed everything for me and for my daughter. The ability to choose meant that I also I had a right to my dreams and hopes just like anyone else. I was able to keep my promises to myself to become the first in my family to graduate from college. I wasn't afraid to explore every opportunity possible—even when they seemed impossible. I studied abroad with my 7-year-old at my side. We moved to France and Spain and I was fortunate to be able to raise her both abroad and in an idyllic New England college town, where I attended undergraduate and graduate school surrounded by ideas, books, and the opportunities that I once fantasized about. It was like living a dream—it was *my* dream.

Today, my daughter is 21 years old and living her own dreams. She will be a college senior this fall at a private liberal arts college in Los Angeles. This is what the right to choose means to me.

Why I Am a Pro-Choice Advocate

Today, I am a pro-choice advocate because I want my daughter to live in a world where she is safe to choose the kind of life she wants to live, just as I did.

I want that for all women, particularly poor working class women, rural women, and women of color, who are the most vulnerable to policy attacks that restrict women's access to reproductive healthcare. All women should feel empowered to choose, with full access to the resources and support systems that they need, without any shame or guilt as they make these very personal and often difficult decisions about their bodies and their families.

North Dakota Republican State Representative Kathy Hawken said it best: "one of the key tenets of the Republican Party is personal responsibility. I am personally pro-life, but I vote pro-choice, because you can't make that decision for anyone else. You just can't."

North Carolina Joins the "War on Women"

This state-by-state, spiteful "war on women" campaign to restrict women's healthcare choices made its way to my home in North Carolina recently. The North Carolina Senate Judiciary Committee unexpectedly added six sweeping anti-abortion measures to an "anti-Sharia" law in a deceptive attempt to shut down all but one Planned Parenthood clinic in the state. The bill parrots almost verbatim what is currently under consideration in places like Texas and around the country—bills which all seek to force abortion clinics to meet very strict and expensive standards, or to close their doors. To add insult to injury, they're calling this bill in North Carolina, "The Family, Faith, and Freedom Protection Act." They have the audacity to use language like "faith," "freedom," and "protection" in a bill that's deeply rooted in the worst parts of patriarchal pathology, sexism, and in the case of the "Sharia" bill, Islamaphobia.

When I heard about the bill, I rushed to join several pro-choice allies and friends to protest HB 695 at the North Carolina State Legislature. Our presence didn't seem to matter to state lawmakers at all. Despite the outcry and outrage of more than 600 people, 29 State Senators, 27 men and 2 women, passed the bill anyway. It's now off to the Republican controlled House where there are enough votes for it to succeed, though hopefully the Republicans in control will heed their peer Kathy Hawken in North Dakota and remember that they can be pro-life personally but vote pro-choice politically.

If not, they will force abortion services underground, which jeopardizes women's safety, and prove once more that they don't see women as whole human-beings or value their right to exercise freedom of choice, any more than they value the cows and pigs that they send to the slaughter house.

Either way, pro-choice advocates will be there and we will remember this moment during the next election cycle.

Crystal M. Hayes, professor of social work at North Carolina State University, is the previous Director of Racial Justice and Maternal Child Wellness at the YWCA, and a community-based mental health clinician with a practice in maternal and pediatric mental health.

EXPLORING THE ISSUE

Should Men Have a Say in Whether Their Partner Has an Abortion?

Critical Thinking and Reflection

1. If a man signs a legal document in which he agrees to raise and financially support a baby that comes from a pregnancy a woman does not wish to carry, should she be required to carry the pregnancy and give birth?
2. If men are given equal say on—or even the right to decide—the outcomes of a woman's pregnancy, what could be the outcomes in cases of rape or incest?
3. What are some of the potential emotional and psychological outcomes on a man who strongly opposes abortion, yet whose female partner chooses to terminate a pregnancy they created together?

Is There Common Ground?

Abortion is one of the most controversial, polarizing issues faced in the United States—and many other countries—today. Strong feelings, rooted in whether one considers a fetus to be a living being or a potential life, fuel discussions into debates into openly adversarial arguments. The United States formerly saw organizations like Operation Rescue and the Army of God whose beliefs were so strong, they espoused stopping abortion using "any means necessary." The Army of God published a manual on how to kill abortion providers, and a list of doctors and clinicians who performed abortions was circulated with their home addresses on them. These organizations were closed down in the 1990s—but not before Dr. Paul Gunn was murdered in Florida, Dr. Barnett Slepian was murdered in Buffalo, NY, Dr. George Tiller was murdered in Wichita, KS, and Shannon Lowney, a receptionist at a Planned Parenthood clinic in Brookline, MA, was murdered and five others injured.

The common ground there was that more reasoned anti-choice individuals and organizations condemned the murders, saying that if they consider abortion murder, how could they possibly condone the killing of other human beings?

This is an extreme example to illustrate how extreme both sides of this debate feel about abortion in general. Add into it the idea that men can have a say in what a woman does with her own body—after the women's rights movement worked so hard to gain social and legal accep-

tance for women's self-determination and agency—and emotions run even higher. What, perhaps, is the common ground here is that in an ideal situation involving a male-female relationship—where the relationship is healthy, the couple has high levels of trust and commitment—one would hope that any significant decisions would be discussed together. Yet in the end, it would be challenging to grant male partners the right to have to consent to their female partners' reproductive decision making. Could, then, a woman legally force her male partner to be sterilized?

Additional Resources

Lee, M. (2014) Sorry, men's rights activists, you don't have abortion "rights." *RH Reality Check.* http://rhrealitycheck.org/article/2014/03/11/sorry -mens-rights-activists-dont-abortion-rights.

Leving, J.M. (No Date). New abortion legislation: Fathers will have final say. http://dadsrights.com /index.php/new-abortion-legislation.

Nicholson, J. (2011). What does the law say about the father's rights on abortion? *LiveStrong.* http:// www.livestrong.com/article/115953-law-say-fathers -rights-abortion.

Rosen, S.J. (2014). Protecting women's right to choose—and their health. *Huffington Post.* http:// www.huffingtonpost.com/sanford-jay-rosen/protecting -womens-right-to-choose_b_5549592.html.

Internet References . . .

American Life League

http://www.all.org/

National Abortion Federation

http://prochoice.org/

NARAL Pro-Choice America

http://www.naral.org/

National Right to Life Committee

http://www.nrlc.org/

Selected, Edited, and with Issue Framing Material by:
Elizabeth Schroeder, EdD, MSW, *Elizabeth Schroeder Consulting*

ISSUE

Are Children Who Are Raised by A Lesbian or Gay Couple Worse Off Than Those Raised by Different-Sex Parents?

YES: Glenn T. Stanton, from "Key Findings of Mark Regnerus' New Family Structure Study," Focusonthefamily .com (2012)

NO: Jeanna Bryner, from "Children Raised by Lesbians Do Just Fine, Studies Show," Livescience.com (2010)

Learning Outcomes

After reading this issue, you will be able to:

- Name at least three pieces of research that support same-sex parenting based on children's social outcomes.
- Describe at least three ways in which the research supporting this approach could be misinterpreted.
- Explain at least two reasons why some people are opposed to same-sex couples or LGBQ single people parenting children.

ISSUE SUMMARY

YES: Glenn T. Stanton from conservative organization Focus on the Family summarizes some of the data from the New Family Structure Study as indicators that children in same-sex headed households are negatively affected by having lesbian or gay parents, and that those impacts extend into adulthood.

NO: Jeanna Bryner describes several studies demonstrating that children born to lesbian parents did just as well developmentally as children born to heterosexual parents. This well-being referred to academic performance, friendships, and overall sense of well-being.

"**S**exual orientation" refers to the gender or genders of the people to whom we are attracted, physically and romantically. The most common categories we have right now for sexual orientation are heterosexual (what some people call "straight"), lesbian or gay (what some people call "homosexual"), bisexual (a category in which gender is not necessarily the deciding factor in who one is attracted to), and queer (which some people use to self-identify if they feel these other terms do not apply to them). More recently, additional identities have been created to better represent the experience of people who do not identify as LGBQ or heterosexual. For example, some people identify as asexual (having feelings of love and love relationships without sexual attraction or behaviors) or pansexual (which goes beyond the gender binary of bisexuality by including the feelings of attraction to transgender people).

Historically, people of non-heterosexual orientations have been met with a range of responses from heterosexual people, from full acceptance and celebration, to slight discomfort, to strong opposition, to overt discrimination and violence. People in countries around the world, including the United States, experience homophobia—the irrational fear of or discomfort with people who are or are perceived to be anything other than heterosexual. More than 81 countries around the world have anti-gay laws, the vast majority of which are located in Africa. These laws pertain to a range of issues, from same-sex sexual behaviors to workplace discrimination, to marriage, to adoption. In at least five of these countries, the punishment for violating these laws is death.

Where does the discomfort with and in some cases outright hatred against lesbian, gay, bisexual and/or queer (LGBQ) people come from? In some cases, it comes from strong cultural or religious teaching that it is wrong to be anything other than heterosexual. In other cases, it comes from pervasive misinformation about what determines a person's sexual orientation—whether that person identifies as heterosexual, lesbian or gay, bisexual, or anything else. Anti-LGBQ individuals and groups have maintained that sexual orientation is a choice, something that people can change if they have the right support for doing so. They have argued that such efforts as prayer and therapy can make a lesbian, gay, or bisexual person heterosexual. In fact, going back to Sigmund Freud's time in the late 19th and early 20th centuries, homosexuality was considered a mental disorder. In the United States, up until 1973, the *Diagnostic and Statistical Manual* of the American Psychological Association had homosexuality and related disorders listed.[1] As research emerged and professional advocacy determined that it was not homosexuality that was a disorder, but rather that disorders were caused by the lack of acceptance and violence perpetuated against LGBQ people, homosexuality was taken out of the DSM. After that time, one category remained for something called "Ego-Dystonic Sexual Orientation," a category that referred to people who were distressed by their feelings of attraction and struggled to accept who they were. This category was eliminated in 1987. But these characterizations of homosexuality as a mental disorder have a terrifying history; women and men have had experiments done on them to determine the "cause" of their orientation; many were subjected to electric shock treatments to try to "cure" their homosexuality or bisexuality. Those who endured this abusive treatment spend decades healing from the trauma; some never do. This practice continues in countries around the world; one recent example in early 2014 involved a man in China who was struggling with accepting that he was gay, sought out therapy, and was subjected to electric shock treatment. As of the writing of this book, he is suing the clinic for this abusive practice.[2]

Over the past 15 years, organizations like the American Psychiatric Association and religious organizations like Faith in America, as well as many other mental health professionals, have determined reparative therapy—trying to convince people they are not the orientation they are—to be emotionally and psychologically harmful to them. (Imagine, if you are heterosexual, being subjected to intensive therapy trying to convince you that you are not). While there is not 100% agreement among professionals, usually influenced by religious backgrounds, most research reinforces that sexual orientation, regardless of which orientation it is, is biologically based—that a lesbian, gay, or bisexual person can no more change their orientation than a heterosexual person can. Yet regardless of what research says, many people still feel strongly that sexual orientation is chosen.

This belief has an impact on how people view LGBQ parents. If sexual orientation is not biologically determined, they argue, then it must be "caused." One significant source of LGBQ orientation is parenting. Offensive stereotypes such as "gay men are gay because they had overbearing mothers," and "girls who are allowed to play sports and with 'boy' toys become lesbians," continue today. Heterosexual parents of lesbian or gay children often wonder themselves whether they did anything to have an impact on their children's orientation. Other people feel that lesbian and gay parents should not be allowed to parent at all, that they will somehow influence their children to "become" lesbian or gay—regardless of the fact that most lesbian, gay, and bisexual children are born to heterosexual parents. More extreme arguments demonstrating ignorance about sexual orientation voice the concern that two same-sex parents who have children of the same gender as they will see that child as a potential sexual or romantic partner, which is why so many LGBQ people—in particular, gay men—are unfairly categorized as pedophiles, when the vast majority of pedophiles in the United States are heterosexual men.[3]

Today, there is greater acceptance of lesbian and gay parents. More and more states in the United States have changed their laws relating to adoption to allow lesbian and gay parents to foster or adopt children. More recent research, which is what the articles in this section discuss, relates to the social adjustment of children who are raised by lesbian or gay parents. This type of research has been done for decades on families in which the parents are not heterosexual, married, and of the same race or ethnicity. Researchers are interested in examining what the impact of having mixed race parents; of being raised by a single more or father; of being raised in poverty, etc. And now that there are more same-sex parenting families, researchers want to get a sense of how children do in these households. The impact of parents' gender(s) and sexual orientation(s) are of significant interest to more socially conservative individuals and organizations, like Focus on the Family, which believes strongly and exclusively in male–female marriage relationships. Equally passionate are researchers like Judith Stacey and Timothy Biblarz, who, as reported by Jeanna Bryner, have found that quality parenting trumps number, gender(s), and sexual orientation of parents.

YES ↵

Glenn T. Stanton

Key Findings of Mark Regnerus' New Family Structure Study

The New Family Structure Study (NFSS) suggests "notable differences on many outcomes do, in fact, exist [between same-sex, intact-married, and biological homes]. This is inconsistent with claims of 'no differences' generated by studies that have commonly employed far narrower samples than this one."

Compared with offspring from married, intact mother/father homes, children raised in same-sex homes are markedly *more likely* to . . .

- Experience poor educational attainment
- Report overall lower levels of happiness, mental and physical health.
- Have impulsive behavior
- Be in counseling or mental health therapy (2xs)
- Suffer from depression (by large margins)
- Have recently thought of suicide (significantly)
- Identify as bisexual, lesbian or gay
- Have male on male or female on female sex partners (dramatically higher)
- Currently be in a same-sex romantic relationship (2x to 3x more likely)
- Be asexual (females with lesbian parents)
- As adults, be unmarried; much more likely to cohabit
- As adults, more likely to be unfaithful in married or cohabiting relationships
- Have a sexually tramsmitted infection (STI)
- Be sexually molested (both inappropriate touching and forced sexual act)
- Feel relationally isolated from bio-mother and -father (Although lesbian-parented children do feel close to their bio-mom—not surprisingly—they are not as close as children with a bio-mom married to father)
- Be unemployed or part-time employed as young adults
- As adults, currently be on public assistance or sometime in their childhood

- Live in homes with lower income levels
- Drink with intention of getting drunk
- To smoke tobacco and marijuana
- Spend more time watching TV
- Have frequency of arrests
- Have pled guilty to minor legal offense

Fuller Analysis of Specific NFSS Findings

This first article from Professor Mark Regnerus' (Professor of Sociology, University of Texas, Austin) New Family Structures Study (NFSS) is published in *Social Science Research*. It is accompanied by published responses from mainstream sociologists, which while critical of a few important points—as academics always are—they are generally in praise of his methodology as well as his unique and needed ground-breaking contribution to the literature on the topic of same-sex parenting. This is key and will go far to rebut the activist's severe, but largely baseless criticisms.

Strengths and Importance of the NFSS

- Regnerus did a remarkably masterful job to be hyper-balanced and guarded in his statements and conclusions.
- The study issues from the highly regarded Population Research Center at UT Austin and its methodology was reviewed pre-start by academic sociological and demographic peers from five different leading American universities.
- This study is absolutely peerless in the strength of its population sample, both in size and representativeness. (It is not longitudinal though.) All the other existing studies on same-sex parenting—99.999% examining only lesbian-headed homes—have such

miniscule and severely non-representative populations that no substantive conclusions can really be drawn from them. One leading family sociologist—Paul Amato (Penn State)—bluntly referred to the existing study's statistical strength as "feeble". Regnerus' study is the first to use a large, nationally representative population sample. In fact, the NFSS is the largest population sample examining same-sex homes, asking this breadth of questions of respondents.

- Regnerus introduces the study by carefully explaining the serious methodological problems endemic in the current literature on this topic in careful detail. (Nearly all of which are done by noted activist lesbian scholars.)
- He is primarily addressing what he calls the "no difference" thesis that is presented in the existing gay family literature and has become a near truism in the current public discussion. This refers to the so-called finding of no differences found between same-sex and mom/dad families.

Important Conclusions from the NFSS

Although there are varying numbers, Regnerus finds that 99,000 is the most reliable general figure for how many same-sex headed homes in America have children present. The overwhelming majority of these are in lesbian homes. (SSM proponents typically offer wildly higher numbers to argue the mainstream nature of such homes.)

Below are a sampling of Regnerus' conclusive statements of his study outcomes:

- The NFSS "suggests that notable differences on many outcomes do in fact exist. This is inconsistent with claims of 'no differences' generated by studies that have commonly employed far more narrow samples than this one."
- "But this study, based on a rare, large probability sample, reveals far greater diversity in experience of lesbian motherhood (and to a lesser extent, gay fatherhood) than has been acknowledged or understood."
- "Nevertheless, to claim that there are few meaningful statistical differences between the different groups evaluated here would be to state something that is empirically inaccurate." [different groups examined are lesbian, gay, married intact bio-, hetero-, step-, divorced, and single-parent families]

Specific numbers on the important and significant differences the NFSS are as follows:

Family Instability

- The NFSS as well as other studies conducted by lesbian activist scholars, find that lesbian relationships are dramatically more likely to break up than those in heterosexual homes. This is true even in parts of the world that are highly affirming of same-sex relationships.[1] And the research is very clear that family instability has a dramatic negative impact on the well-being of children.[2]

Public Assistance Dependence

- *On public assistance at some time in childhood:* Lesbian (69%), gay (57%) and mom/dad (17%) ("mom/dad" throughout indicate intact, married bio-parented homes)
- *Currently on public assistance as young adults:* Lesbian (38%), gay (23%), mom/dad (10%)

Employment as Young Adults

- *Unemployed:* lesbian (28%), gay (20%), mom/dad (8%)
- *Full-time employed, currently:* lesbian (26%), gay (34%), mom/dad (49%)

Voting

- *Young adults voted in 2008 Presidential election:* lesbian (41%), gay (73%), mom/dad (57%) (Note: this is the only instance where gay higher than mom/dad)

Child In Counseling or Therapy/ Mental Health

- *Recently/currently in therapy:* lesbian (19%), gay (19%), mom/dad (8%)
- *Recently thought of suicide:* lesbian (12%), gay (24%), mom/dad (5%)

Sexual Identity and Practice of Children

- *Identify solely as heterosexual:* lesbian (61%), gay (71%), mom/dad (90%)
- *Currently in ss romantic relationship:* lesbian (7%), gay (12%), mom/dad (4%)

[These findings in agreement with many studies conducted by gay activist scholars.][3]

- NFSS explains, "the children of lesbian mothers seem more open to same-sex relationships."

- *Asexual*: female, lesbian parents (4%), female, mom/dad (0.5%).
- *Unfaithful as adult while married/cohabiting*: lesbian (40%), gay homes (25%), mom/dad homes (13%)
- *Same-sex sexual activity*: Substantially higher for offspring from both lesbian and gay parented homes.
- *Opposite-sex sexual activity*: Markedly higher for offspring from lesbian and gay households

Sexual Health and Safety

- *Ever had an STI:* lesbian (20%), gay (25%), mom/dad (8%)
- *Ever been touched sexually by parent or adult:* lesbian (23%), gay (6%), mom/dad (2%)
- *Ever forced to have sex against will:* lesbian (31%), and gay (25%), mom/dad (8%)

[Regarding home where the child might have been victimized, Regnerus explains, "there is no obvious trend to the timing of first victimization and when the respondent may have lived with their biological father or their mother's same-sex partner.]

Own Adult Families

Adult children of three different parented-type homes are . . .

- *Currently Married:* lesbian (36%), gay (35%), mom/dad (43%)
- *Currently Cohabiting:* lesbian (36%), gay (35%), mom/dad (9%) (These vast differences are quite significant for well-being in that cohabitation homes are consistently shown to be markedly poorer in all measures of personal and relational health!)[4]

Over all, lesbian-parented, hetero-step, hetero-single all showed significantly more differences than mom/dad-raised children. Gay-parented children showed fewer (but still substantive) differences in contrast with mom/dad kids.

Concerning the difference in measures contrasted with mom/dad homes, lesbian homes are more similar to step- and single-parented hetero homes. This is a key finding because decades of research (as well as the findings here) show these two hetero-family forms are dramatically more likely than mom/dad homes to be associated with a higher number of seriously harmful outcomes for the children of those homes. In fact, noted Rutgers sociologist, David Popenoe, said that based on the serious negative outcomes from such families, we should do all we can to make sure that step-families become rare.

Regnerus explains that the fewer differences between the mom/dad and gay-parented homes may or may not be due to the much smaller sample size of gay fathers, as well as the significantly fewer children (nearly half) in the study population who lived with their gay father and his partner, compared with those who lived with their mother and her lesbian partner.

The Curiosity of the "No Difference" Claim Regarding Same-Sex Homes

Given the findings—from the existing lesbian activist studies—that children from same-sex homes do as well or better than kids raised in married mother/father homes, Regnerus explains:

"In short, if same-sex parents are able to raise children with no differences, despite the kin distinctions, it

Number of Differences Found Between Intact, Married Mother/Father Homes And the Various Family Forms Examined by NFSS

Family Type	Total # of Qualities Measured	Number of Statistically Significant Differences from Mom/Dad Homes	Numbers of Statistically Significant Differences, After Controls
Hetro-Step	40	24	24
Hetro-Single	40	25	21
Lesbian	40	25	24
Gay	40	11	19

would mean that same-sex couples are able to do something that heterosexuals in step-parenting, adoptive and cohabiting contexts have themselves not been able to do—replicate the optimal childrearing environment of married, biological-parent homes."

This reliable data indicates that same-sex parenting outcomes do not look anything like those from intact, married mother and father families. They look like other family forms that our current family experimentation has created over the last forty years and are shown to markedly hinder child-development.

References

1. Gunnar Andersson, et al., "The Demographics of Same-Sex Marriages in Norway and Sweden," *Demography* 43 (2006): 79–98.
2. Paula Fomby and Andrew J. Cherlin, "Family Instability and Child Well-Being," *American Sociological Review*, 72 (2007): 181–204; Hyun Sik Kim, "Consequences of Parental Divorce for Child Development, *American Sociological Review*, 76 (2011) 487–511.
3. Nanette K. Gartrell, Henny M. W. Bos and Naomi G. Goldberg, "Adolescents of the U.S. National Longitudinal Lesbian Family Study: Sexual Orientation, Sexual Behavior, and Sexual Risk Exposure" *Archive of Sexual Behavior*, 40 (2011):1199–1209, p. 1199; Timothy J. Biblarz and Judith Stacey, "How Does the Gender of Parents Matter?" *Journal of Marriage and Family* 72 (2010): 3–22, p. 15; Fiona L. Tasker and Susan Golombok, *Growing Up in a Lesbian Family: Effects on Child Development*, (The Guilford Press, 1997), p. 111.
4. Glenn T. Stanton, *The Ring Makes All The Difference: The Hidden Consequences of Cohabitation and the Strong Benefits of Marriage* (Moody Publishers, 2011).

GLENN T. STANTON is the Director of Global Family Formation Studies at Focus on the Family in Colorado Springs, Colorado, and the author of *Secure Daughters, Confident Sons: How Parents Guide Their Children into Authentic Masculinity and Femininity* and *The Ring Makes All the Difference*.

Jeanna Bryner

Children Raised by Lesbians Do Just Fine, Studies Show

Children raised by lesbian parents fare as well as they would in heterosexual households, research suggests.

The finding, which comes from a review of essentially all studies on the topic of same-sex parents and the health of their children, helps to tease out politics and science on this highly divisive issue. In general, kids in both heterosexual and lesbian households had similar levels of academic achievement, number of friends and overall well-being.

Whether or not kids from homosexual households are more likely to have a non-heterosexual orientation is still unknown. But if there is a genetic component to sexual orientation, it would make sense that kids born to a lesbian mom, say, would be more likely than other kids to be homosexual, scientists say.

At the end of the day, what matters to kids is far deeper than parents' gender or sexual orientation, the research suggests.

"The family type that is best for children is one that has responsible, committed, stable parenting," said study researcher Judith Stacey of New York University. "Two parents are, on average, better than one, but one really good parent is better than two not-so-good ones."

Here are some highlights of the findings:

- In a study of nearly 90 teens, half living with female same-sex couples and the others with heterosexual couples, both groups fared similarly in school. Teen boys in same-sex households had grade point averages of about 2.9, compared with 2.65 for their counterparts in heterosexual homes. Teen girls showed similar results, with a 2.8 for same-sex households and 2.9 for girls in heterosexual families.
- In another study, teens were asked about delinquent activities, such as damaging others' property, shoplifting and getting into fights, in the previous year. Teens in both same-sex and heterosexual households got essentially the same

average scores of about 1.8 on a scale from 1 to 10 (with higher scores meaning more delinquent behaviors).
- A 2008 study comparing 78 lesbian families in the United States with their counterparts (lesbian households) in the Netherlands, showed American kids were more than twice as likely as the Dutch to be teased about their mothers' sexual orientation.

Stacey says she doesn't think kids growing up in lesbian households get teased more than other kids; it's just that when they do get teased, the target is the non-traditional household, rather than some other aspect of their life or identity. (On another note, gay and lesbian teens are more likely than others to get bullied.)

Studies of gay male families are still limited since the phenomenon of male couples choosing to be parents is relatively new, Stacey said. So results on children raised by gay men are not firm.

Equal Opportunity Parenting

But just because two women seem to be able to parent just as well as a man and a woman doesn't mean that fathers aren't important.

"It's not that men don't matter; it's that men can be just as good as women at parenting," said Karen L. Fingerman of the Child Development & Family Studies at Purdue University, who was not involved in the current study. "The key seems to be that parents have someone who supports them in their parenting (i.e., another parent)."

Fingerman and Others Aren't Surprised by the Findings

"This is an interesting paper, and it doesn't surprise me," Fingerman told LiveScience. "If you think about humans historically and cross-culturally, very few cultures use the model we now consider 'normal' with one woman and one man raising one to three children," Fingerman said. "Humans have evolved to be malleable and adjustable, and a variety of models can meet children's social needs adequately."

Politics and Science

The results, however, may surprise various individuals on different sides of the same-sex marriage and parenting debates.

For instance, in a 2003 Pew survey of more than 1,500 American adults, 56 percent agreed that gay marriage would undermine the traditional American family. Even so more than 50 percent agree that gay and lesbian couples can be as good parents as heterosexual couples, with 37 percent disagreeing.

In terms of adoption, about the same number of Americans say they favor adoption by same-sex couples (46 percent) as say they oppose it (48 percent), according to a Pew survey of more than 2,000 individuals conducted in 2008.

Those who oppose same-sex marriage, or civil unions, tout various arguments, one of which involves the harm done to children of same-sex couples, whether due to the lack of a father or mother figure or the promotion of homosexuality, the study researchers say.

"Significant policy decisions have been swayed by the misconception across party lines that children need both a mother and a father," said study researcher Timothy Biblarz, a sociologist at the University of Southern California. "Yet, there is almost no social science research to support this claim. One problem is that proponents of this view routinely ignore research on same-gender parents."

What research there is, though, has been limited by statistics. In the United States, about 4 percent to 5 percent of adults are not heterosexual, Stacey said. And of those who are in relationships, only about 20 percent of same-sex couples are raising children under age 18, according to the 2000 Census. That means sample sizes are inevitably small, leading to study results that are less robust.

Also, to gather data on a reasonable number of same-sex couples raising children, researchers often take what are called convenient samples—they go to sperm banks or other facilities where they know they'll find homosexual parents. "The problem from [a] statistical point of view is that convenient sample studies don't amount to much," said sociologist Michael J. Rosenfeld of Stanford University, adding it's hard to extrapolate the results to the real world.

But his research, which used U.S. Census data and not convenient samples, looked at thousands of kids raised by same-sex parents and found no difference in grade retention (when a kid gets held back in school) after accounting for demographics, such as income.

"Grade retention is a pretty strong predictor of problems later in life including dropping out of high school and mortality," said Rosenfeld, who wasn't involved in the current research.

Children in Same-Sex Households

To amass the most exhaustive and reliable data pool possible, Stacey and Biblarz analyzed all of the research they could dig up, which amounted to more than 80 relevant studies.

In general, they didn't find evidence for differences in parenting abilities between two moms versus a mom and dad raising kids.

"[The research] pretty much shows that almost no study that has been done on this topic has confirmed this common sense assumption that gender is critical or that a father-mother household works better for kids than a same-sex household," said Brian Powell, a sociologist at Indiana University, who also wasn't involved in this review.

Some detractors of same-sex parents contend the children will grow up to be homosexuals or at the very least confused about their sexuality or gender. Research doesn't support that idea, however.

"There really is no evidence that not having a mother or father produces any sort of gender confusion or insecure gender identity," Stacey said. "It's a big mystery where gender dysphoria in children comes from. But almost all transgender or gender non-conforming people have heterosexual parents."

However, to date there aren't any studies that have tracked a large enough set of kids raised by gay or lesbian parents into adulthood to know their eventual sexual orientation and gender identity, the researchers say.

Another concern has been that boys raised without a "father figure" will not have an appropriate model for masculinity. A study from the U.K., however, suggested that 12-year-olds raised by mother-only families (lesbian or heterosexual) scored the same on masculinity factors as sons raised by a mother and a father. Interestingly, though, the mother-only boys also scored higher on femininity scales.

Are Mom and Dad Different?

While there were few substantial differences between heterosexual and homosexual parents, some gender stereotypes were confirmed.

Compared with heterosexual couples, the review showed that on average, two mothers tended to play with their children more and were less likely to use physical discipline (relative to the time spent with kids). And like heterosexual parents, new parenthood among lesbians increased stress and conflict within the couple. Also, lesbian biological mothers typically assumed greater care-giving responsibility than their partners, reflecting inequities also found between mothers and fathers.

"The bottom line is that the science shows that children raised by two same-gender parents do as well on average as children raised by two different-gender parents," Biblarz said. "This is obviously inconsistent with the widespread claim that children must be raised by a mother and a father to do well."

The Scientists Note They Don't Expect the Results to Change Minds

"There's a huge gap between research and popular belief and public policy, and it's hard for people to believe something that goes so against what they deeply think," Stacey told LiveScience, adding, "I can't say I'm very optimistic that people will believe us, but I'm hopeful it will open up conversation."

JEANNA BRYNER is the managing editor of LiveScience. Prior to this, Ms. Bryner served as a reporter for LiveScience and SPACE.com, and as an assistant editor at *Science World* magazine. She has an English degree from Salisbury University, a master's degree in biogeochemistry and environmental sciences from the University of Maryland, and a science journalism degree from New York University.

EXPLORING THE ISSUE

Are Children Who Are Raised by Lesbian or Gay Parents Worse Off Than Those Raised by Heterosexual Parents?

Critical Thinking and Reflection

1. Aside from the misguided concern that lesbian and gay parents would sexually abuse their children, what do you think opponents to same-sex parenting are most concerned about?
2. What do you think are the three most important components to a household in which children are being raised to promote their overall health and well-being? Do you feel that LGB parents can provide that to their children? If not, why not?
3. If research were to demonstrate that children of same-sex parents do, not just as well as, but actually better than, children who are raised by different-sex parents, what do you think should be done with that knowledge? Is there a way that this information can be used to support parents of all sexual orientations in being stronger parents?

Is There Common Ground?

An important job of being a researcher is to review others' research with a critical eye. Doing so involves reviewing the methods that are used, the size of the sample or population being studied, and determining whether the conclusions the research makes can be claimed. In some cases, biased researchers will want a particular outcome rather than remaining neutral. This bias is usually caught when the research is submitted to a journal for publication in an anonymous review process. The reviewers do not see who has written the research and so cannot be influenced if it is done by a colleague who is known to them.

Whether one is a researcher, a parent, or both, the middle ground is that all people want children to grow up happy, healthy, and well-adjusted. We are a culture of harm reduction and disaster prevention—and those messages and efforts often resonate with the public more than efforts to encourage happiness and adjustment. So regardless of whether children of same-sex or different-sex parents have positive outcomes, it may be easier for some to get their heads around the lack of harm—to get to the common ground that if children do better (or worse), it has to do with factors other than sexual orientation.

Additional Resources

Goldberg, A.E. (2010). Lesbian and gay parents and their children: Research on the family life cycle. Division 44: *Contemporary perspectives on lesbian,*

gay, and bisexual psychology. Washington, DC, US: American Psychological Association.

Regnerus, M. (2012). Parental same-sex relationships, family instability, and subsequent life outcomes for adult children: Answering critics of the new family structures study with additional analyses. *Social Science Research,* 41, 1367–1377.

Tasker, F. (2010). Same-sex parenting and child development: Reviewing the contribution of parental gender. *Journal of Marriage and Family,* 72(1), 35.

References

1. American Psychiatric Association (1968). Diagnostic and statistical manual of mental disorders, 2nd edition. Arlington, VA: APA.
2. Wang, W. and Yangjingjing, X. (2014). Gay activists in China sue over electric shock therapy used to "cure" homosexuality. *The Washington Post,* July 31, 2014. http://www.washingtonpost.com/world /asia_pacific/gay-activists-in-china-sue-over-electric -shock-therapy-used-to-cure-homosexuality/2014/07/31 /cd155d5e-18a9-11e4-9349-84d4a85be981_story.html.
3. Stop Abuse Campaign (2012). Most sex abusers are heterosexual. http://stopabusecampaign.com/feature /most-sex-abusers-are-heterosexual.

Internet References . . .

Catholic Education Resource Center.

Same-Sex Marriage: Not In Kids' Best Interests.

http://www.catholiceducation.org/articles /homosexuality/ho0097.html

Children of Lesbians and Gays Everywhere (COLAGE)

http://www.colage.org

Family Equality Council

http://www.familyequality.org

Family Research Council

Ten Arguments from Social Science against Same-Sex Marriage

http://www.frc.org/get.cfm?i=if04g01

Unit 4

UNIT

Gender in the World Around Us

*T*hroughout this book, it is crystal clear how gendered our world is. From the moment we are born, we are dressed in colors that have been predetermined to indicate and suit our genders. Based on the way people dress, we perceive— sometimes correctly, sometimes incorrectly—what their gender is and then behave accordingly. We are more or less direct with others because that is how we were raised to behave. Or are these older stereotypes that may not even exist anymore? Are men truly more competitive than women, or as more and more women are promoted to higher positions in business, is that no longer the case? Professional distinction aside, the world is made up of numerous religions—the vast majority of which were founded and still are led by men. Over the past few decades, however, that has begun to change selectively. Why are certain religions open to women leaders, and some are not? If a religion was founded by men, is that a sign that they should continue to be led by them, with women having lesser, although still valuable, roles?

Some people will maintain that keeping gender distinctions is important for the social order—others will say that doing so limits boys and girls by pressuring them to fulfill social stereotypes; that it incorrectly sees the world as being comprised exclusively of cisgender men and women, rather than acknowledging transgender and intersex people. In that vein, the questions posted in this unit ask you to reflect on what it means to be one gender or another. Is gender determined by our body parts, our feelings on the inside, a combination of the two? What enables us to have access to gendered spaces, such as restrooms—and how would that be monitored or policed?

Gender in the world around us must be considered, as well, through the lens of sexuality—and perhaps the greatest impact on people's feelings about sexuality right now (particularly teens) is pornography. The impact of porn on people's attitudes, beliefs, and behaviors is still not known for sure—the research is conflicted beyond saying it has some kind of impact on attitudes. But does it have an impact on behaviors? Some maintain it does—but not in the way you would think. Some believe that by watching porn, those who would otherwise violently offend against others, including children, instead find a harmless outlet, thereby reducing the incidence of rape. Others believe that even porn that isn't violent objectifies women—but are women the only ones being objectified? What about porn depicting encounters between two women? Two men?

Selected, Edited, and with Issue Framing Material by:
Elizabeth Schroeder, EdD, MSW, *Elizabeth Schroeder Consulting*

ISSUE

Can Women Have It All?

YES: Gayle Tzemach Lemmon, from "Sheryl Sandberg's Radically Realistic 'And' Solution for Working Mothers," *The Atlantic* Magazine (February 20, 2013)

NO: Anne-Marie Slaughter, from "Why Women Still Can't Have It All," *The Atlantic* Magazine (July 2012)

Learning Outcomes

After reading this issue, you will be able to:

- Understand how people (in this case women) deal with the stress of situations involving the conflict between two very important values. Women have to make life-changing decisions regarding the balance of work and family responsibilities.
- Understand how the conditions affecting these choices have changed over time.
- Explore how the workplaces and family units are changing to accommodate women's needs in this set of conflicting demands.
- Explain, if possible, why these institutions are not more accommodating.
- Form an opinion about whether this issue is largely an individual problem or largely an institutional problem or is both.
- Evaluate what the role of husbands is in this situation.
- Discuss how men tend to handle the stress between work and family.

ISSUE SUMMARY

YES: Gayle Tzemach Lemmon, best-selling author, journalist, and a Senior Fellow with the Council on Foreign Relations' Women and Foreign Policy program, discusses the issues in Sheryl Sandberg's famous book, *Lean In*. Sandberg's advice to career women is not to opt out but to lean in, that is, to firmly choose both career and parenting. Unfortunately men still run the country so the societal changes that could facilitate *Lean In* are missing. Full commitment to both career and family will not be easy.

NO: Anne-Marie Slaughter, the Bert G. Kerstetter '66 University Professor of Politics and International Affairs at Princeton University and formerly dean of Princeton's Woodrow Wilson School of Public and International Affairs, explains why Sandberg is wrong and women cannot successfully pursue career and family at the same time. They must decide which to do well and which to do adequately but not avidly.

The fascinating aspect of social life is how many different trends and changes significantly affect how we live and the choices we make. For example, consider married women and their work–family choices. Ever since the 1950s, married women have increasingly participated in the labor force. Why? The reasons are numerous. Women want the money for themselves. Women need the money for the family. Women want the challenge of a career. Women want the social life that work provides. Women want independence. The list of reasons goes on and on. These reasons change, however, as the context changes.

For example, since 1965 the median price of the one-family home compared to the average income of private nonagricultural workers had doubled in real terms before the housing market crashed. Thus, the single earner family is having much more difficulty buying a house. This trend helps explain why married women increasingly enter or stay in the labor force. Attitudes have also changed. In 1968, a large survey asked young people what they expected to be doing at age 35. About 30 percent of the 20- to 21-year-olds said that they would be working. Seven years later, 65 percent of 20- to 21-year-olds said they would be working. That is an astounding change. The statistical result is that in 1900, women 16 and over constituted 18 percent of the labor force; in 1950, women constituted 30 percent; and since 1995, women constituted 45–47 percent of the labor force.

Educational changes in the past half century have also been dramatic. Females have overtaken males in most aspects of education. Women are now outnumbering men in college and currently earn 58 percent of all bachelor degrees, 60 percent of all master degrees, and 52 percent of PhDs. Women are also more focused on professional degrees while in college as demonstrated by their selection of majors. In 1966, 40 percent of college women graduates majored in education and 17 percent majored in English/literature, but only 2 percent majored in business. Women have stopped shying away from the business world. The percentage of female BA business degrees went from 9 percent in 1971 to 49 percent in 1997, while it went from 4 percent to 39 percent for MA business degrees and from 5 percent to 70 percent for law degrees. Another

trend affecting choices and behaviors is the increasing scarcity of time. The percentage of males working more than 50 hours a week increased from 21.0 to 26.5 and for females from 5.2 to 11.3 during 1970–2000.

Two issues that have received major media attention explore the circumstances of the work–family choice. First, in the 1990s, employers talked about a mommy track for women employees who would be allowed an easier workload that would reduce the conflict between work and family but would slow down their advancement and hold down their income. Second, in the past decade investigators noticed that capable women with prosperous husbands "opted out" of the work world and stayed home with the kids. They had the circumstances that allowed them to make this choice. Could it be that if all women had such circumstances then the majority of them would make the same choice? This is the issue which is debated in the following selections. Gayle Tzemach Lemmon strongly supports Sheryl Sandberg's message in her famous book, *Lean In,* which advises career women not to opt out but to lean in, i.e., to firmly choose both career and parenting. It will not be easy but it is much better than the opt out alternative. Anne-Marie Slaughter attacks Sandberg thesis. She tries to show that women can not successfully pursue both career and family at the same time. They will fail at one or both objectives. They must decide which to do well and which to do adequately but not avidly.

YES

Gayle Tzemach Lemmon

Sheryl Sandberg's Radically Realistic 'And' Solution for Working Mothers

At a wedding this summer, while I was eight months pregnant with twins, an older gentleman sitting next to me asked me whether I still worked in finance.

No, I told him, at the moment I was focused on my next book project, think-tank work, and several magazine pieces.

"Well," he said with a gentle, nearly sympathetic, smile, "in any case, soon you will be pushing three babies in a stroller, right? Won't leave time for much else."

Annoyance swelled up into my already enormous stomach. When our table rose to watch the bride cut the cake I scurried two seats over to my husband and fumed. "I was so irritated I couldn't even come up with a clever answer, other than to say that the kids have a father, too," I said. "No one would *ever* say something like that to you."

My husband laughed and told me not to pay any attention. "It's just because people think that women can only be one thing."

And therein lies the rub.

Somehow, today—even while women learn and earn in greater numbers than ever before—the idea that women live in an "either/or" world stubbornly hangs on. A woman can either be a mother or a professional. Career-driven or family-oriented. A great wife or a great worker. Not both. In other words, the choices are Donna Reed and Murphy Brown (pre-baby). Precious few Clair Huxtables out there.

That is the challenge Sheryl Sandberg's book sets out to tackle. In a women-in-the-workplace discussion consisting mostly of "either/ors," her argument in the upcoming book *Lean In* injects the word "and" into the conversation in a way that urges women to bring their "whole selves" to work. Choice is good, *and* so is aspiration. Ambition is great, and so is telling your boss that you want to have children. Working hard at your job is important, and so is finding a way to leave the office early enough to be home for dinner with your kids.

Already, weeks before the book's publication, criticism is within easy earshot. A 20-something friend told me that several women she respected greatly argued that Sandberg is hardly representative of others and that her advice is impractical for the non-wealthy. But it seems to me that this criticism misses the point. What Sandberg offers is a view that shows 20-somethings like my friend that choices and trade-offs surely exist, but that the "old normal" of blunting ambition so that you can fit in one category or another does not have to be the way it is. And that each of us has a say in what comes next. And that includes men.

We live in an era of immense change when it comes to what women do, how they do it, and with whom. 2011 marked the first year in which more women than men had advanced degrees. Between 1970 and 2009 the number of jobs held by women leapt from 37 percent to close to 48 percent. The boost in productivity resulting from women's increased labor participation accounts for 25 percent of U.S. GDP. Women own nearly 8 million businesses, enterprises that provide more than 20 million jobs. And as researcher Liza Mundy noted in her recent book, nearly 40 percent of wives in the U.S. now earn more than their husbands; Mundy predicts in a generation breadwinning wives will be the majority. Yet no real evolution in our expectations for women's lives and women's ambitions has accompanied these numbers, as Anne-Marie Slaughter's zeitgeist-channeling 2012 *Atlantic* story "Why Women Still Can't Have It All" points out.

Sandberg's proposition, though, looks a lot more like most women's lives than the "either/or" model into which women's lives get shoved. Many women navigate the "ands" every day, juggling a work life and a family life whose demands have meshed into one another in our constantly connected, 24/7-everything world. They don't have the luxury of choosing one or the other because they are too busy doing both. And as I have argued here at *The Atlantic*, all of these are undoubtedly high-class conversations the women I grew up with never had the chance to have.

Still, it is relevant to all women that, as Sandberg notes, "the blunt truth is that men still run the world." Women are fewer than 5 percent of all Fortune 500 CEOs and hold less than 20 percent of all executive board seats. Half the population accounts for barely 10 percent of all heads of state. And it was enormous progress for women to reach the 20-percent mark in the U.S. Senate last year. These dismal numbers and the lack of power they indicate are why it matters that the land of "and" is not only where women live now, but where they should want to stay and prosper. When 50 percent of the country has a kiddie seat at the head table, making room for others gets a whole lot harder. (Sandberg argues that women should, quite literally, sit "at the table" of power in which decisions get made.) Creating a world in which the next generation of talent gets to exercise its potential instead of bumping its head against career-stifling stereotypes or soul-crushing ceilings is in everyone's interest—and the American economy's.

Still, though, even when you succeed in winning fame and fortune in the world of "and", sometimes others make it "either/or" for you.

In a recent *Rolling Stone* piece on the end of the long-running television program *30 Rock*, show creator Tina Fey said the show had run its course, and dropping ratings meant no more. She wanted to do some movies and develop a multi-camera TV show while staying close to home and her two small children.

Her fellow *30 Rock* actor Alec Baldwin had a different and somewhat more detailed explanation.

Baldwin, the magazine wrote, is "convinced that having a second child, in 2011, may have been the breaking point for Fey. 'I saw a real difference in her,' says Baldwin. 'Tina always had her antenna up, but this year was the first time where she came in and laid down on the couch on set, and you could tell, she's a mom. She's fucking wiped out.'"

GAYLE TZEMACH LEMMON is a best-selling author, journalist, and a Senior Fellow with the Council on Foreign Relations' Women and Foreign Policy Program.

Anne-Marie Slaughter    **NO**

Why Women Still Can't Have It All

It's time to stop fooling ourselves, says a woman who left a position of power: the women who have managed to be both mothers and top professionals are superhuman, rich, or self-employed. If we truly believe in equal opportunity for all women, here's what has to change.

Eighteen months into my job as the first woman director of policy planning at the State Department, a foreign-policy dream job that traces its origins back to George Kennan, I found myself in New York, at the United Nations' annual assemblage of every foreign minister and head of state in the world. On a Wednesday evening, President and Mrs. Obama hosted a glamorous reception at the American Museum of Natural History. I sipped champagne, greeted foreign dignitaries, and mingled. But I could not stop thinking about my 14-year-old son, who had started eighth grade three weeks earlier and was already resuming what had become his pattern of skipping homework, disrupting classes, failing math, and tuning out any adult who tried to reach him. Over the summer, we had barely spoken to each other—or, more accurately, he had barely spoken to me. And the previous spring I had received several urgent phone calls—invariably on the day of an important meeting—that required me to take the first train from Washington, D.C., where I worked, back to Princeton, New Jersey, where he lived. My husband, who has always done everything possible to support my career, took care of him and his 12-year-old brother during the week; outside of those midweek emergencies, I came home only on weekends.

As the evening wore on, I ran into a colleague who held a senior position in the White House. She has two sons exactly my sons' ages, but she had chosen to move them from California to D.C. when she got her job, which meant her husband commuted back to California regularly. I told her how difficult I was finding it to be away from my son when he clearly needed me. Then I said, "When this is over, I'm going to write an op-ed titled 'Women Can't Have It All.'"

She was horrified. "You *can't* write that," she said. "You, of all people." What she meant was that such a statement, coming from a high-profile career woman—a role model—would be a terrible signal to younger generations of women. By the end of the evening, she had talked me out of it, but for the remainder of my stint in Washington, I was increasingly aware that the feminist beliefs on which I had built my entire career were shifting under my feet. I had always assumed that if I could get a foreign-policy job in the State Department or the White House while my party was in power, I would stay the course as long as I had the opportunity to do work I loved. But in January 2011, when my two-year public-service leave from Princeton University was up, I hurried home as fast as I could.

A rude epiphany hit me soon after I got there. When people asked why I had left government, I explained that I'd come home not only because of Princeton's rules (after two years of leave, you lose your tenure), but also because of my desire to be with my family and my conclusion that juggling high level government work with the needs of two teenage boys was not possible. I have not exactly left the ranks of full-time career women: I teach a full course load; write regular print and online columns on foreign policy; give 40 to 50 speeches a year; appear regularly on TV and radio; and am working on a new academic book. But I routinely got reactions from other women my age or older that ranged from disappointed ("It's such a pity that you had to leave Washington") to condescending ("I wouldn't generalize from your experience. *I've* never had to compromise, and *my* kids turned out great").

The first set of reactions, with the underlying assumption that my choice was somehow sad or unfortunate, was irksome enough. But it was the second set of reactions—those implying that my parenting and/or my commitment to my profession were somehow substandard—that triggered a blind fury. Suddenly, finally, the penny dropped. All my life, I'd been on the other side of this exchange. I'd been the woman smiling the faintly superior smile while another woman told me she had decided to take some time out or pursue a less competitive career track so that she could spend more time with her family. I'd been the woman congratulating herself on her unswerving commitment to the feminist cause, chatting smugly with her dwindling number of college or law-school friends who had reached and maintained their place on the highest rungs of their profession. I'd been the one telling young women at my lectures that you *can* have it all and do it all, regardless of what field you are in. Which means I'd been part, albeit unwittingly, of making millions of women feel that *they* are to blame if they cannot manage to rise up the ladder as fast as men and also have a family and an active home life (and be thin and beautiful to boot).

Last spring, I flew to Oxford to give a public lecture. At the request of a young Rhodes Scholar I know, I'd agreed to talk to the Rhodes community about "work-family balance." I ended up speaking to a group of about 40 men and women in their mid-20s. What poured out of me was a set of very frank reflections on how unexpectedly hard it was to do the kind of job I wanted to do as a high government official and be the kind of parent I wanted to be, at a demanding time for my children (even though my husband, an academic, was willing to take on the lion's share of parenting for the two years I was in Washington). I concluded by saying that my time in office had convinced me that further government service would be very unlikely while my sons were still at home. The audience was rapt, and asked many thoughtful questions. One of the first was from a young woman who began by thanking me for "not giving just one more fatuous 'You can have it all' talk." Just about all of the women in that room planned to combine careers and family in some way. But almost all assumed and accepted that they would have to make compromises that the men in their lives were far less likely to have to make.

The striking gap between the responses I heard from those young women (and others like them) and the responses I heard from my peers and associates prompted me to write this article. Women of my generation have clung to the feminist credo we were raised with, even as our ranks have been steadily thinned by unresolvable tensions between family and career, because we are determined not to drop the flag for the next generation. But when many members of the younger generation have stopped listening, on the grounds that glibly repeating "you can have it all" is simply airbrushing reality, it is time to talk.

I still strongly believe that women can "have it all" (and that men can too). I believe that we can "have it all at the same time." But not today, not with the way America's economy and society are currently structured. My experiences over the past three years have forced me to confront a number of uncomfortable facts that need to be widely acknowledged—and quickly changed.

Before my service in government, I'd spent my career in academia: as a law professor and then as the dean of Princeton's Woodrow Wilson School of Public and International Affairs. Both were demanding jobs, but I had the ability to set my own schedule most of the time. I could be with my kids when I needed to be, and still get the work done. I had to travel frequently, but I found I could make up for that with an extended period at home or a family vacation.

I knew that I was lucky in my career choice, but I had no idea how lucky until I spent two years in Washington within a rigid bureaucracy, even with bosses as understanding as Hillary Clinton and her chief of staff, Cheryl Mills. My workweek started at 4:20 on Monday morning, when I got up to get the 5:30 train from Trenton to Washington. It ended late on Friday, with the train home. In between, the days were crammed with meetings, and when the meetings stopped, the writing work began—a never-ending stream of memos, reports, and comments on other people's drafts. For two years, I never left the office early enough to go to any stores other than those open 24 hours, which meant that everything from dry cleaning to hair appointments to Christmas shopping had to be done on weekends, amid children's sporting events, music lessons, family meals, and conference calls. I was entitled to four hours of vacation per pay period, which came to one day of vacation a month. And I had it better than many of my peers in D.C.; Secretary Clinton deliberately came in around 8 a.m. and left around 7 p.m., to allow her close staff to have morning and evening time with their families (although of course she worked earlier and later, from home).

In short, the minute I found myself in a job that is typical for the vast majority of working women (and men), working long hours on someone else's schedule, I could no longer be both the parent and the professional I wanted to be—at least not with a child experiencing a rocky adolescence. I realized what should have perhaps been obvious: having it all, at least for me, depended almost entirely on what type of job I had. The flip side is the harder truth: having it all was not possible in many types of jobs, including high government office—at least not for very long.

I am hardly alone in this realization. Michèle Flournoy stepped down after three years as undersecretary of defense for policy, the third-highest job in the department, to spend more time at home with her three children, two of whom are teenagers. Karen Hughes left her position as the counselor to President George W. Bush after a year and a half in Washington to go home to Texas for the sake of her family. Mary Matalin, who spent two years as an assistant to Bush and the counselor to Vice President Dick Cheney before stepping down to spend more time with her daughters, wrote: "Having control over your schedule is the only way that women who want to have a career and a family can make it work."

Yet the decision to step down from a position of power—to value family over professional advancement, even for a time—is directly at odds with the prevailing social pressures on career professionals in the United States. One phrase says it all about current attitudes toward work and family, particularly among elites. In Washington, "leaving to spend time with your family" is a euphemism for being fired. This understanding is so ingrained that when Flournoy announced her resignation last December, *The New York Times* covered her decision as follows:

> Ms. Flournoy's announcement surprised friends and a number of Pentagon officials, but all said they took her reason for resignation at face value and not as a standard Washington excuse for an official who has in reality been forced out. "I can absolutely and unequivocally state that her decision to step down has nothing to do with anything other than her commitment to her family," said Doug Wilson, a top Pentagon spokesman. "She has loved this job and people here love her."

Think about what this "standard Washington excuse" implies: it is so unthinkable that an official would *actually* step down to spend time with his or her family that this must be a cover for something else. How could anyone voluntarily leave the circles of power for the responsibilities of parenthood? Depending on one's vantage point, it is either ironic or maddening that this view abides in the nation's capital, despite the ritual commitments to "family values" that are part of every political campaign. Regardless, this sentiment makes true work-life balance exceptionally difficult. But it cannot change unless top women speak out.

Only recently have I begun to appreciate the extent to which many young professional women feel under assault by women my age and older. After I gave a recent speech in New York, several women in their late 60s or early 70s came up to tell me how glad and proud they were to see me speaking as a foreignpolicy expert. A couple of them went on, however, to contrast my career with the path being traveled by "younger women today." One expressed dismay that many younger women "are just not willing to get out there and do it." Said another, unaware of the circumstances of my recent job change: "They think they have to choose between having a career and having a family."

A similar assumption underlies Facebook Chief Operating Officer Sheryl Sandberg's widely publicized 2011 commencement speech at Barnard, and her earlier TED talk, in which she lamented the dismally small number of women at the top and advised young women not to "leave before you leave." When a woman starts thinking about having children, Sandberg said, "she doesn't raise her hand anymore . . . She starts leaning back." Although couched in terms of encouragement, Sandberg's exhortation contains more than a note of reproach. We who have made it to the top, or are striving to get there, are essentially saying to the women in the generation behind us: "What's the matter with you?"

They have an answer that we don't want to hear. After the speech I gave in New York, I went to dinner with a group of 30-somethings. I sat across from two vibrant women, one of whom worked at the UN and the other at a big New York law firm. As nearly always happens in these situations, they soon began asking me about work-life balance. When I told them I was writing this article, the lawyer said, "I look for role models and can't find any." She said the women in her firm who had become partners and taken on management positions had made tremendous sacrifices, "many of which they don't even seem to realize . . . They take two years off when their kids are young but then work like crazy to get back on track professionally, which means that they see their kids when they are toddlers but not teenagers, or really barely at all." Her friend nodded, mentioning the top professional women she knew, all of whom essentially relied on round-the-clock nannies. Both were very clear that they did not want that life, but could not figure out how to combine professional success and satisfaction with a real commitment to family.

I realize that I am blessed to have been born in the late 1950s instead of the early 1930s, as my mother was, or the beginning of the 20th century, as my grandmothers were. My mother built a successful and rewarding career as a professional artist largely in the years after my brothers and I left home—and after being told in her 20s that she could not go to medical school, as her father had done and her brother would go on to do, because, of course, she was going to get married. I owe my own freedoms and opportunities to the pioneering generation of women ahead of me—the women now in their 60s, 70s, and 80s who faced overt sexism of a kind I see only when watching *Mad Men,* and who knew that the only way to make it as a woman was to act exactly like a man. To admit to, much less act on, maternal longings would have been fatal to their careers.

But precisely thanks to their progress, a different kind of conversation is now possible. It is time for women in leadership positions to recognize that although we are still blazing trails and breaking ceilings, many of us are also reinforcing a falsehood: that "having it all" is, more than anything, a function of personal determination. As Kerry Rubin and Lia Macko, the authors of *Midlife Crisis at 30,* their cri de coeur for Gen-X and Gen-Y women, put it:

> What we discovered in our research is that while the empowerment part of the equation has been loudly celebrated, there has been very little honest discussion among women of our age about the real barriers and flaws that still exist in the system despite the opportunities we inherited.

I am well aware that the majority of American women face problems far greater than any discussed in this article. I am writing for my demographic—highly educated, well-off women who are privileged enough to have choices in the first place. We may not have choices about whether to do paid work, as dual incomes have become indispensable. But we have choices about the type and tempo of the work we do. We are the women who could be leading, and who should be equally represented in the leadership ranks.

Millions of other working women face much more difficult life circumstances. Some are single mothers; many struggle to find any job; others support husbands who cannot find jobs. Many cope with a work life in which good day care is either unavailable or very expensive; school schedules do not match work schedules; and schools themselves are failing to educate their children. Many of these women are worrying not about having it all, but rather about holding on to what they do have. And although women as a group have made substantial gains in wages, educational attainment, and prestige over the past three decades, the economists Justin Wolfers and Betsey Stevenson have shown that women are less happy today than their predecessors were in 1972, both in absolute terms and relative to men.

The best hope for improving the lot of all women, and for closing what Wolfers and Stevenson call a "new gender gap"—measured by well-being rather than wages— is to close the leadership gap: to elect a woman president and 50 women senators; to ensure that women are equally represented in the ranks of corporate executives and judicial leaders. Only when women wield power in sufficient numbers will we create a society that genuinely works for all women. That will be a society that works for everyone.

The Half-Truths We Hold Dear

Let's briefly examine the stories we tell ourselves, the clichés that I and many other women typically fall back on when younger women ask us how we have managed to "have it all." They are not necessarily lies, but at best partial truths. We must clear them out of the way to make room for a more honest and productive discussion about real solutions to the problems faced by professional women.

It's Possible If You Are Just Committed Enough

Our usual starting point, whether we say it explicitly or not, is that having it all depends primarily on the depth and intensity of a woman's commitment to her career. That is precisely the sentiment behind the dismay so many older career women feel about the younger generation. *They are not committed enough,* we say, to make the trade-offs and sacrifices that the women ahead of them made.

Yet instead of chiding, perhaps we should face some basic facts. Very few women reach leadership positions. The pool of female candidates for any top job is small, and will only grow smaller if the women who come after us decide to take time out, or drop out of professional competition altogether, to raise children. That is exactly what has Sheryl Sandberg so upset, and rightly so. In her words, "Women are not making it to the top. A hundred and ninety heads of state; nine are women. Of all the people in parliament in the world, 13 percent are women. In the corporate sector, [the share of] women at the top—C-level jobs, board seats—tops out at 15, 16 percent."

Can "insufficient commitment" even plausibly explain these numbers? To be sure, the women who do make it to the top are highly committed to their profession. On closer examination, however, it turns out that most of them have something else in common: they are genuine superwomen. Consider the number of women recently in the top ranks in Washington—Susan Rice, Elizabeth Sherwood-Randall, Michelle Gavin, Nancy-Ann Min DeParle—who are Rhodes Scholars. Samantha Power, another senior White House official, won a Pulitzer Prize at age 32. Or consider Sandberg herself, who graduated with the prize given to Harvard's top student of economics.

These women cannot possibly be the standard against which even very talented professional women should measure themselves. Such a standard sets up most women for a sense of failure.

What's more, among those who have made it to the top, a balanced life still is more elusive for women than it is for men. A simple measure is how many women in top positions have children compared with their male colleagues. Every male Supreme Court justice has a family. Two of the three female justices are single with no children. And the third, Ruth Bader Ginsburg, began her career as a judge only when her younger child was almost grown. The pattern is the same at the National Security Council: Condoleezza Rice, the first and only woman national-security adviser, is also the only national-security adviser since the 1950s not to have a family.

The line of high-level women appointees in the Obama administration is one woman deep. Virtually all of us who have stepped down have been succeeded by men; searches for women to succeed men in similar positions come up empty. Just about every woman who could plausibly be tapped is already in government. The rest of the foreign-policy world is not much better; Micah Zenko, a fellow at the Council on Foreign Relations, recently surveyed the best data he could find across the government, the military, the academy, and think tanks, and found that women hold fewer than 30 percent of the senior foreign-policy positions in each of these institutions.

These numbers are all the more striking when we look back to the 1980s, when women now in their late 40s and 50s were coming out of graduate school, and remember that our classes were nearly 50–50 men and women. We were sure then that by now, we would be living in a 50–50 world. Something derailed that dream.

Sandberg thinks that "something" is an "ambition gap"—that women do not dream big enough. I am all for encouraging young women to reach for the stars. But I fear that the obstacles that keep women from reaching the top are rather more prosaic than the scope of their ambition. My longtime and invaluable assistant, who has a doctorate and juggles many balls as the mother of teenage twins, e-mailed me while I was working on this article: "You know what would help the vast majority of women with work/family balance? MAKE SCHOOL SCHEDULES MATCH WORK SCHEDULES." The present system, she noted, is based on a society that no longer exists—one in which farming was a major occupation and stay-at-home moms were the norm. Yet the system hasn't changed.

Consider some of the responses of women interviewed by Zenko about why "women are significantly underrepresented in foreign policy and national security positions in government, academia, and think tanks." Juliette Kayyem, who served as an assistant secretary in the Department of Homeland Security from 2009 to 2011 and now writes a foreign-policy and national-security column for *The Boston Globe,* told Zenko that among other reasons,

> the basic truth is also this: the travel sucks. As my youngest of three children is now 6, I can look back at the years when they were all young and realize just how disruptive all the travel was. There were also trips I couldn't take because I was pregnant or on leave, the conferences I couldn't attend because (note to conference organizers: weekends are a bad choice) kids would be home from school, and the various excursions that were offered but just couldn't be managed.

Jolynn Shoemaker, the director of Women in International Security, agreed: "Inflexible schedules, unrelenting travel, and constant pressure to be in the office are common features of these jobs."

These "mundane" issues—the need to travel constantly to succeed, the conflicts between school schedules and work schedules, the insistence that work be done in the office—cannot be solved by exhortations to close the ambition gap. I would hope to see commencement speeches that finger America's social and business policies, rather than women's level of ambition, in explaining the dearth of women at the top. But changing these policies requires much more than speeches. It means fighting the mundane battles—every day, every year—in individual workplaces, in legislatures, and in the media.

It's Possible If You Marry the Right Person

Sandberg's second message in her Barnard commencement address was: "The most important career decision you're going to make is whether or not you have a life partner and who that partner is." Lisa Jackson, the administrator of the Environmental Protection Agency, recently drove that message home to an audience of Princeton students and alumni gathered to hear her acceptance speech for the James Madison Medal. During the Q&A session, an audience member asked her how she managed her career and her family. She laughed and pointed to her husband in the front row, saying: "There's my work-life balance." I could never have had the career I have had without my husband, Andrew Moravcsik, who is a tenured professor of politics and international affairs at Princeton. Andy has spent more time with our sons than I have, not only on homework, but also on baseball, music lessons, photography, card games, and more. When each of them had to bring in a foreign dish for his fourth-grade class dinner, Andy made his grandmother's Hungarian *palacsinta;* when our older son needed to memorize his lines for a lead role in a school play, he turned to Andy for help.

Still, the proposition that women can have high-powered careers as long as their husbands or partners are willing to share the parenting load equally (or disproportionately) assumes that most women will *feel* as comfortable as men do about being away from their children, as long as their partner is home with them. In my experience, that is simply not the case.

Here I step onto treacherous ground, mined with stereotypes. From years of conversations and observations, however, I've come to believe that men and women respond quite differently when problems at home force them to recognize that their absence is hurting a child, or at least that their presence would likely help. I do not believe fathers love their children any less than mothers do, but men do seem more likely to choose their job at a cost to their family, while women seem more likely to choose their family at a cost to their job.

Many factors determine this choice, of course. Men are still socialized to believe that their primary family obligation is to be the breadwinner; women, to believe that their primary family obligation is to be the caregiver. But it may be more than that. When I described the choice between my children and my job to Senator Jeanne Shaheen, she said exactly what I felt: "There's really no choice." She wasn't referring to social expectations, but to a maternal imperative felt so deeply that the "choice" is reflexive.

Men and women also seem to frame the choice differently. In *Midlife Crisis at 30,* Mary Matalin recalls her days working as President Bush's assistant and Vice President Cheney's counselor:

> Even when the stress was overwhelming—those days when I'd cry in the car on the way to work, asking myself "Why am I doing this?"—I always knew the answer to that question: I believe in this president.

But Matalin goes on to describe her choice to leave in words that are again uncannily similar to the explanation I have given so many people since leaving the State Department:

> I finally asked myself, "Who needs me more?" And that's when I realized, it's somebody else's turn to do this job. I'm indispensable to my kids, but I'm not close to indispensable to the White House.

To many men, however, the choice to spend more time with their children, instead of working long hours on issues that affect many lives, seems selfish. Male leaders are routinely praised for having sacrificed their personal life on the altar of public or corporate service. That sacrifice, of course, typically involves their family. Yet their children, too, are trained to value public service over private responsibility. At the diplomat Richard Holbrooke's memorial service, one of his sons told the audience that when he was a child, his father was often gone, not around to teach him to throw a ball or to watch his games. But as he grew older, he said, he realized that Holbrooke's absence was the price of saving people around the world—a price worth paying.

It is not clear to me that this ethical framework makes sense for society. Why should we want leaders who fall short on personal responsibilities? Perhaps leaders who invested time in their own families would be more keenly aware of the toll their public choices—on issues from war to welfare—take on private lives. (Kati Marton, Holbrooke's widow and a noted author, says that although Holbrooke adored his children, he came to appreciate the full importance of family only in his 50s, at which point he became a very present parent and grandparent, while continuing to pursue an extraordinary public career.) Regardless, it is clear which set of choices society values more today. Workers who put their careers first are typically rewarded; workers who choose their families are overlooked, disbelieved, or accused of unprofessionalism.

In sum, having a supportive mate may well be a necessary condition if women are to have it all, but it is not sufficient. If women feel deeply that turning down a promotion that would involve more travel, for instance, is the right thing to do, then they will continue to do that. Ultimately, it is society that must change, coming to value choices to put family ahead of work just as much as those to put work ahead of family. If we really valued those choices, we would value the people who make them; if we valued the people who make them, we would do everything possible to hire and retain them; if we did everything possible to allow them to combine work and family equally over time, then the choices would get a lot easier.

It's Possible If You Sequence It Right

Young women should be wary of the assertion "You can have it all; you just can't have it all at once." This 21st-century addendum to the original line is now proffered by many senior women to their younger mentees. To the extent that it means, in the words of one working mother, "I'm going to do my best and I'm going to keep the long term in mind and know that it's not always going to be this hard to balance," it is sound advice. But to the extent that it means that women can have it all if they just find the right sequence of career and family, it's cheerfully wrong.

The most important sequencing issue is when to have children. Many of the top women leaders of the generation just ahead of me—Madeleine Albright, Hillary Clinton, Ruth Bader Ginsburg, Sandra Day O'Connor, Patricia Wald, Nannerl Keohane—had their children in their 20s and early 30s, as was the norm in the 1950s through the 1970s. A child born when his mother is 25 will finish high school when his mother is 43, an age at which, with full-time immersion in a career, she still has plenty of time and energy for advancement.

Yet this sequence has fallen out of favor with many high-potential women, and understandably so. People tend to marry later now, and anyway, if you have children earlier, you may have difficulty getting a graduate degree, a good first job, and opportunities for advancement in the crucial early years of your career. Making matters worse, you will also have less income while raising your children, and hence less ability to hire the help that can be indispensable to your juggling act.

When I was the dean, the Woodrow Wilson School created a program called Pathways to Public Service, aimed at advising women whose children were almost grown about how to go into public service, and many women still ask me about the best "on-ramps" to careers in their mid-40s. Honestly, I'm not sure what to tell most of them. Unlike the pioneering women who entered the workforce after having children in the 1970s, these women are competing with their younger selves. Government and NGO jobs are an option, but many careers are effectively closed off. Personally, I have never seen a woman in her 40s enter the academic market successfully, or enter a law firm as a junior associate, Alicia Florrick of *The Good Wife* notwithstanding.

These considerations are why so many career women of my generation chose to establish themselves in their careers first and have children in their mid-to-late 30s. But that raises the possibility of spending long, stressful years and a small fortune trying to have a baby. I lived that nightmare: for three years, beginning at age 35, I did everything possible to conceive and was frantic at the thought that I had simply left having a biological child until it was too late.

And when everything does work out? I had my first child at 38 (and counted myself blessed) and my second at 40. That means I will be 58 when both of my children are out of the house. What's more, it means that many peak career opportunities are coinciding precisely with their teenage years, when, experienced parents advise, being available as a parent is just as important as in the first years of a child's life.

Many women of my generation have found themselves, in the prime of their careers, saying no to opportunities they once would have jumped at and hoping those chances come around again later. Many others who have decided to step back for a while, taking on consultant positions or part-time work that lets them spend more time with their children (or aging parents), are worrying about how long they can "stay out" before they lose the competitive edge they worked so hard to acquire.

Given the way our work culture is oriented today, I recommend establishing yourself in your career first but still trying to have kids before you are 35—or else freeze your eggs, whether you are married or not. You may well be a more mature and less frustrated parent in your 30s or 40s; you are also more likely to have found a lasting life partner. But the truth is, neither sequence is optimal, and both involve trade-offs that men do not have to make.

You should be able to have a family if you want one—however and whenever your life circumstances allow—and still have the career you desire. If more women could strike this balance, more women would reach leadership positions. And if more women were in leadership positions, they could make it easier for more women to stay in the workforce. The rest of this essay details how.

Changing the Culture of Face Time

Back in the Reagan administration, a *New York Times* story about the ferociously competitive budget director Dick Darman reported, "Mr. Darman sometimes managed to convey the impression that he was the last one working in the Reagan White House by leaving his suit coat on his chair and his office light burning after he left for home." (Darman claimed that it was just easier to leave his suit jacket in the office so he could put it on again in the morning, but his record of psychological manipulation suggests otherwise.)

The culture of "time macho"—a relentless competition to work harder, stay later, pull more all-nighters, travel around the world and bill the extra hours that the international date line affords you—remains astonishingly prevalent among professionals today. Nothing captures the belief that more time equals more value better than the cult of billable hours afflicting large law firms across the country and providing exactly the wrong incentives for employees who hope to integrate work and family. Yet even in industries that don't explicitly reward sheer quantity of hours spent on the job, the pressure to arrive early, stay late, and be available, always, for in-person meetings at 11 a.m. on Saturdays can be intense. Indeed, by some measures, the problem has gotten worse over time: a study by the Center for American Progress reports that nationwide, the share of all professionals—women and men—working more than 50 hours a week has increased since the late 1970s.

But more time in the office does not always mean more "value added"—and it does not always add up to a more successful organization. In 2009, Sandra Pocharski, a senior female partner at Monitor Group and the head of the firm's Leadership and Organization practice, commissioned a Harvard Business School professor to assess the factors that helped or hindered women's effectiveness and advancement at Monitor. The study found that the company's culture was characterized by an "always on" mode of working, often without due regard to the impact on employees. Pocharski observed:

> Clients come first, always, and sometimes burning the midnight oil really does make the difference between success and failure. But sometimes we were just defaulting to behavior that overloaded our people without improving results much, if at all. We decided we needed managers to get better at distinguishing between these categories, and to recognize the hidden costs of assuming that "time is cheap." When that time doesn't add a lot of value and comes at a high cost to talented employees, who will leave when the personal cost becomes unsustainable—well, that is clearly a bad outcome for everyone.

I have worked very long hours and pulled plenty of all-nighters myself over the course of my career, including a few nights on my office couch during my two years in D.C. Being willing to put the time in when the job simply has to get done is rightfully a hallmark of a successful professional. But looking back, I have to admit that my assumption that I would stay late made me much less efficient over the course of the day than I might have been, and certainly less so than some of my colleagues, who managed to get the same amount of work done and go home at a decent hour. If Dick Darman had a boss who clearly valued prioritization and time management, he might have found reason to turn out the lights and take his jacket home.

Long hours are one thing, and realistically, they are often unavoidable. But do they really need to be spent at the office? To be sure, being in the office *some* of the time is beneficial. In-person meetings can be far more efficient than phone or e-mail tag; trust and collegiality are much more easily built up around the same physical table; and spontaneous conversations often generate good ideas and lasting relationships. Still, armed with e-mail, instant messaging, phones, and videoconferencing technology, we should be able to move to a culture where the office is a base of operations more than the required locus of work.

Being able to work from home—in the evening after children are put to bed, or during their sick days or snow days, and at least some of the time on weekends—can be the key, for mothers, to carrying your full load versus letting a team down at crucial moments. State-of-the-art videoconferencing facilities can dramatically reduce the need for long business trips. These technologies are making inroads, and allowing easier integration of work and family life. According to the Women's Business Center, 61 percent of women business owners use technology to "integrate the responsibilities of work and home"; 44 percent use technology to allow employees "to work off-site or to have flexible work schedules." Yet our work culture still remains more office-centered than it needs to be, especially in light of technological advances.

One way to change that is by changing the "default rules" that govern office work—the baseline expectations about when, where, and how work will be done. As behavioral economists well know, these baselines can make an enormous difference in the way people act. It is one thing, for instance, for an organization to allow phone-ins to a meeting on an ad hoc basis, when parenting and work schedules collide—a system that's better than nothing, but likely to engender guilt among those calling in, and possibly resentment among those in the room. It is quite another for that organization to declare that its policy will be to schedule in-person meetings, whenever possible, during the hours of the school day—a system that might normalize call-ins for those (rarer) meetings still held in the late afternoon.

One real-world example comes from the British Foreign and Commonwealth Office, a place most people are more likely to associate with distinguished gentlemen in pinstripes than with progressive thinking about work-family balance. Like so many other places, however, the FCO worries about losing talented members of two-career couples around the world, particularly women. So it recently changed its basic policy from a default rule that jobs have to be done on-site to one that assumes that some jobs might be done remotely, and invites workers to make the case for remote work. Kara Owen, a career foreign-service officer who was the FCO's diversity director and will soon become the British deputy ambassador to France, writes that she has now done two remote jobs. Before her current maternity leave, she was working a London job from Dublin to be with her partner, using teleconferencing technology and timing her trips to London to coincide "with key meetings where I needed to be in the room (or chatting at the pre-meeting coffee) to have an impact, or to do intensive 'network maintenance.'" In fact, she writes, "I have found the distance and quiet to be a real advantage in a strategic role, providing I have put in the investment up front to develop very strong personal relationships with the game changers." Owen recognizes that not every job can be done this way. But she says that for her part, she has been able to combine family requirements with her career.

Changes in default office rules should not advantage parents over other workers; indeed, done right, they can improve relations among co-workers by raising their awareness of each other's circumstances and instilling a sense of fairness. Two years ago, the ACLU Foundation of Massachusetts decided to replace its "parental leave" policy with a "family leave" policy that provides for as much as 12 weeks of leave not only for new parents, but also for employees who need to care for a spouse, child, or parent with a serious health condition. According to Director Carol Rose, "We wanted a policy that took into account the fact that even employees who do not have children have family obligations." The policy was shaped by the belief that giving women "special treatment" can "backfire if the broader norms shaping the behavior of all employees do not change." When I was the dean of the Wilson School, I managed with the mantra "Family comes first"—any family—and found that my employees were both productive and intensely loyal.

None of these changes will happen by themselves, and reasons to avoid them will seldom be hard to find. But obstacles and inertia are usually surmountable if leaders are open to changing their assumptions about the workplace. The use of technology in many high-level government jobs, for instance, is complicated by the need to have access to classified information. But in 2009, Deputy Secretary of State James Steinberg, who shares the parenting of his two young daughters equally with his wife, made getting such access at home an immediate priority so that he could leave the office at a reasonable hour and participate in important meetings via videoconferencing if necessary. I wonder how many women in similar positions would be afraid to ask, lest they be seen as insufficiently committed to their jobs.

Revaluing Family Values

While employers shouldn't privilege parents over other workers, too often they end up doing the opposite, usually subtly, and usually in ways that make it harder for a primary caregiver to get ahead. Many people in positions of power seem to place a low value on child care in comparison with other outside activities. Consider the following proposition: An employer has two equally talented and productive employees. One trains for and runs marathons when he is not working. The other takes care of two children. What assumptions is the employer likely to make about the marathon runner? That he gets up in the dark every day and logs an hour or two running before even coming into the office, or drives himself to get out there even after a long day. That he is ferociously disciplined and willing to push himself through distraction, exhaustion, and days when nothing seems to go right in the service of a goal far in the distance. That he must manage his time exceptionally well to squeeze all of that in.

Be honest: Do you think the employer makes those same assumptions about the parent? Even though she likely rises in the dark hours before she needs to be at work, organizes her children's day, makes breakfast, packs lunch, gets them off to school, figures out shopping and other errands even if she is lucky enough to have a housekeeper—and does much the same work at the end of the day. Cheryl Mills, Hillary Clinton's indefatigable chief of staff, has twins in elementary school; even with a fully engaged husband, she famously gets up at four every morning to check and send e-mails before her kids wake up. Louise Richardson, now the vice chancellor of the University of St. Andrews, in Scotland, combined an assistant professorship in government at Harvard with mothering three young children. She organized her time so ruthlessly that she always keyed in 1:11 or 2:22 or 3:33 on the microwave rather than 1:00, 2:00, or 3:00, because hitting the same number three times took less time.

Elizabeth Warren, who is now running for the U.S. Senate in Massachusetts, has a similar story. When she had two young children and a part-time law practice, she struggled to find enough time to write the papers and articles that would help get her an academic position. In her words:

I needed a plan. I figured out that writing time was when Alex was asleep. So the minute I put him down for a nap or he fell asleep in the baby swing, I went to my desk and started working on something—footnotes, reading, outlining, writing . . . I learned to do everything else with a baby on my hip.

The discipline, organization, and sheer endurance it takes to succeed at top levels with young children at home is easily comparable to running 20 to 40 miles a week. But that's rarely how employers see things, not only when making allowances, but when making promotions.

Perhaps because people *choose* to have children? People also choose to run marathons.

One final example: I have worked with many Orthodox Jewish men who observed the Sabbath from sundown on Friday until sundown on Saturday. Jack Lew, the two-time director of the Office of Management and Budget, former deputy secretary of state for management and resources, and now White House chief of staff, is a case in point. Jack's wife lived in New York when he worked in the State Department, so he would leave the office early enough on Friday afternoon to take the shuttle to New York and a taxi to his apartment before sundown. He would not work on Friday after sundown or all day Saturday. Everyone who knew him, including me, admired his commitment to his faith and his ability to carve out the time for it, even with an enormously demanding job.

It is hard to imagine, however, that we would have the same response if a mother told us she was blocking out mid-Friday afternoon through the end of the day on Saturday, every week, to spend time with her children. I suspect this would be seen as unprofessional, an imposition of unnecessary costs on co-workers. In fact, of course, one of the great values of the Sabbath—whether Jewish or Christian—is precisely that it carves out a family oasis, with rituals and a mandatory settingaside of work.

Our assumptions are just that: things we believe that are not necessarily so. Yet what we assume has an enormous impact on our perceptions and responses. Fortunately, changing our assumptions is up to us.

Redefining the Arc of a Successful Career

The American definition of a successful professional is someone who can climb the ladder the furthest in the shortest time, generally peaking between ages 45 and 55. It is a definition well suited to the mid-20th century, an era when people had kids in their 20s, stayed in one job, retired at 67, and were dead, on average, by age 71.

It makes far less sense today. Average life expectancy for people in their 20s has increased to 80; men and women in good health can easily work until they are 75. They can expect to have multiple jobs and even multiple careers throughout their working life. Couples marry later, have kids later, and can expect to live on two incomes. They may well retire *earlier*—the average retirement age has gone down from 67 to 63—but that is commonly "retirement" only in the sense of collecting retirement benefits. Many people go on to "encore" careers.

Assuming the priceless gifts of good health and good fortune, a professional woman can thus expect her working life to stretch some 50 years, from her early or mid-20s to her mid-70s. It is reasonable to assume that she will build her credentials and establish herself, at least in her first career, between 22 and 35; she will have children, if she wants them, sometime between 25 and 45; she'll want maximum flexibility and control over her time in the 10 years that her children are 8 to 18; and she should plan to take positions of maximum authority and demands on her time after her children are out of the house. Women who have children in their late 20s can expect to immerse themselves completely in their careers in their late 40s, with plenty of time still to rise to the top in their late 50s and early 60s. Women who make partner, managing director, or senior vice president; get tenure; or establish a medical practice before having children in their late 30s should be coming back on line for the most demanding jobs at almost exactly the same age.

Along the way, women should think about the climb to leadership not in terms of a straight upward slope, but as irregular stair steps, with periodic plateaus (and even dips) when they turn down promotions to remain in a job that works for their family situation; when they leave high-powered jobs and spend a year or two at home on a reduced schedule; or when they step off a conventional professional track to take a consulting position or project-based work for a number of years. I think of these plateaus as "investment intervals." My husband and I took a sabbatical in Shanghai, from August 2007 to May 2008, right in the thick of an election year when many of my friends were advising various candidates on foreign-policy issues. We thought of the move in part as "putting money in the family bank," taking advantage of the opportunity to spend a close year together in a foreign culture. But we were also investing in our children's ability to learn Mandarin and in our own knowledge of Asia.

Peaking in your late 50s and early 60s rather than your late 40s and early 50s makes particular sense for women, who live longer than men. And many of the stereotypes about older workers simply do not hold. A 2006 survey of human-resources professionals shows that only 23 percent think older workers are less flexible than younger workers; only 11 percent think older workers require more training than younger workers; and only 7 percent think older workers have less drive than younger workers.

Whether women will really have the confidence to stair-step their careers, however, will again depend in part on perceptions. Slowing down the rate of promotions, taking time out periodically, pursuing an alternative path during crucial parenting or parent-care years—all have to become more visible and more noticeably accepted as a pause rather than an opt-out. (In an encouraging sign, *Mass Career Customization*, a 2007 book by Cathleen Benko and Anne Weisberg arguing that "today's career is no longer a straight climb up the corporate ladder, but rather a combination of climbs, lateral moves, and planned descents," was a *Wall Street Journal* best seller.)

Institutions can also take concrete steps to promote this acceptance. For instance, in 1970, Princeton established a tenure-extension policy that allowed female assistant professors expecting a child to request a one-year extension on their tenure clocks. This policy was later extended to men, and broadened to include adoptions. In the early 2000s, two reports on the status of female faculty discovered that only about 3 percent of assistant professors requested tenure extensions in a given year. And in response to a survey question, women were much more likely than men to think that a tenure extension would be detrimental to an assistant professor's career.

So in 2005, under President Shirley Tilghman, Princeton changed the default rule. The administration announced that all assistant professors, female and male, who had a new child would *automatically* receive a one-year extension on the tenure clock, with no opt-outs allowed. Instead, assistant professors could request early consideration for tenure if they wished. The number of assistant professors who receive a tenure extension has tripled since the change.

One of the best ways to move social norms in this direction is to choose and celebrate different role models. New Jersey Governor Chris Christie and I are poles apart politically, but he went way up in my estimation when he announced that one reason he decided against running for president in 2012 was the impact his campaign would have had on his children. He reportedly made clear at a fund-raiser in Louisiana that he didn't want to be away from his children for long periods of time; according to a Republican official at the event, he said that "his son [missed] him after being gone for the three days on the road, and that he needed to get back." He may not get my vote if and when he does run for president, but he definitely gets my admiration (providing he doesn't turn around and join the GOP ticket this fall).

If we are looking for high-profile female role models, we might begin with Michelle Obama. She started out with the same résumé as her husband, but has repeatedly made career decisions designed to let her do work she cared about and also be the kind of parent she wanted to be. She moved from a high-powered law firm first to Chicago city government and then to the University of Chicago shortly before her daughters were born, a move that let her work only 10 minutes away from home. She has spoken publicly and often about her initial concerns that her husband's entry into politics would be bad for their family life, and about her determination to limit her participation in the presidential election campaign to have more time at home. Even as first lady, she has been adamant that she be able to balance her official duties with family time. We should see her as a full-time career woman, but one who is taking a very visible investment interval. We should celebrate her not only as a wife, mother, and champion of healthy eating, but also as a woman who has had the courage and judgment to invest in her daughters when they need her most. And we should expect a glittering career from her after she leaves the White House and her daughters leave for college.

Rediscovering the Pursuit of Happiness

One of the most complicated and surprising parts of my journey out of Washington was coming to grips with what I really wanted. I had opportunities to stay on, and I could have tried to work out an arrangement allowing me to spend more time at home. I might have been able to get my family to join me in Washington for a year; I might have been able to get classified technology installed at my house the way Jim Steinberg did; I might have been able to commute only four days a week instead of five. (While this last change would have still left me very little time at home, given the intensity of my job, it might have made the job doable for another year or two.) But I realized that I didn't just *need* to go home. Deep down, I *wanted* to go home. I wanted to be able to spend time with my children in the last few years that they are likely to live at home, crucial years for their development into responsible, productive, happy, and caring adults. But also irreplaceable years for me to enjoy the simple pleasures of parenting—baseball games, piano recitals, waffle breakfasts, family trips, and goofy rituals. My older son is doing very well these days, but even when he gives us a hard time, as all teenagers do, being home to shape his choices and help him make good decisions is deeply satisfying.

The flip side of my realization is captured in Macko and Rubin's ruminations on the importance of bringing the different parts of their lives together as 30-year-old women:

> If we didn't start to learn how to integrate our personal, social, and professional lives, we were about five years away from morphing into the angry woman on the other side of a mahogany

desk who questions her staff's work ethic after standard 12-hour workdays, before heading home to eat moo shoo pork in her lonely apartment.

Women have contributed to the fetish of the one-dimensional life, albeit by necessity. The pioneer generation of feminists walled off their personal lives from their professional personas to ensure that they could never be discriminated against for a lack of commitment to their work. When I was a law student in the 1980s, many women who were then climbing the legal hierarchy in New York firms told me that they never admitted to taking time out for a child's doctor appointment or school performance, but instead invented a much more neutral excuse.

Today, however, women in power can and should change that environment, although change is not easy. When I became dean of the Woodrow Wilson School, in 2002, I decided that one of the advantages of being a woman in power was that I could help change the norms by deliberately talking about my children and my desire to have a balanced life. Thus, I would end faculty meetings at 6 p.m. by saying that I had to go home for dinner; I would also make clear to all student organizations that I would not come to dinner with them, because I needed to be home from six to eight, but that I would often be willing to come back after eight for a meeting. I also once told the Dean's Advisory Committee that the associate dean would chair the next session so I could go to a parent-teacher conference.

After a few months of this, several female assistant professors showed up in my office quite agitated. "You *have* to stop talking about your kids," one said. "You are not showing the gravitas that people expect from a dean, which is particularly damaging precisely because you are the first woman dean of the school." I told them that I was doing it deliberately and continued my practice, but it is interesting that gravitas and parenthood don't seem to go together.

Ten years later, whenever I am introduced at a lecture or other speaking engagement, I insist that the person introducing me mention that I have two sons. It seems odd to me to list degrees, awards, positions, and interests and *not* include the dimension of my life that is most important to me—and takes an enormous amount of my time. As Secretary Clinton once said in a television interview in Beijing when the interviewer asked her about Chelsea's upcoming wedding: "That's my real life." But I notice that my male introducers are typically uncomfortable when I make the request. They frequently say things like "And she particularly wanted me to mention that she has two sons"—thereby drawing attention to the unusual

nature of my request, when my entire purpose is to make family references routine and normal in professional life.

This does not mean that you should insist that your colleagues spend time cooing over pictures of your baby or listening to the prodigious accomplishments of your kindergartner. It does mean that if you are late coming in one week, because it is your turn to drive the kids to school, that you be honest about what you are doing. Indeed, Sheryl Sandberg recently acknowledged not only that she leaves work at 5:30 to have dinner with her family, but also that for many years she did not dare make this admission, even though she would of course make up the work time later in the evening. Her willingness to speak out now is a strong step in the right direction.

Seeking out a more balanced life is not a women's issue; balance would be better for us all. Bronnie Ware, an Australian blogger who worked for years in palliative care and is the author of the 2011 book *The Top Five Regrets of the Dying*, writes that the regret she heard most often was "I wish I'd had the courage to live a life true to myself, not the life others expected of me." The second-most-common regret was "I wish I didn't work so hard." She writes: "This came from every male patient that I nursed. They missed their children's youth and their partner's companionship."

Juliette Kayyem, who several years ago left the Department of Homeland Security soon after her husband, David Barron, left a high position in the Justice Department, says their joint decision to leave Washington and return to Boston sprang from their desire to work on the *"happiness project,"* meaning quality time with their three children. (She borrowed the term from her friend Gretchen Rubin, who wrote a best-selling book and now runs a blog with that name.)

It's time to embrace a national happiness project. As a daughter of Charlottesville, Virginia, the home of Thomas Jefferson and the university he founded, I grew up with the Declaration of Independence in my blood. Last I checked, he did not declare American independence in the name of life, liberty, and professional success. Let us rediscover the pursuit of happiness, and let us start at home.

Innovation Nation

As I write this, I can hear the reaction of some readers to many of the proposals in this essay: It's all fine and well for a tenured professor to write about flexible working hours, investment intervals, and family-comes-first management. But what about the real world? Most American women cannot demand these things, particularly in a bad economy, and their employers have little incentive to grant them voluntarily. Indeed, the most frequent reaction I get in putting forth these ideas is that when the choice is whether to hire a man who will work whenever and wherever needed, or a woman who needs more flexibility, choosing the man will add more value to the company.

In fact, while many of these issues are hard to quantify and measure precisely, the statistics seem to tell a different story. A seminal study of 527 U.S. companies, published in the *Academy of Management Journal* in 2000, suggests that "organizations with more extensive work-family policies have higher perceived firm-level performance" among their industry peers. These findings accorded with a 2003 study conducted by Michelle Arthur at the University of New Mexico. Examining 130 announcements of family-friendly policies in *The Wall Street Journal,* Arthur found that the announcements alone significantly improved share prices. In 2011, a study on flexibility in the workplace by Ellen Galinsky, Kelly Sakai, and Tyler Wigton of the Families and Work Institute showed that increased flexibility correlates positively with job engagement, job satisfaction, employee retention, and employee health.

This is only a small sampling from a large and growing literature trying to pin down the relationship between family-friendly policies and economic performance. Other scholars have concluded that good family policies attract better talent, which in turn raises productivity, but that the policies themselves have no impact on productivity. Still others argue that results attributed to these policies are actually a function of good management overall. What is evident, however, is that many firms that recruit and train well-educated professional women are aware that when a woman leaves because of bad work-family balance, they are losing the money and time they invested in her.

Even the legal industry, built around the billable hour, is taking notice. Deborah Epstein Henry, a former big-firm litigator, is now the president of Flex-Time Lawyers, a national consulting firm focused partly on strategies for the retention of female attorneys. In her book *Law and Reorder,* published by the American Bar Association in 2010, she describes a legal profession "where the billable hour no longer works"; where attorneys, judges, recruiters, and academics all agree that this system of compensation has perverted the industry, leading to brutal work hours, massive inefficiency, and highly inflated costs. The answer—already being deployed in different corners of the industry—is a combination of alternative fee structures, virtual firms, women-owned firms, and the outsourcing of discrete legal jobs to other jurisdictions. Women, and Generation X and Y lawyers more generally, are pushing for these changes on the supply side; clients determined to reduce legal fees and increase flexible service are pulling on the demand side. Slowly, change is happening.

At the core of all this is self-interest. Losing smart and motivated women not only diminishes a company's talent pool; it also reduces the return on its investment in training and mentoring. In trying to address these issues, some firms are finding out that women's ways of working may just be better ways of working, for employees and clients alike.

Experts on creativity and innovation emphasize the value of encouraging nonlinear thinking and cultivating randomness by taking long walks or looking at your environment from unusual angles. In their new book, *A New Culture of Learning: Cultivating the Imagination for a World of Constant Change,* the innovation gurus John Seely Brown and Douglas Thomas write, "We believe that connecting play and imagination may be the single most important step in unleashing the new culture of learning."

Space for play and imagination is exactly what emerges when rigid work schedules and hierarchies loosen up. Skeptics should consider the "California effect." California is the cradle of American innovation—in technology, entertainment, sports, food, and lifestyles. It is also a place where people take leisure as seriously as they take work; where companies like Google deliberately encourage play, with Ping-Pong tables, light sabers, and policies that require employees to spend one day a week working on whatever they wish. Charles Baudelaire wrote: "Genius is nothing more nor less than childhood recovered at will." Google apparently has taken note.

No parent would mistake child care for childhood. Still, seeing the world anew through a child's eyes can be a powerful source of stimulation. When the Nobel laureate Thomas Schelling wrote *The Strategy of Conflict,* a classic text applying game theory to conflicts among nations, he frequently drew on child-rearing for examples of when deterrence might succeed or fail. "It may be easier to articulate the peculiar difficulty of constraining [a ruler] by the use of threats," he wrote, "when one is fresh from a vain attempt at using threats to keep a small child from hurting a dog or a small dog from hurting a child."

The books I've read with my children, the silly movies I've watched, the games I've played, questions I've answered, and people I've met while parenting have broadened my world. Another axiom of the literature on innovation is that the more often people with different perspectives come together, the more likely creative ideas are to emerge. Giving workers the ability to integrate their non-work lives with their work—whether they spend that time mothering or marathoning—will open the door to a much wider range of influences and ideas.

Enlisting Men

Perhaps the most encouraging news of all for achieving the sorts of changes that I have proposed is that men are joining the cause. In commenting on a draft of this article, Martha Minow, the dean of the Harvard Law School, wrote me that one change she has observed during 30 years of teaching law at Harvard is that today many young men are asking questions about how they can manage a work-life balance. And more systematic research on Generation Y confirms that many more men than in the past are asking questions about how they are going to integrate active parenthood with their professional lives.

Abstract aspirations are easier than concrete trade-offs, of course. These young men have not yet faced the question of whether they are prepared to give up that more prestigious clerkship or fellowship, decline a promotion, or delay their professional goals to spend more time with their children and to support their partner's career.

Yet once work practices and work culture begin to evolve, those changes are likely to carry their own momentum. Kara Owen, the British foreign-service officer who worked a London job from Dublin, wrote me in an e-mail:

> I think the culture on flexible working started to change the minute the Board of Management (who were all men at the time) started to work flexibly—quite a few of them started working one day a week from home.

Men have, of course, become much more involved parents over the past couple of decades, and that, too, suggests broad support for big changes in the way we balance work and family. It is noteworthy that both James Steinberg, deputy secretary of state, and William Lynn, deputy secretary of defense, stepped down two years into the Obama administration so that they could spend more time with their children (for real).

Going forward, women would do well to frame work-family balance in terms of the broader social and economic issues that affect both women and men. After all, we have a new generation of young men who have been raised by full-time working mothers. Let us presume, as I do with my sons, that they will understand "supporting their families" to mean more than earning money.

I HAVE BEEN BLESSED to work with and be mentored by some extraordinary women. Watching Hillary Clinton in action makes me incredibly proud—of her intelligence, expertise, professionalism, charisma, and command of any audience. I get a similar rush when I see a frontpage picture of Christine Lagarde, the managing director of the International Monetary Fund, and Angela Merkel, the chancellor of Germany, deep in conversation about some of the most important issues on the world stage; or of Susan Rice, the U.S. ambassador to the United Nations, standing up forcefully for the Syrian people in the Security Council.

These women are extraordinary role models. If I had a daughter, I would encourage her to look to them, and I want a world in which they are extraordinary but not unusual. Yet I also want a world in which, in Lisa Jackson's words, "to be a strong woman, you don't have to give up on the things that define you as a woman." That means respecting, enabling, and indeed celebrating the full range of women's choices. "Empowering yourself," Jackson said in her speech at Princeton, "doesn't have to mean rejecting motherhood, or eliminating the nurturing or feminine aspects of who you are."

I gave a speech at Vassar last November and arrived in time to wander the campus on a lovely fall afternoon. It is a place infused with a spirit of community and generosity, filled with benches, walkways, public art, and quiet places donated by alumnae seeking to encourage contemplation and connection. Turning the pages of the alumni magazine (Vassar is now coed), I was struck by the entries of older alumnae, who greeted their classmates with *Salve* (Latin for "hello") and wrote witty remembrances sprinkled with literary allusions. Theirs was a world in which women wore their learning lightly; their news is mostly of their children's accomplishments. Many of us look back on that earlier era as a time when it was fine to joke that women went to college to get an "M.R.S." And many women of my generation abandoned the Seven Sisters as soon as the formerly all-male Ivy League universities became coed. I would never return to the world of segregated sexes and rampant discrimination. But now is the time to revisit the assumption that women must rush to adapt to the "man's world" that our mothers and mentors warned us about.

I continually push the young women in my classes to speak more. They must gain the confidence to value their own insights and questions, and to present them readily. My husband agrees, but he actually tries to get the young men in his classes to act more like the women—to speak less and listen more. If women are ever to achieve real equality as leaders, then we have to stop accepting male behavior and male choices as the default and the ideal. We must insist on changing social policies and bending career tracks to accommodate *our* choices, too. We have the power to do it if we decide to, and we have many men standing beside us.

We'll create a better society in the process, for *all* women. We may need to put a woman in the White House before we are able to change the conditions of the women working at Walmart. But when we do, we will stop talking about whether women can have it all. We will properly focus on how we can help all Americans have healthy, happy, productive lives, valuing the people they love as much as the success they seek.

ANNE-MARIE SLAUGHTER is the Bert G. Kerstetter '66 University Professor of Politics and International Affairs at Princeton University and formerly dean of Princeton's Woodrow Wilson School of Public and International Affairs. She is currently the president and CEO of the New America Foundation, a public policy institute and idea incubator based in Washington and New York.

EXPLORING THE ISSUE

Can Women Have It All?

Critical Thinking and Reflection

1. The debate about leaning in is largely limited to professional women because that is the group that can afford to choose to lean in or opt out. What hypotheses would you make about the desires of nonprofessional women based on the behavior of professional women?
2. Note two facts. First, the percentage of mothers with at-home children that were working in the labor force increased until the 1990s and then leveled off. Second, a noticeable number of professional women who could afford to were opting out. Linda Hirshman concludes from these facts that "the belief that women are responsible for childrearing and homemaking was largely untouched by decades of workplace feminism." Do a critique of this conclusion.
3. How does the fact that many mothers return to the labor force when their children are of school age and more return when their children leave home impact your view of this debate?
4. What public policies would improve the lives of women with work/family tensions?
5. What is your judgment about the companies that have a "mommy track" policy?

Is There Common Ground?

Both authors want what is best for women and are upset about the situation that they analyze. Both would like societal arrangements to reduce the conflict between work and family. Both want women to be able to have it all. Their debate is over how possible it is to have it all. Gayle Tzemach Lemmon thinks they can have it all but it will not be easy. They will have to "lean in," which involves strength and determination. Anne-Marie Slaughter argues that the cost is generally too high. Women should put family first and career second. They can still have careers but must pursue them in ways that do not sacrifice too much for the family. I know that I would feel very deprived if I had to quit my professor's job to raise children even though children are a great joy. But I do not have to make this choice. This is what is obviously unfair about this issue. It is mostly a female problem. Men are not expected to quit their jobs and stay home and raise their children. Some, in fact, are doing just this since their wives are making far more money than they can, but this is rare. Society and religious groups generally preach that the wife should put family before work, so the stress is generally on women.

Additional Resources

Women who quit careers to go home to raise a family are said to "opt out." For analyses of the opt out phenomenon look at: Pamela Stone, *Opting Out?: Why Women Really Quit Careers and Head Home* (University of California Press, 2007); Lisa A. Mainiero and Sherry E. Sullivan, *The Opt-Out Revolt* (Davies-Black, 2006); Phyllis Moen, *The Career Mystique* (Rowan & Littlefield, 2005); Ann Crittenden, *The Price of Motherhood* (Metropolitan Books, 2001); and Susan Chira, *A Mother's Place: Choosing Work and Family Without Guilt or Shame* (Perennial, 1999).

Some who advocate for "leaning in" and against opting out are: Leslie Bennetts, who strongly advises women not to give up their careers in *The Feminine Mistake* (Voice/Hyperion, 2007), and Sylvia Ann Hewlett does the same in *Off-Ramps and On-Ramps: Keeping Talented Women on the Road to Success* (Harvard Business School Press, 2007).

For discussions of the demands of work and family on women, see: Suzanne M. Bianchi, John P. Robinson, and Melissa Milkie, *Changing Rhythms of Family Life* (American Sociological Association, 2006); Susan Thistle, *From Marriage to the Market* (University of California Press,

2006); Arlie Russell Hochschild, *The Second Shift* (Penguin Books, 2003); and Anna Fels, *Necessary Dreams: Ambition in Women's Changing Lives* (Pantheon Book, 2004). Mary Eberstadt is the major critic of the working mothers who leave much of the childrearing to others. See her *Home-Alone America: The Hidden Toll of Daycare, Behavioral Drugs, and Other Parent Substitutes* (Penguin, 2004).

On the issue of time scarcity and time use, which factors into the debate on the tension between work and family, see: *Fighting for Time: Shifting Boundaries of Work and Social Life,* edited by Cynthia Fuchs-Epstein and Arne L. Kalleberg (Russell Sage Foundation, 2004); Phyllis Moen, *It's About Time: Couples and Careers* (Cornell University Press, 2003); Harriet B. Presser, *Working in a 24/7 Economy: Challenges for American Families* (Russell Sage Foundation, 2003); John Robinson and Geoffrey Godbey, *Time for Life: The Surprising Ways Americans Use Their Time,* 2nd ed. (State University Press, 1999); Juliet Schor, *The Overworked American: The Unexpected Decline of Leisure* (Basic Books, 1991); and Jerry A. Jacobs and Kathleen Gerson, *The Time Divide: Work, Family, and Gender Inequality* (Harvard University Press, 2004).

Internet References . . .

National Council on Family Research

www.ncfr.com

Sociology—Study Sociology Online

http://edu.learnsoc.org/

Sociology Web Resources

www.mhhe.com/socscience/sociology/resources/index.htm

Sociosite

www.topsite.com/goto/sociosite.net

Socioweb

www.topsite.com/goto/socioweb.com

Selected, Edited, and with Issue Framing Material by:
Elizabeth Schroeder, EdD, MSW, *Elizabeth Schroeder Consulting*

ISSUE

Is There Still a Double Standard of Sexuality for Women and Girls?

YES: Michael J. Marks and R. Chris Fraley, from "The Sexual Double Standard: Fact or Fiction?," *Sex Roles* (vol. 52, no. 3/4, February 2005)

NO: Gail Collins, from "The Decline of the Double Standard," in *When Everything Changed: The Amazing Journey of American Women from 1960 to the Present.* (Little, Brown, and Company, 2009)

Learning Outcomes
As you read the issue, focus on the following points:
• What role does pop culture play in setting public norms for sexual behavior?
• How has the widespread availability of affordable birth control changed sexual norms for both men and women?

ISSUE SUMMARY

YES: Michael J. Marks and R. Chris Fraley, in "The Sexual Double Standard: Fact or Fiction?," address contemporary cultural beliefs about the sexual double standard.

NO: Gail Collins, in the chapter titled "The Decline of the Double Standard" from her 2009 book *When Everything Changed: The Amazing Journey of American Women from 1960 to the Present*, discusses how cultural beliefs regarding expectations for women's sexual behaviors have evolved since the 1960s.

The phrase "sexual double standard" refers to the idea that there are different rules for how men and women should conduct their sexual lives. Throughout history, the onus for chastity has largely rested with the party that could experience the postcoital consequence of pregnancy. The advent of the birth control pill and its widespread availability in the latter half of the twentieth century heralded many changes for American women. For many women, reproductive control translated into delayed marriage and the opportunity to earn advanced degrees as well as the chance to pursue careers outside the home.

How do people perceive the sexual behavior of men and women? Is there really a double standard that approves one type of behavior for one sex but not for the other? In "The Sexual Double Standard: Fact or Fiction?"

Michael J. Marks and R. Chris Fraley address beliefs about sexual double standards and examine current research on the subject. To test the limits of existing research on the double standard, Marks and Fraley (2005) conducted an experiment to determine "whether people evaluate men and women differently based on the number of sexual partners they have had" (p. 177). Their objective was to test the hypothesis that a double standard would exist if "as the number of sexual partners reported increases, male targets would be evaluated more positively and female targets more negatively" (Marks & Fraley, 2005, p. 177).

Marks and Fraley's research showed that the sexual double standard exists but is not a simple construct. The fact that people believe a double standard exists becomes, in effect, a self-fulfilling prophecy that is further supported by the phenomenon of confirmation bias. The tendency to notice instances that align with and confirm previously held beliefs while selectively ignoring examples that might disprove the misconception may contribute to the pervasive notion that a sexual double standard exists in contemporary American culture.

In "The Decline of the Double Standard," Gail Collins chronicles the social changes that altered cultural expectations about women's sexual behavior after the 1960s. From widespread acceptance of cohabitation to the relative affordability and widespread availability of the birth control pill, the rules for sexual behavior have changed for both men and women. According to Collins, the sexual revolution that began in the late 1960s and continued into the early 1970s signaled the beginning of the end for the sexual double standard.

The influence of popular culture in setting public norms for sexual behavior cannot be underestimated. Helen Gurley Brown's 1962 novel *Sex and the Single Girl* extolled the virtues of single life and extramarital sex. The book was a bestseller and set the stage for the sexual revolution that would subsequently sweep across cities and college campuses throughout America.

YES

Michael J. Marks and R. Chris Fraley

The Sexual Double Standard: Fact or Fiction?

In contemporary society it is widely believed that women and men are held to different standards of sexual behavior. As [many have] noted, "a man who is successful with many women is likely to be seen as just that—successful . . . [whereas] a woman known to have 'success' with many men is . . . likely to be known as a 'slut.'" The view that men are socially rewarded and women socially derogated for sexual activity has been labeled the *sexual double standard*.

The sexual double standard has received a lot of attention from contemporary critics of Western culture. Tanenbaum (2000), for example, has documented the harassment and distress experienced by adolescent girls who have been branded as "sluts" by their peers. Other writers have critiqued the way the media help to create and reinforce negative stereotypes of sexually active women and how these stereotypes may contribute to violence against women. Given the attention the sexual double standard has received in contemporary discourse, one might assume that behavioral scientists have documented the double standard extensively and elucidated many of the mechanisms that generate and sustain it. Despite much systematic research, however, there is virtually no consistent evidence for the existence of this allegedly pervasive phenomenon.

We have three objectives in this [paper]. Our first is to review briefly the empirical literature on the sexual double standard. As we discuss, research findings concerning the double standard do not strongly support its existence. Next, we discuss several methodological reasons why previous researchers may not have been able to document a double standard even if one exists. Finally, we report a study that was designed to determine whether the sexual double standard exists by rectifying the methodological limitations of previous studies.

Empirical Research on the Sexual Double Standard

The sexual double standard seems to be a ubiquitous phenomenon in contemporary society; one recent survey revealed that 85% of people believe that a double standard exists in our culture. The double standard is frequently publicized by the media. For example, MTV, a popular cable television channel that specializes in contemporary culture, recently aired a program called "Fight for Your Rights: Busting the Double Standard" that was designed to convey the idea that a sexual double standard exists and that people should try to transcend it by exhibiting more egalitarian thinking.

Although the sexual double standard seems pervasive, empirical research does not necessarily show that people evaluate sexually active men and women differently. In fact, much of the literature reveals little or no evidence of a double standard. O'Sullivan (1995), for example, conducted a person perception study in which individual participants read vignettes of a male or female target who reported a high or low number of past sexual partners. Participants then evaluated the targets in domains such as likeability, morality, and desirability as a spouse. Although men and women who engaged in casual intercourse were evaluated more negatively than those whose sexual experiences occurred in committed relationships, a double standard was not found. Gentry (1998) also employed a person perception task and found that raters judged both male and female targets who had relatively few past sexual partners and who were in monogamous relationships more positively than targets who had a high number of partners and had frequent casual sex. Again, no evidence of a double standard was found. Sprecher et al. (1988) examined how appropriate certain sexual acts were for men and women of various ages. Although older targets received more permissive responses (i.e., they were allowed more sexual freedom), there were few differences in the standards used for men versus women for any age group.

Researchers have also documented many characteristics of respondents that influence attitudes toward sexuality, but few, if any, of these findings are consistent with a double standard. For instance, Garcia (1982) found that respondents' degree of androgyny was related to the sexual stereotypes they held. Androgynous participants (i.e., people who possess high levels of both masculine and feminine psychological traits) displayed a single standard, whereas gender-typed respondents (i.e., masculine men and feminine women) displayed a slight preference for female targets in the low-sexual experience condition. However, a preference for high-experience male targets over low-experience male targets was not found.

The number of sexual partners respondents have had also appears to influence their judgments of targets. Milhausen and Herold (1999), for example, found that women with many sexual partners were more tolerant of highly sexually active men than were women with few sexual partners. However, the interaction between target gender, target experience, and participant experience was not tested. The gender of the respondent has also been shown to influence views on sexuality. Women tend to hold sexual standards that are stricter than those of men, but do not necessarily apply those standards differently as a function of the gender of the person being evaluated.

In summary, although it appears that people *do* evaluate others with respect to the number of sexual partners those people have had, research does not consistently show that those evaluations differ for male and female targets. Even in situations in which men and women are evaluated differently, the associations usually vary only in magnitude, not in sign. In other words, there are some situations in which both women and men may be evaluated more negatively as the number of sexual partners they report increases, but this association is only slightly stronger for women than it is for men. As we will explain below, this pattern can be characterized as a "weak" rather than "strong" double standard. If the sexual double standard is as pervasive and powerful as many people believe, empirical research should reveal cross-over interactions such that the association between sexual experience and evaluations is negative for women but positive for men.

Sexual Double Standard Research Methodology

Although the empirical literature would seem to suggest that the sexual double standard is not in operation, it may be the case that behavioral scientists have failed to tap it properly. Commonly used paradigms for studying the sexual double standard may have methodological limitations that prevent the double standard from emerging. If this is the case, changes are needed in the methodology used in sexual double standard research.

One limitation of past research is the likely existence of demand characteristics. For example, if a study explicitly requires participants to rate the appropriateness of certain sexual behaviors for men, immediately followed by identical questions regarding women, participants may try to answer either in an egalitarian manner or in a manner that is consistent with what they believe to be the norm. Given that many people have preconceived notions about the sexual double standard, it is important to minimize demand characteristics when researching attitudes toward sexuality.

A second limitation of past research involves the presentation of sexual activity in a valenced fashion. For example, some researchers have used materials that imply that premarital sexual intercourse "is just wrong" or have described a target as having a number of past sexual partners that is "a lot above average." This kind of language implies that there is something abnormal or inappropriate about the target's activity. Describing sexual activity with value-laden terms or implying that a person is involved in *any* behavior to an excess may lead to biased evaluations of that person, regardless of whether that person is male or female. If a sexual double standard exists, the use of these kinds of descriptors may occlude researchers' ability to document it clearly.

Finally, much of the past double standard research has not differentiated between attitudes and evaluations. *Attitudes* toward sexual behavior may include general beliefs about the norms of the culture, personal decisions about when sex is permissible, and the perceived appropriateness of certain sexual behaviors. *Evaluations* concern real judgments made about specific people who engage in sexual activity. Attitudes may be independent of the way people actually evaluate one another. Because of this, results concerning attitudinal differences (e.g., women hold less permissive sexual standards than men do) as evidence of the double standard's existence may conflict with results concerning evaluations of others' behavior. We believe that at the core of popular interest in the sexual double standard is the notion that men and women are evaluated differently depending on their sexual experience. Although the general attitudes that people hold about sexuality are of interest to psychologists, these attitudes may not be reflected in the actual evaluations that people make about one another. Therefore, it is imperative to focus on the evaluations that people make about specific individuals.

Overview of the Present Study

The objective of the present experiment was to determine whether people evaluate men and women differently based on the number of sexual partners they have had. To do this, we asked participants to rate a target on a number of evaluative dimensions. We manipulated both (a) the sex of the target and (b) the number of sexual partners reported by the target. This experiment was explicitly designed to rectify some of the limitations of previous research on the sexual double standard. For example, we focused on the evaluations people made about specific targets rather than general perceptions of social norms. We did not include valenced or biased descriptions of sexual activity (e.g., "promiscuous," "above average number of partners"). Moreover, we employed a between-subjects design to reduce potential demand characteristics. These features enabled us to draw attention away from the sexual focus of the study and allowed us to tap the way people evaluate others who vary in gender and sexual experience. . . .

Competing Hypotheses

If a traditional or "strong" sexual double standard exists, then as the number of sexual partners reported increases, male targets would be evaluated more positively and female targets more negatively. . . .

It is also possible that a "weak" double standard exists, such that both men and women are derogated for high levels of sexual experience, but to different degrees. . . . Finally, if there is no sexual double standard, then we would observe equivalent slopes for male and female targets. . . .

Method

Participants

. . . The . . . sample consisted of 144 undergraduates from a large midwestern university (44 men, 100 women) who participated in fulfillment of partial course credit. The mean participant age in this sample was 19.66 ($SD = 3.14$, range 18–30 years). . . .

Design

We employed a 2 (target sex) $\times$ 6 (number of partners: 0, 1, 3, 7, 12, or 19) between-subjects design. . . .

Procedure

A page (constructed by the experimenters) that contained five questions and the answers to those questions was given to the participants to read. Participants were told that the page was a section from a general public survey that had been completed by an anonymous individual. The page contained answers to questions such as "What are your hobbies?" and "How do you see yourself?" Information about the target's sexual experience was conveyed in response to the question "What is something not many people know about you?" The key phrase in the response was "I've had sex with [number] [guys/girls]. I don't really have much to say about it. It's just sort of the way I've lived my life."

After reading the page that contained the target's answers, participants were asked to rate 30 evaluative statements about the target. Participants rated each item on a *Disagree* [to] *Agree* [scale]. These items . . . power, intelligence, likeability, morality, quality as a date, quality as a spouse, physical appeal, and friendship [comprised] four evaluative factors: *values . . . , peer popularity . . . , power/success . . . , and intelligence. . . .*

Results

. . . [A statistical technique, called multiple regression was used to analyse the results.]

In the values domain, there was a main effect of number of sexual partners. . . . Targets with more partners were evaluated more negatively. . . . There was no main effect of target sex and no . . . interaction [of number of sexual partners and target sex.]

In the domain of peer popularity, there was a main effect of number of sexual partners. . . . Targets with more partners were evaluated more negatively. . . . There was no main effect of target sex and no . . . interaction [of number of sexual partners and target sex].

In the domain of power/success, there were no main effects of target sex or number of sexual partners, although there was a tendency for participants to evaluate targets with many partners more negatively. . . . There was no . . . interaction [of number of sexual partners and target sex].

In the domain of intelligence, again there was a main effect of number of sexual partners. . . . Targets with more partners were evaluated more negatively. . . . There was no . . . interaction [of number of sexual partners and target sex].

Discussion

To date, there has been little evidence that women are evaluated more negatively than men for having many sexual partners. However, if the double standard exists, methodological limitations of previous research may have prevented it from emerging clearly. In the present research, we sought to provide a rigorous test of whether or not the sexual double standard exists by rectifying methodological limitations of previous studies. Our data reveal virtually no evidence of a traditional, or "strong," sexual double standard. . . .

These results . . . suggest that although the double standard may not operate in overall evaluations of persons, it may play a role in shaping perceptions of sexually active people in specific domains. Concerning the domain of intelligence, for example, engaging in frequent casual sex may not be a "smart" thing to do in light of the dangers of sexually transmitted diseases (especially AIDS). . . .

These results suggest that even after addressing some of the methodological limitations of previous research, traditional accounts of the sexual double standard do not appear to characterize the manner in which sexually active men and women are evaluated. This raises the question of whether the sexual double standard is more a cultural illusion than an actual phenomenon. If the double standard does not accurately characterize the manner in which people evaluate sexually active others, why does belief in it persist?

One possibility is that people are sensitive to our culture's "sexual lexicon." Many writers have observed that there are more slang terms in our language that degrade sexually active women than sexually active men. On the basis of such observations, people may conclude that a sexual double standard exists. However, one must be cautious when citing sexual slang as evidence of a double standard. It may be more valuable to consider the relative frequency of the use of slang terms than to consider solely the number of slang terms that exist. When Milhausen and Herold (2001) analyzed the frequency of sexual slang used to describe men and women in actual discourse, they found that the majority of men and women used negative terms to describe both sexually experienced men *and* women. They reported that a minority of men (25%) and women (8%) actually used words such as "stud" to describe sexually active men. Moreover, sexually active men were frequently described with words that fall into the category of *sexual predator* (e.g., "womanizer") or *promiscuous* (e.g., "slut," "dirty"). So although a difference exists in the *number* of sexual slang terms to describe men and women, it is not nearly analogous to the difference in the frequency of their *use* for men and women.

The confirmation bias may also help to explain why people believe that the sexual double standard exists. Confirmation bias refers to a type of selective thinking in which one tends to notice evidence that confirms one's

beliefs and to ignore or undervalue evidence that contradicts one's beliefs. Confirmation biases may lead people to notice cases that are consistent with the double standard (e.g., a woman being referred to as a "slut") and fail to notice cases inconsistent with the double standard (e.g., a man being referred to as a "whore"). Because the vast majority of people believe that a sexual double standard exists, it is likely that people will process social information that seemingly corroborates the sexual double standard and will ignore information that refutes it. In short, although men and women may have an equal probability of being derogated (or rewarded) for having had many sexual partners, people may tend to notice only the instances in which women are derogated and men are rewarded. Attending to cases that are consistent with the double standard while ignoring cases inconsistent with it may create the illusion that the sexual double standard is more pervasive than it really is.

Limitations of the Present Study

Although we sought to correct some limitations of past research, other limitations remain. First, the statistical power of the student sample was low because of the relatively small sample size. . . .

Second, the results reported here may not generalize to populations outside of Western culture. Culture can be a powerful sculptor of sexual attitudes and behavior; the double standard may exist in one culture, but be absent from another. For instance, a review of the anthropological literature on sex and sexuality in Africa reveals much evidence of a double standard in African culture.

Third, this study, like much previous research, employs an experimental person perception paradigm. Studying the double standard in more naturalistic settings may reveal dynamics not otherwise tapped by more artificial methodologies. For example, observing "hot spots" where social interactions are possibly centered on sex (e.g., bars, locker rooms) may offer insight to the kinds of attitudes expressed concerning the sexual activity of men and women.

Finally, the present research is relatively atheoretical, partly because we believe that it is necessary to document the phenomenon of the double standard systematically (if it exists) before bringing theoretical perspectives to bear on it. Nonetheless, there may be theoretical perspectives that would help guide us in a more effective search for this phenomenon. For example, social psychological theory suggests that people tend to conform to social norms in the presence of others. Because there are strong gender norms concerning the appropriate sexual behavior of men and women, people may behave in accordance with these norms in social situations. Our study, like other studies on the double standard, only focused on individuals in non-group situations. Social psychological theory suggests that social interaction in group contexts may be a necessary precondition for the emergence of the double standard.

Conclusions

In an effort to denounce the sexual double standard, contemporary authors, critics, and the media may actually be *perpetuating* it by unintentionally providing confirming evidence for the double standard while ignoring disconfirming evidence. Most accounts from these sources cite numerous cases of women being derogated for sexual activity, perhaps in an effort to elicit empathy from the audience. Empathy is a commendable (and desirable) goal, but these writings may also serve to embed the double standard in our collective conscious. Suggesting that a societal double standard is the basis of the derogation of women shifts focus away from those who are truly at fault—those who are engaging in or permitting sexual harassment and other forms of derogation.

In closing, we believe that it may be beneficial to shift the emphasis of sexual double standard research from the question of *whether* the double standard exists to *why* the double standard appears to be such a pervasive phenomenon when it really is not. By addressing this question, future researchers should be able to elucidate the disparity between popular intuitions and the research literature and open doors to novel avenues for our understanding of attitudes toward sexuality.

References

Garcia, L. T. (1982). Sex-role orientation and stereotypes about male-female sexuality. *Sex Roles, 8,* 863–876.

Gentry, M. (1998). The sexual double standard. The influence of number of relationships and level of sexual activity on judgments of women and men. *Psychology of Women Quarterly, 22,* 505–511.

Milhausen, R. R., & Herold, E. S. (1999). Does the sexual double standard still exist? Perceptions of university women. *Journal of Sex Research, 36,* 361–368.

Milhausen, R. R., & Herold, E. S. (2001). Reconceptualizing the sexual double standard. *Journal of Psychology and Human Sexuality, 13,* 63–83.

O'Sullivan, L. F. (1995). Less is more: The effects of sexual experience on judgments of men's and women's personality characteristics and relationship desirability. *Sex Roles, 33,* 159–181.

Sprecher, S., McKinney, K., Walsh, R., & Anderson, C. (1988). A revision of the Reiss Premarital Sexual Permissiveness Scale. *Journal of Marriage and the Family, 50,* 821–828.

Tanenbaum, L. (2000). *Slut!* New York: Harper Collins.

MICHAEL J. MARKS is an associate professor in the Department of Psychology at New Mexico State University.

R. CHRIS FRALEY is an associate professor of psychology at the University of Illinois at Urbana-Champaign.

Gail Collins

 **NO**

The Decline of the Double Standard

"They Think I'm a Good Girl."

In 1968 the *New York Times* took note of a startling new trend: "cohabiting." A feature story introduced readers to several couples, mainly New York City college students, who were living together without the benefit of a marriage license. Everyone's identity was disguised in deference to the controversial nature of the subject. "Joan," whose parents believed she was rooming with a girlfriend, said even the mailman was conspiring with her to hide the truth from her family. "It's funny . . . my parents have a lot of confidence in me. They think I'm a good girl," said Joan, who clearly believed that if her parents got a load of her real roommate, "Charles," they might change their minds.

The lead anecdote, however, belonged to "Peter" and "Susan," who were part of a youthful counterculture that the *Times* was still slowly introducing to its readers. The couple was sharing a four-room apartment with "no bed in the bedroom—just six mattresses for their use and that of fellow students who need a place to sleep." And the paper reported that although Peter and Susan had been together for two years, they "had no plans for a wedding because they regard marriage as 'too serious a step.'" Susan was a student at Barnard College, which generally prohibited off-campus living arrangements. But she had gotten around the rule by having a friend tell the college employment bureau she wanted to hire Susan as a live-in nanny.

That was a little too much detail, as it turned out. It didn't take the Barnard administration long to figure out that "Susan" was actually Linda LeClair, a 20-year-old sophomore. When confronted, LeClair admitted she had deceived the housing administrator and broken school regulations. Rather than apologizing, she and her boyfriend, Peter Behr, a junior at Columbia, began leafleting the campus, asking students to demand changes in the rules. Endless debate and newspaper headlines ensued. A student-faculty committee was called to consider the case. After five hours of deliberation, the committee announced that as punishment for deceiving the administration about where she lived, LeClair would be "denied the privilege of using the following college facilities: the snack bar, the cafeteria, and the James Room," a student lounge.

A snack-bar ban was clearly not the kind of penalty likely to deter future cohabitation, and the alumnae wrote to complain. Barnard's president, Martha Peterson, seemed torn between respecting the committee's decision and showing the college's donors that she was not going to let the matter drop. So she sent an open letter to LeClair, asking her opinion on "the importance of integrity among individuals in the college" and "the importance of respect for regularized procedures." She also wanted a letter from LeClair's parents stating whether they approved of their daughter's behavior. The result of all this was another *Times* story, titled "Father Despairs of Barnard Daughter," and an editorial noting that Barnard could have saved itself a lot of grief "by letting sleeping coeds lie."

By May, Peterson was hinting very strongly that Linda LeClair ought to go away (". . . no useful purpose can be served by your continued enrollment in Barnard College"). Yet she insisted that the final judgment would be based neither on sex nor on failure to follow procedures, but on the final grades of a student who, it appeared, had been spending more time passing out leaflets than attending classes. The *Times*, which had been covering the story as if it involved the threat of nuclear war, tracked down LeClair among "a student group flying paper airplanes on the Columbia campus" and found her rather indifferent to her future as an undergraduate. The next time she made an appearance in the paper would be as one of hundreds of students arrested during sit-ins and protests over Columbia's plan to build a gym in Harlem. Ultimately, LeClair dropped out at the end of the semester, went off with Peter Behr to live in a commune in Vermont, hitchhiked to the West Coast, and returned to New York so her boyfriend could refuse induction into the army. On her arrival, LeClair told a *Times* reporter that she had a certain sympathy for President Peterson. "She is aware . . . that recognizing sexual intercourse would cause embarrassment to the ladies that give money to the college."

"... While I Wasn't Allowed Out After Nine Thirty."

Of all the social uprisings of the late 1960s and early 1970s, none was more popular than the sexual revolution. And while men took an enthusiastic part, it was basically a story about women. Most of the world had always operated under a double standard in which girls were supposed to remain chaste until marriage while boys were allowed—sometimes encouraged—to press for whatever sex they could get. But Linda LeClair's generation had learned from the civil rights movement that just because something had always been the rule did not mean it was right—particularly if that rule gave some people more privileges than others. Even the authority figures had lost some of their confidence in the old morality. The Barnard administration, while trying to get a handle on the LeClair situation, skirted any suggestion that it was wrong for a young woman to shack up with a man she did not intend to marry. Instead, President Peterson focused on the fact that LeClair had lied about where she was living. Even in 1968, everyone on campus tended to agree that lying was bad.

Colleges had always given their unspoken endorsement to the double standard by setting far stricter regulations in girls' dormitories. In her precohabitation days, LeClair would get back to her room in time for curfew, then look out the window to watch her boyfriend walking away. "I can still see the image," she said recently, "of him going across Broadway to do whatever the heck he wanted to do while I wasn't allowed out after nine thirty at night." It was a tradition as old as women's higher education. But by the late 1960s, Barnard was hardly the only college on the defensive. Within a few years, many schools were in full-scale retreat. When Nora Ephron returned to Wellesley for the tenth reunion of the Class of 1962, she heard that one of her old classmates had gone into a dormitory bathroom and seen "a boy and a girl taking a shower together." No one, Ephron said, could believe it. "Ten years ago we were allowed to have men in the rooms on Sunday afternoons only, on the condition the door be left fourteen inches ajar." And Anne Wallach, visiting her daughter at Antioch, prided herself on not reacting when she passed a naked man on her way to Alison's room.

"... The Technical Virgins Association."

The female warriors of the sexual revolution had been born into a world where the importance of remaining a virgin until marriage was seldom questioned. Nothing

was worse than being suspected of casual sleeping around. Ellen Miller, who grew up in Kentucky, remembers that adults were extremely tolerant of their children smoking and that parents routinely chaperoned parties in which underage boys and girls drank alcohol. But permissiveness went only so far. Nobody wanted to hang out with a girl who had "a reputation," Miller said. "I guess the social mores accepted smoking, accepted drinking, but did not accept early sex."

There were, of course, many women who had clear-cut religious reasons for avoiding sex outside wedlock. But for a great many others, virginity had become a social convention without any real ethical roots. Rather, they saw it as a commodity that made women more valuable in the marriage market, and they tried to divert their boyfriends into sexual activity that would leave them satisfied without risking penetration. "We called it the TVA—the Technical Virgins Association," said one coed of the mid-'60s. The task was made all the more challenging because many women of the era found oral sex disgusting. "Now don't turn up your nose and make that ugly face," warned the author of *The Sensuous Woman* in 1969 before embarking on a discussion of oral sex.

The country had been wedded to the old Victorian belief that women had a much lower sex drive than men and that women were the ones responsible for drawing the line. For a boy, manliness meant pressing his dates to go farther, ever farther. It was the girl's duty to call a halt. "A man will go as far as a woman will let him. The girl has to set the standard," a college student told George Gallup. It was the girl who had to decide whether French-kissing on the second date was too fast, how much touching could take place and where. Advice columnists doled out leaflets with titles such as "Necking and Petting and How Far to Go," and boys reported to their friends whether they had gotten to second base or third.

If a home run had been hit, a gentleman never told—unless, of course, the girl in question had a reputation and was therefore fair game. Girls with reputations got asked out on dates for only "one thing," and most people believed they forfeited their chance of a good marriage. In the movies, unmarried women who were sexually active were punished with a life of lonely solitude or sudden death. (Elizabeth Taylor won the 1960 best actress award for *BUtterfield 8*, in which she played a "party girl" whose decision to reform wasn't enough to save her from a fatal car crash.) The most popular actress of the early 1960s was Doris Day, who specialized in playing a working woman protecting her virtue against handsome men who schemed to deflower her. Since Day was well into her 30s at the time, the films drove home the point that a woman was never too old to resist extramarital sex.

The virginity rule was a reason for early marriage—any delay would increase the chances of straying from the path of virtue. And it was an excellent argument against training women for serious careers. If unmarried women—even those as old as Doris Day—were expected to avoid sex, and if married women were not supposed to work, pursuing a career became something very close to taking the veil.

"... A Lot More Fun by the Dozen."

In 1961 *Ladies' Home Journal* offered its readers an essay that asked, "Is the Double Standard Out of Date?" In it, writer Betsy Marvin McKinney answered her own question with a definite no. Sex for the sake of sex, without the chance of procreation, could be satisfying for a man, she conceded. His only job, after all, was to release some sperm. But a woman was built to have babies, and for her, sex for pleasure alone was far more frustrating than simply remaining chaste. Doris Day knew what she was doing, and once women started behaving like men in the bedroom, life tilted out of balance. "The end of the world would come as surely as atomic warfare could bring it," McKinney warned grimly.

One reader who came away less than convinced was Helen Gurley Brown, an ad-agency executive in her late 30s who had worked her way up from typist to secretary to a high-salaried copywriter in Los Angeles, all the while sleeping with whatever men took her fancy. She paid her own way in the world, supporting her widowed mother and disabled sister back in Little Rock and plunking down cash for an expensive, if used, Mercedes-Benz. That car impressed David Brown, a film producer who had been burned in the past by extravagant women who expected him to pay the bills. They married, and Brown urged his new wife to write an advice book for young women on how to live a modern single life. McKinney's article got Gurley Brown focused, and her response, *Sex and the Single Girl,* was published in 1962. It became a bestseller "that torpedoed the myth that a girl must be married to enjoy a satisfying life," as the cover bragged in bright yellow letters.

It also became one of those books that define an era. Whether Gurley Brown converted large numbers of people to a new way of thinking or simply announced a change that was already well under way, she captured the mood of the moment. Many American women were beginning to realize that they might be fated to be single for a long time, whether they liked it or not. Those who left school without a mate found the demographics stacked against them. Tradition dictated that they marry a man somewhat older than they were, which meant searching among the scanty population born during the war or competing with younger girls for the first wave of male baby boomers. Georgia Panter, who began a career as a stewardess at 23, said that even a job that put her in constant contact with planes full of businessmen didn't produce many prospects: "It was rare that I met single men." Gurley Brown suggested that her readers should just enjoy affairs with other people's husbands: "The statistics merely state that there are not enough *marriageable* men to go around. Nobody said a word about a shortage of *men.*"

Sex and the Single Girl announced that the single woman, "far from being a creature to be pitied and patronized, is emerging as the newest glamour girl of our times." Unlike her married sisters, Gurley Brown declared breezily, the single woman got to spend her life in the interesting public world of men. She could have almost all the fruits of marriage—financial security, a nice home in which to entertain, an active social life. Children could be put off till later or borrowed for the occasional day from a harried friend or relative. "Her world is a far more colorful world than the one of PTA, Dr. Spock, and a jammed clothes dryer," Gurley Brown declared. It was the polar opposite of the conviction that George Gallup brought back from his surveys—that married women were much happier than their single sisters.

The section of the book that really caused a stir was the one in which Brown gave her single girl the right to extramarital sex—lots of extramarital sex. ("You do need a man of course every step of the way, and they are often cheaper emotionally and a lot more fun by the dozen.") For the new breed of single girl, sex was simply another part of her full, exciting life, just like dinner parties and a well-decorated apartment. It was pretty much the same game plan that *Playboy* had been urging on its male readers with so much success and profitability—except that *Sex and the Single Girl,* with a keen eye to its audience, also promised that at the end of all this glamorous independence, there would still probably be a husband. A *better* husband, in fact. Gurley Brown warned the young women of the 1960s that the men who were real catches were not looking for innocence and submission anymore; they wanted a wife who was both interesting and capable of pulling in a good paycheck. She caught her "brainy, charming, and sexy" movie producer because she had spent seventeen years becoming the kind of woman a rich, fascinating man would want to live with. "And when he finally walked into my life I was just worldly enough, relaxed enough, financially secure enough . . . and adorned with enough glitter to attract him."

"We Weren't of the Mind-Set of Saving It for the Husbands Anymore."

The sexual revolution hit hardest and fastest in big cities and in campus communities. But no one who read a newspaper or went to the movies could miss that something new was going on. A series of court decisions had made it far more difficult to ban pornography of any stripe, and the nation's ever-vigilant marketing community responded by churning out sexually explicit movies, books, magazines, and plays. On Broadway, audiences poured in to see the musical *Hair*, which featured onstage nudity and a cast that cheerfully sang, "Masturbation can be fun." A well-known designer introduced a topless women's swimsuit, and although only a few thousand customers actually bought one, the publicity and jokes made it seem as if everybody was going to the beach clad in just a bikini bottom. A fad for topless dancers in bars started in San Francisco, and everyone knew that at the fashionable Playboy Clubs, drinks were served by those glamorous "Bunnies" in their scanty costumes. (Before her incarnation as a feminist leader, Gloria Steinem was famous for her article "I Was a Playboy Bunny," in which she went under cover to discover that the costumes were extremely uncomfortable, the pay low, and the turnover rapid.)

There was certainly a lot more talk about sex, but it's hard to tell how much of it translated into real-world activity. Women had never shared all that much information about their sexual behavior, even with friends. Marie Monsky, who was living on her own in Manhattan and working her way through night school in the early 1960s, hung out with a fairly sophisticated crowd. But she still doesn't remember having a frank discussion about sexual experience. "There was a line you never crossed," she said. "It was a privacy issue." So it's possible that what looked like a great deal of sexual freedom was actually just a great deal more sexual frankness.

Alfred Kinsey had stunned the nation in 1953 with his famous study that found half of American women had had sex before they were married. (The study was limited to white women—Kinsey, like most of the nation, seemed indifferent to what African-Americans, Hispanics, Asians, or other minorities were doing with their private lives.) His findings were denounced as absurd, unbelievable, and morally suspect—the American Medical Association accused him of setting off a "wave of sex hysteria," and given the fact that Kinsey interviewed only people who had volunteered to talk about the most private aspects

of their lives, there was reason to question whether the results were representative of the population as a whole. But his conclusions about women and premarital sex were probably close to the mark. Most of the sexually active single women he found had slept with the men they believed would be their future husbands, something that had always been common, if not readily admitted. (As far back as 1695, a minister visiting New York wrote home that young people there seldom married until "a great belly puts it so forward that they must either submit to that, or to shame and disgrace.")

But as the '60s rolled along, it seemed clear that quite a few respectable middle-class young women had ditched the double standard completely. And the respectable middle-class young men responded enthusiastically. "There was a tremendous amount of sex," said Barbara Arnold, who was a nursing student at the University of Bridgeport. "There was a tremendous amount of, literally, free love. There were just orgies all over the place. . . . It was a very crazy time, it really was." Pam Andrews—whose mother, Lillian, was one of the post-war housewives who enjoyed the new suburbs so much—arrived at Wellesley in 1968 and quickly went to a Planned Parenthood clinic and got a diaphragm. "I think I was one of the early ones," she said. But her classmates soon caught up with her, and when she transferred to the University of Wisconsin in 1970, Andrews found that the spirit of free love was completely in bloom. "You could sleep with everybody. Everybody was very open. It was such an unreal world." Sex in those days, she remembered, "was nothing special—just another way to get to know somebody."

In 1972 a survey of eight colleges found that less than a quarter of the women were still virgins in their junior year—the same proportion as men. "We weren't of the mind-set of saving it for the husbands anymore," said Tawana Hinton, who started college in 1970. "You know, it's like, if it feels good, do it. That was the rule. I don't have to be madly in love. It's not all about love; it's really just . . . no big deal. Pretty much everybody was on the Pill . . . and STDs and HIV wasn't of concern. Your only concern back then was, don't get pregnant."

"I Probably Wouldn't Have Done This if It Weren't for the Pill."

The young Americans who took part in the sexual revolution were living at a very particular moment in time, a brief window in which having sex with multiple partners posed very little physical peril. For most of human history, syphilis had been a scourge, and a good deal of the Victorian hysteria about sex—and prostitution in particular—had to do with women's fear that their husbands would stray and infect them with an incurable disease that could put them in peril of sterility, insanity, and death. Parents who feared their children would not be impressed by the moral arguments against premarital sex had an excellent follow-up: the Victorian version of sex education involved lantern shows of pictures of the grisly effects of syphilis. Then penicillin, which became widely available during World War II, provided a cure. By the 1960s sexually transmitted diseases were being treated like a joke by middle-class people who, as the decade went on, began experimenting with group sex, wife-swapping, and other kinds of behavior that would have been regarded as near suicidal by earlier generations.

And then there was the birth control pill, or—as the media called it in deference to its awesome powers—the Pill. The *Times,* in its survey of college cohabitation, noted that all the female roommates described in the story were taking it. "I probably wouldn't have done this if it weren't for the Pill," said Joan, the student who wistfully noted that her parents still thought she was a good girl. The older generation tended to agree with Joan—they blamed the birth control pill for what they saw as a frightening upsurge in premarital sex. "I think that's when morals started to deteriorate, because women weren't afraid they were going to get pregnant anymore, so why not?" said Louise Meyer in Wyoming. Her youngest daughter, who was born in 1968, wound up living with her future husband before they were married, she noted. It was something she felt her older girls, who had been born in the early '50s, "would never have done."

The fact that the birth control pill had been invented did not necessarily mean a woman could get it. In 1960, the year the Pill went on sale, thirty states had laws restricting the sale or advertising of virtually anything related to birth control. The most draconian was in Connecticut, where anyone convicted of using, buying, or helping someone to acquire a birth control device could be fined or sentenced to up to a year in prison. The law was not one of those moldy pieces of antique legislation that the lawmakers had simply forgotten to repeal. Margaret Sanger, the birth control pioneer, had launched an attempt to eliminate it in 1923, and a bill to modify or repeal it had come up continually ever since. "It is a ridiculous and unenforceable law," complained a state senator from Greenwich in 1953, one of the few years in which advocates for change ever managed to get as far as a full debate. (The repeal bill was defeated on a voice vote by what the *Times* reported as an "overwhelming" majority.)

The law did not have much effect on middle-class married women, who could quietly get a prescription from the family doctor. But anyone who needed to go to a clinic—poor women or unmarried women seeking anonymity—was out of luck. Connecticut's Planned Parenthood League ran a van service transporting women in need of birth control pills across the state line to clinics in Rhode Island or New York. (Driving to Massachusetts would have been no help for unmarried women, since the law there barred anyone—even doctors—from helping them obtain contraceptives.) In 1958 the head of Connecticut Planned Parenthood, Estelle Griswold, designed a plan of attack. Griswold, a gray-haired, middle-aged woman of eminent respectability and an equal amount of feistiness, invited Dr. Charles Lee Buxton, the chairman of Yale Medical School's Department of Obstetrics, and Fowler Harper, a Yale law professor, to her home for cocktails. "Her martinis were always notorious," said Catherine Roraback, a New Haven attorney. Soon after, Harper called Roraback and asked her to join the team that was going to challenge the law.

"Are you calling me as an attorney or a single woman?" asked Roraback.

Harper laughed and acknowledged that having a counsel who represented the people who suffered most under the Connecticut law would be a fine thing.

"Well, I'm not taking it," rejoined Roraback, who did not want to be a token. But she added quickly, "I'll do it as an attorney."

Harper was both a Yale professor and a famous free-speech advocate who had been an outspoken critic of the anti-Communist witch hunts of Senator Joseph McCarthy and his followers. Roraback had defended some of the victims of McCarthyism for little or no fee, and it was for that reason that Harper wanted to invite her into what everyone believed might be a history-making, career-building case.

"I think you deserve something like this," he said.

They brought their first case on behalf of a group of clients that included Dr. Buxton, who argued that he was being denied his right to practice medicine; a woman who had been warned that she would die from another pregnancy; and a couple who had had three disabled children. The case went up to the Supreme Court, which rejected it on the grounds that the laws were not actually being enforced.

That was true only if you were a middle-class woman with a private physician. "All of us knew—and Lee Buxton especially knew—that poor women couldn't get contraceptive advice," said Roraback. The last family-planning clinic had closed long ago, and hospitals did not deal in birth control because they knew they would be prosecuted. But because there were no clinics to prosecute, there were no plaintiffs who had standing to bring a case. A Catch-22.

So Griswold and Buxton opened a clinic. The Connecticut Planned Parenthood Center of New Haven immediately attracted customers, even though the women were warned that the police might arrive at any moment. "If they do that, we'll just sit down here until we get the information we came for," replied one patient. But Roraback was worried that the women's privacy might be compromised during a raid. She went to see the local prosecutor and arranged for three volunteer clinic patients to testify that they had indeed received contraceptives. Griswold and Buxton were given the choice of appearing at the police station on their own or being dramatically arrested, handcuffed, and hauled off before the TV cameras. Representatives of an older, more discreet generation, they opted for the police station. They were fined $100—and given the legal grounding they needed to go to court to challenge the law.

In 1965 the Supreme Court ruled 7 to 2 that Connecticut's law violated married couples' constitutional rights, and in 1972 the Court closed the circle by tossing out the Massachusetts law as well, making it clear that the right to use birth control belonged to everyone, not just to married couples. (In 1973, in the ultimate American benediction, the Internal Revenue Service declared that the Pill was a tax-deductible medicine.) All around the nation, women lined up to get prescriptions. "We had an option, so you took it," said June LaValleur, who had always felt using a diaphragm "kind of broke up the spontaneity of things."

Unmarried women who did not have a personal physician—or whose family doctor might disapprove—continued to have a harder time, especially if they were not living in big cities with liberal attitudes toward sex. In the 1960s, in most states, the age of adulthood was 21, and it was illegal for a doctor to prescribe birth control to an unmarried woman under that age without a parent's consent. It was not until the 1970s that Congress, embarrassed by the fact that young men of 18 were being sent off to the war in Vietnam while they were still legally children, passed the Twenty-sixth Amendment, which reduced the age of majority to 18. Until then, even unmarried 20-year-olds generally had to claim they were engaged and on the verge of marriage to cadge a birth control prescription from a physician.

College health services slowly began prescribing birth control pills for students who wanted them, and some parents made sure their children arrived on campus with a supply already in hand. When Tawana Hinton started college in 1970, her mother marched her off to the gynecologist. "It was like, 'You will go to college on the Pill,'" Hinton recalled. "And I did."

Planned Parenthood clinics were another crucial source—Alison Foster remembered that her boarding school ferried interested students to the nearest clinic. "And when I was in college, it was like candy," she said. "You just went to the health center and they gave them to you." But only 4 percent of the women who were taking the Pill in 1969 got it through Planned Parenthood, and even those who had the name of a sympathetic doctor were sometimes too embarrassed to follow through. Wendy Woythaler got the Pill while she was at Mount Holyoke in the late '60s, and when she looks back, she remembers searching for an office down a dark alley: "It was probably a fine, upstanding gynecologist somewhere in town. But when you're thinking, 'I'm not supposed to be doing this', it feels like you're going down a dark alley."

"There was a stigma attached to it if you weren't married," said Maria K. "I didn't want to go to the drugstore and buy birth control pills because everybody would know I was having sex. Oh, heavens!"

"Whores Don't Get Pregnant."

For every Linda LeClair, who seemed to have her finger right on the '60s zeitgeist, there were many more young women like Maria K. Maria—whose mother had wound up cooking in a home for elderly women when her father died—walked into the new morality without the sophistication to protect herself from its consequences. She got the news she was pregnant while she was working as a secretary at a local college in a small town in upstate New York. "At that time, if you got pregnant, you either got married or you went away and came back unpregnant," she said.

In 1967, when Maria had her child, the idea that an unmarried woman would simply raise a baby herself was almost unheard-of, particularly in small towns. Most girls just married the father. Others got abortions or went off to homes for unwed mothers, where they gave the baby up for adoption and returned from what was generally described as a long stay with an out-of-town relative. Judy Riff remembered that one of her friends at their all-girls Catholic college got pregnant her sophomore year, "and one minute she was there and the next minute she was gone. It was like she was never there. . . . I don't know what happened to her." The very idea of having a baby out of wedlock "was just so awful. . .," Riff said, "that probably would have to be the worst thing that could have happened to any of us."

Most women had no idea how to obtain an abortion, which was illegal everywhere until the late 1960s. Maria, who was Catholic, never considered the option. Consulting her parish priest, she went to a home for unwed mothers in a nearby city. She was interviewed on arrival by a "kind, compassionate, and practical" woman who told her that the baby's chances of being adopted would be low. The man who fathered Maria's baby was blind, and at a time when adoptive parents had a large supply of illegitimate babies to choose from, any hint of a possible imperfection could be disqualifying. "She said even though it couldn't be genetically passed on to my son, that he would be very difficult to adopt if it was known that one of his parents was not sighted. And she told me that I seemed like a nice girl and she believed . . . that I would make a good mother."

When Maria decided to keep her son, her mother told her that a baby is always a wonderful thing and behaved "like an angel," her daughter recalled. But otherwise, "I became an outcast." She had trouble finding a landlord who would rent to an unmarried mother, and she lost her job. "I think they probably thought I was a bad example in the college atmosphere and so forth." And far worse trouble was around the corner. "About a year and a half later, I was pregnant again. And I was really up a creek."

When she got the news, Maria broke down in the doctor's office. "Everybody's going to think that I'm a whore," she cried.

"Whores don't get pregnant," the doctor said. "They're smarter than that."

"Remember, All of Us Had Taken the Pill."

The Pill had been developed by Dr. Gregory Pincus, a biologist recruited by Margaret Sanger, who was more successful in revolutionizing medical contraception than she was in lobbying the Connecticut state legislature. It posed unique questions when it came to safety. Unlike most medication, it was intended to be taken over long periods of time by healthy women. Risks that might seem acceptable if you were, say, controlling diabetes loomed a lot larger if there was no disease to cure. Cases of blood clotting were reported, and women began to worry that they were being put at risk of heart attacks or strokes. The Food and Drug Administration began research, and in 1970 a Senate committee headed by Gaylord Nelson of Wisconsin held hearings on the Pill's safety. Some women

immediately noticed that all the senators doing the investigating were male—no small surprise, since 99 percent of the Senate was of one gender and Margaret Chase Smith couldn't be everywhere. But all the people invited to speak were men as well. Barbara Seaman, the author of the powerful book *The Doctors' Case Against the Pill,* had not been invited. There were no women scientists or consumers who had experienced bad effects. "Remember, all of us had taken the Pill, so we were there as activists, but also as concerned women," said Alice Wolfson, who led a protest that disrupted the proceedings.

The FDA eventually ordered that birth control pills come with an insert describing possible health risks, and a Gallup survey found that 18 percent of those who had been taking the Pill stopped. Many turned to intrauterine devices (IUDs)—until the most popular model, known as the Dalkon Shield, had to be pulled from the market due to questions about its own safety. Meanwhile, researchers were discovering that the Pill was far stronger than necessary. Gradually, the amount of estrogen dropped to less than a third of what was in the earliest versions, and progesterone to less than a tenth. The controversy over the Pill died away, but it turned out to be only the first shot in what would become a long-running feud between American women and the traditional medical community.

For generations, women had been American doctors' best clients and abused guinea pigs. When physicians learned how to use a hypodermic syringe in the mid-nineteenth century, one of the first things they did was to inject opium or morphine into their patients, sometimes on a daily basis, creating legions of addicted housewives. Surgeons removed reproductive organs in women who showed signs of promiscuity or masturbation, and castrated more than 100,000 around the turn of the century. And although those abuses were long over by the 1960s, there was still a widespread presumption that a woman's uterus became useless once she passed childbearing age and should be removed—often along with her ovaries—for minor problems or as a precaution against disease developing in the future. When a doctor discovered a lump in a patient's breast, it was standard procedure to have the woman sign a form consenting to have the entire breast removed even before the biopsy was performed. (Susan Ford, whose mother, Betty, saved many American women's lives by being open about her mastectomy when she was first lady, noted that in those days, the patient woke up to discover she "either had a Band-Aid or no breast.")

Doctors, who were overwhelmingly male, had an authoritarian attitude toward all patients in the postwar era, but they saw more women, and they were particularly inclined to treat female patients as children who panicked easily and were better off knowing as little as possible. When 23-year-old Barbara Winslow of Seattle found a lump in her breast, she and her husband went to a doctor. He told them that he would do a biopsy and that if it proved malignant, he would immediately perform a complete mastectomy. He then handed a consent form to her husband to sign. When Winslow asked why she was not the one asked to give permission, the doctor said, "Because women are too emotionally and irrationally tied to their breasts." Nora Ephron wrote that it seemed every week brought "a new gynecological atrocity tale. A friend who specifically asks not to be sedated during childbirth is sedated. Another friend who has a simple infection is treated instead for gonorrhea, and develops a serious infection as a side effect of penicillin. Another woman tells of going to see her doctor one month after he has delivered her first child, a deformed baby, born dead. His first question: 'Why haven't you been to see me in two years?'"

In 1969 a small group of women in Boston decided to get together and share their "feelings of frustration and anger toward . . . doctors who were condescending, paternalistic, judgmental, and noninformative." As time went on, the group felt it was on to something worth sharing. The members created a course on women and their bodies that in turn became the basis for *Our Bodies, Ourselves,* a book that talked simply and explicitly about sex, birth control, venereal disease, lesbianism, childbirth, and menopause. Lessons on anatomy and basic biology were interspersed with personal testimony, offering the reader the comforting sense that whatever she was feeling or was worried about had happened to somebody else before. "I will tell you that a book we all had was *Our Bodies, Ourselves,*" said Kathy Hinder-hofer, who went to college in the early '70s. "You had to have that." Other women started medical self-help projects, some focusing on informal classes that trained students in basics such as breast examinations, and others evolving into full-blown medical clinics. (A few went over the deep end and began urging women to extract their monthly menstrual flow and perform do-it-yourself abortions with a syringe.) By 1975 nearly two thousand projects were scattered across the United States.

"It Is as Easy as Being the Log Itself."

The sexual revolution was about more than whether women should be able to feel as free as men to have sex before marriage. It was also about whether women—single or married—had as much right to *enjoy* sex. Most postwar manuals on how couples could improve their physical relationship centered on the man. The woman's

role pretty much involved lying there. The experts did not generally go as far as the authors of *Modern Woman: The Lost Sex,* an influential postwar diatribe against the nontraditional female that decreed that for a woman, having sex was "not as easy as rolling off a log. . . . It is easier. It is as easy as being the log itself." But they almost all seemed to disapprove of too much aggressive activity on her part. And there was a virtual consensus that women should attain satisfaction from conventional penetration.

Many women had little information about what went on in other people's bedrooms. The popular magazines were vague, and what specifics they did impart were about how to make husbands happy, not how to give wives sexual satisfaction. In a 1957 article called "How to Love Your Husband" in *Coronet,* for instance, author Hannah Lees approvingly described an interview with an "unselfish" wife who admitted, in the language of the era, to faking orgasms:

> "I have never had that feeling," she said, "that wild emotion that many other women have. But my husband, he expects it. I love him. So I try to make him happy." She spread her hands and shrugged, and her face was soft and tender. . . . Maybe her husband was missing something by not having a wife who could match his strong physical need with hers. But I had an idea it made no difference.

Even Helen Gurley Brown, so eager to encourage her readers to have affairs, was silent about what a single girl should do if she didn't enjoy the sex—except to suggest seeing a psychiatrist. And less than half of married women and 38 percent of single women said they talked frankly about sex with their friends or female relatives, according to that famous Gallup survey. Even if they did share confidences, what they learned could often be misleading. Jane Alpert, a high school student in the early '60s, was part of a cool bohemian crowd in Queens. Her role model, Beatrice, "the first girl I knew who claimed not to be a virgin," bragged to Alpert that she had had vaginal orgasms, "which were the best kind."

While their mothers had not necessarily been reared to expect real physical pleasure from lovemaking, the postwar generation wanted intimacy and partnership in every aspect of marriage. Many women who failed to get much pleasure themselves found solace in creating the illusion of success by writhing, moaning, and simulating orgasm. (Robin Morgan said that when she confessed to her husband that she often faked orgasm with him, she was convinced "I was the only woman in the world sick enough to have done this.") It was no wonder that experts suspected more than half of American women were "frigid."

Many women got reeducated by *Human Sexual Response*. The book, which was published in 1966 by William Masters and Virginia Johnson, was the product of eleven years of direct laboratory observation of nearly seven hundred people who had volunteered to have sex while the authors ran cameras and measured their heart and brain activity. Masters and Johnson found, among many, many other things, that women were capable of more intense and enduring sexual response than men, and that, contrary to what Jane Alpert's best friend told her, vaginal orgasms were not the best kind. While the book itself was written in hard-to-read scientific terminology, it was interpreted, summarized, explained, and debated all over the mainstream media for the rest of the decade.

Women began to argue—out loud—that the right to satisfying sexual experience was important, perhaps right up there with equal pay. In 1970 "Myth of the Vaginal Orgasm," an essay by Anne Koedt, explained that the reason "the so-called frigidity rate among women is phenomenally high" was because men were looking for their mates' orgasms in the wrong place. In a call to action that was copied, reprinted, and shared all around the country, Koedt urged, "We must begin to demand that if certain sexual positions now defined as 'standard' are not mutually conducive to orgasm, they no longer be defined as standard."

American society had always given women only one big responsibility when it came to sex—stopping boyfriends from going too far. Now they seemed to be in charge of everything, from providing the birth control to making sure they had orgasms. A great deal of research was obviously required. Workshops sprouted up on college campuses, offering women tips on all sorts of hitherto-undiscussed matters. Arriving at Antioch as a freshman, Alison Foster showed up for a meeting of the campus women's group. About half an hour into the proceedings, she recalled, "everybody was supposed to look at their cervix. We all got little mirrors." Nora Ephron, reporting on similar gatherings in New York, commented, "It is hard not to long for the days when an evening with the girls meant bridge."

"... This Velvet Bathrobe."

The sexual revolution was only one part of an extraordinary era, when a large number of relatively privileged young people felt free to plan the reinvention of the world, confident that the world would pay attention. They had an unprecedented amount of time to devote to the task because the still-booming economy made it easy to drop in and out of the job market at will. The cost of living was very low, particularly for those who were willing to share space in a rural farmhouse or urban tenement. Travel was cheap, and airlines gave students special passes that allowed them to fly standby for cut-rate prices. When you got to wherever you were going, there was almost always a bed where you could crash for the night in the apartments of fellow members of the youth culture.

Political activists shut down their universities over the war in Vietnam, free speech, or the administration's failure to accept their advice on matters ranging from how to invest the endowment to where to locate the new gym. And even the most apolitical took part in the cultural revolution—a '60s watchword for everything from hippie communes to the Beatles. Standards for fashion and physical appearance underwent a drastic makeover. Clothes became comfortable, colorful, and dramatic. Girls tie-dyed everything, dipping knotted fabric into bright colors to produce psychedelic patterns. ("I ruined many a sink in the dorm," recalled Barbara Arnold.) They bought long, loose-fitting peasant dresses and blouses and vintage clothes. "I was really part of that hippie, thrift-store, make-your-own-blouses-out-of-your-mother's-linen-tablecloth scene," said Alison Foster. She still has a very clear memory of the moment she stopped liking anything the department stores sold and gave her patronage to the secondhand shops downtown. "I'd go to the East Village and buy funky furs and velvet coats. . . . I loved that stuff." When it was time to dress up for Sunday dinner at her boarding school, Foster donned "this velvet bathrobe—which I thought was the height of sophistication. It wasn't even mine. It was my roommate's, but I wore it as many times as I could get away with it." The whole point, she concluded, was being creative "and not looking like our parents. That was very important to me. I look at kids now and I'm wearing very similar clothes to what a lot of the girls wear. But those days I didn't want to look like my parents."

It was nothing personal. Alison Foster got along very well with her mother, Anne Wallach. She had not minded being the only girl in her circle whose mother worked, "and I liked it that she didn't hover." Still, whether a young woman adored her mother or loathed her, if she grew up in the '60s, she probably vowed that her life would be far different—more exciting, less concerned about what the neighbors would think, more in touch with her feelings, more *real*. (Or, as Wellesley College's 1969 student commencement speaker, Hillary Rodham, put it: "A more immediate, ecstatic, and penetrating mode of living.") And no matter what else she did to align herself with the revolutions at hand, clothing marked her as part of the brave new world of change and adventure.

Everything was supposed to be natural. Some women stopped shaving their legs, which quickly turned into a political issue. There was, recalled Anselma Dell'Olio, "a tendency to gauge one's feminist credentials by look, address, and degree of hairiness." (A letter writer to the *Times* denounced "arm-pit Feminists, women whose involvement with the ethic of body hair has overpowered other considerations.") It was easy to wear shorter skirts because panty hose had arrived on the scene. Basically the same leotards that dancers had always worn, panty hose quickly displaced stockings as the undergarment of choice. (Wendy Woythaler's mother was shocked at the idea of throwing out two legs' worth of panty hose when only one had a run in it, so she cut off the offending legs and told her daughter to wear a pair with a good right leg over a pair with a good left. "Oh God, it was awful." Woythaler sighed.) And it was easy not to bother with skirts at all, because by the end of the decade women had given themselves permission to spend their entire lives in jeans if they felt like it. "I used to have to go to an army/navy store to buy blue jeans," recalled Alison Foster. "There was a point where nobody sold blue jeans. And then everybody sold blue jeans."

Black women let their hair blossom out into Afros, and white college students let theirs fall straight down their backs, banishing the nighttime roller routine. Neither style, unfortunately, was always as easy to achieve in reality as in theory. Most white women did not actually have perfectly straight hair, and many resorted to ironing it. Some black women discovered that their hair, when left to its own volition, just hung there. "I decided I was going to show some of my blackness and have this Afro," said Tawana Hinton. "My hair was long, and I did it by trying to roll it and wet it. . . . It didn't work. It didn't last but a minute, you know." Josie Bass, who had given up trying to get her hair to cooperate, was invited to a dance at the University of Maryland by a student she fancied, who himself sported an impressive Afro, so she went downtown and invested in an Afro wig. She was so intent on her errand she didn't really notice that one of the many urban riots of the era was beginning to break out. "The dance was canceled and I never wore that wig." She laughed.

"I Thought I Was the Only Person Like that in the World."

It looked for a while as though the sexual revolution applied to only heterosexuals. "The whole idea of homosexuality made me profoundly uneasy," said Betty Friedan. The leader of the National Organization for Women had a tactical concern about the fact that opponents had tried to undermine the movement by depicting it as a lesbian cabal. But beyond that, it was pretty clear Friedan, like many Americans, was just uncomfortable with "the whole idea."

For most of history, lesbianism was so little understood that it was actually pretty easy for gay women to live out their lives in peace and quiet. (When Martha Peterson, the Barnard president who fought the Linda LeClair wars, died in 2006 at the age of 90, the *Times* obituary surprised many alumnae when it reported that she was "survived by her companion, Dr. Maxine Bennett.") Women had always slept together—the draftiness of most homes made cuddling up in bed extremely popular. And they had traditionally expressed their friendship for one another in intense terms that involved kissing and hugging and declarations of love. The shortage of men after major wars created a large population of unmarried women who often lived together. No one ever thought they were sharing their lives for any reason beyond companionship and convenience.

A woman who was attracted to members of her own sex thus had an easy time hiding it, if she chose to do so. But she probably had a hard time putting her feelings in any positive context. "I thought I was the only person like that in the world," said Carol Rumsey, who was 18 in 1960 when she felt stirrings for her girlfriend, the Jackie Kennedy look-alike. They were spending a last day together before the friend's impending marriage, "and we went to the movies and it was cold in Connecticut—and we got in the backseat and we snuggled up and we were just talking and all of a sudden we kissed and that was, you know, the first time that ever happened to me." And like many other women in her circumstances, Rumsey responded to her discovery by pretending nothing had changed and getting unhappily married.

At the time, while conservatives saw homosexuality as a sin, liberals saw it as an illness. (When *Ms.* began publication in 1971, an early issue assured readers that letting their sons play with dolls would not lead them into homosexuality, since "boys become homosexual because of disturbed family relationships, not because their parents allow them to do so-called feminine things.") No one had much of anything positive to say about it. *Time,* which had put the author Kate Millett on the cover when it wrote a glowing article about the women's liberation movement in 1970, rethought the whole issue when Millett acknowledged she was gay. The revelation about Millett's sexuality, *Time* said, was "bound to discredit her as a spokesman for her cause, cast further doubt on her theories, and reinforce the views of those skeptics who routinely dismiss all liberationists as lesbians."

Homosexuality was almost never referred to in the mainstream media, and when it was, the references were generally oblique—jokes that could go over the heads of more innocent readers and viewers. In the movies, gay characters were the cause of problems, if not disaster. In 1961 *The Children's Hour,* starring Audrey Hepburn and Shirley MacLaine, tackled the subject of lesbianism with sensitivity and an ending depressing enough to make the *BUtterfield 8* finale look like a situation comedy. Hepburn's and MacLaine's characters, the owners of a boarding school for young girls, are falsely accused of having an "unnatural" affair by an extraordinarily unpleasant student. They sue unsuccessfully for libel, and the school is destroyed. Curiosity-seekers come to gawk outside the house, and MacLaine—who turns out to have been nursing a secret passion for her friend all along—hangs herself in the bedroom.

The first attempt by lesbians to organize publicly may have been the Daughters of Bilitis, founded in 1953 in San Francisco. (By 1970 the editors of their magazine, *The Ladder,* felt they had made enormous progress when they proudly estimated that each issue was read or at least seen by "approximately 1,200 people.") Gene Damon, a writer for the magazine, said that to be a lesbian was to be regarded as "automatically out of the human race" and that she was constantly being asked questions such as "But what do you Lesbians do in the daytime?" Damon contributed an essay to the feminist book *Sisterhood Is Powerful* in 1970 that captured the feelings of persecution: "Run, reader, run right past this article, because most of you reading this will be women . . . and you are going to be frightened when you hear what this is all about. I am social anathema, even to you brave ones, for I am a Lesbian."

"Society Has Begun to Make It as Rough for Virgins . . ."

The prophets of the sexual revolution had more in mind than simply eliminating the double standard. The big thought of the 1960s was that sex should become a perfectly natural part of everyday life, not much more dramatic and profound than a handshake. If people would just give up the idea of sex as a sacred act between a man and a woman eternally bonded together, the argument went, they could throw off their repressions and inhibitions. Sharing and good feeling would triumph over jealousy and negativism. The world could make love, not war. The other famous slogan of the '60s—"If it feels good, do it"— might mean more than just an excuse for self-indulgence. It might mean a happier society or even world peace. The hippie movement in particular gave great credence to the idea that if people were busy taking off their clothes and coupling, they were not likely to be in the mood for more negative activity.

Alison Foster experienced that side of the sexual revolution very suddenly, after spending her first two years of high school at a private all-girls school in Manhattan with a very strong sense of decorum. "We had dances where they literally had a ruler—if you were dancing too close, the ladies would come and separate you." She transferred in 1970 to a progressive boarding school, where she discovered a very different world. "Everybody was sleeping with everybody. Professors were sleeping with students. I had a poetry teacher sleeping with a tenth grader. "We had professors modeling in the nude in our art classes. We had a lake that we would all skinny-dip in. So I went from what I thought was this very sophisticated New York girl to—oh my God, I am so over my head." She loved the school. ("Everybody was talking about feelings. It was just the kind of thing I liked.") But she saw the damage that the new theories about free love could do. "I had friends— they acted like it didn't bother them, but they felt very bad the next morning when he didn't call. I figured out pretty early on that I wasn't going to do that. That I could figure out."

The pressure to give in to the code of free love was a lot more difficult to resist when it was ideological as well as personal. A 1966 novel called *The Harrad Experiment* was an enormous hit on college campuses (to the tune of 2.5 million copies sold in a year and a half), and it was one of those bestsellers that attracts readers with its ideas, not riveting prose or well-drawn characters. *Harrad* was the tale of a group of wholesome college students brought together to learn how to experience sex in a completely honest, open atmosphere. By graduation, the heroes and heroines have, as promised, taken "the long step away from primitive emotions of hate and jealousy" and formed a six-person group marriage. "Every Sunday when my new husband for the week joins me in my room, I feel like a new bride all over again," reported one of the women. "Sometimes I wake up in the night and for a sleepy moment I may forget whether I am with Stanley, Jack, or Harry, and then I feel warm and bubbly." As the curtain fell, they were on their way to settle in an underpopulated state out west, where they planned to take over the legislature and create a utopia where every young citizen would have the right to a free college education, along with cohabitation, nude beaches, and humanistic group sex.

The ideology of the sexual revolution meshed into another '60s phenomenon, the political upheaval known as the New Left. Although young leftists came in all sorts of packages, many saw monogamy as just another form of private property, and free love as a kind of socialism of the flesh. "Certainly it was a time of fairly extensive sleeping around, a time when couples who remained monogamous were not proclaiming the fact from the rooftops," said Priscilla Long, a writer and political activist. Jane Alpert, who had traveled a long road from her high school in Queens to a Lower East Side household of two men and two women in intertwining relationships, became suspicious of a new couple her lover wanted to bring into the circle. "I considered their intention to marry reason enough to exclude them," she said.

Of course, if sex was all about *sharing*, anyone who refused to share was seen, in some quarters, as selfish or repressed or both. "I think there was subtle pressure," said Pam Andrews. "You were a truly liberated person that was going to build a new world, a new idealistic world." Women were still in charge of drawing the lines but were left with fewer arguments against going all the way. Rejected men told them they were sexually repressed or accused them of

failing to sympathize with the fact that the men might be drafted for the war in Vietnam. At the time, one woman compared the men she knew to "rabbits," adding, "It was so boring you could die." While most women would not have wanted to go back to a time when they were expected to save themselves for the man they would marry, some did feel that things had gone overboard. "The invention of the Pill made millions for the drug companies, made guinea pigs of us, and made us all the more 'available' as sex objects," raged Robin Morgan. "If a woman didn't want to go to bed with a man *now* she must be hung up." Gloria Steinem wrote that "in the fine old American tradition of conformity, society has begun to make it as rough for virgins . . . as it once did for those who had affairs before marrying."

GAIL COLLINS is an American journalist, op-ed columnist, and author who is most recognized for her work with *The New York Times*.

EXPLORING THE ISSUE

Is There Still a Double Standard of Sexuality for Women and Girls?

Critical Thinking and Reflection

1. How do legislative measures to limit access to birth control represent the perpetuation of traditional sexual double standards?
2. How do media discourses on women, women's appearance, and expressions of women's sexuality support public notions of a sexual standard?

Is There Common Ground?

Do men gain social status from engaging in casual sex from multiple partners? Is there a social stigma attached to women who engage in this behavior? These questions underlie the debate about the existence of a sexual double standard. Further complicating the notion of the sexual double standard are the gendered perceptions about men, women, and statutory rape. Women, such as teachers, who engage in sexual behavior with younger males or underage boys, perhaps students, may be perceived more negatively than men who commit similar non-forcible transgressions.

Issues of power and control relative to women's sexual agency and traditional subjectivity as a sexual object raise cultural hackles over what constitutes acceptable social behavior. The gendered application of rules premised on culture-based constructs of femininity and masculinity continue to create figurative boxes for social interaction. Such rules continue to have very real and restrictive implications for how people enact and experience the social scripts that guide the individual expression of sexuality.

Additional Resources

Koon-Magnin, S. and Ruback, R. (2012). "Young Adults' Perceptions of Non-Forcible Sexual Activity: The Effects of Participant Gender, Respondent Gender, and Sexual Act." *Sex Roles*, *67*(11/12), 646–658.

Lai, Y. and Hynie, M. (2011). "A Tale of Two Standards: An Examination of Young Adults' Endorsement of Gendered and Ageist Sexual Double Standards." *Sex Roles*, *64*(5/6), 360–371.

Rudman, L., Fetteroif, J., and Sanchez, D. (2013). "What Motivates the Sexual Double Standard? More Support for Male Versus Female Control Theory." *Personality & Social Psychology Bulletin*, *39*(2), 250–263.

Internet References . . .

AlterNet: Alternative news

http://www.alternet.org/story/86736/he%27s_a_
stud%2C_she%27s_a_slut%3A_the_sexual_double_
standard

The Good Men Project

http://goodmenproject.com/sex-relationships/
the-sexual-double-standard-and-you/

Selected, Edited, and with Issue Framing Material by:
Elizabeth Schroeder, EdD, MSW, *Elizabeth Schroeder Consulting*

ISSUE

Does Anatomy Predict Gender?

YES: Cornelieke van de Beek et al., from "Prenatal Sex Hormones (Maternal and Amniotic Fluid) and Gender-Related Play Behavior in 13-Month-Old Infant," *Archives of Sexual Behavior* (2009)

NO: Vasanti Jadva, Melissa Hines, and Susan Golombok, from "Infants' Preferences for Toys, Colors, and Shapes: Sex Differences and Similarities," *Archives of Sexual Behavior* (2010)

Learning Outcomes

After reading this issue, you will be able to:

- Distinguish correlation from causation. Correlations between hormonal levels and behavior do not always mean that biological factors drive the behavior.
- Consider how various factors, such as environmental ones, might explain various hormonal—behavioral relations, especially at very young ages. You should be able to think about other factors that might account for a correlation between two variables.
- Consider why it is important to use experimental research designs to answer research questions related to hormonal–behavioral relations.

ISSUE SUMMARY

YES: Cornelieke van de Beek and colleagues demonstrated that testosterone, estradiol, and progesterone levels measured during pregnancy are related to gender-related play in 13-month-old girls and boys and found clear sex differences in preferences for masculine and feminine toys.

NO: Vasanti Jadva, Melissa Hines, and Susan Golombok, using a preferential looking task, found sex similarities in infants' preferences for shapes and colors and suggest that later gender-related patterns of toy preferences may be related to socialization or cognitive development factors rather than inborn differences.

Do we really know what constitutes one's "sex" and "gender"? Why do girls and boys, women and men behave the way they do? Typically, people assume that being male or female is a clear and absolute distinction. Biologically based theories of sex differentiation support the argument that genetic make-up and resultant hormonal influences determine fundamental differences between women and men. Given the ethical constraints associated with doing research on humans, researchers have had to rely on animal experimentation to demonstrate, for example, that hormones contribute to sexual dimorphism (i.e., sexual differentiation) on neural systems, brains, temperament,

and behavior. The assumption is that sex is an unquestionably natural dichotomy rooted in an organism's genetics. Various research traditions have attempted to validate the biological basis of sex differences. These include animal studies, anthropological and cultural studies, and studies of newborns. Examples of each are provided below.

A review of animal studies has found "every imaginable mode of relationship between the sexes exists in different species." Some animal studies offer evidence of the effects of environment on something as fundamental as biological sex. For example, it is known that the depth at which sea turtle eggs are buried and the resultant temperature determine whether the turtle will be female or male (known as temperature-dependent sex determination). Even with scientific experiments (i.e., with manipulation of variables and random assignment of animals to experimental conditions), no sweeping conclusions can be drawn because, depending on the species studied, diametrically opposed results have been found.

In contrast to animal studies, anthropologists have studied various cultures in the search of universal patterns of sex differences, premised on the assumption that such patterns would be evidence for some biological basis. However, they have found that humans are incredibly malleable. Cultural analyses question the immunity of biological constructs and suggest that we must recognize that the practice of science occurs within a sociopolitical context. Therefore, notions about the biological basis of sex differences result from a dynamic interplay of cultural, social, religious, and political thought and practice. Scholars have uncovered compelling evidence that even when a binary view of sex is embraced, there are still cultural underpinnings. For example, within both Judeo-Christian and Islamic traditions, sex is seen as binary; a person is either male or female. These dominant views of sex delineate two "normal" categories: male and female. Notions of gender follow suit, typically contrasting masculine and feminine behavior patterns. However, religious traditions also deal with the reality of gender/sexual diversity in different ways. The medical procedure of a sexual reassignment surgery is understood very differently by religious leaders: for instance, while the Vatican does not think individuals can "change" sex through hormone replacement or plastic surgery, there are some Shii clerics who believe this transformation may be required in cases where the gender identity does not match external genital.

However, is this dichotomy universal? Some scholars argue that when looking for binaries, we observe only a dichotomous reality. But what remains unseen—gender diversity—is also an important reality. Dichotomous definitions of sex are not universal. Instead, many cultures acknowledge multiple genders. For example, the *Turnim man* (meaning "expected to become a man") has been recognized in Sambian society (New Guinea). As a result of a genetic variation known as delta-4-steroid-5-alpha-reductase deficiency, individuals are born with a pseudo-female appearance and may be raised as a boy or girl; however, at puberty, as a result of an increase in testosterone, the individual becomes male-like. However, they typically experience a life of ridicule and rejection. This is unlike the treatment that individuals with the same genetic variation receive in the Dominican Republic. Here,

the transformation of these individuals, called *guevedoces,* is celebrated. Contrast these two examples with that of the *berdache* (now considered an outdated term by some anthropologists) in Navajo society, where not only are three sexes recognized, but the berdache ("two spirits") are valued. Among various indigenous peoples more than two sexes are recognized, with remarkable variation in how they are treated by their own cultures. However, whether reviled or celebrated, for the purpose of this discussion, the point is that many cultures acknowledge more than the two traditional sexes, male and female.

Another research tradition relies on studies of newborns, on the assumption that the environment has not yet had a chance to shape gender-related patterns. However, there is the question of whether any of these can be truly unbiased. The YES and NO selections you will read for this issue were based on studies of newborn infants. These studies attempt to establish explanations for often-observed sex differences in color, shape, and toy preferences among children.

What we do know is that females and males differ in the amount of various sex-related hormones in their system, sex hormones enter the brain and affect its activity, but research is inconclusive regarding causality and behavioral ramifications. Indeed, a large body of research with numerous species of animals, as well as with humans, suggests that environmental factors provide the major determinants of gender-related patterns of behavior. That is, gender is a socially constructed constellation of feelings, attitudes, and behaviors, thus strongly influenced by cultural forces.

Some revisionists have begun to "reinvent sex" by replacing dichotomous conceptions of sex with arrays reflecting the complexities of sexual variability in natural characteristics of humans. For example, terms such as "gender-crossing" have been coined. The problem with such concepts is that they still rely on the fixed binary of male/female, and they problematize deviations. As an alternative, sexologists have grappled with the idea of fluidity, such as in the "lovemap," a term first coined in 1981 by sexologist John Money. It is a "a developmental representation or template in the mind and in the brain depicting the idealized lover and the idealized program of sexual and erotic activity projected in imagery or actually engaged in with that lover." He claims that each person's map is as unique as a fingerprint. He describes the lovemap as an "entity," the facets of which include one's reproductive structure, one's sexual identity, mechanisms of reproduction, sexual orientation, and patterns and roles that are related to gender.

Whether or not you find the idea of a lovemap compelling, such a conceptualization challenges us to stretch our understanding of sex and gender in more complicated, nuanced, and multidimensional ways than most of us typically think. We may be able to more easily conceive of the possibility of multiple genders, transcend binary notions, and reconsider the notion of deviance typically associated with nonmale and nonfemale genders.

YES

Cornelieke van de Beek et al.

Prenatal Sex Hormones (Maternal and Amniotic Fluid) and Gender-Related Play Behavior in 13-Month-Old Infants

Introduction

Toy preference is one of the earliest manifestations of gender-related behavior. Girls have been found to prefer playing with toys such as dolls and household supplies, whereas boys prefer playing with toys such as vehicles and weapons. Several studies have demonstrated that sex differences in play behavior are present in the second year of life. One study showed that girls and boys chose different toys as early as the age of 12 months.

The fact that parents engage in some form of sex typing of their infant's play behavior in the first year of life suggests that socializing influences already may play a role. However, there are also indications that the child himself or herself may have certain innate preferences, i.e., the tendency to be focused on specific aspects of objects, like movement, color or form, which may prime them to prefer specific toy categories. The findings of sex differences in toy preferences in non-human primates, in which the influence of social learning and cognitive concepts or beliefs on toy preference can be considered nil, give additional reason to assume that there is a biological basis for the development of sex-typed toy preferences.

Among the biological determinants of play behavior, sex hormones are likely candidates. Prenatal sex hormones can permanently influence postnatal human sex-typed behaviors by altering fetal brain development. Moreover, since there is also much within-sex variation in gender-typical behaviors, such as tomboy behavior, sex hormones are probably not only responsible for behavioral sex differences, but also for within-sex variations in gender-related behavior.

Animal studies have shown that there are a few critical periods in development in which the brain regions that are responsible for the regulation of the sex-typed behavior are highly sensitive to the effects of sex hormones. In humans, the period between weeks 8 and 24 of gestation may be particularly important for sexual differentiation because this is the period when the male fetus shows a peak in serum testosterone (at its highest at about week 16).

It has been clearly shown that prenatal androgens can have masculinizing and defeminizing effects on postnatal human behaviors. Very little is known about the function of "female-typical" hormones in sexual differentiation and their effects on human behavioral differentiation. Although rodent studies indicate that estradiol is very important in behavioral masculinization and defeminization, its role in humans is less obvious. Findings in both girls and boys, exposed to diethystilbestrol (DES) (a synthetic estrogen), suggest a general lack of influences on childhood gender typical play.

Studies that have investigated the behavioral effects of prenatal progestagens mostly focused on exogenously administered synthetic progestins. The interpretations of the findings are complicated by the fact that different types of progestins were used. Prenatal exposure of girls to androgen-based synthetic progestins seemed to result in more male-typical behavior, such as more tomboyism and a stronger preference for male-typical toys, whereas exposure of girls to progesterone-based synthetic progestins produced fewer and opposite effects. Similar but less pronounced effects of these two types of exogenous progestins were found in boys. Less is known about the effects of normal circulating progesterone levels during pregnancy, although an antiandrogenic effect on the fetus has been proposed.

Currently, most evidence of a prenatal effect of androgens on human play behavior comes from studies in girls with congenital adrenal hyperplasia (CAH). CAH is a genetic condition that results in the production of high adrenal androgens beginning very early in gestation. Girls with CAH show both masculinization and defeminization of behavior: they have a stronger preference for traditionally masculine toys and activities than unaffected control girls (relatives or matched comparisons). Indications for a dose–response relationship have also been found: more severely affected girls with CAH were more interested in masculine careers and toys than less affected girls. Furthermore, the timing of exposure on behavior has been demonstrated: prenatal androgen exposure, but not early or later postnatal exposure, was related to more male-typical play behavior. In boys with CAH, elevated prenatal adrenal androgen exposure does not seem to result in more masculine play behavior.

There is also evidence that normal variations in androgen levels are systematically related to early sex differences and within-sex variations in gender-typical play behavior of children without clinical conditions. This evidence comes from studies using maternal blood to infer hormonal effects on the fetus. . . . Recently, a positive correlation was found between maternal and fetal blood testosterone. This suggests that testosterone may cross the placenta, but it may also reflect a genetic relationship. However, maternal androgens do not appear to come from the fetus, as several studies have failed to find a difference in serum second trimester testosterone levels between women carrying a male and those carrying a female fetus.

Another approach to investigate the organizational effects of prenatal sex hormones is used by amniotic fluid studies. Amniotic fluid can only be obtained from amniocentesis conducted for purposes of diagnosing fetal anomalies. Coincidentally, this medical intervention usually takes place around week 16 of gestation, a time that appears to correspond well to the male testosterone peak. Amniotic fluid seems to provide information about the sex steroid production by the fetus since several studies have found large sex differences in amniotic androgens. However, currently there is no hard evidence of a direct relationship between amniotic testosterone and fetal serum testosterone. The mostly low and/or nonsignificant correlations between androgens measured in amniotic fluid and in maternal serum suggest that these measures reflect something different. In addition, there is also another methodological difference between these two measures: amniotic fluid measures are only available for a specific population, which contains generally older mothers, while maternal blood measures can be relatively easily measured in a representative sample of the general population. Therefore, both measures have their advantages and disadvantages, and might provide convergent evidence of the relationship between prenatal hormones and postnatal behavior.

Until now, there are two groups of investigators that have examined the relationship between early androgen exposure by investigating prenatal amniotic hormones and postnatal behavior. One research group mainly looked at measures of cognition and cerebral lateralization. The other group of investigators primarily focused on aspects of early social development, but also included one aspect of gender role behavior in their design, namely game participation. They did not find amniotic testosterone to be related to individual differences on the Masculinity and Femininity scales of the Children's Play Questionnaire at age 5/6 years, despite the fact that this measure showed large sex differences in the same sample. However, this parent report instrument might not have been sufficiently sensitive to within sex variability in behavior, as opposed to between-sex differences. Also, the very small sample size may have increased the chance of negative results.

In the current study, we focused on toy preference observed in a laboratory situation. Rather than using parental reports, play behavior was scored by trained observers. Our first goal was to replicate previously reported sex differences in masculine and feminine toy preference in normally developing 13-month-old infants. Furthermore, we investigated whether prenatal testosterone, estradiol, and progesterone levels, as assessed in amniotic fluid and maternal serum, were related to sex differences and within-sex variations in gender-related play behavior.

Since the literature suggests most clearly an effect of prenatal androgens on play behavior, we hypothesized that higher levels of testosterone would be related to more masculine and less feminine play behavior. Previous studies on children with CAH indicate that these effects are clearly observed in girls, but are absent in boys. [T]he maternal blood study reported the same pattern in a normative population. Therefore, we predicted that this relationship would be sex-specific, i.e., more clearly present in girls than boys. We did not have clear predictions with respect to the behavioral effects of variations in estradiol and progesterone.

Method

Participants

All participants were enrolled in a prospective longitudinal project on the effects of prenatal sex hormones on gender development. Participants were recruited from a consecutive series of referrals, between January 1999 and August 2000, to the Department of Obstetrics at the University Medical Centre in Utrecht (UMCU) to undergo an amniocentesis because of prenatal diagnostic screening. All participants lived in relative close vicinity (30 km) of the UMCU. Amniotic fluid samples were provided by 153 participants with a normal healthy singleton pregnancy. Each participant gave informed consent to the procedure and the UMCU Medical Ethical Committee approved the study.

For the majority of the women (96%), the reason for amniocentesis was a higher risk of age-related (36 years or older) genetic changes and their implications. The others had an amniocentesis because of their medical history (e.g., a previous child with Down syndrome or radiation cancer treatment) (3.3%) and one participant had a high result on the triple test (indicating an increased risk for Down syndrome) (0.7%). Seven participants reported that they did not become pregnant spontaneously; $n = 4$ had ovulation induction of which one also had donor insemination, $n = 1$ had artificial insemination, and $n = 2$ had in vitro fertilization (IVF).

For 18 participants, data could not be collected at follow-up. Three children could not be tested because of illness or pregnancy of their mothers. Two children were excluded when their mother's command of the Dutch language appeared to be insufficient to complete questionnaires. One child was excluded because of extreme prematurity (gestational period less than 35 weeks) at birth. Furthermore, we lost participants ($n = 12$) because they moved abroad ($n = 1$) or were no longer interested to participate in the study ($n = 11$).

In total, 135 children were seen at the age of 13 months. Two girls were so timid that behavioral observations were not possible. The observations of three other children were not reliable because of illness or fatigue and the play behavior of four children could not be scored because of technical problems. In the end, the data of 126 children (63 boys and 63 girls) were used for further analyses. The mean age of the children was 56.4 weeks ($SD = 1.2$, range, 53.6–60.6). The mean age of the mothers at amniocentesis was 37.5 years ($SD = 2.1$, range, 28–45). The mean parental education score was 9.8 ($SD = 3.1$, range, 2–14). With respect to the presence of older siblings, there were: no older brother ($n = 69$), one older brother ($n = 43$), two or more older brothers ($n = 10$), no older sister ($n = 86$), one older sister ($n = 31$), and two or more older sisters ($n = 5$). None of these variables differed significantly between boys and girls.

Measures

Sex Hormones in Amniotic Fluid

The amniotic fluid samples were collected between week 15.3 and 18.0 of pregnancy ($M = 16.3$, $SD = .46$). The length of gestation was determined by the last menstrual period and/or ultrasonic measurement of crown-rump length (CRL). Because we had to adjust to the time schedule of the clinic, it was not possible to standardize the hormone sampling time completely; however, all samples were taken between 8:00 am and 13:00 pm. The material was stored at –30°C until assayed. The lab employees who analyzed the samples were masked to the behavioral data. Testosterone was determined by radioimmunoassay (RIA) after extraction with diethyl ether. . . .

Sex Hormones in Maternal Serum

We were able to collect serum in 115 mothers-to-be (57 boys, 58 girls). The maternal serum samples were collected immediately following the amniocentesis. The hormonal analyses were conducted as described above except for testosterone. In maternal serum, free testosterone, the biologically active part of this sex hormone, was calculated using existing procedures. . . .

One girl with an extremely high (because of skewed distributions, a criterion of >4 SD was used) amnion testosterone level (2.50 nmol/l) and whose mother had an extremely high progesterone level (2,860.0 nmol/l) and one girl whose mother had an extremely high plasma testosterone level (42.40 nmol/l) were not included in the data analyses.

Play Observations

In a structured toy play session, nine different toys that previously had been classified by parents and non-parents as masculine, feminine, or neutral were used. Each toy category was equally presented. Neutral toys were a plastic friction dog, a wooden puzzle, and a stacking pole with rings. Masculine toys were a trailer with four cars, a garbage truck, and a set of three plastic pieces of equipment. Feminine toys were a teapot with a cup, a soft doll in a cradle with a blanket, and a doll with beauty set (brush, comb, and mirror).

The toys were arranged in a standard order in a semicircle (from left to right: tea set, dog, trailer, doll in cradle, rings, truck, doll with beauty set, puzzle, and equipment). The mother was asked to place the child in the center of the semicircle, at the same distance from all toys, and then take a seat in the chair just outside the semicircle (1.5 m). She was instructed to let the child play on his or her own, but was allowed to give neutral verbal reactions if the child specifically asked her attention. When giving verbal reactions, she was asked to avoid naming the objects and guiding the child in its actions. The child was videotaped for 7 min, starting by the first touch of a toy. If play behavior was not present for longer than 30 s (e.g., if the child started to cry and sought comfort with his/her mother), this time was added to the original 7 min. In this way, every child had 7 min real playing time. The play session took place at the beginning of a more extensive testing session, after a short (5–10 min) talk with the mother. The entire visit took approximately 1 h.

For each toy, we recorded the number of seconds the child played with that particular toy. Each "play action" was scored from the moment that physical contact started until the physical contact stopped, unless there was still obvious "involvement" (e.g., pushing a car and crawling behind it). "Involvement" was defined as looking at, pointing at, and moving behind the object. If the child played with several toys simultaneously, physical contact time was scored for each toy separately. Thus, the total playing time of a child (all time spent with the different objects in sum) sometimes was longer than the 7 min of play observation. For each toy category, the total amount of time was counted and the percentage of the total playing time was calculated, resulting in the variables "% masculine play," "% feminine play," and "% neutral play." Two participants with a deviant total playing time (>3 SD) were excluded; one boy showed an extremely high (730 s) and another boy an extremely low (36 s) total playing time.

The videotapes were scored by trained observers who were masked to the hormonal values. The inter-rater reliability was high. Kendall's tau correlations ranged from .95 to 1.00 for masculine play, from .94 to .99 for feminine play, and from .99 to 1.00 for neutral play.

Developmental Assessment
A home visit took place within a week after the play session. During this visit, the Bayley Scales of Infant Development II (BSID II) was administered to assess motor and mental development.

Background Variables
Information was collected on several social and demographic variables by means of a short questionnaire. The following variables were used in the analyses: age of the mother at the time of amniocentesis, parental educational level, and number of older brothers and sisters. For each parent, the educational level was scored on a 7-point scale, with a score of 1 indicating "no formal qualifications" to 7 representing "a university degree." The scores of both parents were combined. . . .

Results

Prenatal Sex Hormones
There were no significant sex differences in maternal serum. In amniotic fluid, male fetuses had significantly higher testosterone levels, and female fetuses had significantly higher estradiol levels. No significant sex difference was found with respect to amniotic progesterone levels.

No significant relationship was found between maternal age and the hormone levels, and the same applied for gestational age at sampling and maternal hormones. In male fetuses, but not in female fetuses, there was a gestational age effect with respect to the amniotic data. With the progression of pregnancy, a significant decrease was found in testosterone, progesterone, and estradiol. To control for these effects, we used in further analyses the standardized residual of the calculated regression lines instead of the actual hormone levels.

Play Behavior
The total sample had a mean total playing time of 415 s (SD = 87; range, 181–692). There was no significant sex difference in the total time that the toys were handled.

. . . Boys (M = 40.96, SEM = 3.59) spent a significantly higher percentage of time playing with the masculine toys than girls (M = 27.10, SEM = 2.87). . . . The percentage of time with feminine toys was significantly higher for girls (M = 45.74, SEM = 3.43) than for boys (M = 36.62, SEM = 3.56). . . . Boys and girls did not differ significantly with respect to neutral play.

Gender-Related Play and Non-Hormonal Variables
In boys, no clear relationships were found between the age of mother, parental education, the number of older sisters, and mental and motor development, on the one hand, and masculine and feminine play behavior, on the other, except for a marginally significant positive relationship between parental educational level and masculine play behavior. For feminine play, a marginally significant relationship was found for boys, but in the opposite direction. In addition, the percentage of masculine play behavior tended to be lower, and feminine play higher, with an increase in the number of older brothers.

In girls, no significant relationships were found between any of the background variables and gender-related play, except for a significant negative relation between percentage of feminine play and number of older sisters.

Prenatal Hormones and Gender-Related Play
No significant relations were found between maternal sex hormones levels and masculine or feminine play behavior in either boys or girls. With regard to the sex hormones measured in amniotic fluid, a positive correlation between progesterone and time spent with masculine toys . . . was observed in boys. No other significant relationships with masculine or feminine play were found in either boys or girls.

Regression Analysis Within the Sexes

Because there were no significant relationships between prenatal hormones and feminine play in boys or girls, and because there was no relationship between prenatal hormone levels and masculine play behavior in girls, we further explored the relationship between hormones and masculine behavior in boys only. First, the variables that were related to masculine play (at a $p < .10$ level) were entered in the model simultaneously. These variables were progesterone in amniotic fluid, parental educational level, and the number of older brothers. Although amniotic testosterone was not significantly correlated with masculine play, we included it in the regression, because amniotic testosterone and progesterone were positively related. . . . In the final model, only progesterone in amniotic fluid significantly and positively predicted masculine play. With respect to the non-hormonal variables, masculine play was predicted by the number of older brothers (less masculine play with more older brothers) and parental educational level (less masculine play with lower educational level).

Regression Analysis Including Both Sexes

Using a similar procedure, we also entered sex, and the interactions between sex and amniotic progesterone and testosterone, respectively, in the model. Again, progesterone positively predicted masculine play, but now at a trend level. Sex of child strongly predicted masculine play, as did parental educational level. Finally, at a trend level, an inverse relation was found between the number of older brothers and masculine play.

Discussion

In the present study, we observed significantly higher amniotic testosterone levels in male pregnancies, significantly higher amniotic estradiol levels in female pregnancies, and no sex difference in maternal plasma sex hormone levels. This is in line with previous findings. Furthermore, sex differences in toy preference were clearly present at the age of 13 months. Boys spent significantly more time playing with masculine toys than girls and girls played significantly more with feminine toys than boys.

For both sexes, no significant relations were found between amniotic testosterone or other hormones and masculine or feminine play behavior, except for an unexpected positive relationship between amniotic progesterone and masculine play. This effect was clearly present in boys and was present at a trend level in the total sample (girls and boys together).

We can think of several reasons for the absence of a significant relationship between amniotic testosterone and play behavior. In our study, there are several methodological gaps that may have led to insufficient experimental power. First, it may be that one single sample of hormones does not represent actual individual differences in fetal hormone exposure. Little is known about circadian rhythms of sex hormones during pregnancy, but it has been reported that several hormones show fluctuations within a day and across days, even in fetuses. Furthermore, the relationship between testosterone measured in amniotic fluid and fetal blood is not established, so it is still uncertain what the amniotic level really represents.

Second, it may be that, at the age of 13 months, sex differences in play behavior were too small to study hormone–play relationships in the currently used sample size. At 13 months of age, we found clear sex differences in masculine and feminine toy preference, but the effect sizes were small (feminine play: $d = .35$) to moderate (masculine play: $d = .53$). This is much smaller than what is usually reported in studies in somewhat older pre-school children (e.g., $d = 1.92$ for masculine toys and $d = 1.23$ for feminine toys in 3-year-olds. However, other hormone studies did find a relationship between amniotic testosterone and behaviors that show sex differences of moderate effect size, i.e., eye-contact ($d = .53$) and vocabulary size ($d = .67$). Therefore, we expected to find at least significant results for masculine play.

Third, in a study on hormone–behavior relationships, an instrument is needed that captures behavioral differences between boys and girls, but that is also sensitive to within sex differences. Despite the fact that we did find sex differences, it may be that our method was not sensitive enough to measure within sex variability. Although the mothers in our study were instructed not to interfere, it may be that their presence has caused some error.

The positive and unexpected relationship between amniotic progesterone and masculine play behavior in boys may have reflected a Type I error, considering the multiple comparisons. Yet, in the Stanford Longitudinal Study, which used umbilical cord blood assessments, some significant relationships were found between progesterone and traits that can be labeled masculine. However, it is questionable whether umbilical cord blood levels are a good index of organizational effects of sex hormones and little is known about the relationship between progesterone levels from cord blood at birth and progesterone levels in second trimester amniotic fluid.

Finally, some attention should be paid to the few potentially relevant non-hormonal variables we incorporated in our study to control for their possible effects. Although the design of the study does not allow for definite conclusions, the results indicate that, already at

13 months of age, variables such as parental education and the number of older brothers are related to gender-related play behavior. In boys, there were indications for a tendency of masculine play to be less frequent, and feminine play to be more frequent, when the child had more older brothers. Although having one older brother is associated with more masculine gender role behavior, studies that included families with more than one sibling suggest that having two or more brothers is related to a decrease in masculine behavior. Rather than considering sibship as a social factor some researchers consider it as a biological factor, propos[ing] that each succeeding male fetus leads to the production of antibodies that can pass through the placental barrier, enter the fetal brain, and impede the sexual differentiation of the brain in the male-typical direction.

Although both biological and social factors play a role in gender role development, there is no real consensus as to if and how the different factors interact and whether there is a specific point in time at which social or cultural factors might, in fact, overrule potential biological influences. Parental behavior may strengthen biologically based differences, augmenting small differences present at 13 months. However, parents may also modify individual preferences, and overrule biological predispositions, for example in the case of very feminine boys. It is important to follow up the participants of this study and establish whether the studied relationships between prenatal hormones and gender-related play behavior increase or change over time or only appear later in development.

CORNELIEKE VAN DE BEEK is with the Department of Child and Adolescent Psychiatry, University Medical Centre Utrecht, and the Rudolf Magnus Institute for Neurosciences, Utrecht, the Netherlands.

STEPHANIE H. M. VAN GOOZEN is a biological psychologist interested in developmental psychopathology. Her research focuses on individual factors that explain or accentuate risk of developing antisocial behavior to those who live with early social adversity.

JAN K. BUITELAAR is a professor of psychiatry and child and adolescent psychiatry in the Department of Psychiatry at St. Radboud University Nijmegen Medical Center, Nijmegen, the Netherlands. His primary focus is on child psychiatry and he has published widely on ADHD, conduct disorder, and autism spectrum disorder. He currently serves as head of Karakter Child and Adolescent Psychiatry University Centre and as editor-in-chief of *European Child and Adolescent Psychiatry*.

PEGGY T. COHEN-KETTENIS is the head of the Department of Medical Psychology and director of the Center of Expertise on Gender Dysphoria at VU University Medical Center, Amsterdam, the Netherlands. Her primary research focus is on disorders of sex and gender development and sex hormone–behavior relationships. Current projects include studies of the effects of pubertal delay in adolescent transsexuals on psychological functioning, psychiatric comorbidity, and brain structure.

**Vasanti Jadva, Melissa Hines,
and Susan Golombok**

 **NO**

Infants' Preferences for Toys, Colors, and Shapes: Sex Differences and Similarities

Introduction

Children show clear sex-typed toy preferences, with girls showing more interest than boys do in dolls and boys showing more interest than girls do in vehicles. In addition to these differences between the sexes, within sex analyses show that boys play more with masculine toys, like vehicles and weapons, than with feminine toys, like dolls and tea sets. In contrast, although girls play more with feminine toys than with masculine toys when the feminine toys are sufficiently interesting, they sometimes show no significant preference for feminine over masculine toys. The strong male preference for same-sex toys has sometimes been described as boys avoiding girls' toys.

Sex-typed toy preferences have been seen in infants grow larger as childhood progresses and have been reported into young adulthood. These sex differences have been documented using an array of research methodologies, including inventories of children's toys at home, observation of children's toy contact in a playroom, parental interviews and questionnaires, and visual preferences and eye-tracking.

Perspectives on the acquisition of sex-typed play, including toy preferences, can be categorized broadly into social learning theories, cognitive theories, and hormonal theories. Social learning theories posit that children are socialized into different gender role behaviors, including toy play. Boys are reinforced for engaging with male-typical toys and girls for engaging with female-typical toys. Opposite sex-typed behavior is punished or not rewarded, which leads to extinction. Children can also learn which behaviors to adopt by modeling individuals of the same sex as themselves or by complying with labels identifying behaviors as appropriate for children of one sex or the other.

From a social learning perspective, infants' preferences for sex-typed toys would suggest that the differential treatment of boys and girls begins at an early age. In support of this view, studies have found that fathers of 12-month-old infants were less likely to give dolls to their sons than to their daughters. In one study, parents of boys called their sons' attention to the clown more than the doll and parents of girls called their daughters' attention to the doll more than the clown. Similarly, parents of infants aged 5–25 months may create different home environments for boys and girls. Boys have more sports equipment, tools and vehicles, and girls have more dolls and fictional characters. Thus, socialization of very young infants may be occurring not only through parents' interactions with their sons and daughters, but also in the way in which they design their infants' home environments.

Cognitive theories include cognitive developmental theories and gender schema theories. According to cognitive developmental theories, gender role acquisition involves three stages: gender labeling, gender stability, and gender constancy. It is at this last stage, where the child understands that gender remains the same across different situations, that sex-typed preferences were originally thought to emerge. More recently, researchers have suggested that gender constancy is not a prerequisite for gender-typed behavior and, indeed, young children show sex-typed preferences before gender constancy is attained. Gender schema theorists posit that children develop gender schemas to organize and structure gender-related information from their environment. The process of gender typing is thought to begin once the child is able to categorize him/herself as belonging to a particular gender. For cognitive theorists, sex-typed behavior follows from a child knowing his or her own gender and becoming aware of the stereotypes that exist in the social environment.

From the hormonal perspective, sex differences arise, in part, from early hormonal differences between boys and girls. In particular, sex differences in the prenatal hormonal environment are thought to produce differences in neural organization, such that high concentrations of androgens, hormones typically produced in large amounts by the male fetus, lead to brain masculinization and increased male-typical behavior. One approach to understanding the

From *Archives of Sexual Behavior*, vol. 39, 2010, pp. 1261–1273. Copyright © 2010 by the International Academy of Sex Research. Reprinted with kind permission of Springer Science + Business Media via Rightslink.

effects of sex hormones has been to study children with congenital adrenal hyperplasia (CAH), a genetic condition where the female fetus is exposed to abnormally high concentrations of androgens. These studies have shown that girls with CAH spend more time playing with masculine toys and less time playing with feminine toys compared to control group girls. The suggestion that this may result from parents encouraging male-typical toy play in girls with CAH has not been supported by research finding that parents encourage feminine toy play, not masculine toy play, more in their daughters with CAH than in their unaffected daughters. Normal variability in androgen exposure prenatally also relates to male-typical childhood behavior, suggesting that the findings for girls with CAH relate to their androgen exposure, not to other aspects of the disorder. Sex-typed toy preferences similar to those seen in children have also been reported in two species of non-human primates, vervet monkeys and rhesus monkeys, providing additional evidence of some innate contribution.

Given the evidence that sex differences in toy preferences emerge early in life and appear to relate, in part, to hormonal or other inborn influences, some researchers have begun to ask what properties of sex-typed toys differentially attract boys and girls. For example, are boys attracted to wheels and motion, and girls to faces and imaginary role-play? Perhaps toy preferences result from what the toy can do, rather than from children knowing that a toy is appropriate for their own gender. Similarly . . . sex-typed toy preferences may result from a preference for different object features, including color, movement, or form.

Sex-Typed Toys and Color

Toys for boys and girls tend to differ in many ways. One of the most obvious is color. [G]irls' toys tended to be colored in pastel shades, especially pink and lavender, and boys' toys tended to be colored in intense colors, such as red, blue, and black. These colors are also differentially preferred by girls and boys. One study asked 3- to 7-year-old children to choose their favorite felt pig from a choice of pigs colored in either stereotypically masculine colors (navy blue, brown, maroon) or stereotypically feminine colors (light pink, bright pink, lavender), and found that they were likely to choose a pig in a color stereotyped as for their own sex. . . . Girls use more "warm" colors, including pink, than boys, whereas boys use more "cold" colors, such as gray and blue, compared to girls. Sex-typed color preferences appear to persist into adulthood; . . . females prefer reddish purple and males . . . prefer blue-green.

Few studies have examined the color preferences of children below the age of 3 years, and none have looked at sex differences in infants' preferences. However, babies as young as 3 months can see color and both male and female infants between the ages of 3 and 5 months appear to like red most and green least. It is not known, however, if infants display sex-typed color preferences similar to those of older children and adults or, if so, when these sex differences emerge.

Sex-Typed Toys and Shape

In addition to color, sex-typed toys differ in their shape. For instance, cars and other vehicles tend to be angular, whereas dolls tend to be rounded. Although research has not examined preferences for different shaped toys per se, some studies have examined the content of drawings, finding sex differences in images produced by adults, as well as children. [M]en tend to "close off" stimuli, to enlarge images (mainly by extending the image upwards), and to emphasize sharp or angular lines, while women tend to leave the stimulus areas "open", to elaborate the drawing within the confines of the presented lines and to blunt or round off any angular lines. Among children, girls are more likely than boys to draw flowers, butterflies, the sun, and human motifs, whereas boys are more likely than girls to draw mobile objects, such as vehicles, trains, aircraft, and rockets.

The present study examined toy preferences, as well as color and shape preferences, in infants ages 12, 18, and 24 months. We evaluated the hypotheses that these young children show preferences for sex-typical toys and colors, for sex-typed toys in sex-typed colors, and for angular versus rounded shapes. Infants across a range of ages were studied in anticipation of determining not only infants' sex-typed preferences, but also the age at which any such preferences emerge.

Method
Participants

Parents of infants were contacted through nurseries and mother and baby groups in London, UK. Infants were recruited into three age categories: 12 months . . . , 18 months, and 24 months. Each age category consisted of 20 boys and 20 girls. Most infants ($N = 116$) participated with their mothers; four infants participated with their fathers. Each parent–infant pair was paid £10 sterling (about $20) for taking part in the study.

The majority of mothers (72, 60%) and fathers (81, 67.5%) had a professional occupation, . . . and 94 (78.3%) mothers and 96 (80%) fathers held a university degree.

Sixty-six (55%) of the mothers were not working at the time of study, 13 (10.8%) worked full-time, and 41 (34.2%) worked part-time. Ninety-eight (81.7%) infants were Caucasian. . . .

Measures

We used a preferential looking task, whereby two images were shown simultaneously to the infant in a darkened room. Each image in each stimulus pair was mounted in a square, colored in gray. . . . The infant's face was recorded by videotape and later coded for the length of time that the infant looked at each image. The stimuli used for the preferential looking task were chosen to test specific hypotheses, and these stimuli, and the hypotheses they were chosen to assess, are described below.

Color Stimuli

Four pairs of stimuli were used to evaluate infants' preferences for colors on their own. These stimulus pairs examined the hypotheses that boys prefer blue and girls prefer pink, as well as that infants show these sex-typed color preferences when brightness is controlled. Two pairs of stimuli compared pink . . . and blue. . . . To ensure that the color of the stimuli matched the shades of pink and blue of existing toys, two toys (a doll's dress and a building block) were scanned directly into the computer and their shades of pink and blue were recorded. Because pink and blue are made up of different brightness (luminance) levels, with pink being brighter than blue, and because differences in the brightness levels of colors have been shown to modify infants' color preferences two additional stimulus pairs were used to control for brightness. The pink was matched for brightness with the blue to produce red, and the blue was matched for brightness with the pink to produce pale blue. Thus, there were four pairings: pink/blue; red/pale blue; pink/pale blue; and red/blue.

Toy Stimuli

Two sex-typed toys (a doll and a car) provided the toy stimulus pairings. Simple line drawings of a doll and a car were scanned into a computer to create the stimuli. To allow assessment of relationships between toy and color, as well as toy preferences on their own, the car and the doll were colored in the same four colors used for the color stimuli (pink, blue, red, pale blue).

The stimuli were paired to examine specific hypotheses. To test the hypothesis that boys and girls prefer sex-typed toys in sex-typed colors, we compared the doll to the car when colored in sex congruent colors, i.e., pink doll/blue car. To test the hypothesis that the preference for sex-typed toys would be weaker when they are colored in cross sex-typed colors, we compared the doll to the car when colored in sex incongruent colors, i.e., blue doll/pink car. To examine the same hypotheses with brightness controlled, we paired the doll to the car when colored in sex congruent colors and sex incongruent colors controlling for the difference in brightness levels of pink and blue. As all possible color combinations were included, this resulted in four pairings: two pairings of toys colored in sex congruent colors (i.e., red doll/blue car and pink doll/pale blue car) and two parings of toys colored in sex incongruent colors (i.e., red car/blue doll and pale blue doll/pink car).

We also tested the hypothesis that boys and girls differ in their preference for the car and doll when both toys were of the same color or no color, by pairing the doll with the car of the same color, i.e., pink car/pink doll, blue doll/blue car, and by pairing a colorless car with a colorless doll. Finally, to test the hypothesis that boys and girls differ in preferences for the colors pink and blue, we paired pink to blue with the toy held constant: blue doll/pink doll and pink car/blue car.

Shape Stimuli

Three pairs of stimuli tested the hypothesis that boys and girls differ in their preferences for angular shapes versus rounded shapes: an angular triangle paired with a triangle with rounded edges (rounded triangle), an angular star paired with a star with rounded edges (rounded star), and an overlapping square and rectangle (rectangles) paired with an overlapping circle and oval (circles). The shapes were colored in white.

Procedure

. . . On arrival, parents and infants were taken into a reception room where they were informed about the procedure for the study and parental consent was obtained. They were then taken into the laboratory where parents were asked to seat their infants in their laps. In front of them, at a distance of 2 m, was a large white screen onto which the prepared images were projected. Hidden behind the screen was a stand holding a video camera and speakers. Only the lens of the video camera, which protruded from a hole cut out of the screen, was visible from the front of the screen. Parents were advised not to direct their child to a particular stimulus, either verbally or physically. They were also told that they could stop the testing procedure at any time by getting up from their seat. The experimenter sat in the observation room, separated from the laboratory by a one-way mirror.

As in other preferential looking studies, two stimuli were presented simultaneously, one on either side of the child's central gaze. The stimuli measured 45 × 45 cm and were located approximately 45 cm apart when projected onto the screen. The experimenter waited for the child to have a central gaze before showing each pair of stimuli. The infant could also be encouraged to look centrally at the screen by projecting a red spot onto the central point of the screen (used when the infant was looking in the direction of the screen) or by playing a sound (used when the infant was looking away from the screen area or was being especially fidgety). Generally, these devices were only required before the first pair of stimuli were presented.

The first sets of stimuli shown were the four pairs of color stimuli combined with the 11 pairs of toy stimuli. To ensure counterbalancing, each pairing was shown twice, with each stimulus within a pair appearing once on the left and once on the right side of the child's gaze. Thus, 30 pairs of stimuli were shown for 5 s each. The shape stimuli were shown after the color and toy stimuli. The three pairs of shape stimuli were counterbalanced producing six pairs shown for 5 s each. Order of presentation was randomized within each of the two groups of stimuli.

Data Analysis

Coding of the videotapes from the toy, color, and shape presentations was carried out by playing the tape on a VHS video-recorder and freezing the initial image. The frame advance function was then used to move the picture frame by frame. Data were coded directly onto a spreadsheet where it was noted whether the infant was looking at the left hand image, the right hand image or neither image during each frame. There were a total of 25 frames per second. . . . To assess inter-rater reliability, a randomly selected sample of the videotapes was coded by two scorers. Pearson correlation coefficients for the pairings, calculated using the combined raw scores for each pair of stimuli, ranged from .80 to .99 with an average correlation of .95. . . .

Some infants looked longer at the pairings than others. To adjust for these differences, scores were converted into the proportion of time spent looking at one stimulus over the total looking time for both stimuli. Proportions were transformed into percentage values; thus, an infant looking at a particular stimulus for 50% of the time meant that no preference was shown. All subsequent analyses were conducted using these percentage values.

Results

Mean proportions of time that infants looked at each of the color, toy, and shape stimulus pairings [were] broken down by sex and age. . . . Sex and age differences and their interaction were evaluated using analysis of variance for each of the pairings.

Color Stimuli

No main effects of sex were found for any of the four color pairings. A significant main effect of age was found only for the red/pale blue pairing, . . . with l2-month-olds looking significantly longer at red compared to 24-month-olds. . . . There were no significant interaction effects. A composite score was computed to examine sex and age influences on preferences for pink/red versus blue/pale blue collapsed across all four pairings. There were no significant main effects of sex or age and no interaction between sex and age.

Toy Stimuli

Five of the 11 pairings designed to test specific hypotheses were significant, and, contrary to the expectation that sex-typed toys would be of most interest when of sex-typed colors, findings suggested that infants preferred looking at sex-typed toys whether or not they were of sex-typed colors, but only when the brightness of colors was matched. In addition, means, even when not significant, were in the direction consistent with a preference for sex-typed toys, regardless of their color.

Shape Stimuli

No main effects of sex or age and no interactions were found for any of the three shape pairings comparing rounded shapes to angular shapes. An overall score, collapsed across all three pairings, also showed no main effects of sex or age and no interaction between sex and age.

Composite Stimuli

We next combined stimulus pairs to provide more reliable, composite estimates of children's preferences for sex-typed toys and sex-typed colors. Preferences for sex-typed toys were assessed by computing infants' average scores for looking at the doll versus the car, irrespective of color, across all pairings. Preferences for sex-typed colors were assessed by computing infants' average scores for looking at pink/red versus blue/pale blue, across all color pairings and, irrespective of the toy, across all toy pairings. . . .

The combined analysis of toy type revealed a main effect of sex. Girls looked longer at the doll than boys did, and boys looked longer at the car than girls did. . . . There also was a main effect of age. . . . Infants looked significantly longer at the doll at 12 months of age than at either

18 months . . . or 24 months . . . , but 18- and 24-month-olds did not differ. There was no significant interaction between sex and age. The combined analysis of color preferences across all toys and color pairings showed no significant main effects of sex or age and no significant interaction.

Using the composite scores, we also looked at within sex preferences for same sex-typed toys over other sex-typed toys (i.e., boys' preferences for cars over dolls and girls' preferences for dolls over cars) in each age group. Girls showed a significant preference for the doll over the car at ages 12 months . . . and 18 months . . . , but this difference, though in the same direction, was not statistically significant at 24 months. Boys also showed a significant preference for the doll over the car at 12 months. . . . At ages 18 and 24 months, boys no longer showed a preference for the doll, and, although they looked longer at the car than the doll at these later ages, their preference for the car was not statistically significant.

Finally, at the suggestion of a reviewer, we analyzed difference scores, obtained by subtracting percentage looking time at the colorless doll and car from percentage looking time at the same stimuli when colored. These analyses also suggested that infants did not show sex typed color preferences. There were no significant main or interaction effects for the composite color difference scores, and only one main effect and no interactions for any of the individual pairings.

Infant Preferences Regardless of Sex and Age
Because no sex or age differences emerged for the color or shape stimuli, we examined color and shape preferences, irrespective of sex and age. For the color stimuli, infants looked longer at red than blue and longer at red than pale blue. For the shape stimuli, infants looked longer at circles than squares and longer at rounded triangles than triangles. For the four color stimuli combined, infants looked longer at pink/red than blue/pale blue. . . . For the three shape stimuli combined, infants looked longer at rounded images than angular images. . . .

Discussion

Our results found both sex differences and sex similarities in infants' toy, color, and shape preferences. We saw the expected sex differences in toy preferences, with girls showing more interest than boys in dolls, and boys showing more interest than girls in cars. These results did not interact with age. The differences were most apparent in stimulus pairings when colors were controlled for brightness. Contrary to prediction, however, sex-typed toy pref-

erences were not stronger when toys were of sex-typed colors. In addition, infants did not show the predicted sex differences in color or shape preferences. Instead, we saw sex similarities in these areas. Both boys and girls preferred reddish colors to blue colors, and rounded shapes to angular shapes. There was also an age effect for interest in the doll. Both boys and girls looked longer at the doll at age 12 months, than at 18 or 24 months.

Controlling the brightness of colors was a novel aspect of the current study and, given that sex differences in toy preferences were most obvious when brightness was controlled, this could be a useful design feature for future studies. Controlling brightness may be particularly important in studies such as ours, which present images in a darkened room, allowing the brightness of a color, as well as its hue or other characteristics to influence its attractiveness.

Our observations that 12- to 24-month-old boys show more interest than girls do in cars, and that girls of this age show more interest than boys do in dolls, resemble observations of sex differences in toy preferences in older children, and add to evidence that these sex differences emerge at a very young age. Such early sex differences could reflect inborn tendencies for girls and boys to prefer different toys. This interpretation is consistent with findings linking prenatal androgen exposure to toy preferences in children and with findings of similar sex differences in toy preferences in non-human primates. Additionally, early socialization could contribute to sex differences in infants, since they have already been provided with sex-typed toys. Thus, their looking preferences may reflect the type of toys that they have been exposed to in their environment. This interpretation would suggest that children learn sex-typed behaviors at a very young age.

Cognitive developmental processes related to gender are not likely to explain sex-typed toy preferences in 12- to 24-month-old infants. At this age, many infants would not have reached even the first stage of gender acquisition (gender labeling). In addition, although there is evidence that female infants may display some understanding of gender by the age of 18 months, this is apparently not the case for boys. The role of gender identity in the acquisition of gender role learning needs to be re-evaluated, because toy preferences are found in male infants, even though they do not appear to be aware of their gender identity. Our findings also argue for reconsidering the role of cognitive understanding of gender, at least in the initial phase of children's acquisition of sex-typed toy preferences. Cognitive factors may play a role in later years, however, as sex-typed toy preferences become increasingly evident.

We did not see sex differences in preferences for pink or reddish colors over blue, nor did we see sex differences in preferences for angular versus rounded shapes. Therefore, our findings did not support [the] suggestion that differences in color or shape preferences explain sex differences in toy preferences, at least at this early stage of development. Indeed, the causal relationships may be the opposite. Sex differences in toy preferences may contribute to sex differences in preferences for colors or shapes. For example, girls may learn to like pink because many of the toys they play with are pink. Alternatively, or additionally, they may learn this color preference through social or cognitive mechanisms. For example, girls may learn to prefer pink through modeling older girls who like pink, or through cultural labeling of pink as for girls. Similar mechanisms could explain sex differences in shape preferences. In addition to suggesting that the different colors of sex-typed toys could drive boys and girls differential interest in them, [it] has [been] suggested that females and males may have evolved to prefer pink and blue, respectively, a suggestion that has been reiterated by others. Our findings argue against these suggestions as well.

Our observation that boys at 12 months of age, like girls, prefer the doll to the car . . . argue against suggestions that boys' strong preference for masculine toys or avoidance of feminine toys, such as dolls, is inborn, and argue instead for the importance of social learning or cognitive developmental processes in the development of this particular aspect of sex-typed toy preferences. Consistent with this argument, boys' avoidance of feminine toys has been found to increase with age, and to be stronger when an observer is present. Boys also receive stronger reinforcement than girls do to avoid cross sex toy play, and they are more likely than girls are to imitate the behavior of same sex models. Thus, reinforcement and modeling could play an important role in boys' eventual strong preference for masculine toys or avoidance of feminine toys.

Instead of providing evidence of sex differences in infants' visual preference for pink and blue, our findings suggest that infants prefer red, irrespective of their sex. Other studies also have reported that infants from as young as 2 months of age look longer at red than at other colors. . . . The absence of sex differences in infants' and young children's color preferences, coupled with findings that older children display sex-typed color choices, suggests that children learn these preferences. The timing of the emergence of sex-typed color preference (after age two, or maybe even five, years) is also consistent with cognitive developmental perspectives, which suggest that sex differences in children's behavior emerge as children develop a cognitive understanding of their gender and its stability and constancy, a process that continues after the age of two until as late as age seven years or older.

Our results also suggest sex similarity rather than difference in infants' shape preferences; irrespective of sex, infants looked longer at rounded shapes (circles, rounded triangles) than at angular shapes (squares, triangles). The preference for rounded over angular shapes could relate to the emotional responses that different shapes elicit. A study asking college students to rate their emotional response to stimuli consisting of either an ellipse or a straight line found that roundedness conveyed warmth and acute angles conveyed threat. . . . Sharp angles may convey a sense of threat which results in a negative bias. It also has been suggested that the visual properties of angularity could reflect the facial attributes of an angry face and roundedness could reflect the facial attributes of a happy face. . . .

In addition to seeing unexpected sex similarities in the color and shape preferences of infants, we saw an unpredicted effect of age. Regardless of sex, infants looked longer at the doll at age 12 months than at later ages. The interest of 12-month-old infants of both sexes in dolls might relate to infants' interest in faces. If so, our results suggest that this interest is more pronounced in younger infants than in older infants. . . .

The current study adds to growing evidence that infants younger than 2 years of age display sex-typed toy preferences, with boys showing more interest than girls do in cars, and girls showing more interest than boys do in dolls. Within sex analyses found that the female preference for dolls over cars begins as early as 12 months of age, whereas boys of this age also prefer dolls to cars. The male preference for cars over dolls, or avoidance of dolls, emerges later, suggesting that socialization or cognitive development, rather than inborn factors, causes the male avoidance of feminine toys. Similarly the lack of sex differences in color or shape preferences in infants suggests that sex differences in these areas emerge later, perhaps also under the influence of socialization or cognitive developmental processes. In addition to seeing sex differences in infants, we also observed sex similarities. Infants of both sexes preferred reddish colors to blue and rounded shapes to angular shapes. One implication of our findings is that sex differences in toy preferences in infancy are not driven by sex-linked preferences for different colors or shapes, since sex differences in these areas are not yet present. Instead, the direction of influence could be the opposite. Girls may learn to prefer pink, for instance, because the toys that they enjoy playing with are often colored pink. Finally, our results suggest that different types of factors influence different aspects of children's sex-typed preferences. Inborn factors, such as the prenatal testosterone surge in male fetuses, may be particularly important for boys' greater interest than girls in vehicles and girls' greater interest than boys in dolls. In contrast, sex-typed color and shape preferences, and the male avoidance of girls' toys, which appear to emerge later in life, may depend more extensively on sex-related differences in socialization or cognitive developmental processes.

Vasanti Jadva is a research associate in the Center for Family Research, Faculty of Social and Political Sciences, University of Cambridge, Cambridge, UK. Her current focus is on families created using donor insemination, egg donation, and surrogacy, and she has also studied the experiences of individuals searching for, and finding, their donor relations, including donor offspring searching for their donors and donor siblings.

Melissa Hines specializes in human gender development and is the director of the Hormones and Behaviour Research Lab at the University of Cambridge.

Susan Golombok is a psychology professor and director of the Family and Child Psychology Research Centre at the City University, London.

EXPLORING THE ISSUE

Does Anatomy Predict Gender?

Critical Thinking and Reflection

1. Jadva and colleagues describe a number of different theories that might account for sex differences in toy preferences. What are these theories?
2. Given that toy preferences, especially the nature of sex differences, appear to change with age, how might these age-related changes be explained? Do some theoretical accounts do a better job of explaining such changes than others?
3. Explain the concepts of sex-similarities and sex-differences.
4. What findings might argue against explanations that focus on inborn causes of the differences? Make a list of what these might be, including such things as parents' educational level or number and sex of older siblings in the home.
5. What findings might argue against explanations that focus on environmental causes of the differences? Make a list of what these might be, including such things as prenatal hormonal levels.
6. Do studies such as these shed light on the question of whether anatomy is destiny? Why or why not?
7. How might the issue of gender-related patterns in toy preferences be studied cross-culturally?

Is There Common Ground?

Both YES and NO selections suggest that clear gender-related preferences for toys exist, but the question of why remains to be answered. Van de Beek and colleagues note that although their focus was on the relation between prenatal hormones and toy preferences, there is clearly room for various environmental factors to affect toy preferences. Conversely, Javda and her colleagues do admit that although socialization and cognitive development factors probably account for sex similarities and differences, inborn biological factors including hormones may also make a contribution. Thus, although different authors may emphasize one set of factors over another, they do leave room for the possibility that there is a dynamic interaction between the biological and the environmental factors.

Nature versus nurture? Biology versus social determinism? Just as some scholars argue that we need to move beyond gender binaries to better understand human complexity, we must also move beyond neat either/or propositions about the causes of sex and gender. Traditional thought dictates that biology affects or determines behavior and that anatomy is destiny. But behavior can also alter physiology. Recent advances explore the complex interaction between biology (genes, hormones, brain structure) and environment. We have learned that it is impossible to determine how much of our behavior is biologically based and how much is environmental. Moreover, definitions of gendered behavior are temporally and culturally relative. Yet why do researchers continue to try to isolate biological factors from environmental factors? Advancements in the study of biological bases of sex and critiques of applications of biological theory to human behavior challenge many long-held assertions. Many traditional biologists recognize species diversity in hormone–brain–behavior relationships, which makes the general application of theories based on animal physiology and behavior to humans problematic. Moreover, species diversity challenges male/female binaries. The validity of the presence/absence model of sex dimorphism has been challenged. In embryonic development, do females "just happen" by default in the absence of testosterone? No, all individuals actively develop through various genetic processes that are integrally linked to environmental factors that either activate or alter these processes. Moreover, the sexes are similar in the presence of, and need for, both androgens and estrogens; in fact, the chemical structures and derivation of estrogen and testosterone are interconnected and imbalances of either in females and males cause serious anomalies in the development and lifetime functioning.

Additional Resources

Delamont, S. (2012). Sex roles and the school, Volume 71. London and New York: Routledge.

Lindsey, L.L. (2011). Gender roles: A sociological perspective. Boston: Prentice Hall.

Suar, D. and Gochhayat, J. (2014). Influence of biological sex and gender roles on ethicality. *Journal of Business Ethics*, October 8.

Internet References . . .

Good Men Project

http://goodmenproject.com/

True Child

http://www.truechild.org/

UN Women

http://www.unwomen.org/en

Selected, Edited, and with Issue Framing Material by:
Elizabeth Schroeder, EdD, MSW, *Elizabeth Schroeder Consulting*

ISSUE

Are Barriers to Women's Success as Leaders Due to Societal Obstacles?

YES: Alice H. Eagly and Linda L. Carli, from "Women and the Labyrinth of Leadership," *Harvard Business Review* (2007)

NO: Mark van Vugt and Anjana Ahuja, from *Naturally Selected: The Evolutionary Science of Leadership* (Harper Business, 2011)

Learning Outcomes

After reading this issue, you will be able to:

- Provide an evolutionary explanation of leadership styles that accounts for gender-related patterns.
- Describe at least one strength and one weakness of the glass ceiling and labyrinth analogies in describing women's barriers to success as leaders.
- Define at least two gender-related patterns in leadership styles.

ISSUE SUMMARY

YES: Alice Eagly and Linda Carli contend that barriers exist for women at every stage of their career trajectories, resulting in, not a glass ceiling, but a labyrinth.

NO: Mark van Vugt and Anjana Ahuja assert that the division of labor by sex is rooted in biologically based differences between women and men. Evolutionarily based natural selection has led to inclinations that make women and men better suited for different types of jobs.

Women continue to face career barriers. Although women hold 40 percent of managerial positions in the United States today, only 2 percent of *Fortune* 500 CEOs are women. The question remains as to why. Explanations tend to fall into one of two camps: human capital theory and discrimination theory. Human capital theories focus on obstacles from within the person. These theories focus on explanations such as differences in women's and men's abilities, interests, education, qualifications, personal investment in their careers and leadership style, as well as choices related to family-work conflicts that are more likely to result in job discontinuity and turnover for women than for men. On the other hand, discrimination theorists focus on sociocultural factors that result in differential treatment of women and men. Three forms of

employment discrimination have been identified. *Within-job wage discrimination* occurs when there are disparities in the same job or unequal pay for equal work. *Valuative discrimination* is associated with lower wages in female- rather than male-dominated fields. Finally, *allocative discrimination* occurs when there are biases in hiring, promotion, and dismissal. This latter form of discrimination has evoked various descriptors of discrimination, including the "glass ceiling," "concrete wall," "sticky floor," and "glass escalator." The image of the glass ceiling suggests that women ascend the career ladder with the top in sight, but at some rung on that ladder they hit the glass ceiling. This image was transformed to that of a concrete wall to describe the even greater challenges faced by ethnic minority women. The glass elevator was a term coined to express the rapid career advancement of men who enter nontraditional, historically female-dominated fields, such as nursing. The sticky floor refers to the finding that when there is a critical mass of members of a particular under-valued group in the workplace, one of their own may be more likely to achieve a position of mid-management, but it is very difficult to rise higher.

Power operates as a social structure that affects how people respond to female leaders. Lips has identified four ways in which women are responded to differently and which can undermine their effectiveness as leaders: (1) women are expected to combine leadership with compassion; (2) people do not listen to or take direction from women as comfortably as from men; (3) women who promote themselves and their abilities reap disapproval; and (4) women require more external validation then do men in some contexts. Furthermore, women in leadership positions are quite aware of these reactions. Some are more comfortable than others taking on the negative reactions of others if they are seen as too bossy, aggressive, or domineering. They also realize the double bind created if they try to counter such judgments by toning down their actions, actions that may ultimately undermine their authority. Lips has noted that women cope with this conundrum by finding rewards in their leadership roles. She says these rewards include a sense of competence and of positive impact and the opportunity to empower others. She further suggests that organizations committed to supporting female leaders can do so by not isolating women as tokens in male-dominated department; by endorsing and legitimating them; and by ensuring that differential standards are not used to evaluate male and female leaders. These issues raise questions about what women should do if they wish to continue to strive for higher levels of leadership. Is there some leadership style that is most likely to ensure success?

Research has identified several different leadership styles. Autocratic leaders exercise a great deal of personal control, whereas democratic leaders involve group members in the decision-making process. One extreme, laissez-faire leadership, entails a hands-off approach in which the followers are expected to solve problems and make decisions on their own. Management by exception is the style wherein the leader allows the group to handle routine matters and gets involved only with matters that are non-routine. In contrast, transactional leadership involves interactions with group members, but ultimately the leader makes the decisions and is very focused on rewards and punishments. Transformational leaders provide yet another contrast. They are focused on the goals of individuals and organizations and lead in ways that result in change within the organization. Their goals are to inspire and be a role model. There are numerous stereotypical beliefs, both descriptive and prescriptive, about women in leadership that have implications for what leadership styles might be best suited for women who are interested in being successful. Given that stereotypically men are seen as agentic and women as communal, it is not surprising that stereotypes about leadership styles reflect this distinction. In general, people believe that women are more transformational and use more contingent rewards than men, whereas men are thought to lead in a more laissez-faire style and use more management by exception then do women. Furthermore, it appears that the leadership style used by women and men leaders affects the likelihood that they are judged worthy of promotion. Alice Eagly and her colleagues conducted a study in which they found that of all the various dimensions of transformational leadership, only inspirational motivation (being optimistic and excited about goals in the future) was judged more important for male than female leaders as a criterion for promotion, especially promotion to CEO. For female leaders, while inspirational motivation was seen as relevant, so too was individualized consideration, paying attention to the needs and goals of individuals, which is another component of transformational leadership. This was seen as particularly relevant for promoting women to senior management positions. Eagly and her colleagues concluded that for women the inclusion of individualized consideration into their leadership style, along with inspirational motivation, may enable them "to fulfill prescriptive gender norms and avoid backlash."

In contrast, Eagly and Carli's selection represents a discrimination theory perspective. In addition to describing all the various ways in which women can be targets of discrimination in the workplace, they coined a new term for allocative discrimination, "the labyrinth." That is, women must navigate a maze of obstacles to succeed. In the selection that follows, the excerpt from Mark van Vogt and Anjana Ahuja is an example of an explanation from the human capital perspective in which they argue that by nature women and men have different interests and talents that better suit them for different jobs. They argue from an evolutionary perspective that women and men are designed to lead differently.

YES ←

Alice H. Eagly and Linda L. Carli

Women and the Labyrinth of Leadership

If one has misdiagnosed a problem, then one is unlikely to prescribe an effective cure. This is the situation regarding the scarcity of women in top leadership. Because people with the best of intentions have misread the symptoms, the solutions that managers are investing in are not making enough of a difference.

That there is a problem is not in doubt. Despite years of progress by women in the workforce (they now occupy more than 40% of all managerial positions in the United States), within the C-suite they remain as rare as hens' teeth. Consider the most highly paid executives of *Fortune 500* companies—those with titles such as chairman, president, chief executive officer, and chief operating officer. Of this group, only 6% are women. Most notably, only 2% of the CEOs are women, and only 15% of the seats on the boards of directors are held by women. The situation is not much different in other industrialized countries. In the 50 largest publicly traded corporations in each nation of the European Union, women make up, on average, 11% of the top executives and 4% of the CEOs and heads of boards. Just seven companies, or 1%, of *Fortune* magazine's Global 500 have female CEOs. What is to blame for the pronounced lack of women in positions of power and authority?

In 1986 the *Wall Street Journal's* Carol Hymowitz and Timothy Schellhardt gave the world an answer: "Even those few women who rose steadily through the ranks eventually crashed into an invisible barrier. The executive suite seemed within their grasp, but they just couldn't break through the glass ceiling." The metaphor, driven home by the article's accompanying illustration, resonated; it captured the frustration of a goal within sight but somehow unattainable. To be sure, there was a time when the barriers were absolute. Even within the career spans of 1980s-era executives, access to top posts had been explicitly denied. . . .

Times have changed, however, and the glass ceiling metaphor is now more wrong than right. For one thing, it describes an absolute barrier at a specific high level in organizations. The fact that there have been female chief executives, university presidents, state governors, and presidents of nations gives the lie to that charge. At the same time, the metaphor implies that women and men have equal access to entry- and mid-level positions. They do not. The image of a transparent obstruction also suggests that women are being misled about their opportunities, because the impediment is not easy for them to see from a distance. But some impediments are not subtle. Worst of all, by depicting a single, unvarying obstacle, the glass ceiling fails to incorporate the complexity and variety of challenges that women can face in their leadership journeys. In truth, women are not turned away only as they reach the penultimate stage of a distinguished career. They disappear in various numbers at many points leading up to that stage.

Metaphors matter because they are part of the storytelling that can compel change. Believing in the existence of a glass ceiling, people emphasize certain kinds of interventions: top-to-top networking, mentoring to increase board memberships, requirements for diverse candidates in high-profile succession horse races, litigation aimed at punishing discrimination in the C-suite. None of these is counterproductive; all have a role to play. The danger arises when they draw attention and resources away from other kinds of interventions that might attack the problem more potently. If we want to make better progress, it's time to rename the challenge.

Walls All Around

A better metaphor for what confronts women in their professional endeavors is the labyrinth. It's an image with a long and varied history in ancient Greece, India, Nepal, native North and South America, medieval Europe, and elsewhere. As a contemporary symbol, it conveys the idea of a complex journey toward a goal worth striving for. Passage through a labyrinth is not simple or direct, but requires persistence, awareness of one's progress, and a careful analysis of the puzzles that lie ahead. It is this meaning that we intend to convey. For women who aspire to top leadership, routes exist but are full of twists and turns, both unexpected and expected. Because all labyrinths have a viable route to the center, it is understood that goals are attainable. The metaphor acknowledges obstacles but is not ultimately discouraging.

If we can understand the various barriers that make up this labyrinth, and how some women find their way around them, we can work more effectively to improve the situation. What are the obstructions that women run up against? Let's explore them in turn.

Vestiges of prejudice. It is a well-established fact that men as a group still have the benefit of higher wages and faster promotions. In the United States in 2005, for example, women employed full-time earned 81 cents for every dollar that men earned. . . .

One of the most comprehensive of these studies was conducted by the U.S. Government Accountability Office. The study was based on survey data from 1983 through 2000 from a representative sample of Americans. Because the same people responded to the survey repeatedly over the years, the study provided accurate estimates of past work experience, which is important for explaining later wages.

The GAO researchers tested whether individuals' total wages could be predicted by sex and other characteristics. They included part-time and full-time employees in the surveys and took into account all the factors that they could estimate and that might affect earnings, such as education and work experience. Without controls for these variables, the data showed that women earned about 44% less than men, averaged over the entire period from 1983 to 2000. With these controls in place, the gap was only about half as large, but still substantial. The control factors that reduced the wage gap most were the different employment patterns of men and women: Men undertook more hours of paid labor per year than women and had more years of job experience.

Although most variables affected the wages of men and women similarly, there were exceptions. Marriage and parenthood, for instance, were associated with higher wages for men but not for women. In contrast, other characteristics, especially years of education, had a more positive effect on women's wages than on men's. Even after adjusting wages for all of the ways men and women differ, the GAO study, like similar studies, showed that women's wages remained lower than men's. The unexplained gender gap is consistent with the presence of wage discrimination.

Similar methods have been applied to the question of whether discrimination affects promotions. Evidently it does. Promotions come more slowly for women than

for men with equivalent qualifications. . . . Even in culturally feminine settings such as nursing, librarianship, elementary education, and social work, men ascend to supervisory and administrative positions more quickly than women.

The findings of correlational studies are supported by experimental research, in which subjects are asked to evaluate hypothetical individuals as managers or job candidates, and all characteristics of these individuals are held constant except for their sex. Such efforts continue the tradition of the Goldberg paradigm, named for a 1968 experiment by Philip Goldberg. His simple, elegant study had student participants evaluate written essays that were identical except for the attached male or female name. The students were unaware that other students had received identical material ascribed to a writer of the other sex. This initial experiment demonstrated an overall gender bias: Women received lower evaluations unless the essay was on a feminine topic. Some 40 years later, unfortunately, experiments continue to reveal the same kind of bias in work settings. Men are advantaged over equivalent women as candidates for jobs traditionally held by men as well as for more gender-integrated jobs. Similarly, male leaders receive somewhat more favorable evaluations than equivalent female leaders, especially in roles usually occupied by men.

. . . [A] general bias against women appears to operate with approximately equal strength at all levels. The scarcity of female corporate officers is the sum of discrimination that has operated at all ranks, not evidence of a particular obstacle to advancement as women approach the top. The problem, in other words, is not a glass ceiling.

Resistance to women's leadership. What's behind the discrimination we've been describing? Essentially, a set of widely shared conscious and unconscious mental associations about women, men, and leaders. Study after study has affirmed that people associate women and men with different traits and link men with more of the traits that connote leadership. . . .

In the language of psychologists, the clash is between two sets of associations: communal and agentic. Women are associated with communal qualities, which convey a concern for the compassionate treatment of others. They include being especially affectionate, helpful, friendly, kind, and sympathetic, as well as interpersonally sensitive, gentle, and soft-spoken. In contrast, men are associated with agentic qualities, which convey assertion and control. They include being especially aggressive, ambitious, dominant, self-confident, and forceful, as well as self-reliant and individualistic. The agentic traits are also associated in most people's minds with effective leadership—perhaps because a long history of male domination of leadership roles has made it difficult to separate the leader associations from the male associations.

As a result, women leaders find themselves in a double bind. If they are highly communal, they may be criticized for not being agentic enough. But if they are highly agentic, they may be criticized for lacking communion. Either way, they may leave the impression that they don't have "the right stuff" for powerful jobs.

Given this double bind, it is hardly surprising that people are more resistant to women's influence than to men's. . . .

Studies have gauged reactions to men and women engaging in various types of dominant behavior. The findings are quite consistent. Nonverbal dominance, such as staring at others while speaking to them or pointing at people, is a more damaging behavior for women than for men. Verbally intimidating others can undermine a woman's influence, and assertive behavior can reduce her chances of getting a job or advancing in her career. Simply disagreeing can sometimes get women into trouble. Men who disagree or otherwise act dominant get away with it more often than women do.

Self-promotion is similarly risky for women. Although it can convey status and competence, it is not at all communal. So while men can use bluster to get themselves noticed, modesty is expected even of highly accomplished women. . . .

Another way the double bind penalizes women is by denying them the full benefits of being warm and considerate. Because people expect it of women, nice behavior that seems noteworthy in men seems unimpressive in women. For example, in one study, helpful men reaped a lot of approval, but helpful women did not. Likewise, men got away with being unhelpful, but women did not. . . .

While one might suppose that men would have a double bind of their own, they in fact have more freedom. Several experiments and organizational studies have assessed reactions to behavior that is warm and friendly versus dominant and assertive. The findings show that men can communicate in a warm or a dominant manner, with no penalty either way. People like men equally well and are equally influenced by them regardless of their warmth.

It all amounts to a clash of assumptions when the average person confronts a woman in management. . . . In the absence of any evidence to the contrary, people suspect that such highly effective women must not be very likable or nice.

Issues of leadership style. In response to the challenges presented by the double bind, female leaders often struggle to cultivate an appropriate and effective leadership style—one that reconciles the communal qualities people prefer in women with the agentic qualities people think leaders need to succeed. . . .

It's difficult to pull off such a transformation while maintaining a sense of authenticity as a leader. Sometimes the whole effort can backfire. In the words of another female leader, "I think that there is a real penalty for a woman who behaves like a man. The men don't like her and the women don't either." Women leaders worry a lot about these things, complicating the labyrinth that they negotiate. For example, Catalyst's study of *Fortune* 1000 female executives found that 96% of them rated as critical or fairly important that they develop "a style with which male managers are comfortable."

Does a distinct "female" leadership style exist? There seems to be a popular consensus that it does. . . .

More scientifically, a recent meta-analysis integrated the results of 45 studies addressing the question [comparing three leadership styles]. . . . Transformational leaders establish themselves as role models by gaining followers' trust and confidence. They state future goals, develop plans to achieve those goals, and innovate, even when their organizations are generally successful. Such leaders mentor and empower followers, encouraging them to develop their full potential and thus to contribute more effectively to their organizations. By contrast, transactional leaders establish give-and-take relationships that appeal to subordinates' self-interest. Such leaders manage in the conventional manner of clarifying subordinates' responsibilities, rewarding them for meeting objectives, and correcting them for failing to meet objectives. Although transformational and transactional leadership styles are different, most leaders adopt at least some behaviors of both types. The researchers also allowed for a third category, called the laissez-faire style—a sort of non-leadership that concerns itself with none of the above, despite rank authority.

The meta-analysis found that, in general, female leaders were somewhat more transformational than male leaders, especially when it came to giving support and encouragement to subordinates. They also engaged in more of the rewarding behaviors that are one aspect of transactional leadership. Meanwhile, men exceeded women on the aspects of transactional leadership involving corrective and disciplinary actions that are either active (timely) or passive (belated). Men were also more likely than women to be laissez-faire leaders, who take little responsibility for managing. These findings add up to a startling conclusion, given that most leadership research has found the transformational style (along with the rewards and positive incentives associated with the transactional style) to be more suited to leading the modern organization. The research tells us not only that men and women do have somewhat different leadership styles, but also that women's approaches are the more generally effective—while men's often are only somewhat effective or actually hinder effectiveness.

Another part of this picture, based on a separate meta-analysis, is that women adopt a more participative and collaborative style than men typically favor. The reason for this difference is unlikely to be genetic. Rather, it may be that collaboration can get results without seeming particularly masculine. As women navigate their way through the double bind, they seek ways to project authority without relying on the autocratic behaviors that people find so jarring in women. A viable path is to bring others into decision making and to lead as an encouraging teacher and positive role model. . . .

Demands of family life. For many women, the most fateful turns in the labyrinth are the ones taken under pressure of family responsibilities. Women continue to be the ones who interrupt their careers, take more days off, and work part-time. As a result, they have fewer years of job experience and fewer hours of employment per year, which slows their career progress and reduces their earnings. . . .

There is no question that, while men increasingly share housework and child rearing, the bulk of domestic work still falls on women's shoulders. We know this from time-diary studies, in which people record what they are doing during each hour of a 24-hour day. So, for example, in the United States married women devoted 19 hours per week on average to housework in 2005, while married men contributed 11 hours. That's a huge improvement over 1965 numbers, when women spent a whopping 34 hours per week to men's five, but it is still a major inequity. And the situation looks worse when child care hours are added.

Although it is common knowledge that mothers provide more child care than fathers, few people realize that mothers provide more than they did in earlier generations—despite the fact that fathers are putting in a lot more time than in the past. . . . Thus, though husbands have taken on more domestic work, the work/family conflict has not eased for women; the gain has been offset by escalating pressures for intensive parenting and the increasing time demands of most high-level careers.

Even women who have found a way to relieve pressures from the home front by sharing child care with husbands, other family members, or paid workers may not enjoy the full workplace benefit of having done so. Decision makers often assume that mothers have domestic responsibilities that make it inappropriate to promote them to demanding positions. . . .

Underinvestment in social capital. Perhaps the most destructive result of the work/family balancing act so many women must perform is that it leaves very little time for socializing with colleagues and building professional networks. The social capital that accrues from such "nonessential" parts of work turns out to be quite essential indeed. One study yielded the following description of managers who advanced rapidly in hierarchies: Fast-track managers "spent relatively more time and effort socializing, politicking, and interacting with outsiders than did their less successful counterparts . . . [and] did not give much time or attention to the traditional management activities of planning, decision making, and controlling or to the human resource management activities of motivating/reinforcing, staffing, training/developing, and managing conflict." . . .

Even given sufficient time, women can find it difficult to engage in and benefit from informal networking if they are a small minority. In such settings, the influential networks are composed entirely or almost entirely of men. Breaking into those male networks can be hard, especially when men center their networks on masculine activities. The recent gender discrimination lawsuit against Wal-Mart provides examples of this. For instance, an executive retreat took the form of a quail-hunting expedition at Sam Walton's ranch in Texas. Middle managers' meetings included visits to strip clubs and Hooters restaurants, and a sales conference attended by thousands of store managers featured a football theme. One executive received feedback that she probably would not advance in the company because she didn't hunt or fish.

Management Interventions That Work

Taking the measure of the labyrinth that confronts women leaders, we see that it begins with prejudices that benefit men and penalize women, continues with particular resistance to women's leadership, includes questions of leadership style and authenticity, and—most dramatically for many women—features the challenge of balancing work and family responsibilities. It becomes clear that a woman's situation as she reaches her peak career years is the result of many turns at many challenging junctures. Only a few individual women have made the right combination of moves to land at the center of power—but as for the rest, there is usually no single turning point where their progress was diverted and the prize was lost.

What's to be done in the face of such a multifaceted problem? A solution that is often proposed is for governments to implement and enforce antidiscrimination legislation and thereby require organizations to eliminate inequitable practices. However, analysis of discrimination cases that have gone to court has shown that legal remedies can be elusive when gender inequality results from norms embedded in organizational structure and culture. The more effective approach is for organizations to appreciate the subtlety and complexity of the problem and to attack its many roots simultaneously. More specifically, if a company wants to see more women arrive in its executive suite, it should do the following:

Increase people's awareness of the psychological drivers of prejudice toward female leaders, and work to dispel those perceptions. . . .

Change the long-hours norm. . . . To the extent an organization can shift the focus to objective measures of productivity, women with family demands on their time but highly productive work habits will receive the rewards and encouragement they deserve.

Reduce the subjectivity of performance evaluation. . . . To ensure fairness, criteria should be explicit and evaluation processes designed to limit the influence of decision makers' conscious and unconscious biases.

Use open-recruitment tools, such as advertising and employment agencies, rather than relying on informal social networks and referrals to fill positions. . . . Research has shown that such personnel practices increase the numbers of women in managerial roles.

Ensure a critical mass of women in executive positions—not just one or two women—to head off the problems that come with tokenism. Token women tend to be pegged into narrow stereotypical roles such as "seductress," "mother," "pet," or "iron maiden." . . . When women are not a small minority, their identities as women become less salient, and colleagues are more likely to react to them in terms of their individual competencies.

Avoid having a sole female member of any team. Top management tends to divide its small population of women managers among many projects in the interests of introducing diversity to them all. But several studies have found that, so outnumbered, the women tend to be ignored by the men. . . . This is part of the reason that the glass ceiling metaphor resonates with so many. But in fact, the problem can be present at any level.

Help shore up social capital. As we've discussed, the call of family responsibilities is mainly to blame for women's underinvestment in networking. When time is scarce, this social activity is the first thing to go by the wayside. . . . When a well-placed individual who possesses greater legitimacy (often a man) takes an interest in a woman's career, her efforts to build social capital can proceed far more efficiently.

Prepare women for line management with appropriately demanding assignments. Women, like men, must have the benefit of developmental job experiences if they are to qualify for promotions. . . .

Establish family-friendly human resources practices. These may include flextime, job sharing, telecommuting, elder care provisions, adoption benefits, dependent child care options, and employee-sponsored on-site child care. Such support can allow women to stay in their jobs during the most demanding years of child rearing, build social capital, keep up to date in their fields, and eventually compete for higher positions. . . .

Allow employees who have significant parental responsibility more time to prove themselves worthy of promotion. This recommendation is particularly directed to organizations, many of them professional services firms, that have established "up or out" career progressions. People not ready for promotion at the same time as the top performers in their cohort aren't simply left in place—they're asked to leave. But many parents (most often mothers), while fully capable of reaching that level of achievement, need extra time—perhaps a year or two—to get there. . . .

Welcome women back. It makes sense to give high-performing women who step away from the workforce an opportunity to return to responsible positions when their circumstances change. . . .

Encourage male participation in family-friendly benefits. Dangers lurk in family-friendly benefits that are used only by women. Exercising options such as generous parental leave and part-time work slows down women's careers. More profoundly, having many more women than men take such benefits can harm the careers of women in general because of the expectation that they may well exercise those options. Any effort toward greater family friendliness should actively recruit male participation to avoid inadvertently making it harder for women to gain access to essential managerial roles.

Managers can be forgiven if they find the foregoing list a tall order. It's a wide-ranging set of interventions and still far from exhaustive. The point, however, is just that: Organizations will succeed in filling half their top management slots with women—and women who are the true performance equals of their male counterparts—only by attacking all the reasons they are absent today. Glass ceiling-inspired programs and projects can do just so much if the leakage of talented women is happening on every lower floor of the building. Individually, each of these interventions has been shown to make a difference. Collectively, we believe, they can make all the difference.

The View from Above

Imagine visiting a formal garden and finding within it a high hedgerow. At a point along its vertical face, you spot a rectangle—a neatly pruned and inviting doorway.

Are you aware as you step through that you are entering a labyrinth? And, three doorways later, as the reality of the puzzle settles in, do you have any idea how to proceed? This is the situation in which many women find themselves in their career endeavors. Ground-level perplexity and frustration make every move uncertain.

Labyrinths become infinitely more tractable when seen from above. When the eye can take in the whole of the puzzle—the starting position, the goal, and the maze of walls—solutions begin to suggest themselves. This has been the goal of our research. Our hope is that women, equipped with a map of the barriers they will confront on their path to professional achievement, will make more informed choices. We hope that managers, too, will understand where their efforts can facilitate the progress of women. If women are to achieve equality, women and men will have to share leadership equally. With a greater understanding of what stands in the way of gender-balanced leadership, we draw nearer to attaining it in our time.

ALICE H. EAGLY, a social psychologist, is the James Padilla Chair of Arts and Sciences, professor of psychology, faculty fellow of the Institute for Policy Research, and department chair of psychology, all at Northwestern University. She has received numerous awards including the 2007 Interamerican Psychologist Award from Interamerican Society of Psychology for contributions to psychology as a science and profession in the Americas, as well as the 2005 Carolyn Wood Sherif Award from the Society for the Psychology of Women for contributions to the field of the psychology of women as a scholar, teacher, mentor, and leader.

LINDA L. CARLI is an associate professor in the psychology department at Wellesley College, where she has been since 1991. Her current research focuses on women's leadership, particularly the obstacles that women leaders face and ways to overcome those obstacles. Dr. Carli teaches a variety of courses, including organizational psychology, the psychology of law, and research in applied psychology.

Mark van Vugt and Anjana Ahuja

 **NO**

Naturally Selected: The Evolutionary Science of Leadership

Our brand new theory of leadership [is] grounded in evolutionary science. . . . [W]hen viewed in the context of this theory, much of human behaviour—the leadership styles we prefer, and those we abhor—begins to make sense: why we don't like middle managers, why we prefer the political devil we know to the angel we don't, why we bristle at extravagance among leaders, and why there is universal interest in the domestic minutiae of political figures. Our theory accommodates all the familiar features of the leadership landscape—charisma, personality traits, alpha males, the glass ceiling for women, nature versus nurture—but, unlike other leadership theories, brings them together in a way that makes sense.

We have a name for this bigger picture: evolutionary leadership theory (ELT). Its name reflects our contention, backed up by observations and experiment, that leadership and followership emerged during the course of human evolution and that their foundations were laid long before humans evolved. We call them adaptive behaviours. When scientists use the word 'adaptive' to describe a behaviour, they mean that it emerged during the course of evolution in order to enhance an organism's chances of reproduction by enabling it to adapt to the environment. Evolution selected for a combination of leaders and followers in human society; a template for these behaviours eventually became 'hard-wired' into the human brain. As you'll see, there is an abundance of evidence that leadership and followership are automatic and (usually) beneficial. Groups of strangers speedily and spontaneously arrange themselves into a led group when asked to carry out a task, and led groups invariably fare better than groups without leaders. There is, as all of us already know, something instinctive and unforced about human leadership. The ubiquity of leadership and followership in the hierarchy of life—from fish to bees to humans—also suggests that tagging behind a competent leader is a smart way for any species, not just *Homo sapiens*, to prosper.

This brings us to the distinctive and unique feature of evolutionary leadership theory. We tackle leadership by doing something startlingly simple: turning back the clock and revisiting its origins. Human leadership as we know it had to start somewhere, and it began more than two million years ago on the African savannah with the birth of the species *Homo*. Our ancestors teamed up to hunt, to fight, to live, to love—and, because tribes showing strong leadership thrived, leadership and followership came to be part of the fabric of human life. This perspective makes *Naturally Selected* very different from most of the other books on leadership psychology, which often start by scrutinising a great leader and then combing through his background to fathom what makes him tick (no apologies for the male bias here; accounts of successful female leaders are rare, and we'll explain why later on). Such biographies, while making compelling reading, rarely provide insight beyond the psychology of the lantern-jawed hero gazing out assertively from the front cover.

Naturally Selected, on the other hand, applies to each and every one of us. It goes back to basics. It transports us back to the beginning, to trace how leadership emerged and changed over an evolutionary time period of several million years. If there is any central figure in the book, it is evolution's Everyman. Conceptually, we believe that the psychology of leadership and followership emerged in our species (as well as in many others) as a response to the challenges of survival and reproduction, which are the ultimate aim of any organism. We should note here that we are adopting an evolutionary perspective which applies insights from evolutionary biology and evolutionary psychology to questions concerning leadership. An evolutionary perspective assumes that certain cognitive capacities, such as language, evolved to solve certain problems that would have preoccupied our ancestors, such as finding shelter and food. . . . Combining and integrating insights about leadership from psychology, biology, neuroscience, economics, anthropology and primatology, evolutionary leadership theory investigates what those evolutionary pressures may have been, how they might have prompted differing leadership styles throughout human history, and, finally, attempts to cast some light on what this means for us today. . . .

You'll discover that, when it comes to the workplace, the pinstripes conceal an ancient brain. That statement is not intended as an insult either to you or your ancestors; it's a fact. First, evolution works on such long timescales that all of us have, more or less, the brains that our African ancestors did, even if your entire white-skinned family has blond hair and blue eyes. Second, we are not entitled to disrespect our forebears: it is thanks to their resourcefulness that *Homo sapiens* has risen to become the most successful species on earth. Whether your distant African relatives were despots or peacemakers, you would not exist were it not for their instinct for survival. Still, the fact is that we are ancient brains trying to make our way in an ultra-modern world; when shiny new corporate ideas rub up against our creaking millennia-old psyches, the clash can make us feel uneasy. . . .

We survey evidence that voters prize traits such as height, physique, facial structure, oratorical skill—and a Y chromosome. These make little sense from a political theorist's point of view, because none of these traits (except the power of oratory, which is correlated with intelligence) is obviously linked to being able to govern well. They fit neatly, however, with what we would expect from evolutionary leadership theory. We show that our ancestral biases towards tall men with square jawlines, who look like 'one of us', often exclude better-qualified candidates. We yearn for personal information about potential leaders too—in the absence of CVs and job appraisals, this is how our ancestors gauged the quality of potential leaders within their tribes. . . .

Often, the shared objective is the leader's objective. So becoming a leader is a good way of achieving whatever it is you want to achieve, whether it is building a well or building up support for an ideology. Not only that, but leaders reap benefits, both financial (top executives get paid more than middle-ranking ones) and sexual, because (generally male) leaders appear to get their pick of (female) followers. They also enjoy an elevated social status. We will call these perks the three S's—representing salary, status and sex—and that this triumvirate of factors drives power-seeking behaviour, because they enhance the reproductive potential of the (usually) men who pursue them. Political leaders, for example, have a long and ignoble history of polygamy and infidelity.

In fact, the three S's have a clear relationship to each other, and to ELT: the ultimate evolutionary aim is reproductive success, which must be achieved through sex, which means catching the eye of sexual partners, which

means being a man of status. And how is status signified today? Through salary. And so, thanks to evolutionary leadership theory, we have a thread linking money to power to sex.

This has to be one explanation for the preponderance of books about leadership: people buy them in the hope they can achieve leadership positions, and an accompanying helping of the three S's. This would suggest there are hundreds of authors who understand what leadership is about. If this is true, why do we still have so many leaders in business and politics made of the wrong stuff? Why do half of chief executives fail in their jobs? Why do political leaders lead us into unwinnable wars? Why do incompetence and immorality so often come as part of the whole human leadership package.

For the answers, we do something that no other students of leadership have yet done: travel back in time to explore the origins of human leadership. *Naturally Selected* is about how and why leadership evolved in our species. The 'why' of leadership is very rarely addressed: despite the trillions of words on the different forms leadership can take, and whether people are born to lead or can be schooled for greatness, few have paused to ask why we bother with leaders at all. Why is it that almost every social grouping—from countries to companies, councils to cults—has a figurehead out in front? Why don't individuals break from the crowd and do their own thing? This gaping hole must be plugged if we are to truly understand the human instinct to lead and the accompanying instinct to follow.

Naturally Selected is that intellectual stopper—by stepping back deep into human history, into the societies inhabited by our ancestors, we can arrive at a deeper, more complete and pleasingly concise understanding of how the twin phenomena of leadership and followership evolved in our own and other species. It allows us to identify the ingredients of good leadership ('good' in the sense of both competent and moral; as we know from the besieged financial world, leadership is frequently amoral, even immoral, and incompetent)—and to understand why bad leadership flourishes. Evolutionary leadership theory proposes a brand-new framework for answering the 'why' question: it contends that, since humans are evolutionarily adapted to live in groups, and since groups with leaders do much better than groups without leaders, it follows that leadership and followership became prerequisites for reproductive success (which is the only kind of success that matters when it comes to evolution). Simply, groups without effective leaders died out. All of us who live today carry the psychological legacy gifted to us by our forebears: we are programmed to live in led groups and, most of the time, be obedient group members. . . .

We . . . discover that when we select our leaders, we consistently favour tall, fit-looking males. We call this the Savannah Hypothesis, and it contends that we still choose our leaders as if we are appointing Big Men to protect us from aggressors and predators on the savannah. . . . Sometimes we want our leaders to look warm, sometimes steely. All those traits that we pay close attention to—height, age, perceived masculinity, gender and reputation—can be thought of as 'savannah traits' of leaders. We have folded the Savannah Hypothesis into the Mismatch Hypothesis . . . because focusing on savannah traits can blind us to better candidates with proven competence, and ranks as an obvious example of a mismatch. . . .

Mismatch is a concept from evolutionary science. All organisms, including people, possess traits (biological and behavioural) that have been passed down through generations through natural selection. . . .

[But] traits that were adaptive, or useful, in ancestral times are no longer necessarily adaptive in these new, different surroundings. As the experimental psychologist Steven Pinker writes: '. . . our ordeals come from a mismatch between the sources of our passions in evolutionary history and the goals we set for ourselves today'. Witness, for example, the rising rate of obesity in the West, where energy-dense foods are widely and cheaply available. Our ancestors did not live in a time when food was so plentiful; when they came across such bounty, they made the most of it. Unfortunately, we still carry the ancestral propensity to tuck into fatty, sugary foods whenever we can. Couple that with a more sedentary way of life today, and it is no wonder that our waistlines are expanding. . . .

An important aspect of Big Men leadership is that they exercise influence through persuasion rather than coercion. Big Men would be foolish to throw their weight around members of hunter-gatherer societies don't like being bossed around and, it is not unknown for them to ignore, disobey or even kill a person who assumes too much power and authority (murder is thousands of times more common in these tribes than in modern society). In an echo of our ancestral past, we still dislike bossy, self-centred and corrupt leaders today. The GLOBE project data are useful here. Dominance, despotism and selfishness are universally loathed, as are leaders regarded as arrogant, vindictive, untrustworthy, emotional, compulsive, over-controlling, insensitive, abrasive, aloof, too ambitious, or unable to delegate or make decisions.

The challenge, then, for any evolutionary framework, is to explain why leaders with these attributes still make it to the top. One possibility is that they appear benign when angling for power but show their true dictatorial colours once in office. This is where, we suggest, the Dark Triad comes into play: men who score highly on all three traits—narcissism, Machiavellianism and psychopathy—often rise to leadership positions because their cunning allows them to present a likable face to the world. Only once enthroned do they unveil their manipulative, selfish and power-hungry personalities.

In the absence of a personality test result, we do not know for sure whether Robert Mugabe, who started life as a freedom fighter in Zimbabwe against British colonialists, is a member of the Dark Triad fraternity, but we can be certain he is no longer seen as a noble liberator of his people. In 2009, while Zimbabwe starved, Mugabe ordered tons of lobster, champagne and chocolates to be flown into the country for his 85th birthday celebrations. Today, despotic leaders such as Mugabe can stay in power with the help of the army (because armies benefit from being 'in' with the ruler) and maintain the monopoly on violence. In traditional societies, such behaviour would not be tolerated for long. . . .

Women

[The] innate favouritism for 'people like us' can work against success. . . . Sometimes, the most competent leader is a different colour, a different gender or a different social class from us; and yet our evolved psychology prevents us from fully embracing this fact. For example, there are very few women directors on the boards of companies (and even fewer CEOs). A study of the 500 top US companies in 2006, however, as listed by *Fortune* magazine, showed that those with women directors are more profitable than those with no women on the board. The women-friendly companies are especially strong on corporate governance. A study from Leeds University Business School has found the same phenomenon: the data suggest that a 50:50 ratio of men and women on a board makes for a healthy balance sheet. All male boards are not good: adding just one female director cuts the risk of bankruptcy by 20 per cent. The Savannah Hypothesis will show how our gender bias is very probably a consequence of the time our species spent on the savannah. . . .

Tall, Fit, Male Leaders (or the Savannah Hypothesis)

The Savannah Hypothesis is the conceptual cocktail you get when you blend evolutionary leadership theory with the Mismatch Hypothesis. And we can give you an inkling of what we mean by asking you to consider the word 'statesmanlike'. What does it mean? You could answer: it means looking or acting like a statesman. We have certain expectations of a 'statesman': he should be male, authoritative, wise, benevolent. But to earn this epithet a leader must also have a special demeanour or even physique about him. It is hard for a nervy beanpole who stutters to look statesmanlike; a short, tubby fellow with a high-pitched voice would be similarly challenged. Where do we get this mental image of what a statesman should be like?

The truth is, voters approve of candidates who look, sound and behave in a certain way. Height, physique and attractiveness matter. Political scientists have consistently noted that taller presidential candidates are more likely to be voted in; rotund hopefuls are extremely unlikely to become wedged behind the desk in the Oval Office (the last overweight candidate to roll into the White House was William Howard Taft, in 1909). Voters also generally favour mature leaders over young ones. Barack Obama bucked the maturity trend, partly because some voters thought that, at 72, John McCain was a little too mature to start ruling. Not that Obama coveted the gift of youth: there were rumours that the dynamic lawyer dyed his hair grey in order to heighten his air of authority.

Traditional leadership theories have some difficulty explaining the seemingly irrelevant correlations with age, height, weight, health and gender, and tend to see them as spurious (and the preference for male leaders as an example of social conditioning). After all, ruling is more of a cerebral activity than a physical one. But view these same correlations through the lens of evolutionary leadership theory, and these preferences begin to make sense. In ancestral environments, choosing a poor leader was potentially so costly that any notable personal trait would be folded into the selection process. After all, hunter-gatherer tribes didn't do interview boards, leaving physical appearance and personality as the only viable metrics for competence. For leadership activities requiring physical strength and stamina, such as group hunting or warfare, our ancestors would have wanted the physically fittest man for the job (in retrospect, a wise judgement, because you are testament to their success). Height, weight and health would have pointed to fitness. Evolutionary leadership theory explains it like this: evolution has burned into our brains a set of templates for selecting those who lead us, and these templates are activated whenever we encounter a specific problem requiring coordination (such as in times of war or recession). The Savannah Hypothesis spells out what those criteria, or savannah traits, are.

Our Savannah Hypothesis contains four broad ingredients. First, it proposes that individuals with a particular set of physical features and psychological traits were more likely to emerge as leaders in ancestral societies. To the extent that these traits were reliable predictors of effective leadership, followers started to pay closer attention to these cues. Over time, using these cues, followers built up cognitive profiles or prototypes of good leadership, and individuals who slotted most closely into these moulds were more likely to be accorded leadership status.

Second, the Savannah Hypothesis maintains that these cognitive ancestral leader prototypes (let's call them CALPs for short) varied according to the task in hand. For instance, the CALP of a peacetime leader would look very different from the CALP of a war leader, because different leadership traits are required for fighting wars and maintaining peace.

A third plank of the hypothesis is that, over time, these CALPs became hard-wired in our brains. This is how it works: if a particular action (say, following Thor to go hunting) is consistently associated with a particular, positive outcome (say, filling one's belly), the mental association between action and outcome becomes reinforced over time. So, whenever Thor dons his hunting boots, he attracts followers. This cognitive association can then be generalised to other situations in which Thor wants to take the lead—such as going into battle with another group—as well as to situations in which people who look or behave like Thor want to take the reins. Over many generations, this reinforced association becomes a cognitive template. So, people lacking in experience might still become leaders simply because they fit the CALP template.

A fourth and final implication is that we still spontaneously evaluate aspiring leaders based on these CALPs, even though the templates are no longer relevant (because most of us don't need to hunt for food). Think of the automatic fear response towards snakes and spiders. Although they hardly threaten modern humans, these creatures—and even pictures of them—consistently elicit a powerful fear response. We don't respond in anything like the same way to cars, which are much more threatening to human survival in terms of the number of genetic lines they bring to a premature end. So, our brains seem to be primed to instantly respond to dangers that were lethal in ancestral times, rather than to modern killers; and we are similarly psychologically primed to this day to seek out leaders who would have surpassed themselves on the savannah. Astonishingly, young children who are shown photographs of election candidates are extremely accurate at forecasting the winner, even though they base their judgements on looks alone. [T]he savannah traits that appear to influence the perception of leadership potential . . . [include] overall health, height, age, a masculine appearance, gender, reputation and, finally, charisma. . . .

Gender

. . . We invited four people at a time to our laboratory to play an investment game. Half the groups were told that the aim of the game was 'to earn more money with your team than the other teams in the game' (we call this the war scenario, because teams are pitted against one another). The other half were told that the aim of the game was 'to earn more money than the other players in your team' (the peace scenario).

Each group was then asked to choose a leader from two candidates, described like this: 'Sarah, a 21-year-old university student in law. Her hobbies are exercise, travelling, and going out with friends' and 'Peter, a 20-year-old university student in English literature. His hobbies are reading, music, and attending parties.' In other words, the only salient difference between the two leaders was gender. Predictably, most players (78 per cent) voted for Peter in the war scenario, and there was an overwhelming preference for Sarah (93 per cent) as leader in the peace scenario. Furthermore, these leaders were also more effective in the situations that members thought them most suited to; Peter raised more contributions in the war scenario and Sarah in the peace scenario.

Interestingly, there was also a version of the game which combined elements of both war and peace. The players were told that the goal was 'to earn more money than other teams and to earn more than the other players in your team'. In these hybrid cases the players preferred Sarah to lead (75 per cent). There is some evidence from other research that women have a more flexible leadership style, making them exceptionally capable of dealing with situations involving high degrees of complexity, such as when there are simultaneous opportunities for conflict and collaboration (and those women diplomats come to mind again).

Our relative reluctance to choose women leaders explains their absence in the top echelons of politics and business; only a third of the FTSE100 companies boast women directors, and most of those are non-executive. Just 3 percent of executive directors are female. Female presidents and prime ministers are few and far between, and tend to be daughters or widows of previous leaders (Benazir Bhutto and Corazon Aquino, for example). Where does this reluctance come from? In hunter-gatherer societies, leadership often includes a physical component.

Duties include spearheading group hunts, organising raids and breaking up group fights. Because men are usually bigger and stronger than women, they are more likely to rise to prominence.

We must also remember that the perks of leadership—salary, status and sex—militate against women. Men hunger for high-status positions because it makes them more desirable to women (Darwinian logic explains the sexual allure of rich men: women know their babies will be well provided for). Women don't benefit evolutionarily from acquiring personal status and riches in quite the same way: they can best serve evolution's end (which is the propagation of the species) by nurturing their children rather than chasing a promotion or salary increase (in fact, there is some indication that career women have fertility problems because of job-related stress). These evolved differences in the way men and women view status—men care about it much more than women do—might be responsible for strengthening the already robust bias towards male leaders.

Some women do make it the top but they seem to be penalised for excelling at stereotypically masculine tasks. Carly Fiorina, the former CEO of Hewlett Packard, has often remarked on how sexist the coverage of her tenure was. It is true: we don't ask male CEOs what it's like to be a man at the top.

Society tends to assume it is the natural order of things; a woman wielding great power is still somehow seen as unnatural, especially if she is of childbearing age. We find it hard to shake the feeling that she should be at home looking after her brood. Post-menopausal women, however, appear to be taken more seriously in politics and business. Angela Merkel, the Chancellor of Germany, Hillary Clinton and Kraft CEO Irene Rosenfeld are all highly respected. In *Fortune's* 2009 ranking of America's leading businesswomen, only two were under 40. . . .

To recap, we hope we've convinced you that the way we choose our leaders owes much to our time on the savannah, where our psychology evolved to help us operate in small hunter-gatherer tribes. But, because society today is much larger and socially more complex, we've become wedged in the gap between savannah and suburbia. However much we may employ our intellect, our brains have tunnel vision when it comes to leadership psychology. And we have been in that evolutionary tunnel for perhaps two million years since the emergence of the genus *Homo*: the 13,000 years since agriculture, which fuelled the growth of large settlements, don't even register on our evolutionary radar. And so we still hanker after certain leader prototypes: we like to be led by tall, strong, lantern-jawed men who know us personally. They must possess self-belief but not self-regard; they should be charismatic, but not charlatans. These revered figures should receive extra rewards and privileges, but not too many. Today, though, leadership is very rarely about foraging and fighting in 100-strong tribes of blood relatives; it's about ruling nations of millions (a billion, in the case of China), running multinational corporations with thousand of employees, and rubbing along in a global village where people don't look and behave the same way as you do. Is it any wonder that the leaders we choose today so often disappoint?

. . . What does this mean for leadership and followership? As evolutionary leadership theory explains, our psychology has been sculpted to thrive in small, flattened communities. So, we make the kind of instinctive judgements that our ancestors made. We follow people with charisma because we use it as a proxy for competence, but we often find out to our cost that a charismatic exterior can conceal a vacuous, even vindictive, nature. We vote for tall, fit men because those are the kind of people whom our ancestors sought out to provide tribal protection. We tend to exclude women (because they were confined to traditional roles in tribal life) and minorities (because we instinctively feel suspicious of people who are not like us). Today, there is no rational reason why height, age, weight, colour and gender should be used as sole qualifications for jobs or roles. Yet these savannah instincts continue to prevent us from picking the best person to fill a particular role, which we hypothesise contributes to the substantial failure rate of managers in corporate America. . . .

Again, although male leadership is the norm in preindustrial societies we should be wary of excluding women. In today's global village, business and politics bring people of different cultures together. Interpersonal skills and network-building are supremely valuable abilities. There is good evidence that women leaders, armed with superior empathic and verbal skills, cope better in these novel environments. While our 'think leader think male' bias might be difficult to overcome, we should be aware that it might prejudice our consideration of talented women candidates.

Status is a major factor in the gender debate: evolution has selected men to be more ambitious and status-obsessed than women because, for them, these behaviours translated into ancestral reproductive success. When men and women work together, men are quicker to assume the position of a leader even when a better-qualified woman is present. Illuminatingly, Charles A. O'Reilly III, a Stanford University business professor, concludes it is not gender per se which leads to the glass ceiling for women, but the overwhelming male desire to compete. It is an interesting rewording of the evolutionary imperative we've already discussed (and he found it was the most masculine men who excelled). . . .

MARK VAN VUGT is a professor of social and organizational psychology at the VU University Amsterdam and a Research Associate at Oxford University. His research is in evolutionary social and organizational psychology, leadership, cooperation, and other group processes. He is the author of numerous books, including *Naturally Selected: The Evolutionary Science of Leadership.*

ANJANA AHUJA is a former science journalist and columnist for the *Times,* with a degree in space physics from Imperial College London. She is a two-time nominee for the National Science Writing Awards and recipient of the EMMA award for Best Print Journalism. She recently collaborated with Mark van Vugt to write *Naturally Selected: The Evolutionary Science of Leadership.*

EXPLORING THE ISSUE

Are Barriers to Women's Success as Leaders Due to Societal Obstacles?

Critical Thinking and Reflection

1. Are leaders born or made?
2. How do circumstances help determine the attributes most likely to portend success?
3. Should women deliberately adjust their leadership style to achieve promotion in the workplace?
4. What strategies should workplaces adopt to ensure that the best leaders, women and men, make it to the top?
5. Are workplaces better for having a diversity of people in various leadership roles?

Is There Common Ground?

Women's leadership style has been cited frequently as a barrier to success at the top of the corporate ladder. Leadership can be viewed from either the human capital perspective or the discrimination perspective. The human capital view would suggest that women, due to their natures, simply do not have the dominance-related and assertive dispositions that are presumed to be correlates of leadership. From a discrimination perspective, one can argue that women have not been given opportunities to learn and practice leadership skills. Furthermore, research shows that many people prefer a male to a female boss. The irony is that much of the research suggests that women's leadership styles, when they different from those of men, can be more effective, although the job description rather than the sex of the person usually better predicts what type of leadership style one will use. How can the contradictions between women being effective leaders and still having difficulty exercising leadership be resolved? Alice Eagly has suggested that the view of female leadership is complex and is a mixture of advantage and disadvantage. On the one hand, women's styles have been described as transformative, in that they promote innovation, trust, and empowerment in followers. On the other hand, expectations regarding competitiveness and toughness, coupled with old-fashioned prejudice against women, can interfere with effective leadership, especially in male-dominated domains.

Additional Resources

Paxton, P. and Hughes, M.M. (2007). Women, politics, and power: A global perspective. Los Angeles: Pine Forge Press.

Sanchez-Hucles, J.V. and Davis, D.D. (2010). Women and women of color in leadership: Complexity, identity, and intersectionality. *American Psychologist*, 65(3), 171–181.

Shames, S.L. (2010). Women's leadership in political science. In Karen O'Connor, ed., *Gender and women's leadership: A reference handbook*. Thousand Oaks, CA: Sage, 669–678.

Internet References . . .

American Business Women's Association

http://www.abwa.org/pages/abwa-home-page

Women in Business and Industry

http://www.wib-i.com/

Women Unlimited

http://www.women-unlimited.com/home/

Selected, Edited, and with Issue Framing Material by:
Elizabeth Schroeder, EdD, MSW, *Elizabeth Schroeder Consulting*

ISSUE

Does Pornography Reduce the Incidence of Rape?

YES: Anthony D'Amato, from "Porn Up, Rape Down," Northwestern University School of Law, Public Law and Legal Theory Research Paper Series (June 26, 2012)

NO: Darwin, from "Does Porn Prevent Rape?" Catholicexchange.com (2012)

Learning Outcomes

After reading this issue, you will be able to:

- Explain the definition of pornography, and how it differs from erotica.
- Understand whether or not viewing pornography encourages young people to become sexually active at earlier ages, and if viewing pornography psychologically damages kids.
- Explain what mechanisms might account for the argument that pornography is related to increases in violence against women. If it is related to a reduction in the incidence of rape, what mechanisms might explain this effect?

ISSUE SUMMARY

YES: Professor of law Anthony D'Amato highlights statistics from the most recent National Crime Victimization Survey that demonstrate a correlation between the increased consumption of pornography over the years with the decreased incidence of rape. Some people, he argues, watch pornography in order to push any desire to rape out of their minds, and thus have no further desire to go out and actually do it.

NO: Blogger Darwin argues that the while sexual crimes have gone down over the years, the consumption of sexually explicit material cannot be given credit, and that trying to associate pornography with a decrease in the incidence of rape is an attempt to justify condoning its existence and use.

According to the Family Safe Media Web site, every second, $3,075.64 is being spent on pornography, 28,258 Internet users are viewing pornography, and 372 Internet users are typing adult search terms into search engines. The site also claims that every 39 minutes a new pornographic video is being created in the United States. The total worldwide revenue of the pornography industry is estimated to be over $96 billion dollars annually, with the United States contributing approximately $13 billion to this total. The site states, "The pornography industry is larger than the revenues of the top technology companies combined: Microsoft, Google, Amazon, eBay, Yahoo!, Apple, Netflix

and EarthLink." With these staggering numbers and the huge economic impact, it is little surprise that there is so much interest in the impact of pornography on people's lives. Furthermore, while researchers, practitioners, and activists are arguing for the dangers of pornography, the industry itself argues that pornography is not harmful and is a matter of free speech.

Since the creation of the Internet, the world has seen a huge increase in the amount and manner in which information is exchanged with others. This includes the adult entertainment industry, which has become an enormous, multi-billion dollar industry thanks in part to the anonymity and privacy that online pornography provides adults. One challenge, many argue, is that adults are far from the only ones who are able to access porn sites online. Children as young as middle school age are accessing images online, some of which they search for and some of which is targeted to them through spam e-mails or pornographic websites that purchase the domain of a similarly sounding website; they count on minors to arrive at these sites by accident. The debates about the effects of porn on its users are nearly endless.

There has been a recent interest in the effect of media images on girls, especially as they result in the objectification of the female body with effects on body image and self-esteem. Consequences can range from eating disorders to increased risk for sexual violence victimization. In 2005, the Violence in Video Games and Interactive Media policy was adopted by the American Psychological Association (APA). The review of the literature that led to this resolution summarized results of studies documenting the negative impact of exposure to violent interactive media on children and youth. However, in recognition that this policy did not address issues of sexualization that result from media images, the APA convened the Task Force on the Sexualization of Girls. The task force defined sexualization as occurring when

- a person's value comes only from his or her sexual appeal or behavior, to the exclusion of other characteristics;
- a person is held to a standard that equates physical attractiveness (narrowly defined) with being sexy;
- a person is sexually objectified—that is, made into a thing for others' sexual use, rather than seen as a person with the capacity for independent action and decision making; and/or
- sexuality is inappropriately imposed upon a person.

Guided by this definition, the task force documented the negative impact of media images on girls' cognitive functioning, such as impaired performance on mental activities like math tests. Emotional functioning, in the form of shame and self-disgust, can result from exposure to unrealistic pictures of female bodies. Health, both mental and physical, can be compromised. For example, sexualization of the female body can lead to low self-esteem and depression, as well as eating disorders. Unrealistic expectations about the ideal female body and what sexual relations should be like can impair healthy sexuality. Sexualization can also affect various attitudes and beliefs, such as the acceptance of sexual stereotypes. Furthermore, it is not just girls and young women who are affected by sexualized images of females; others and society are also affected. Men's expectations regarding "ideal" women can undermine healthy relationships and sexism in general can increase. Of particular concern for the present discussion was the task force's finding that the sexualization of girls through media images was associated with increased rates of sexual harassment and sexual violence and an increased demand for child pornography. Scholars who have been studying human trafficking, such as Norma Ramos with the Coalition Against Trafficking of Women, have argued that pornography is "erotized bigotry." For many, trafficking begins in childhood and takes the form of prostitution, and pornographic images both arouse the appetite for child victims and suggest ways to rape. Ramos has suggested that prostitution is nothing more than pre-paid rape and the world's oldest oppression.

This issue looks at the effects of visual pornography on the incidence of rape in the United States. Since pornography became available, there are many proponents who maintain that by depicting certain sexual acts, sexually explicit media encourages people to try these acts out. In particular, they say, porn that shows rape makes this type of behavior real and, in the rapists' mind, acceptable, thereby encouraging rape. Others maintain that there is no causality between viewing Internet porn and the incidence of rape, that people are exposed to a wide range of information, images, and behaviors every day and do not engage in all of the behaviors they see. These include, they say, sexual behaviors. It has been difficult to demonstrate the causal role of pornography in increasing the likelihood of violence against women. Many studies, such as described in the Anthony D'Amato selection to follow, rely on correlational analyses. With these analyses it is impossible to know whether the presence of pornography causes certain behaviors to increase or decrease, whether people prone to those behaviors or more or less likely to seek out pornography, or whether there is some third factor, such as women's status in a society, that affects both the amount of pornography consumed and the level of violence against women.

In the following selections, D'Amato provides analyses that suggest a negative correlation: A decrease in rapes in the United States is associated with the increase of pornography availability. He maintains that having pornography available actually *decreases* the incidence of rape. Depicting rape, which is a socially unacceptable (and criminal) behavior, this author argues, actually provides a potential rapist with an outlet for his unacceptable fantasies, thereby keeping him from acting upon them. Darwin analyzes the data relating to causality and asserts that the causality argument, from a data standpoint, cannot be made.

YES

Anthony D'Amato

Porn Up, Rape Down

Today's headlines are shouting RAPE IN DECLINE![1] Official figures just released show a plunge in the number of rapes per capita in the United States since the 1970s. Even when measured in different ways, including police reports and survey interviews, the results are in agreement; there has been an 85% reduction in sexual violence in the past 25 years. The decline, steeper than the stock market crash that led to the Great Depression, is depicted in this chart prepared by the United States Department of Justice.

As the chart shows, there were 2.7 rapes for every 1,000 people in 1980; by 2004, the same survey found the rate had decreased to 0.4 per 1,000 people, a decline of 85%.

Official explanations for the unexpected decline include (a) less lawlessness associated with crack cocaine; (b) women have been taught to avoid unsafe situations; (c) more would-be rapists already in prison for other crimes; (d) sex education classes telling boys that "no means no." But these minor factors cannot begin to explain such a sharp decline in the incidence of rape.

There is, however, one social factor that correlates almost exactly with the rape statistics. The American public is probably not ready to believe it. My theory is that the sharp rise in access to pornography accounts for the decline in rape. The correlation is inverse: the more pornography, the less rape. It is like the inverse correlation: the more police officers on the street, the less crime.

The pornographic movie "Deep Throat" which started the flood of X-rated VHS and later DVD films, was released in 1972. Movie rental shops at first catered primarily to the adult film trade. Pornographic magazines also sharply increased in numbers in the 1970s and 1980s.

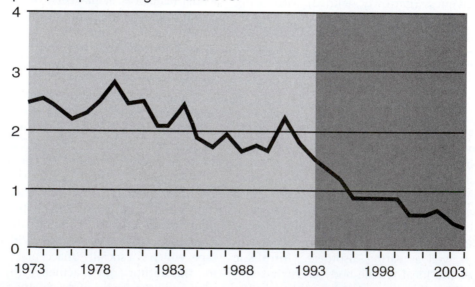

Rape rates

Adjusted victimization rate
per 1,000 persons age 12 and over

Source: The National Crime Victimization Survey. Includes both attempted and completed rapes.

Anthony D'Amato, "Porn Up, Rape Down," *Northwestern University of Law, Public Law and Legal Theory Research Paper Series,* June 26, 2012. Copyright © 2012 Anthony D'Amato. All rights reserved. Used with permission.

Then came a seismic change: pornography became available on the new Internet. Today, purveyors of Internet porn earn a combined annual income exceeding the total of the major networks ABC, CBS, and NBC.

> "Deep Throat" has moved from the adult theatre to a laptop near you.

National trends are one thing; what do the figures for the states show? From data compiled by the National Telecommunications and Information Administration in 2001, the four states with the *lowest* per capita access to the Internet were Arkansas, Kentucky, Minnesota, and West Virginia. The four states with the *highest* Internet access were Alaska, Colorado, New Jersey, and Washington. (I would not have guessed this.)

Next I took the figures for forcible rape compiled by police reports by the Disaster Center for the years 1980 and 2000. The following two charts display the results:

Table 1

States with Lowest Internet Access[2]

State	Internet 2001	Rape 1980	Rape 2000
Arkansas	36.9	26.7	31.7
Kentucky	40.2	19.2	27.4
Minnesota	36.1	23.2	45.5
W. Virginia	40.7	15.8	18.3

All figures are per capita.

Table 2

States with Highest Internet Access[3]

Alaska	64.1	56.8	70.3
Colorado	58.5	52.5	41.2
New Jersey	61.6	30.7	16.1
Washington	60.4	52.7	46.4

All figures are per capita.

While the nationwide incidence of rape was showing a drastic decline, the incidence of rape in the four states having the *least* access to the Internet showed an actual *increase* in rape over the same time period. This result was almost too clear and convincing, so to check it I

compiled figures for the four states having the *most* access to the Internet. Three out of four of these states showed declines (in New Jersey, an almost 50% decline). Alaska was an anomaly: it increased both in Internet access and incidence of rape. However, the population of Alaska is less than one-tenth that of the other three states in its category. To adjust for the disparity in population, I took the combined population of the four states in each table and calculated the percentage change in the rape statistics:

Table 3

Combined Per Capita Percentage Change in Incidence of Rape

Aggregate per capita increase or decline in rape	
Four states with lowest Internet access	Increase in rape of 53%
Four states with highest Internet access	Decrease in rape of 27%

I find these results to be statistically significant beyond the 95 confidence interval.

Yet proof of correlation is not the same thing as causation. If autumn regularly precedes winter, that doesn't mean that autumn causes winter. When six years ago my former Northwestern colleague John Donohue, together with Steven Levitt,[4] found that legalized abortion correlated with a reduction in crime, theirs would have only been an academically curious thesis if they had not identified a causal factor. But they did identify one: that prior to legalization there were many unwanted babies born due to the lack of a legal abortion alternative. Those unwanted children became the most likely group to turn to crime.

My own interest in the rape-pornography question began in 1970 when I served as a consultant to President Nixon's Commission on Obscenity and Pornography. The Commission concluded that there was no causal relationship between exposure to sexually explicit materials and delinquent or criminal behavior. The President was furious when he learned of the conclusion.

Later President Reagan tried the same thing, except unlike his predecessor he packed the Commission with persons who passed his ideological litmus test (small wonder that I was not asked to participate). This time, Reagan's Commission on Pornography reached the approved result: that there does exist a causal relationship between pornography and violent sex crimes.

The drafter of the Commission's report was Frederich Schauer, a prominent law professor. In a separate statement, he assured readers that neither he nor the other

Commissioners were at all influenced by their personal moral values.[5] . . .

Although the Reagan Commission had at its disposal all the evidence gathered by psychology and social-science departments throughout the world on the question whether a student's exposure to pornography increased his tendency to commit antisocial acts, I found that the Commission was unable to adduce a shred of evidence to support its affirmative conclusion. No scientist had ever found that pornography raised the probability of rape. However, the Commission was not seeking truth; rather, as I said in the title to my article, it sought political truth.

If pornography does not *produce* rape, I thought, then maybe it *reduces* rape. But no one apparently had any incentive to investigate the latter proposition. But the just-released rape statistics provide the necessary evidence.

Although neither Professor Schauer nor the other Commissioners ever responded to my William & Mary article, now they can forget it. For if they had been right that exposure to pornography leads to an increase in social violence, then the vast exposure to pornography furnished by the Internet would by now have resulted in scores of rapes per day on university campuses, hundreds of rapes daily in every town, and thousands of rapes per day in every city. Instead, the Commissioners were so incredibly wrong that the incidence of rape has actually declined by the astounding rate of 85%.

Correlations aside, could access to pornography actually reduce the incidence of rape as a matter of causation? In my article I mentioned one possibility: that some people watching pornography may "get it out of their system" and thus have no further desire to go out and actually try it. Another possibility might be labeled "Victorian effect": the more that people covered up their bodies with clothes in those days, the greater the mystery of what they looked like in the nude. The sight of a woman's ankle was considered shocking and erotic. But today, Internet porn has thoroughly de-mystified sex. . . .

I am sure there will be other explanations forthcoming as to why access to pornography is the most important causal factor in the decline of rape. Once one accepts the observation that there is a precise negative correlation between the two, the rest can safely be left to the imagination.

Notes

1. E.g., *Washington Post,* June 19, 2006; *Chicago Tribune,* June 21, 2006.
2. Statistics on Internet Access compiled from National Telecommunications and Information Administration. . . .
3. Statistics on forcible rape compiled from. . . .
4. Author of *Freakonimics* (2005).
5. U.S. Dept. of Justice, Final Report: Attorney General's Commission on Pornography 176–79 (1986) (personal statement of Commissioner Schauer).

ANTHONY D'AMATO's interest is in the theory of law. He writes in the areas of international law and jurisprudence, focusing upon their underlying analytic structure.

Darwin

 **NO**

Does Porn Prevent Rape?

People will often go to great length to convince themselves that their vices are actually virtues or, short of that, at least that their vices are somehow a bulwark against worse vices. Sometimes pseudoscience is utilized to lend an empirical veneer to this self-justication. Someone recently sent me a link to a Scientific American article from last summer which attempts to make the case that porn is actually good for society:

Perhaps the most serious accusation against pornography is that it incites sexual aggression. But not only do rape statistics suggest otherwise, some experts believe the consumption of pornography may actually reduce the desire to rape by offering a safe, private outlet for deviant sexual desires.

"Rates of rapes and sexual assault in the U.S. are at their lowest levels since the 1960s," says Christopher J. Ferguson, a professor of psychology and criminal justice at Texas A&M International University. The same goes for other countries: as access to pornography grew in once restrictive Japan, China and Denmark in the past 40 years, rape statistics plummeted. Within the U.S., the states with the least Internet access between 1980 and 2000—and therefore the least access to Internet pornography—experienced a 53 percent increase in rape incidence, whereas the states with the most access experienced a 27 percent drop in the number of reported rapes, according to a paper published in 2006 by Anthony D'Amato, a law professor at Northwestern University.

Obviously, even if there is a social correlation between porn availability and decreased rates of rape, this doesn't mean that use or creation of porn is moral. Lots of highly immoral activities may happen to correlate with (or even cause) decreases in other immoral activities, and the fact that one of these is immoral doesn't change the immoral status of the other.

However, the whole set of claims sounded fishy to me. "Lowest levels since the 1960s" seems like one of those statement which might, while technically true, still mask a huge difference, rather like "worst economic downturn since the Great Depression". Similarly, measuring statistics based on "the states with the least Internet access between 1980 and 2000—and therefore the least access to Internet pornography" seemed incredibly vague. The internet wasn't even particularly useful for pornography before the advent of the World Wide Web in the early '90s, so the 1980 to 2000 time frame intentionally included a lot of irrelevant time, and measuring the states with the least internet access was likely to simply get you the poorest and most rural states.

Further, I just found the whole proposed causal mechanism doubtful. It sounded like the sort of thing where someone fished for a some correlations that worked just a little bit, but they were probably really just seeing some wider trend. My going hypothesis was that the rate of rape would mirror the rate of other violent crimes such as murder. If the rate of rape deviated from the rate of other violent crimes a lot, it would suggest that rape had different causal mechanisms than other forms of violent crime. If it rose and fell in a similar pattern (and I knew that violent crime as a whole had been falling since peaking in the early '90s) that would suggest that rape was just another, particularly nasty, form of social violence.

Searching around, I found two major sources of crime statistics that track the incidence of rape in the population as a whole. The first of these is the Uniform Crime Reporting Statistics database maintained by the FBI. This database is compiled from local law enforcement agencies by the FBI and statistically adjusted to make up for missing, over-reported or under-reported data. From there I was able to pull data on the rate per 100,000 of population of the set of violent crimes the database tracks: murder, aggravated assault, forcible rape, and robbery. The some total of these is the Violent Crime Rate.

The pattern match is very strong. The lowest correlation is between murder and rape, a 54% correlation. Robbery has an 84% correlation and aggravated assault has a 96% correlation. The overall violent crime rate has a 97% correlation with the rate of forcible rape. With correlations that high, if you ask me to tell you what the rate of rape is in the US in any given year, I'm not going to ask you, "Gee, how available was porn that year?" No, I'll ask you, "What was the overall rate of violent crime?" That is a far,

far more predictive indicator than anything vague association with porn availability. And predictability is what science is all about. All the rest of what we're hearing is hand waving and self justification.

I then ran averages for each decade. In the 1960s the rape rate was 12.3 per 100,000 of population.

In the 1970s, 26.0.

In the 1980s, 36.5.

In the 1990s, 38.3.

In the 2000s, 32.2.

So Prof. Ferguson's statement is actually false, the rape rate is not at its lowest since the 1960s (it was lower in the '70s than it was in 2010 at 27.5) and the current rape rate is more than 2x the rate for the 1960s, when pornography was unquestionably much less available than now. The only way that this pseudo correlation comes to be is that the web has only existed since the early '90s and by coincidence all forms of violent crime have been on a steady decline since the early '90s. Unless one wants to claim that burglary and aggravated assault rates are being driven down by the availability of internet porn, we don't have much of a causal case to make here.

There's a second major source of government data on violent crime called the National Crime Victimization Survey. Whereas the UCR data is based on crimes reported to law enforcement, the NCVS is compiled by the Justice Department by contacting 40,000 randomly selected households annually and asking all the members of those households who are over twelve years old about any crimes which they have personally been victims of during the last year. The idea behind using this methodology is that some people may not report crimes they suffer to the police. Since rape victims in particular are often afraid to come forward to authorities (whether because they fear retaliation from the rapist or out of shame) many sociologists believe that the NCVS provides a truer view of the incidence of rape in society.

I obtained the NCVS data (which unfortunately only goes back to 1973) and analyzed that as well. This source shows a much higher incidence of rape (and of other violent crimes) than the UCR data, and the shape of the trend is different: it shows a steady decline in all crime categories since the early seventies. However, the correlation between rape and other violent crimes is similar to in the UCR data.

Running the correlation between the sets of annual data for rape and total violent crime, I get a correlation of 89%. There's also a correlation of 91% between robbery

and rape and of 91% between aggravated assault and rape. Simple assault shows a correlation of 82% with rape.

This means both that the rate of decline in the rape rate, as shown in the NCVS's survey methodology is not unprecedented, and that one can predict the number of rapes likely to have occurred in a year with a fair degree of accuracy by knowing the amount of overall violent crime. The availability of pornography does not have this predictive value—or at least, none of these "studies" which attempt to show a connection between the availability of porn and the number of rapes even attempts to put together some sort of annual number which can be used to measure porn consumption or availability, and so any attempt at prediction is impossible.

Really the only thing that the porn-reduces-rape thesis has going for it, according to the NCVS's data is that the incidence of rape took a sharp down turn in 1991 which was three years before the overall violent crime rate took a sharp downturn in 1994. However, since that time the rape and violent crime as a whole have decreased at almost exactly the same rate. I think it would be virtually impossible to attribute this 1991–1994 divergence in the trends to internet pornography, given how comparatively small the internet was at the time. If internet porn were truly a "safety valve" which prevented men with deviant sexual urges from assaulting real women, we would expect the effect to become more pronounced (for the incidence of rape to decrease much faster than violent crime as a whole) as internet pornography became more prevalent in the last decade.

What we see, I think, in this attempt to associate pornography with a decrease in rape is self-justifying behavior. In a society in which far too many men satisfy their sexual urges alone by watching the exploitation and objectification of women in pornography, those who make this claim are attempting to deflect attention from the one fault (using pornography) by associating this vice with a decrease in an even worse exploitation and objectification of women: rape.

Strictly looking at the data, rape is simply a form of violence: a particularly exploitative and personal form of violence, and one primarily directed against women, but a form a violence which increases and decreases in society as the overall rate of violence increases and decreases. As such, it is not surprising that crime statistics show the incidence of rape to be highly correlated with those of other violent crimes. However, at the moral level, rape is simply a more extreme form of the desire to use and objectify others which is also at the root of the pornography industry.

EXPLORING THE ISSUE

Does Pornography Reduce the Incidence of Rape?

Critical Thinking and Reflection

1. Should pornography be protected as a First Amendment free speech right?
2. Is pornography ever okay? What if it is only consumed only by adults?
3. Does the content of the explicit images make a difference? Does it depend on what it depicts?
4. Do adults who view porn develop unrealistic expectations of beauty and sexual expression in their own relationships?
5. If some kind of causality could be shown, that pornography *does* indeed increase behavior, what role do you think the government should or should not play in regulating the industry?

Is There Common Ground?

Throughout history, people have looked for answers to why people perpetrate violent crimes on others. Mental health professionals, law enforcement officials, politicians, parents, and others have pointed fingers at many different potential causes without coming up with a clear answer. Is a person biologically determined to be a rapist? Is a rapist "created," and if so, by what or by whom? One of the first sources people go to for these reasons is the media. One type of indictment against the media focuses on their role as the pulse of the culture. The claim is that media depictions of behavior cause viewers to take actions that they would not otherwise take. Some argue, for example, that depictions of violence in the media lead to greater violence in real life. These arguments have even been brought to the legal system and used during trials. In a well-known court case at the time (*Huceg v. Hustler Magazine*, 1983), a family brought suit against *Hustler*, an adult pornographic magazine, in which a description appeared of autoerotic asphyxiation, a sexual practice in which a person restricts her or his breathing through partial hanging or other method, masturbates, and releases the air restriction at the moment of orgasm. The family's underage son tried this, did it incorrectly, and ended up hanging himself. The family sued *Hustler* magazine, arguing that if this had not been printed, their son would not have done it and died. The Court ruled for the magazine, saying that just reading a description of something does not necessarily encourage someone to do it—especially a young person for whom the material was not created. To say, however,

that the media have *no* effect on people's attitudes or behaviors would be inaccurate. Advertisers spend billions of dollars every year on television, print, Internet, and other ads to sell a wide variety of products. The ads are designed to influence people's behaviors—that if we see a particular commercial or hear a particular song, we will be more likely to purchase one product over another. If advertisers are successful at this—at actually influencing people enough to purchase something they may not have necessarily known they wanted—is it possible that the creators and producers of adult sexually explicit media could be doing the same? For right now, the data are inconclusive—and there seem to be as many reports supporting each side of the debate. Be sure to consider a range of reasoning as you establish your own opinion on this topic.

Additional Resources

Emmers-Sommer, T., Hertlein K., and Kennedy, A. (2013). Pornography use and attitudes: An examination of relational and sexual openness variables between and within gender. *Marriage & Family Review*, 49(4), 201e, 349–365.

Fisher, W.A., Kohut, T., Di Gioacchino, L.A., and Federoff, P. (2013). Pornography, sex crime, and paraphilia. *Current Psychiatry Reports*,15, 362.

Foubert, J.D., Brosi, M.W., and Bannon, R. S. (2011). Pornography viewing among fraternity men: Effects on bystander intervention, rape myth acceptance and behavioral intent to commit sexual assault. *Sexual Addiction & Compulsivity: The Journal of Treatment & Prevention*, 8(4), 212–231.

Freakonomics (2011). Porn and rape: The debate continues. August 4. http://freakonomics.com/2011/08/04/porn-and-rape-the-debate-continues.

Internet References . . .

Anti-Porn.org

http://www.antipornography.org/

Stop Porn Culture

http://stoppornculture.org/

Selected, Edited, and with Issue Framing Material by:
Elizabeth Schroeder, EdD, MSW, *Elizabeth Schroeder Consulting*

ISSUE

Are Women More at Risk for Crimes Using Digital Technology?

YES: Danielle Keats Citron, from "Law's Expressive Value in Combating Cyber Gender Harassment," *Michigan Law Review* (vol. 108, no. 3, 2009)

NO: Rebecca Eckler, from "Finding Out What Men Are Up To: Some Women Pride Themselves on Their Cyber-Sleuth Skills," *Macleans* (September 28, 2009)

Learning Outcomes

As you read the issue, focus on the following points:

- Does online anonymity increase abuse and harassment? Why?
- Is the preservation of anonymity for the sake of the masses worth the cost of abuse to the few?

ISSUE SUMMARY

YES: Professor of law at University of Maryland Law School, Danielle Keats Citron argues that women face higher rates of gender-based cyber harassment and it creates a gender divide online where women are disenfranchised from full participation.

NO: Rebecca Eckler asserts that women are equal opportunity offenders in the realm of digital crime and that women have used online tactics to harass men in increasingly greater numbers.

The online universe of the Internet along with other computer-assisted digital technologies has, for many, opened a virtual "wild west" of criminal opportunities. The relative anonymity of digital interactions in digital and virtual environments creates a fertile environment for abuse and harassment.

While law enforcement agencies report increased incidences of digital stalking and other forms of cyber harassment, research suggests that cyber crime does not divide neatly along gender lines.

In the YES and NO selections, two different perspectives on the gendered patterns of cyber-based behavior are presented. Citron examines the scope of cyber harassment arguing that the prevalence of gender-based online abuse inhibits women's potential participation in digital environments. Eckler presents a counter-narrative in which women have embraced technology as a way to engage in male-focused harassment and stalking behavior.

In "Law's Expressive Value in Combating Cyber Gender Harassment," Citron examines how the bulk of cyber gender harassment is focused on women. This online targeting of women, Citron posits, inhibits women from free and full participation in the Internet world. According to Citron, while cyber gender harassment "encompasses various behaviors," three core features characterize cyber gender harassment and make it a gendered form of abuse that is primarily experienced by women: "(1) its victims are female, (2) the harassment is aimed at particular women, and (3) the abuse invokes the targeted individual's gender in sexually threatening and degrading ways" (p. 378).

In "Finding Out What Men Are Up To: Some Women Pride Themselves on Their Cyber-Sleuth Skills," Eckler examines how women appropriate technology to flip the power narrative in order to cyber-stalk men. The anonymity of new technology and the relative ease of access the technology provides afford opportunities for anyone with the inclination to engage in invasive online activities. Women's online activities allow them to furtively spy on current and former relationships using purloined passwords. Other technological advances allow both men and women to engage in mischief that ranges from prank calls to fake text messages.

YES

Danielle Keats Citron

Law's Expressive Value in Combating Cyber Gender Harassment

Introduction

The harassment of women online is a pernicious and widespread problem.[1] It can be severe, involving threats of sexual violence, doctored photographs of women being suffocated, postings of women's home addresses alongside the suggestion that they should be raped, and technological attacks that shut down feminist blogs and websites.[2] Cyber harassment is a uniquely gendered phenomenon—the majority of targeted individuals are women,[3] and the abuse of female victims invokes gender in threatening and demeaning terms.[4]

Such harassment has a profound effect on targeted women. It discourages them from writing and earning a living online.[5] It interferes with their professional lives. It raises their vulnerability to offline sexual violence. It brands them as incompetent workers and inferior sexual objects. The harassment causes considerable emotional distress.[6] Some women have committed suicide.[7]

To avoid future abuse, women assume gender-neutral pseudonyms or go offline, even if it costs them work opportunities.[8] Others curtail their online activities.[9] For the "digital native"[10] generation, forsaking aspects of the internet means missing innumerable social connections. Although online harassment inflicts the most direct costs on targeted individuals, it harms society as well by entrenching male hierarchy online.

But no matter how serious the harm that cyber gender harassment inflicts, the public tends to trivialize it. Commentators dismiss it as harmless locker-room talk, characterizing perpetrators as juvenile pranksters and targeted individuals as overly sensitive complainers.[11] Others consider cyber gender harassment as an inconvenience that victims can ignore or defeat with counterspeech.[12] Some argue that women who benefit from the internet have assumed the risks of its Wild West norms.[13] Although the arguments differ, their message is the same—women need to tolerate these cyber "pranks" or opt out of life

online. This message has the unfortunate consequence of discouraging women from reporting cyber gender harassment and preventing law enforcement from pursuing cyber-harassment complaints.[14]

The trivialization of harms suffered by women is nothing new.[15] Society ignored or downplayed domestic violence's brutality for over 200 years.[16] No term even existed to describe sexual harassment in the workplace until the 1970s, despite the pervasiveness of the practice.[17] In light of this history, the current refusal to take seriously the cyber harassment of women is as unsurprising as it is disappointing.

Due to the internet's relative youth, this is an auspicious time to combat the trivialization of cyber gender harassment before it becomes too entrenched. If it continues unabated, cyber harassment could very well be the central front of struggles against sexual harassment in the coming decades given our increasing dependence on the net. More people make friends, apply for jobs, and discuss policy online than ever before, shifting their social and professional interactions to the net and with it the risk of sexual harassment.[18] As the market leans toward more realistic sensory experiences in virtual worlds and as these sites become more popular, cyber gender harassment may more closely approximate conventional notions of sexual violence. For instance, Second Life users' avatars have reportedly been forced to perform sexually explicit acts after being given malicious code.[19] These developments, and others like them, would further threaten gender equality in our digital age.

Wrestling with the marginalization of cyber sexual harassment is a crucial step in combating its gender-specific harms. Law has a crucial role to play in this effort. Law serves different functions here. It can deter online harassment's harms by raising the costs of noncompliance beyond its expected benefits. Law can also remedy such harm with monetary damages, injunctions, and criminal convictions. My article *Cyber Civil Rights* explored antidiscrimination, criminal, and tort law's role in preventing, punishing, and redressing cyber harassment.[20] In this piece, I explore law's other crucial role: educating the public about women's unique suffering in the wake of cyber harassment and potentially changing societal responses to it. Because law is expressive, it constructs our understanding of harms that are not trivial. The application of a cyber civil rights legal agenda would reveal online harassment for what it truly is—harmful gender discrimination. It would recognize the distinct suffering of women, suffering that men ordinarily do not experience or appreciate as harmful.

Once cyber harassment is understood as gender discrimination and not as a triviality to be ignored, women are more likely to complain about it rather than suffer in silence. Law enforcement could pursue cyber harassment complaints rather than just counseling women to get off their computers and seek help only if their harassers confront them offline. As a result, some perpetrators might curtail their bigoted assaults. Viewing cyber harassment as gender discrimination could become part of our cultural understandings and practices. As with workplace sexual harassment and domestic violence, changing the norms of acceptable conduct may be the most potent force in regulating behavior in cyberspace. An antidiscrimination message is crucial to harness law's moral and coercive power.[21]

. . . [This article] explores the gendered nature of online harassment.[22] It first defines the phenomenon of cyber gender harassment. It then explores the distinct harms that such online abuse inflicts on targeted women and society.

Cyber Harassment Through a Feminist Lens

Online harassment is a problem that has a profound impact on women's lives but is little understood. Just as society ignored sexual harassment until scholars and courts recognized it as sex discrimination, a definition of cyber gender harassment is crucial to understanding and tackling its distinct harms to women. No working definition has been constructed, perhaps because cyber gender harassment has been relegated to the shadows of our thinking. This [article] fills that void and provides an account of the gendered nature of online harassment, highlighting its distinct effect on targeted women and society.

Understanding Cyber Gender Harassment

Although cyber gender harassment encompasses various behaviors, it has a set of core features: (1) its victims are female, (2) the harassment is aimed at particular women, and (3) the abuse invokes the targeted individual's gender in sexually threatening and degrading ways.[23]

While cyber attackers target men, more often their victims are female.[24] The nonprofit organization *Working to Halt Online Abuse* has compiled statistics about individuals harassed online. In 2007, 61% of the individuals reporting online abuse identified themselves as women while 21% identified themselves as men.[25] In 2006, 70% of online harassment complainants identified themselves as women.[26] Overall, from 2000 to 2008, 72.5% of the 2,519 individuals reporting cyber harassment were female and 22% were male.[27] Forty-four percent of the victims were between the ages of 18 and 40,[28] and 49% reportedly had no relationship with their attackers.[29] Similarly, the Stalking Resource Center, a branch of the National Center for Victims of Crimes, reports that approximately 60% of online harassment cases involve male attackers and female targets.[30]

Academic research supports this statistical evidence. The University of Maryland's Electrical Engineering and Computer Department recently studied the threat of attacks associated with the chat medium Internet Relay Chat.[31] Researchers found that users with female names received on average 100 "malicious private messages," which the study defined as "sexually explicit or threatening language," whereas users with male names received only 3.7.[32] According to the study, the "experiment show[ed] that the user gender has a significant impact on one component of the attack thread (i.e., the number of malicious private messages received for which the female bots received more than 25 times more private messages than the male bots . . .)" and "no significant impact on the other components on the attack threat[,]" such as attempts to send files to users and links sent to users.[33] The study explained that attacks came from human chat users who selected their targets, not automated scripts programmed to send attacks to everyone on the channel, and that "male human users specifically targeted female users. . . ."[34]

Distinct Impact on Targeted Women

Cyber gender harassment invokes women's sexuality and gender in ways that interfere with their agency, livelihood, identity, dignity, and well-being. The subsequent injuries are unique to women because men do not typically experience sexual threats and demeaning comments suggesting their inferiority due to their gender.[35]

First, cyber gender harassment undermines women's agency over their own lives. Online threats of sexual violence "literally, albeit not physically, penetrate[]" women's bodies.[36] They expose women's sexuality, conveying the message that attackers control targeted women's physical safety.[37] The rape threats are particularly frightening to women as one in every six women has experienced an attempted or completed rape as a child or adult.[38] Such threats discourage women from pursuing their interests in cyberspace. For instance, women shut down their blogs and websites.[39] They retreat from chat rooms. A 2005 Pew Internet and American Life Project study attributed an 11 percent decline in women's use of chat rooms to menacing comments.[40] Women limit their websites' connectivity to a wider, and potentially threatening, audience by password protecting their sites.[41] They close comments on blog posts, foreclosing positive conversations along with abusive ones.[42] The harassment scares women away from online discourse "by making an example of those females who [do] participate" with "very real threats of rape."[43]

Cyber harassment also affects women's agency in their offline lives. For instance, a woman stopped going to the gym because her anonymous harassers encouraged her law school classmates to take cell phone pictures of her and post them online.[44] After posters warned a female blogger that she needed to watch her back because they knew where she lived, the woman "g[o]t an alarm" and "started [carrying a] bat to and from the car when [she] went to work at night."[45] Kathy Sierra's cyber harassment experience left her fearful to attend speaking engagements and even to leave her yard: "I will never feel the same. I will never *be* the same."[46] Another woman explained: cyber threats had a "major impact on me both online and offline—I removed my name from my Website and my Internet registration. I rented a mailbox to handle all snail mail related to the Website, and I changed my business and home phone numbers . . ."[47] As Ms. Sierra noted, "[h]ow many rape/fantasy threats does it take to make women want to lay low? Not many. . . ."[48]

Online harassment replicates in cyberspace the autonomy erosion that female employees have long experienced in real space. Workplace sexual harassment exposes and exploits a female employees' sexuality. Verbal sexual abuse and displays of pornography make female employees "feel physically vulnerable" to attack.[49] Female employees leave their jobs or seek transfers to escape hostile work environments in much the same way that women shut down income-generating sites or limit access to their blogs to avoid cyber abuse.

Second, cyber gender harassment undermines women's ability to achieve their professional goals. It may impair women's work directly, such as technological attacks designed to shutter feminist websites or

postings designed to discourage employees from hiring women.[50] It may take a more indirect form of professional sabotage by discrediting women's competence in their careers.[51] Assertions that "[t]his is why women are TOO STUPID to think critically and intelligently about film; AND business for that matter" and "why don't you make yourself useful and go have a baby"[52] appear designed to generate feelings of inferiority and to discourage women from engaging in professional activities online. Rape threats and sexually menacing comments have a similar effect. This sort of intimidation is unique to women—men are not routinely told that they belong in the kitchen or bedroom instead of earning a living online.

The abuse harms targeted individuals' careers because employers routinely rely on search engines to collect intelligence on job applicants and may discover negative postings about them. Employers may decline to interview or hire targeted women not because they believe the malicious postings but because it is simply easier to hire individuals who don't come with such baggage. Moreover, candidates with impressive online reputations are more attractive to employers than those who lack them. Indeed, an online presence is crucial to obtaining work in certain fields. Noted technology blogger Robert Scoble explains that women who don't blog are "never going to be included in the [technology] industry."[53] This parallels workplace sexual harassment's interference with women's economic opportunities.[54] Demeaning verbal abuse can be so severe that women leave their jobs,[55] just as online intimidation has pushed women out of the blogosphere.[56] It impairs women's work opportunities by making clear to them that they will be viewed and judged by traditional and subordinate female roles,[57] in much the way that cyber gender harassment does.

Third, women sustain harm to their identities *as women*. Women may feel impelled to compromise their female identity by "passing" as men to prevent discrimination.[58] . . .

Fourth, cyber harassment harms women's dignity and sense of equal worth.[59] Online assaults objectify women, reducing them to their body parts.[60] For instance, posters on the message board AutoAdmit described one targeted female student as a "dumbass bitch . . . [who] I wish to rape . . . in the ass"[61] and stated that another has "huge fake titties."[62] Harassers further humiliate women by reducing them to *diseased* body parts. For example, a poster says of one woman, "just don't FUCK her, she has herpes."[63] They make clear that women have worth only as sex objects.

Such objectification injures women by signaling that they are nothing but things to be used by men, not persons with feelings.[64] Online rape threats say to women "[y]ou claim to be a full human being, but you are much less than that. You are a mere thing . . . . [whose] autonomy can be snatched away, your feelings ignored or violated."[65] Women feel rejected and less worthy.[66] A victim explained: "someone who writes 'You're just a cunt!' is not trying to convince me of anything but my own worthlessness."[67] Martha Nussbaum considers the online objectification of women an attempt to "restor[e] the patriarchal world before the advent of sex equality, the world in which women were just tools of male purposes . . . . [and] had no right to be more than tits and cunt."[68]

Sexual harassment in the workplace similarly treats women as moral subordinates and undermines their self-respect.[69] Employers and co-workers who refer to female workers as "nice pieces of ass" or "stupid pair of boobs" cause women to see themselves as less equal and able than men.[70] As Kathryn Abrams develops in her work, sexual inquiries, jokes, and innuendos in the workplace have the effect of reminding women that they are viewed as objects of sexual derision, not colleagues worthy of respect and equal treatment.[71]

Last, cyber harassment inflicts unique harms to women's physical and emotional well-being. Posts providing women's home addresses alongside the suggestion that they have rape fantasies or should be raped have led to offline stalking and rape. Women also fear that online threats of sexual violence will be realized. Women's anxiety may be particularly acute as the posters' anonymity eliminates cues—such as the identity or location of the person who made the threat or a joking tone of voice— that might diminish concerns about the threat. Women's emotional distress often produces physical symptoms, such as anorexia nervosa, depression, and suicide. Women experience similar symptoms in the face of workplace sexual harassment.

This destructive phenomenon not only has profound consequences for individual women, but for society as well, as the next Section demonstrates. . . .

Notes

1. Although its scope is difficult to estimate, one study suggests that approximately 40 percent of female internet users have experienced cyber harassment. Azy Barak. *Sexual Harassment on the Internet,* 23 Soc. Sci. Computer Rev. 77, 81 (2005); *see also* Francesca Philips & Gabrielle Morrissey, *Cyberstalking and Cyberpredators: A Threat to Safe Sexuality on the Internet,* 10 Convergence: Int'l J.

Res. into New Media Techs. 66, 72 (2004) (estimating that one-third of female internet users have been harassed online). Any existing statistical evidence surrounding cyber gender harassment is likely to underestimate the phenomenon as women tend to underreport it due to feelings of shame and embarrassment. *See* Att'y Gen. to Vice President, Cyberstalking: A New Challenge for Law Enforcement and Industry (1999), http://www.usdoj.gov/criminal/cybercrime/cyberstalking .htm [hereinafter Rep. on Cyberstalking]. This is unsurprising given women's underreporting of workplace sexual harassment. Louise Fitzgerald et al., *Why Didn't She Just Report Him?,* 51 J. Soc. Issues 117, 119–21 (1995).

2. Danielle Keats Citron, *Cyber Civil Rights,* 89 B.U.L. Rev. 61, 69–75 (2009).

3. L.P. Sheridan & T. Grant, *Is Cyberstalking Different?,* 13 Psychol., Crime & L. 627, 637 (2007) (citing various studies suggesting that the majority of cyber stalking victims were female and their online stalkers were less likely to be ex-partners of the victims).

4. *See* Barak, *supra* note 1, at 78–79.

5. Posting of Louisa Garib to On the Identity Trail, *Blogging White Female, Online Equality and the Law,* http://www.anonequity.org/weblog/archives/2007/08/ blogging_while_female_online_i.php (Aug. 21, 2007, 23:59 EST).

6. *See* Ellen Nakashima, *Sexual Threats Stifle Some Female Bloggers,* Wash. Post. Apr. 30, 2007, at A1.

7. *See* B.J. Lee. *When Words Kill: Suicide spurs bid to regulate the net in South Korea,* Newsweek.com, Oct. 15, 2008. http://www.newsweek.com/id/164013.

8. Nakashima, *supra* note 6; *see also, e.g.,* Posting of womensspace to Women's Space, *Blogging White Female. Hacking as Sexual Terrorism,* http:// www.womensspace.org/phpBB2/2007/08/06/blogging- while-female-men-win-hacking-as-sexual-terrorism/ (Aug. 6. 2007) (explaining that she shut down her women's issues website due to cyber harassment that included threats of violence, technological attacks, and publication of her home address).

9. *See* Posting of Louisa Garib to On the Identity Trail, *supra* note 5.

10. A digital native is "a person for whom digital technologies already existed when they were born." and who has "grown up with digital technology such as computers, the Internet, mobile phones and MP3s." Wikipedia, Digital Native, http://en.wikipedia.org/wiki/Digital_native (last visited Aug. 29. 2009).

11. Posting of Rev. Billy Bob Gisher to Less People Less Idiots. *Silence of the hams,* http://lessidiots.blogspot. com/2007/04/silence-of-hams.html (Apr. 3, 2007, 16:19 EST) (on file with author).

12. Posting of Markos Moulitsas to Daily Kos, *Death threats and blogging,* http://www.dailykos.com/story/2007/4/l2/22533/9224 (Apr. 11, 2007, 23:45 PDT).

13. Posting of Susannah Breslin to The XX Factor, *Is Blogging While Female Really So "Perilous"?,* SLATE, http://www.slate.com/blogs/blogs/xxfactor/archive/2009/03/13/is-blogging-while-female-really-so-perilous.aspx (Mar. 13, 2009. 17:03 EST) (arguing that the web is an equal-opportunity attack forum and thus urging women to "get over yourselves"); Comment of Fistandantalus to Posting of Rev. Billy Bob Gisher to Less People Less Idiots, *Silence of the hams,* http://lessidiots.blogspot.com/2007/04/silence-of-hams.html (on file with author).

14. *See, e.g.,* PAUL BOCIJ, CYBERSTALKING: HARASSMENT IN THE INTERNET AGE AND HOW TO PROTECT YOUR FAMILY 17 (2004).

15. ROBIN WEST. CARING FOR JUSTICE 96 (1997).

16. *Id.*

17. CATHARINE A. MACKINNON, SEXUAL HARASSMENT OF WORKING WOMEN: A CASE OF SEX DISCRIMINATION xi (1979).

18. *See, e.g.,* Posting of Danielle Citron to Concurring Opinions, *Zuckerberg's Law on Data Sharing, Not Puffery,* http://www.concurringopinions.com/archives/2009/07/zuckerbergs-law-on-data-sharing-not-puffery.html (July 16, 2009, 12:32 EST) (explaining that as of July 2009, Facebook had 250 million members, up from 150 million in January 2009).

19. Michael Tennesen, *Avatar Acts: When the Matrix Has You, What Laws Apply to Settle Conflicts?,* SCI. AM., July 2009, at 27; *see also* Regina Lynn, *Virtual Rape Is Traumatic, but Is It A Crime?,* WIRED.COM COMMENT.—SEX DRIVE, May 4, 2007, http://www.wired.com/culture/lifestyle/commentary/sexdrive/2007/05/sexdrive_0504; Posting on Tech FAQ, *Second Life virtual rape,* http://www.tech-faq.com/blog/second-life-virtual-rape.html (last visited Aug. 29. 2009) (explaining that a Belgian user of Second Life was forced to perform sexually explicit acts after being given a "voodoo doll," a piece of code that takes the form of a regular object such as a cup or pen but in fact takes control of your avatar).

20. Citron, *supra* note 2.

21. *Cf.* Kimberlé Williams Crenshaw, *Race, Reform, and Retrenchment: Transformation and Legitimation in Antidiscrimination Law,* 101 HARV. L. REV. 1331, 1335 (1988) (describing the importance of an antidiscrimination message to combat racial subordination).

22. Brian Leiter aptly calls social networking sites that house and encourage such gender harassment "cyber–cesspools." Brian Leiter, Cleaning Cyber–Cesspools: Google and Free Speech 1 (Nov. 21, 2008) (unpublished manuscript, on file with author).

23. Online harassment is also targeted at gay men—the harassment similarly invokes targeted individuals' gender in a sexually threatening manner. For instance, anonymous posters on the high school gossip site Peoples Dirt noted that named male students were gay and threatened them with violence. A posting under a male student's name asserted "we know your [sic] g@y . . . just come out of the closet . . . and you should choke on a dick and die." Posting of Danielle Citron to Concurring Opinions, *Peoples Dirt, Now Terrorizing High Schoolers Everywhere,* http://www.concurringopinions.com/archives/2009/05/peoples-dirt-now-terrorizing-high-schoolers-everywhere.html (May 18, 2009, 15:05 EST) (alteration in original). Anonymous posters on the Encyclopedia Dramatica site direct sexually threatening taunts to named gay men. Posters accused a man of having an incestuous relationship with his brother and a bestial relationship with his dog. Encyclopedia Dramatica, Chris Cocker, http://www.encyclopedia-dramatica.com/Chris_Crocker (last visited Aug. 29, 2009).

24. Sheridan & Grant, *supra* note 3, at 67. A 2003 study of 169 individuals who reportedly experienced cyber harassment found that 62.5 percent of the respondents were female. Paul Bocij, *Victims of Cyberstalking: An Exploratory Study of Harassment Perpetrated via the Internet,* FIRST MONDAY, Oct. 6, 2003, http://firstmonday.org/htbin/cgiwrap/bin/ojs/index.php/fm/articlc/view/1086/1006. The harassment consisted of threatening or abusive email messages, threats or abusive comments via IM messages, threats or abusive comments in chat rooms, the posting of false rumors in chat rooms, impersonation of individuals in e-mail messages to friends, and encouragement of others to harass or threaten the respondent. *Id.*

25. WORKING TO HALT ONLINE ABUSE, 2007 CYBERSTALKING STATISTICS 1, http://www.haltabuse.org/resources/stats/2007Statistics.pdf. Eighteen percent of those reporting cyber harassment did not report their gender. *Id.*

26. WORKING TO HALT ONLINE ABUSE, 2006 CYBERSTALKING STATISTICS 1. http://www.haltabuse.org/resources/stats/2006Statistics.pdf.

27. WORKING TO HALT ONLINE ABUSE, CYBERSTALKING COMPARISON STATISTICS 2000–2008 1. http://www.haltabuse.org/resources/stats/Cumulative2000–2008.pdf. Five and one-half percent of the reporting individuals refused to provide their gender to the organization. *Id.*

28. *Id.*

29. *Id.* at 2.

30. Christine Petrozzo & Sarah Stapp, *To catch a predator: How some cyber–agencies help victims fight back against online aggression.* DAILY ORANGE (Syracuse. N.Y.), Jan. 24. 2008. http://media .www.dailyorange.eom/media/storage/paper522/ news/2008/01/24/News/To.Catch.A.Predator-3165676 .shtml#cp_article_tools.

31. *See* Robert Meyer & Michael Cukier, *Assessing the Attack Threat due to IRC Channels, in* PROCEEDINGS OF THE INTERNATIONAL CONFERENCE ON DEPENDABLE SYSTEMS AND NETWORKS 467 (2006), *available at* http://www.enre.umd.edu/content/rmeyer-assessing .pdf. Chat rooms using IRC protocol permit live conversations via the internet, containing as many as several thousand people, whereas other chat programs such as MSN messenger and Yahoo focus on two-person conversations. *Id.* Users can join existing discussions or create new ones. BOCIJ. *supra* note 14, at 126. "Estimates of the number of publicly accessible channels available [on IRC] range from 100,000 to more than 580,000." *Id.* (citation omitted).

32. Meyer & Cukier, *supra* note 31, at 469. The researchers used simulated users with female names Cathy, Elyse, Irene, Melissa, and Stephanie, and simulated users with male names Andy, Brad, Dan, Gregg, and Kevin. *Id.* at 469–70.

33. *Id.* at 470.

34. *Id.* at 471.

35. This statement is particularly true for heterosexual men who are less likely to face sexual intimidation by women or homosexual men, but less true for gay men who confront sexual taunts when others perceive them as effeminate. *See* Jerry Finn, *A Survey of Online Harassment at a University Campus,* 19 J. INTERPERSONAL VIOLENCE 468 (2004).

36. WEST, *supra* note 15, at 102–03 (discussing real space rape) (emphasis omitted).

37. *See* Martha Nussbaum, *Objectification and Ressentiment* 18–20 (Nov. 21–22, 2008) (unpublished manuscript, on file with author).

38. LENORA M. LAPIDUS ET AL., THE RIGHTS OF WOMEN: THE AUTHORITATIVE ACLU GUIDE TO WOMEN'S RIGHTS 180 (4th ed. 2009) (describing incidence of rape in United States). To the extent that we see men experience threats of sexual violence online, the victims are gay men. *See* Posting of Danielle Citron to Concurring Opinions, *supra* note 23.

39. Sheridan & Grant, *supra* note 3, at 637.

40. *See Female Bloggers Face Harassment,* WOMEN IN HIGHER EDUC., June 2007, at 5.

41. Nakashima, *supra* note 6 (explaining that women attacked online by anonymous posters suspend their blogging, turn to private forums, or use gender-neutral pseudonyms).

42. *See* Comment of Alyssa Royse to Posting of Alyssa Royse to BlogHer, *supra* note 71.

43. Comment of C.L. to Posting of Danielle Citron to Concurring Opinions. *Cyber Harassment: Yes, It is a Woman's Thing,* http://www.concurringopinions .com/archives/2009/03/cyber_harassmen.html (March 12, 2009, 22:37 EST).

44. *See* Ellen Nakashima, *Harsh Words Die Hard on the Web; Law Students Feel Lasting Effects of Anonymous Attacks,* WASH. POST, Mar. 7, 2007, at A1.

45. Tracy L.M. Kennedy, *An Exploratory Study of Feminist Experiences In Cyberspace,* 3 CYBERPSYCHOL., & BEHAV. 707, 716 (2000).

46. Dahlia Lithwick, *Fear of Blogging: Why women shouldn't apologize for being afraid of threats on the Web.* SLATE, May 4, 2007. http://www.slate.com/ id/2165654 (internal quotation marks omitted).

47. Kennedy, *supra* note 99, at 716.

48. Valenti, *supra* note 35 (internal quotation marks omitted).

49. Kathryn Abrams, *Gender Discrimination and the Transformation of Workplace Norms,* 42 VAND. L. REV. 1183, 1206 (1989) [hereinafter Abrams, *Transformation*].

50. *See supra* notes 80–81 and accompanying text (describing activities of Anonymous).

51. *See, e.g.,* Posting of Alyssa Royse to BlogHer, *supra* note 38.

52. *Id.*

53. Nakashima. *supra* note 6 (internal quotation marks omitted).

54. *See* Vicki Schultz. *Reconceptualizing Sexual Harassment,* 107 YALE L.J. 1683. 1763–65 (1998) (conceptualizing hostile-work-environment harassment as a means for men to preserve dominance in favored types of work by undermining women's effectiveness on the job through demeaning comments, deliberate sabotage, and refusals to provide women support they need on the job).

55. Kathryn Abrams, *The New Jurisprudence of Sexual Harassment,* 83 CORNELL L. REV. 1169, 1207 (1998) [hereinafter Abrams, *New Jurisprudence*].

56. Posting of John Hawkins to Right Wing News, *Blogging While Female Part 2: Five Women Bloggers Talk About Gender Issues And The Blogosphere,* http:// www.rightwingnews.com/mt331/2008/03/blogging_ while_female_part_2_5_l.php (Mar. 18, 2008 11:30 EST) (interviewing blogger Ann Althouse).

57. Abrams, *New Jurisprudence, supra* note 109, at 1208.

58. *See* KENJI YOSHINO, COVERING: THE HIDDEN ASSAULT ON OUR CIVIL RIGHTS 22, 144 (2006) [hereinafter YOSHINO, COVERING]. Discrimination has long forced women to pass as men to gain access to professions or

relationships that would otherwise have remained unavailable to them. *See also. e.g.,* Marjorie Garber, Vested Interests: Cross–Dressing & Cultural Anxiety 67–70 (1992). Kenji Yoshino identifies films such as *Yentl* and *Boys Don't Cry* as examples of female passing. Kenji Yoshino, *Covering,* 111 Yale L.J. 769, 926 & n.880 (2002) [hereinafter Yoshino, *Covering*].

59. As Leslie Meitzer elegantly develops in her article *Spheres of Dignity: Conceptions and Functions in Constitutional Law* (on file with author), the term dignity implicates a variety of values, including dignity as equality. I aim to use the term dignity here to refer to the value harmed by conduct that demeans, devalues, and denigrates women due to their gender.

60. Nussbaum, *supra* note 91, at 5–6; *see also* West, *supra* note 15. at 146 (explaining that sexual harassment objectifies women, inflicting a dignitary injury).

61. First Amended Complaint at ¶ 25. Doe v. Ciolli, No. 307CV00909 CFD (D. Conn. Nov. 8. 2007) (internal quotation marks omitted).

62. *Id.* at ¶ 18 (internal quotation marks omitted).
63. *Id.* at ¶ 21 (internal quotation marks omitted).
64. Nussbaum. *supra* note 91, at 3–4.
65. *Id.* at 8 (internal quotation marks omitted).
66. Kennedy, *supra* note 99, at 717.
67. *Id.* at 715 (internal quotation marks omitted).
68. Nussbaum, *supra* note 91, at 19.
69. Abrams, *Transformation, supra* note 103, at 1208. *See generally* Deborah Hellman, When is Discrimination Wrong? (2008) (exploring when and why discrimination is morally wrong).
70. Kathryn Abrams, *Title VII and the Complex Female Subject,* 92 Mich. L. Rev. 2479, 2529–30 (1994).
71 *E.g.,* Abrams, *New Jurisprudence, supra* note 109, at 1207–08.

Danielle Keats Citron is the Lois K. Macht Research Professor of Law at the University of Maryland Francis King Carey School of Law.

Rebecca Eckler

Finding Out What Men Are Up To: Some Women Pride Themselves on Their Cyber-Sleuth Skills

On a recent episode of the reality show *Keeping Up with the Kardashians,* Kourtney Kardashian tells her sister Kim she has her boyfriend's old phone. "Have you gone through it?" Kim asks Kourtney excitedly. What's the point, Kourtney wants to know. "What do you mean what is the point?" Kim asks. "You want to know what your boyfriend is up to." Then, speaking directly to the camera, Kim proudly says, "I can break into any phone, can get any code, can get into any voice mail." She's not the only phone-email snooper out there. One of the main characters on the show *Entourage* just dropped a woman who listened to one of his phone messages when he was in the shower.

Ali Wise, a stunning 32-year-old New Yorker, was arrested in July on felony charges of computer trespass and eavesdropping after allegedly hacking into the voice mail of Nina Freudenberger, an interior designer and socialite. Hacking "isn't the sort of crime that normally comes to mind when you think of a pretty young publicist who attends glam parties on a nightly basis," says Remy Stern, founder of Cityfile, a gossip website that has followed the story. "It was a little more juicy because she wasn't accused of hacking into her boyfriend's voice mail; the victim was another woman . . . who may have been involved with an ex-boyfriend of hers."

Wise used software called SpoofCard to hack into the voice mail. The SpoofCard can be bought online and, according to information on the product's website, "offers the ability to change what someone sees on their caller ID display when they receive a phone call." You simply dial SpoofCard's toll-free number or local access number in your country and then enter your PIN (like a calling card). What comes up on a person's phone is a number that's not yours.

The SpoofCard is meant to be used, mostly it seems, for crank calls and for other times people want to hide their number. But, obviously, it's being misused. The Internet is rife with information about how to break into someone's voice mail using a SpoofCard. "I'll tell you how," writes one snooper. "Call up SpoofCard and when they ask you to enter the number you want to show [up] on the caller ID, you enter your boyfriend's number.

When they ask you to enter the number you want to call, you enter your boyfriend's number again, and, bingo, you'll get into his messages. This works because it tricks the cellphone to think the cell is calling into the voice message system." The deviousness doesn't end there. "Now remember," another writes, "when you get into the voice message, you must quickly change the password so you can always access the voice mail messages."

According to a friend of Wise's, when the police asked her if she had used a SpoofCard, her answer was, "Of course I used a SpoofCard." It was as if they had asked a meat lover if they ate steak.

Wise stepped down from her job at Dolce & Gabbana, and has become fodder for New York gossip rags. But to some women she's become, if not a hero, at least relatable. Movie producers have begged to option her story.

On a recent night out, five women laughed at stories of breaking into men's voice mails. "I would wait until he went into the shower," said one, "and I would manically try and figure out his password." Another admitted that for years she has broken into her boyfriend's, and ex-boyfriend's, email and voice mail accounts. "It's really not that hard. Men are stupid. If you know their Interac password, that's generally their code for all their other PDAs," she said. One woman is so skilled at figuring out passwords, she can hear someone type in the phone digits, and from the tones of the numbers, figure out the code. "I want to see if they're up to no good," she laughs.

Obviously, serial snooping isn't just for the rich and famous. The founder of Toronto-based Blue Star

Investigations Inc. International, Allen Brik, has been a private detective for 15 years. He says this kind of invasion of privacy has exploded in the past five years. "It's not always easy, but it's certainly doable." It's strictly illegal, he says, and shouldn't be done, "but people want to know they can trust someone. They're not thinking with their heads about right or wrong."

Brik agrees that men "don't often change their password. They usually use their date of birth or their middle names. Women are more creative." (He hasn't changed any of his passwords in 12 years.) It's not only females who snoop, he says, but the majority are women. "I think it comes down to men cheating more."

A judge could turn Wise's case, due in court in October, into an "example" à la Paris Hilton's jail stint. "I do hope that no prison time is involved," says Stern. "A much better punishment would be to require her to have those godawful orange jumpsuits worn by American prisoners redesigned by Dolce & Gabbana. That might make it all worth it."

REBECCA ECKLER is a Canadian journalist and an author whose work has appeared in *Elle, Maclean's,* and *Mademoiselle.* She is also a columnist for *Post City Magazines* in Toronto.

EXPLORING THE ISSUE

Are Women More at Risk for Crimes Using Digital Technology?

Critical Thinking and Reflection

1. How does the Internet pose greater dangers to women than men?
2. How might technological advances level the playing field in a way that allows women to be online aggressors in greater numbers?

Is There Common Ground?

Schenk (2008) developed the Cyber-Sexual Experiences Questionnaire to study sexual harassment that occurs online via the Internet. While Schenk's study focused on how women experience cyber-sexual harassment, her findings can also help explain how women can become aggressors in the online environment. The Internet can be a power equalizer that serves to empower both men and women to engage in cyber harassment. The "dissociative anonymity" that people experience within the online environment may allow both men and women to engage in behavior on the Internet that seems separate from their day-to-day offline personas (Schenk, 2008, p. 84). Online disinhibition may also occur due to the relative invisibility of easily navigating Internet sites without the need to self-identify. Schenk's (2008) review of the literature additionally noted the "minimization of authority" that occurs in the online world where people are empowered to speak freely without regard to relative social status (p. 84). All of these factors may contribute to a potential leveling of the power field that would permit both men and women to engage in harassment behavior using the Internet.

Cook (2010) reviewed the world of online gossip sites and how their proliferation has impacted campus life at colleges around the nation. The posting of gossip, including photos, has created new challenges for higher education student personnel professionals in combating campus harassment. Officials find that men and women can be equal opportunity offenders as well as harassment targets.

Additional Resources

Cook, S. G. (2010, July). "Gossip on Steroids: Cyber-Bullying, Stalking, Harassing." *Women in Higher Education, 19*(7), 18–19.

Schenk, S. (2008). "Cyber-Sexual Harassment: The Development of the Cyber-Sexual Experiences Questionnaire," *McNair Scholars Journal, 12*(1), Article 8.

Internet Reference . . .

Electronic Crime Technology Center of Excellence

http://ectcoe.net/

Selected, Edited, and with Issue Framing Material by:
Elizabeth Schroeder, EdD, MSW, *Elizabeth Schroeder Consulting*

ISSUE

Can a Woman with Conservative Political Views Be a Feminist?

YES: Christina Hoff Sommers, from "Feminism and Freedom," *The American Spectator* (July/August 2008)

NO: Jessica Valenti, from "Who Stole Feminism?" *The Nation* (October 18, 2010)

Learning Outcomes

As you read the issue, focus on the following points:

- How has feminism evolved over the past decade?
- How is the influence of various subgroups expressed in feminism?

ISSUE SUMMARY

YES: Christina Hoff Sommers, in "Feminism and Freedom," makes an argument for a broader representation and a redefinition of feminism that diverges from what she characterizes as a revisionist and radical feminist agenda.

NO: Jessica Valenti, in "Who Stole Feminism?," makes an argument against what she frames as a co-optation and re-branding of feminism by conservative women.

The fragmentation of the women's movement is not a recent phenomenon. Scholars who study the suffrage efforts of the late ninteenth and early twentieth century would note that a single monolithic movement wholly representative of all women has never existed. The contemporary battle for ownership of the feminist title and, by association, the women's movement has gained particular notoriety in recent years due to an eagerness on the part of both pundits and politicians to claim the sobriquet.

During the 2008 election cycle, vice presidential candidate Sarah Palin claimed the feminist designation and inspired young conservative women throughout the nation to try the label on for size. In "Feminism and Freedom," conservative scholar Christina Hoff Sommers reexamines the women's movement of the eighteenth and nineteenth century. Sommers characterizes egalitarian feminism as radical and conservative feminism as family-centered. She credits egalitarian feminism with earning women important legal rights but makes a case for the

conservative feminism school of thought as an option for living a feminist life.

Sommers characterizes the conservative women's movement as one of philanthropy and volunteerism. Historically, the conservative women's movement embraced and celebrated the "Angel in the house" role for women. In fact, the conservative branch of the suffrage movement depicted the fight for the women's vote as a battle for the "home protection ballot." This conservative home-focused messaging would prove successful with talking points that framed the political enfranchisement of women as "a mother's sacred duty to vote."

In "Who Stole Feminism?," Jessica Valenti examines how conservative women co-opted feminism during the 2008 presidential cycle. The popularity of conservative GOP women who became national political stars in the months leading up to the historic election of President Barack Obama was underscored by the subversion of progressive feminist labels by members of the nascent Tea Party movement. The conservative spin on feminism was hailed by pundits as the "new feminism" and the standard bearer of the movement was Alaska's Governor Sarah Palin, tapped to run as president candidate John McCain's running mate. Valenti makes the argument that feminism is not simply about women ascending to positions of power and influence but encompasses much larger and harder to achieve goals of equity and social justice.

Modern-day conservative women represent a diverse demographic group. Conservative women hold political office and serve as CEOs of Fortune 500 companies. The dividing line between conservative and liberal women often rests on issues of choice. Liberal feminists posit that a key tenet of feminism is a woman's right to choose. Conservative women who embrace the feminist label believe that feminism is not a single issue movement and that being a feminist is about economic opportunity and shattering glass ceilings in the workplace.

YES ↵

Christina Hoff Sommers

Feminism and Freedom

On February 10, 2001, 18,000 women filled Madison Square Garden for one of the more notable feminist gatherings of our time. The event—"Take Back the Garden"—centered on a performance of Eve Ensler's raunchy play, *The Vagina Monologues*. The "Vulva Choir" sang; self-described "Vagina Warriors"—including Gloria Steinem, Jane Fonda, and Donna Hanover (Rudolph Giuliani's ex-wife)—recited pet names for vaginas: Mimi, Gladys. Glenn Close led the crowd in spelling out the obscene word for women's intimate anatomy, "Give me a C...!!!" A huge banner declared the Garden to be a "RAPE FREE ZONE." The mood grew solemn when Oprah Winfrey came forward to read a new monologue called "Under the Burqa," which described the plight of Afghan women living under the Taliban. At its climax, an actual Afghan woman named Zoya, who represented RAWA—the Revolutionary Association of the Women of Afghanistan—appeared on stage covered from head to toe in a burqa. Oprah approached her and, with a dramatic sweep of her arm, lifted and removed it. The crowd roared in delight.

Later, an exposé in the progressive *American Prospect* would reveal that RAWA is a Maoist organization whose fanatical members are so feared by Afghan women that one human rights activist has dubbed them the "Talibabes." According to the *Prospect,* when *Ms.* magazine tried to distance itself from RAWA in 2002, a RAWA spokeswoman denounced *Ms.* as the "mouthpiece of hegemonic, U.S.-centric corporate feminism." But on that magical February night at the Garden, few knew or cared about Zoya's political views or affiliations.

The evening was a near-perfect distillation of contemporary feminism. Pick up a women's studies textbook, visit a college women's center, or look at the websites of leading feminist organizations and you will be likely to find the same fixation on intimate anatomy, combined with left-wing politics, and a poisonous antipathy to men. (Campus feminists were among the most vocal and zealous accusers of the young men on the Duke University lacrosse team who were falsely indicted for rape in 2006.) Contemporary feminism routinely depicts American society as a dangerous patriarchy where women are under siege—that is the message of the "RAPE FREE ZONE" banner in the Garden. It therefore presents itself as a movement of "liberation," defying the patriarchal oppressor and offering women everywhere the opportunity to make contact with their "real selves."

But modern "women's liberation" has little to do with liberty. It aims not to free women to pursue their own interests and inclinations, but rather to re-educate them to attitudes often profoundly contrary to their natures. In *Professing Feminism: Education and Indoctrination in Women's Studies* (2003), two once-committed women's studies professors, Daphne Patai and Noretta Koertge, describe how the feminist classroom transforms idealistic female students into "relentless grievance collectors." In 1991, the culture critic and dissident feminist Camille Paglia put the matter even more bluntly: she described women's studies as "a jumble of vulgarians, bunglers, whiners, French faddists, apparatchiks, dough-faced party-liners, pie-in-the-sky utopians and bullying sanctimonious sermonizers. Reasonable, moderate feminists hang back and keep silent in the face of fascism."

The embarrassing spectacle at Madison Square Garden, the erratic state of women's studies, the outbreak of feminist vigilantism at Duke University may tempt some to conclude that the women's movement in the United States is in a state of hopeless, hapless, and permanent disarray. Perhaps American feminism has become hysterical because it has ceased to be useful. After all, women in this country have their freedom; they have achieved parity with men in most of the ways that count. Why not let the feminist movement fade from the scene? The sooner the better. Good riddance.

That is an understandable but unwarranted reaction. Women in the West *did* form a movement and *did* liberate themselves in ways of vital importance to the evolution of liberal society. Feminism, in its classical phase, was a critical chapter in the history of freedom. For most of the world's women, that history has just begun; for them, classical feminism offers a tried and true roadmap to equality and freedom. And even in the West there are unresolved equity issues and the work of feminism is not over. Who needs feminism? We do. The world does. Women everywhere need the liberty to be what they are—not, as contemporary feminism insists, liberation *from* what they are. This we can see if we look back at the history of women's liberation—not as it is taught in women's studies departments, but as it truly was.

The classical feminism of the 18th and 19th centuries embodied two distinct schools of thought and social activism. The first, egalitarian feminism, was progressive (in the view of many contemporaries of both sexes, radical), and it centered on women as independent agents rather than wives and mothers. It held that men and women are, in their essential nature, the same, and it sought to liberate women through abstract appeals to social justice and universal rights. The second school, conservative feminism, was traditionalist and family-centered. It embraced rather than rejected women's established roles as homemakers, caregivers, and providers of domestic tranquility—and it promoted women's rights by redefining, strengthening, and expanding those roles. Conservative feminists argued that a practical, responsible femininity could be a force for good in the world beyond the family, through charitable works and more enlightened politics and government.

Of the two schools, conservative feminism was much the more influential. Unlike its more radical sister, conservative feminism has always had great appeal to large majorities of women. By contrast, egalitarian feminists often appeared strange and frightening with their salons and little journals. It is not, however, my purpose to denigrate egalitarian feminism—quite the contrary. Historically, proponents of the two schools were forthright and sometimes fierce competitors, but their competition sharpened the arguments on both sides, and they often cooperated on practical causes to great effect. The two movements were (and will remain) rivals in principle but complementary in practice. Thanks to egalitarian feminism, women now have the same rights and opportunities as men. But, as conservative feminists have always insisted, free women seldom aspire to be just like men, but rather employ their freedom in distinctive ways and for distinctive purposes.

Egalitarian feminism had its historical beginnings in the writings of the British philosopher Mary Wollstonecraft (1759–1797). Wollstonecraft, a rebel and a free thinker, believed that women were as intelligent as men and as

worthy of respect. Her *A Vindication of the Rights of Woman* became an instant sensation. She wrote it in the spirit of the European Enlightenment—whose primary principle was the essential dignity and moral equality of all rational beings. However, Wollstonecraft's insistence that women too are rational and deserving of the same rights as men was then a contentious thesis.

Wollstonecraft's demand was a dramatic break with the past. In 1776, Abigail Adams famously wrote a letter to her husband, John, urging him and his colleagues in the Continental Congress to "remember the ladies. . . and to be more generous and favorable to them than your ancestors." Adams was appealing to a tradition of chivalry and gallantry that enjoined male protectiveness toward women. Sixteen years later, in her *Vindication*, Wollstonecraft was doing something markedly different. She was not urging legislators in France and England to "remember the ladies" or appealing to their generous or protective impulses. Reason, she said, demanded that women be granted the same rights as men. She wanted nothing less than total political and moral equality. Wollstonecraft was perhaps the first woman in history to insist that biology is not destiny: "I view with indignation the mistaken notions that enslave my sex."

For Wollstonecraft, education was the key to female liberation: "Strengthen the female mind by enlarging it, and there will be an end to blind obedience." She was a proponent of co-education and insisted that women be educated on a par with men—with all fields and disciplines being open to them. In the opening lines of *Vindication*, she expresses her "profound conviction that the neglected education of [women] is the grand source of the misery I deplore."

Wollstonecraft led one of the most daring, dramatic, and consequential lives of the 18th century. She was a lower-middle-class, semi-educated "nobody" (as one British historian has described her) who was to become the first woman to enter the Western canon of political philosophy. Her friends included Thomas Paine, William Wordsworth, and William Blake. She carried on a famous debate with Edmund Burke about the merits of the French Revolution. Soon after she published her *Vindication of the Rights of Woman* she ran off to Paris to write about the revolution.

After her death, her husband William Godwin wrote what he thought was an adulatory biography. He talked honestly about her unorthodox lifestyle that included love affairs, an out-of-wedlock child, and two suicide attempts over her faithless American lover. He even praised her—completely inaccurately—for having rejected Christianity.

Godwin all but destroyed her reputation for the next hundred years. The public reaction to his disclosures was fascination, horror, and repulsion. Former friends denounced her. Feminists distanced themselves. Political enemies called her a "whore." Today, however, her reputation is secure. In an essay published in 1932, Virginia Woolf wrote, "One form of immortality is hers undoubtedly: she is alive and active, she argues and experiments, we hear her voice and trace her influence even now among the living." Woolf summarizes Wollstonecraft's egalitarian teachings in one sentence: "The staple of her doctrine was that nothing matters save independence." Another way of putting it is to say that what Wollstonecraft wanted for women was the full liberty of citizenship.

At the time Wollstonecraft was writing, Hannah More (1745–1833)—novelist, poet, pamphleteer, political activist, evangelical reformer, and abolitionist—was waging a very different campaign to improve the status of women. More is well-known to scholars who specialize in eighteenth century culture. The late UCLA literary historian Mitzi Myers calls her a "female crusader infinitely more successful than Wollstonecraft or any other competitor," but More is rarely given the credit she deserves. The story of what she initiated and how she did it is integral to the story of women's quest for freedom. But few contemporary feminist historians have wanted that story to be told.

Virginia Woolf once said that if she were in charge of assigning names to critical historical epochs, along with the Crusades, or the War of the Roses, she would give a special name to that world-transforming period at the end of the 18th century in England when, in her words, "The middleclass woman began to write." One disparaging historian called this unprecedented cohort of writing women (borrowing a phrase from the 16th-century religious reformer John Knox) "a monstrous regiment." It was a regiment that was destined to win decisive battles in women's struggle for freedom and opportunity. Its three most important members were Mary Wollstonecraft, Jane Austen, and Hannah More.

If Wollstonecraft was the founder of egalitarian feminism, More was the founder of conservative feminism. Like Wollstonecraft, More was a religiously inspired, self-made woman who became an intellectual peer of several of the most accomplished men of her age. But whereas Wollstonecraft befriended Paine and debated Burke, More was a friend and admirer of Burke, a close friend of Samuel Johnson and of Horace Walpole, and an indispensable ally and confidante to William Wilberforce, a father of British abolitionism. Concerning the French revolution which Wollstonecraft initially championed, More wrote, "From

liberty, equality, and the rights of man, good Lord deliver *us*." And she was surely the most prominent woman of her age. As one biographer notes, "In her time she was better known than Mary Wollstonecraft and her books outsold Jane Austen's many times over." Her various pamphlets sold in the millions and her tract against the French revolution enjoyed a greater circulation than Burke's *Reflections* or Paine's *Rights of Man*. Some historians credit her political writings with saving England from the kind of brutal revolutionary upheaval that traumatized France.

More (who never married) was active in the Bluestocking society. The "Blues" were a group of intellectual women (and men) who would meet to discuss politics, literature, science, and philosophy. It was started in 1750 by intelligent but education-starved upper- and middle-class women who yearned for serious conversation rather than the customary chatter and gossip typical of elite gatherings. "I was educated at random," More would say, and women's education became one of her most passionate causes.

More is hard to classify politically. It is possible to find passages in her novels, pamphlets, and letters that make her look like an arch conservative; others show her as a progressive reformer. Through selective citation she can be made to seem like an insufferable prude—Lord Byron dismissed her as "Morality's prim personification"—but it is doubtful that a "prim personification" would have attracted the devotion and respect of men like Johnson, Walpole, and Wilberforce.

More was a British patriot, a champion of constitutional monarchy, and a friend and admirer of Edmund Burke, but she was no defender of the status quo. She called for revolutionary change—not in politics, but in morals. In her novels and pamphlets, she sharply reproached members of the upper classes for their amorality, hedonism, indifference to the poor, and tolerance of the crime of slavery. In the many Sunday schools she established she encouraged the poor to be sober, thrifty, hard-working, and religious. More shared Adam Smith's enthusiasm for the free market as a force for good. But for the market to thrive, she believed England's poor and rich would need to develop good moral habits and virtuous characters.

Historians have referred to her as "bourgeois progressivist," a "Christian capitalist," "Burke for beginners," the "first Victorian." She could also be called the first conservative feminist. Unlike Wollstonecraft, More believed the sexes were significantly different in their propensities, aptitudes, and life preferences. She envisioned a society where women's characteristic virtues and graces could be developed, refined, and freely expressed.

She was persuaded that these virtues could be realized only when women were given more freedom and a serious education:

> [T]ill women shall be more reasonably educated, and until the native growth of their mind shall cease to be stilted and cramped, we shall have no juster ground for pronouncing that their understanding has already reached its highest attainable perfection, than the Chinese would have for affirming that their women have attained to the greatest possible perfection in walking, while their first care is, during their infancy, to cripple their feet.

She loathed the mindless pastimes that absorbed upper-class women of her day, and encouraged middle- and upper-class women to leave their homes and salons so as to take up serious philanthropic pursuits. According to More, women were more tender-minded than men and were the natural caretakers of the nation. She told women that it was their patriotic duty to apply their natural gifts—nurturing, organizing, and educating—not merely to their own households, but to society at large. "Charity," said one of More's fictional characters, "is the calling of a lady: the care of the poor is her profession." More envisioned armies of intelligent, informed, and well-trained women working in hospitals, orphanages, and schools. She appealed to women to exert themselves "with a patriotism at once firm and feminine for the greater good of all." And women listened.

Her didactic 1880 novel, *Coelebs in Search of a Wife*, which valorized a new kind of wise, effective, active, and responsible femininity, went into 11 editions in nine months, and to 30 by the time of More's death. UCLA literary scholar Anne Mellor comments on the extent of More's influence:

> She urged her women readers to participate actively in the organization of voluntary benevolent societies and in the foundation of hospitals, orphanages, Sunday Schools. . . .And her call was heard: literally thousands of voluntary societies sprang up in the opening decades of the nineteenth century to serve the needs of every imaginable group of sufferers.

It is hard to overstate the positive impact of widespread volunteerism on the fate of women. As women became engaged in charitable works, other parts of the public sphere became accessible. British historian F.K. Prochaska, in his seminal *Women and Philanthropy in Nineteenth-Century England* (1980), wrote, "The charitable experience of women was a lever which they used to open the doors closed to them in other spheres." According to Prochaska, as women began to become active in the outside world and form philanthropic organizations, they became interested in "government, administration and the law." Their volunteer work in charity schools focused their minds on education reform—for women of their own social class and for the poor women they sought to help. Prochaska, who calls More "probably the most influential woman of her day," concludes, "It should not come as a surprise that in 1866 women trained in charitable society were prominent among those who petitioned the House of Commons praying for the enfranchisement of their sex."

It was taken for granted in More's time that women were less intelligent and less serious than men, and thus less worthy as human beings. More flatly rejected these assumptions. She did so without rejecting the idea of a special women's sphere. She embraced that sphere, giving it greater dignity and power. That was her signature Burkean style of feminism. More initiated a humane revolution in the relations of the sexes that was decorous, civilized, and in no way socially divisive. Above all, it was a feminism that women themselves could comfortably embrace: a feminism that granted women the liberty to be themselves without ceasing to be women. Indeed, if More's name and fame had not been brushed out of women's history, many women today might well be identifying with a modernized version of her femalefriendly feminism.

Fortunately, her ideals and her style of feminism are well represented in the novels of Jane Austen. We don't know for sure whether Austen read More, but scholars claim to see the unmistakable influence in her writings of both More and Wollstonecraft. Her heroines are paragons of rational, merciful, and responsible womanhood. Austen also honors a style of enlightened and chivalrous manhood. Austen's heroes—men like Mr. Darcy, Captain Wentworth, and Mr. Knightley—esteem female strength, rationality, and intelligence.

Egalitarian feminists like Wollstonecraft (and later, John Stuart Mill and Harriet Taylor) are staple figures in the intellectual history of feminism, but they have never attracted a very large following among the rank and file of women of their time. More succeeded brilliantly with all classes of women. She awakened a nation and changed the way it saw itself. What she achieved was unprecedented. But the feminist scholar Elizabeth Kowaleski Wallace speaks for many when she describes More as a case study of "patriarchal complicity" and an "univited guest" who "makes the process of celebrating our HERITAGE as women more difficult."

Hannah More is not the only once-famous women's advocate to have vanished from the official "herstorical" record. Ken Burns, the celebrated documentarian, followed his award-winning *Civil War* with a 1999 film about Elizabeth Cady Stanton (1815–1902) and Susan B. Anthony (1820–1906) and their struggle to win the vote for American women. There is one brief sequence in which the narrator explains that in the last quarter of the 19th century, Anthony forged coalitions with conservative mainstream groups. The mood darkens and a pioneer in the field of women's studies—Professor Sally Roesch Wagner—appears on the screen. Wagner informs viewers that Anthony was so determined to win the vote, she established alliances with pro-suffrage women who were "enemies of freedom in every other way—Frances Willard is a case in point." The camera then shows a photo of a menacing-looking Willard.

One would never imagine from Burns's film that Frances Willard (1839–1898) was one of the most beloved and respected women of the 19th century. When she died, one newspaper wrote, "No woman's name is better known in the English-speaking world than that of Miss Willard, save that of England's great queen." Because of her prodigious good works and kindly nature, Willard was often called the "Saint Frances of American Womanhood."

But Willard, a suffragist and leader of the Women's Christian Temperance Union, is another once esteemed figure in women's history who is today unmentioned and unmentionable. Willard brought mainstream women into the suffrage movement, and some historians credit her with doing far more to win the vote for women than any other suffragist. But her fondness for saying things like "Womanliness first—afterwards what you will" was her ticket to historical obliquy.

Approved feminist founders like Elizabeth Cady Stanton and Susan B. Anthony promoted women's suffrage through Wollstonecraft-like appeals to universal rights. Their inspirations were John Locke, Thomas Jefferson, and Wollstonecraft herself. Stanton wrote affectingly on "the individuality of each human soul," and on a woman's need to be the "arbiter of her own destiny." She and her sister suffragists brought a feminist Enlightenment to women, but to their abiding disappointment, American women greeted the offer with a mixture of indifference and hostility. Stanton's words were effective with a relatively small coterie of educated women, mostly on the East Coast. When a suffrage amendment failed dismally in the state of Colorado in 1877, one newspaper editorial called the suffragists "carpetbaggers" promoting an elitist "eastern issue." The headline read: "Good-bye to the Female Tramps of Boston."

For many decades the average American woman simply ignored the cause of suffrage. In a 1902 history of women's suffrage, Anthony and her co-author wrote, "the indifference and inertia, the apathy of women lies the greatest obstacle to their enfranchisement." Throughout the 1880s and 1890s many women actively organized against it. Stanford historian Carl Degler, in his classic 1980 social history, *At Odds: Women and the Family in America from the Revolution to the Present,* notes that in 1890, more than 20,000 women had joined an *anti*-suffrage group in New York State alone.

To prove once and for all that the majority of women wanted the vote, suffragists organized a referendum in Massachusetts in 1895. Both men and women were allowed to take part. The initiative lost, with 187,000 voting against the franchise and only 110,000 in favor—and of those who voted yes, only 23,000 were women! According to Anthony, "The average man would not vote against granting women the suffrage if all those of his own family brought a strong pressure to bear upon him in its favor." It is the conventional wisdom that men denied women the ballot. But even a cursory look at the historical record suggests that men were not the only problem.

Degler and other historians believe that, because the vote was associated with individualism and personal assertiveness, many women saw it as both selfish and an attack on their unique and valued place in the family. Feminist historians denigrate what they call the "cult of domesticity" that proved so beguiling to nineteenth century women. But they forget that this "cult" freed many rural women from manual labor, improved the material conditions of women's lives and coincided with an increase in female life expectancy. Furthermore, as Degler shows, in nineteenth-century America, both the public and private spheres were prized and valued. The companionate marriages described by Jane Austen were the American domestic ideal. Alexis de Tocqueville commented on the essential equality of the male and female spheres in *Democracy in America* (1840) "Americans," he said, did not think that men and women should perform the same tasks, "but they show an equal regard for both their perspective parts; and though their lot is different, they consider both of them as being of equal value."

Hence as long as women saw the vote as a threat to their sphere, suffrage was a lost cause. Impassioned feminist rhetoric about freedom, dignity, autonomy, and individual rights fell on deaf ears. If the American women's movement was going to move forward, the suffrage movement needed new arguments and new ways of thinking that were more respectful and protective of women's role. Frances Willard showed the way.

Frances Willard served as president of the Woman's Christian Temperance Union from 1879 until her death in 1898. Under her leadership it grew to be the largest and most influential women's organization in the nation. Today we associate temperance with Puritanism. But in the late 19th century, most feminists, including Elizabeth Cady Stanton and Susan B. Anthony, supported it. Temperance advocates believed that a ban on the sale of alcohol would greatly diminish wife abuse, desertion, destitution, and crime. In other words, temperance was a movement in defense of the home—the female sphere.

Willard was proud of women's role as the "Angel in the house." But why, she asked, limit these angels to the home? With the vote, said Willard, women could greatly increase their civilizing and humane influence on society. With the vote, they could protect the homes they so dearly loved. Indeed, Willard referred to the "vote" as "the home protection ballot." Women were moved by this, and men were disarmed.

Anthony admired Willard; Stanton, a skeptic in religious matters, was leery. Both were startled by her ability to attract unprecedented numbers of dedicated women to the suffrage cause. The membership figures for the various women's organizations are striking. In 1890, two leading egalitarian suffragist groups merged because they were worried that the cause was dying. They formed the National American Woman Suffrage Association and elected Elizabeth Cady Stanton president. The total membership of these combined groups, according to University of Michigan historian Ruth Bordin, was 13,000. By comparison, Willard had built an organization with more than ten times that number; by 1890 she had 150,000 adult dues-paying members. Moreover, Willard and her followers began to bring the suffrage movement something new and unfamiliar: victories.

In 1893 the state of Colorado held a second election on women's suffrage. Unlike 1877, when the suffragists lost and the so-called "tramps of Boston" were sent packing, this time the suffragists won the vote by a 55 percent majority. Many historians agree that Willard's new conservative approach explains the success. She had persuaded large numbers of men and women that it was a mother's sacred duty to vote.

Thomas Carlyle has ascribed the insights of genius to "cooperation with the tendency of the world." Like Hannah More before her, Willard cooperated with the world and discerned novel and effective ways to improve it. Feminists do not honor the memory of these women. Indeed, with the exception of a small group of professional historians and literary critics, almost no one knows who they are. Still, it is interesting to note, today the Hannah More/ Frances Willard style of conservative feminism is on the verge of a powerful resurgence.

In her 1990 book, *In Search of Islamic Feminism,* the University of Texas Middle Eastern studies professor Elizabeth Warnock Fernea described a new style of feminism coming to life throughout the Muslim world. Traveling through Uzbekistan, Saudi Arabia, Morocco, Turkey, and Iraq, Fernea met great numbers of women's advocates working hard to improve the status of women. There have always been Western-style egalitarian feminists in these countries. But they are small in number and tend to be found among the most educated elites. The "Islamic feminists" Fernea was meeting were different. They were traditional, religious, and family-centered—and they had a following among women from all social classes. They were proud of women's role as mother, wife, and caregiver. Several rejected what they see as divisiveness in today's American women's movement. As one Iraqi women's advocate, Haifa Abdul Rahman, told her, "We see feminism in America as dividing women from men, separating women from the family. This is bad for everyone." Fernea settled on the term "family feminism" to describe this new movement. Experts on the history of Western feminism will here recognize its affinities with Frances Willard's long-lost teachings. Today, almost 20 years after Fernea's book, conservative feminism is surging in the Muslim world.

When Frances Willard died in 1898, her younger feminist colleague Carrie Chapman Catt remarked, "There has never been a woman leader in this country greater than Frances Willard." But today's feminists remain implacably hostile to Willard's notions of "womanly virtue" and have no sympathy with her family-centered feminism. These are unforgivable defects in their eyes, but they are precisely the traits that make Willard's style of feminism highly relevant to the many millions of women all over the world who are struggling for their rights and freedoms in strongly traditional societies, and who do not want to be liberated from their love for family, children, and husband.

Truth be told, there are also great numbers of contemporary American women who would today readily label themselves as feminists were they aware of a conservative alternative, in which liberty rather than "liberation" is the dominant idea. Today, more than 70 percent of American women reject the label "feminist," largely because the label has been appropriated by those who reject the very idea of a feminine sphere.

Clare Boothe Luce, a conservative feminist who in her heyday in the 1940s was a popular playwright and a member of the United States Congress, wrote and spoke about women at a time when feminism's Second Wave was still more than 20 years away. Luce's exemplary remarks on Mother Nature and sex differences are especially relevant today.

> It is time to leave the question of the role of women in society up to Mother Nature—a difficult lady to fool. You have only to give women the same opportunities as men, and you will soon find out what is or is not in their nature. What is in women's nature to do they will do, and you won't be able to stop them. But you will also find, and so will they, that what is not in their nature, even if they are given every opportunity, they will not do, and you won't be able to make them do it.

Camille Paglia once told me she found these words powerful, persuasive, and even awe-inspiring. So do I. Luce takes the best of both egalitarian and conservative feminism. She is careful to say that women's nature can be made known only in conditions of freedom and opportunity. It is in such conditions of respect and fairness that woman can reveal their true preferences. Clearly Luce does not expect that women will turn out to be interchangeable with men.

When Luce wrote her cautionary words, sex role stereotypes still powerfully limited women's choices and opportunities. Today, women enjoy the equality of opportunity that Luce alluded to. The conventional constraints, confinements, and rigid expectations are largely things of the past. It is now possible to observe "the role of women in society" by taking note of the roles women themselves freely choose. Was Wollstonecraft right to insist that under conditions of freedom the sexes would make similar choices? Or was Hannah More closer to the truth when she suggested that women will always prevail in the private sphere and express themselves as the natural caregivers of the species?

We know from common observation that women are markedly more nurturing and empathetic than men. The female tendency to be empathic and caring shows up very early in life. Female infants, for example, show greater distress and concern than male infants over the plight of others; this difference persists into adulthood. Women don't merely say they want to help others; they enter the helping and caring professions in great numbers. Even today, in an era when equal rights feminism is dominant in education, the media, and the women's movement, women continue to be vastly over-represented in fields like nursing, social work, pediatrics, veterinary medicine, and early childhood education. The great 19th-century psychologist William James said that for men "the world is a theater for heroism." That may be an overstatement, but it finds a lot of support in modern social science—and evidence of everyday life. Women are numerically dominant in the helping professions; men prevail in the saving and rescuing vocations such as policemen, firefighters, and soldiers.

Here we come to the central paradox of egalitarian feminism: when women are liberated from the domestic sphere and no longer forced into the role of nurturers, when they are granted their full Lockean/Jeffersonian freedoms to pursue happiness in all the multitudinous ways a free society has to offer, many, perhaps most, still give priority to the domestic sphere.

In a 1975 exchange in the *Saturday Review*, the feminist pioneer Betty Friedan and the French philosopher and women's rights advocate Simone de Beauvoir discussed the "problem" of stay-at-home mothers. Friedan told Beauvoir that she believed women should have the choice to stay home to raise their children if that is what they wished to do. Beauvoir candidly disagreed:

> No, we don't believe that any woman should have this choice. No woman should be authorized to stay at home to raise her children. Society should be totally different. Women should not have that choice, precisely because if there is such a choice, too many women will make that one . . .

In Simone de Beauvoir, we see how starkly the ideology of liberation has come to oppose actual, practical liberty—even "choice." Her intolerance and condescension toward family-centered women is shared by many in today's feminist establishment, and has affected the education of American students. Historian Christine Rosen, in a recent survey of women's studies texts, found that every one disparaged traditional marriage, stay-at-home mothers, and the culture of romance. Perhaps there is a sensible women's studies text out there somewhere, but, for the most part, the sphere of life that has the greatest appeal to most women, and is inseparable from traditional ideas of feminine fulfillment, is rejected in the name of liberation.

Today's feminist establishment in the United States is dominated by the radical wing of the egalitarian tradition. Not only do its members not cooperate with their conservative sisters, but they also often denigrate and vilify them; indeed they have all but eliminated them from the history of American feminism. Revisionist history is never a pretty sight. But feminist revisionists are destructive in special ways. They seek to obliterate not only feminist history but the femininity that made it a success.

Contemporary feminism needs to make peace with Hannah More and Frances Willard and their modern-day heirs or face a complete loss of appeal and effectiveness. Eve Ensler and her most devoted disciple, Jane Fonda, may not be amenable to change. But there is hope for the younger generation. Over the years, I have lectured on more than 100 college campuses where I meet both conservative and radical women activists. The former invite me and the latter come to jeer and wrangle—but as a rule we all part as friends. "Why do you like the Vagina Monologues so much?", I ask them. Most tell me that, by acting in the play or support-ing it, they are both having fun (girls, too, like to push the limits) and serving a good cause (funds raised by the perfor-mances support local domestic violence shelters). I have yet to meet a single one who shares the play's misandry.

These young women can be reasoned with and many are fully capable of allying themselves with moderate and conservative women to work for common interests. My advice to them: Don't bother "taking back the Garden." Take back feminism. Restore its lost history. Make the movement attractive once again to the silent majority of American women, who really don't want to be liberated from their womanhood. And then take on the cause of the women who have yet to find the liberty that western women have won for themselves and that all women eve-rywhere deserve.

CHRISTINA HOFF SOMMERS is an associate professor of phi-losophy at Clark University.

Jessica Valenti

 **NO**

Who Stole Feminism?

Sarah Palin opposes abortion and comprehensive sex education. While mayor of Wasilla she made sexual assault victims pay for their own rape kits. She also calls herself a feminist. Delaware GOP Senate nominee Christine O'Donnell has said that allowing women to attend military academies "cripples the readiness of our defense" and that wives should "graciously submit" to their husbands—but her website touts her "commitment to the women's movement." Pundits who once mocked women's rights activists as ugly bra burners are abuzz over the "new conservative feminism," and the Tea Party is lauding itself as a women's movement.

The right once disparaged feminism as man-hating and baby-killing, but now "feminist" is the must-have label for women on the right. Whether or not this rebranding strategy actually succeeds in overcoming the GOP's anti-women reputation is unclear (see Betsy Reed, "Sex and the GOP," page 11). After all, Republicans have long supported overturning *Roe v. Wade*, voted against family and maternity leave, and fought groundbreaking legislation like the Lilly Ledbettter Fair Pay Act. When it comes to wooing women's votes for the GOP, there's a lot of damage control to do.

Feminists are understandably horrified—the movement we've fought so hard for is suddenly being appropriated by the very people who are trying to dismantle it. But this co-opting hasn't happened in a vacuum; the mainstream feminist movement's instability and stalled ideology have made stealing it that much easier. The failure of feminists to prop up the next generation of activists, and the focus on gender as the sole requisite for feminism, has led to a crisis of our own making.

Conservative women have been trying to steal feminism for more than a decade—organizations like the Independent Women's Forum and Feminists for Life have long fought for antiwomen policies while identifying themselves as the "real" feminists. But their "prowoman" messaging didn't garner national attention until actual feminists paved the way for them in the 2008 presidential election. During the Democratic primary, feminist icons and leaders of mainstream women's organizations insisted that the

only acceptable vote was for Hillary Clinton; female Barack Obama supporters were derided as traitors or chided for their naïveté. I even heard from women working in feminist organizations who kept mum on their vote for fear of losing their jobs. Perhaps most representative of the internal strife was a *New York Times* op-ed (and the fallout that followed) by Gloria Steinem in which the icon wrote, "Gender is probably the most restricting force in American life."

Soon after, Melissa Harris-Lacewell, an associate professor of politics and African-American studies at Princeton University, responded in a *Democracy Now!* segment, "Part of what, again, has been sort of an anxiety for African-American women feminists like myself is that we're often asked to join up with white women's feminism, but only on their own terms, as long as we sort of remain silent about the ways in which our gender, our class, our sexual identity doesn't intersect, as long as we can be quiet about those things and join onto a single agenda."

The argument was not a new one—women of color and younger feminists have often taken white second-wave feminists to task for focusing on gender inequities over a more intersectional approach that also takes race, class and sexuality into account. But this intrafeminist skirmish over identity politics took on a life of its own in the aftermath of the bitter primary struggle. By pushing a vote for Clinton on the basis of her gender alone, establishment feminists not only rehashed internal grievances—they opened the door for conservatives to demand support for Palin for the very same reason. Unwittingly, the feminist argument for Clinton gave credence to the GOP's hope that the mere presence of a female on the ticket would deliver women's votes.

Is it any wonder, then, that everyone from Palin's supporters to the mainstream media was eager to paint the vice presidential candidate as a feminist? If all it took was being a woman, well, then Palin was it! The *Wall Street Journal* called it "Sarah Palin Feminism." The *New York Post* called her "a feminist dream," while the *Los Angeles Times* ran a piece headlined "Sarah Palin's 'New Feminism' Is Hailed."

In much the same way Obama-supporting feminists were criticized, women who didn't back Palin were swiftly denounced as hypocrites by those on the right. Rick Santorum called Palin the "Clarence Thomas for feminists," blasting women who didn't support her. Janice Shaw Crouse of Concerned Women for America said, "Even feminists—who supposedly promote women's equality and the so-called 'women's rights' agenda—are questioning a female candidate's ability to get the job done." The criticism of women who failed to back Palin even indulged in sexism. Dennis Miller said that women who weren't behind Palin were simply jealous of the candidate's sex life, and *Time* magazine reporter Belinda Luscombe wrote that some women had a "hatred" for Palin simply because she was "too pretty." (My favorite, however, was Kevin Burke's argument in *National Review* that women who didn't support Palin were suffering from "post-abortion symptoms.") Palin even managed to divide some feminists. Elaine Lafferty—a former editor of *Ms.* magazine who had endorsed Clinton but then signed on as a consultant to the McCain campaign—condemned feminist leaders for "sink[ing] this low" and called feminism an "exclusionary club" for not welcoming Palin with open arms.

If there was ever proof that the feminist movement needs to leave gender essentialism at the door—this is it. If powerful feminists continue to insist that gender matters above all else, the movement will become meaningless. If any woman can be a feminist simply because of her gender, then the right will continue to use this faux feminism to advance conservative values and roll back women's rights.

Ensuring feminism's future doesn't stop at embracing intersectionality—we must also shine a spotlight on the real feminists. Part of the reason Palin and her cohort are so successful at positioning themselves as the "new" women's movement is because we fail to push forward and support new feminists of our own. This is not to say that younger women aren't at the forefront of the movement—they certainly are. But their work is often made invisible by an older generation of feminists who prefer to believe young women are apathetic rather than admitting their movement is shifting into something they don't recognize and can't control.

For example, in an April *Newsweek* article about young people's supposed apathy over reproductive rights, NARAL Pro-Choice America President Nancy Keenan suggested that it was only the "postmenopausal militia" on the front lines of reproductive justice. Yet when I asked a NARAL spokesperson about employee demographics, I was told that people younger than 35 make up around 60 percent of the organization. And when they're not ignored, young feminists are painted as vapid and sexualized. Take

feminist writer Debra Dickerson, who wrote in a 2009 *Mother Jones* article that today's feminists are all about "pole-dancing, walking around half-naked, posting drunk photos on Facebook and blogging about [their] sex lives." This insistence that a new wave doesn't exist or isn't worth paying attention to has left open the cultural space for antifeminist women like O'Donnell and Palin to swoop in and lay claim to the movement

If the new wave of feminists—the leaders of small grassroots organizations across the country, the bloggers who are organizing hundreds of thousands of women online, the advocates for reproductive justice, racial equality and queer rights—aren't recognized as the real advocates for women, then the future of the movement will be lost.

Women vote for their interests—not their gender or age—but they still want to see themselves represented. If the only young women Americans see identified as "feminists" are those on the right, we run the risk of losing the larger cultural battle and the many younger women who are seeking an answer to the mixed messages about what feminism really is. And frankly, if we position vibrant young activists front and center, there will be no question as to who is creating the best change for women.

So instead of wringing our hands every time a new female candidate with distinctly antiwoman policies pops up, let's use it as an opportunity to re-establish what feminism is about and to support the up-and-comers in our midst. Let's focus on building power for the new wave of feminists by giving money to the organizations that best represent the future of the movement (like SAFER, NY Abortion Access Fund and Girls for Gender Equity); by providing media training and placing young activists on television and in the op-ed pages (as the great Women's Media Center does); and by pushing young feminists—not just women—to run for office.

Feminism isn't simply about being a woman in a position of power. It's battling systemic inequities; it's a social justice movement that believes sexism, racism and classism exist and interconnect, and that they should be consistently challenged. What's most important to remember as we fight back against conservative appropriation is that the battle over who "owns" the movement is not just about feminists; feminism's future affects all American women. And if we let the lie of conservative feminism stand—if real feminists don't lay claim to the movement and outline their vision for the future—all of us will suffer.

JESSICA VALENTI is an American blogger and feminist writer, known for having founded the feminist blog *Feministing*.

EXPLORING THE ISSUE

Can a Woman with Conservative Political Views Be a Feminist?

Critical Thinking and Reflection

1. How did conservative perspectives come to be perceived as antithetical to the dominant feminist viewpoint?
2. How do the competing voices in the feminist movement contribute to the contested terrain of the feminist narrative?

Is There Common Ground?

Sarah Palin, the former governor of Alaska and 2008 Republican vice presidential candidate, categorized herself as a "conservative feminist." When she accepted the role of vice presidential candidate to form the McCain–Palin ticket, she referenced Hillary Clinton's unsuccessful effort to become the Democratic nominee for president and talked about shattering glass ceilings. In doing so, Palin attempted to carve out a place within the realm of feminism for conservative women. If the Margaret Thatchers and Sarah Palins of the world can be trailblazers and serve as role models for young women, is it possible that there might also be a place for them in a feminist continuum that does not skew to the left of left in liberal ideology? Along the same lines, the role of Condoleeza Rice in breaking new ground to lift the aspirations for young African American women should not be discounted.

Additional Resources

Celis, K. and Childs, S. (2012). "The Substantive Representation of Women: What to Do with Conservative Claims?" *Political Studies*, 60(1), 213–225.

McCarver, V. (2012). "The New Oxymoron: Socially Conservative Feminism." *Women & Language*, 35(1), 57–76.

Internet References . . .

Feministing

http://feministing.com/

The Heritage Foundation

http://www.heritage.org/events/2013/05/cwn-christina-hoff-sommers-freedom-feminism

Selected, Edited, and with Issue Framing Material by:
Elizabeth Schroeder, EdD, MSW, *Elizabeth Schroeder Consulting*

ISSUE

Should "Transgender" Women Benefit from Gender Equity Policies?

YES: Laurel Anderson, from "Punishing the Innocent: How the Classification of Male-to-Female Transgender Individuals in Immigration Detention Constitutes Illegal Punishment Under the Fifth Amendment," *Berkeley Journal of Gender, Law & Justice,* vol. 25, issue 1 (Spring 2010)

NO: Stephanie Bloyd, from "'Bathroom Bill' Sparks Accessibility Debate," *Club Industry* (Fitness Business Pro section, Penton Media, August 2009)

Learning Outcomes

As you read the issues, focus on the following points:

- Are current gender equity policies sufficient to protect the rights of transgender individuals?
- Is segregation of transgender individuals a viable option?

ISSUE SUMMARY

YES: Laurel Anderson examines the gap in the justice system's current policies relative to the concerns of the transgender community. She suggests that the detention policies currently in place provide insufficient protection to female detainees and place the safety of "trans" women in particular in jeopardy.

NO: Stephanie Bloyd examines bathroom parity and accessibility within the framework of gender equity relative to the experiences of transgender men and women.

Petra L. Doan, a post-operative transsexual woman, is an urban and regional planning professor who writes about issues related to planning for queer populations. Her research suggests that "trans" women experience greater levels of victimization across all spheres of society (Doan, 2009). Issues of accessibility, discrimination, and safety are key factors in policy discussions concerning accommodations for members of the transgender community.

Part of the challenge in determining how to address the needs of the gender variant community is to consider what framework to apply. Anti-discrimination proponents frame the discourse within civil rights language, while issues surrounding privacy rights further complicate legal considerations in the courts.

In "Punishing the Innocent: How the Classification of Male-to-Female Transgender Individuals in Immigration

Detention Constitutes Illegal Punishment Under the Fifth Amendment," Anderson examines how the current policies of such agencies as Immigration and Customs Enforcement (ICE) hold transgender women in conditions that may violate the Due Process Clause. She suggests that policy reform alone will not ensure the safety of transgender female detainees. According to Anderson, specialized diversity training designed to create a culture of respect and understanding will ultimately be effective in reducing violence toward incarcerated transgender women.

In "'Bathroom Bill' Sparks Accessibility Debate," Bloyd addresses the conflict between anti-discrimination and privacy issues inherent in the debate over accessibility for transgender women. The issue of accessibility and the provision of non-discriminatory, private, and safe space continue to be a source of controversy as states struggle to determine questions of gender in public venues.

YES ↵

Laurel Anderson

Punishing the Innocent: How the Classification of Male-to-Female Transgender Individuals in Immigration Detention Constitutes Illegal Punishment Under the Fifth Amendment

Christina Madrazo, a male-to-female pre-operative transgender immigrant, was detained in Krome Detention Center in Miami, Florida awaiting an appeal of her asylum claim. She fled Mexico after she was violently attacked for being transgender. Madrazo was placed in solitary confinement at Krome because officials were unsure whether to house her with men or women. Solitary confinement was isolating and made her extremely vulnerable to attacks by prison guards. One of the guards, in charge of bringing her meals and watching over her safety, raped her on two separate occasions. The first time, the guard attacked Madrazo in her cell and tried to force her to perform oral sex on him. When she refused, he sodomized her until he heard another person approaching. Madrazo reported the rape, but the officer was still allowed to serve her food the next day. Later that night, he raped her a second time. Unfortunately, this tragic story is not uncommon; transgender detainees, particularly male-to-female transgender women, are at a high risk of sexual assault and harassment.

Although immigrant detainees are technically held in civil custody, there is an inherent inconsistency between their legal status and their detention conditions. Most are housed in jails and prisons, while others are held in prison-like conditions in detention centers without having been convicted of a crime. Detainees are often treated like prisoners: shackled, forced to wear jumpsuits, and permitted to visit with relatives only through glass. Despite their identification as women, most transgender detainees are housed with men. Abuse in male facilities is rampant, and male-to-female transgender women are often the targets. They experience harassment and sexual assault at rates much higher than the general population.

For example, a recent study by the University of California, Irvine found that 59 percent of transgender prisoners in California reported being victims of sexual assault, compared to 4.4 percent of the general prison population.

In men's detention facilities, a strict hierarchy is enforced that rewards masculinity and aggression with power and punishes femininity and passivity with violence. An informal but highly enforced code of conduct requires men to "'act tough, lift weights, and be willing to fight to settle grudges,' or risk being labeled weak and subjected to beatings and rape." Detainees and staff victimize other detainees who are perceived as weak or feminine. As one inmate explained, "Smaller, weaker, meeker individuals are usually targets. Meeker individuals tend to 'act Gay' is how it's described here and in turn invites [sic] assault. . . ." Transgender women in men's facilities immediately stand out due to their femininity. Consequently, they find themselves at the bottom of the hierarchy and become targets of sexual victimization and harassment from other inmates and guards.

This commentary focuses on the plight of male-to-female transgender immigrants in men's detention facilities. The term "transgender" signifies people who have a gender identity or expression that is different from the one associated with their assigned sex. A male-to-female transgender person, or a transgender woman, is a person who was deemed a man at birth but who currently identifies as a woman. This paper uses the term "transgender detainees" to refer to transgender women, who are the focus of this inquiry. Additionally, the term "detention facilities" is used as a general term meant to encompass all types of facilities—including prisons, jails, and detention centers—that detain immigrants for immigration purposes.

Anderson, Laurel. From *Berkeley Journal of Gender, Law & Justice,* vol. 25, issue 1 (Spring 2010), pp. 1–11, 13–16, 30–31. Copyright © 2010 by the Regents of the University of California. Reprinted by permission of Berkeley Law Journal Publications, University of California.

I argue that the detention policies of Immigration and Customs Enforcement (ICE)—when applied to transgender immigrants—create an environment that constitutes punishment in violation of the Due Process Clause. This note seeks to identify the efficacy of using a due process challenge to force ICE to make the reforms necessary to reduce the punitive nature of immigrant detention and protect the heath and safety of transgender detainees. I identify two necessary reforms: reworking the current gender classification system to reflect gender identity and limiting the use of administrative segregation as the primary means of providing detainee safety. I argue that a successful due process claim is possible to compel these reforms. Previous constitutional challenges to conditions of confinement brought by other groups serve as a litigation guide. Cases that define the constitutional rights of convicted prisoners can be utilized to define the rights of detainees as well as support a due process claim. Successful constitutional challenges brought in the context of juvenile immigrant detention provide strategies for shaping this claim.

In [the following sections,] I will give a brief background of ways in which transgender immigrants end up in ICE detention [and] identify the problems caused by the current gender classification system and administrative segregation protocols. I propose changes to these current practices that would increase the safety of transgender detainees and create accountability for the detention centers. [I] will explore the possibility of bringing a constitutional challenge against detention centers to force ICE to implement these proposed changes. By examining the ways in which the courts have defined the proper conditions of confinement for a similar group, namely transgender prisoners, and by proposing several challenges to the current prison jurisprudence, I will provide a roadmap for a successful legal claim by transgender detainees. In fleshing out this roadmap, I look to the successes achieved by juvenile immigrant detainees and suggest that a transgender detainee challenge would benefit from highlighting the similarities between these two groups.

Avenues to Detention

There are two common ways in which a transgender immigrant ends up in detention. The first occurs when ICE arrests a transgender immigrant either crossing the border or living in the United States without proper immigration status. Many male-to-female transgender women migrate to the United States in order to escape persecution on the basis of their gender identity. Because they lack the immigration status necessary to enter or remain in the country legally, they are vulnerable to being detained by

ICE. Federal statute requires mandatory detention of all immigrants who do not have valid visas or who entered the country without inspection, even if the immigrant has expressed an intention to file for asylum. Between 2003 and 2009, ICE detained over 48,000 asylum seekers. In 2007 and 2008 alone, over 6,000 asylum seekers were caught while crossing the border or shortly after entering the country. If detained, transgender immigrants can file an asylum application as a defense to deportation, but it rarely results in their release. They are automatically held until they can prove a credible fear of returning home. As a result, an asylum seeker can spend anywhere from several months up to a year in detention waiting for a decision.

Transgender immigrants of any status can also be detained by ICE after completing a jail or prison sentence for a deportable crime. Federal statute requires mandatory detention until removal for non-citizens who have committed crimes of moral turpitude, aggravated felonies, most controlled substance offenses, or firearms offenses. Crimes of moral turpitude include, but are not limited to, prostitution, fraud, and theft.

Transgender people in general, particularly transgender people of color, have been subjected to extremely high levels of incarceration. One possible explanation for this phenomenon is poverty. Transgender immigrants often experience multiple layers of oppression; the discrimination they face as immigrants is compounded with the discrimination they face because of their transgender status. Their transgender status excludes them from the network of jobs and financial support usually available to immigrants. Additionally, because of pervasive discrimination, transgender people often have difficulty accessing safety nets such as homeless shelters, foster care, and other public services that are supposed to provide for impoverished people. Due to crippling poverty and minimal access to social services, many transgender people turn to illegal economies, such as sex work and the drug trade, to survive.

A second cause of the high incarceration rates is police profiling. Discrimination based on gender identity and race makes transgender individuals especially vulnerable to law enforcement profiling, prosecution, and incarceration. Police profiling of transgender women as sex workers, particularly women of color, is common. Police officers harass and arrest female transgender sex workers even when they have not witnessed sex work related behavior, and even when sex workers are not engaging in work at the time. Many transgender sex workers have reported sexual assaults by police officers. Sometimes sex workers are forced to have sexual relations with the officers; they face arrest if they refuse.

Transgender immigrants who have been convicted of a crime also have the right to apply for asylum defensively, but have to wait in detention until their asylum claims have been adjudicated. They are detained in the meantime, not for their former crime but for the civil violation of living in the U.S. without proper status, and often in deplorable conditions.

Problems with the Current System

The government holds transgender detainees against their will, often for long periods of time, but does not have proper standards set in place to protect their safety. This section will identify the reasons why the current gender classification system creates a dangerous environment for transgender detainees. It will then explain how the current solution to these dangers, administrative segregation, does not alleviate the problems but instead creates additional ones.

Inappropriate Gender Classification System

Whether transgender detainees are defined as male or female for housing purposes has a significant impact on their health and safety. A male-to-female transgender woman is far more likely to experience violence if housed with men instead of women. As victims of sexual assault, harassment, and humiliation, transgender women in detention are likely to suffer serious physical injury and mental anguish. On the extreme end, transgender women are raped and fear for their lives. They also suffer smaller indignities daily: they are spit on, sexually objectified, propositioned, and insulted. Guards may perform sexualized pat downs or strip searches in front of other detainees. Transgender women regularly complain of being watched in the shower by other detainees or guards. They are also denied hormone treatments and grooming products necessary to maintain a feminine appearance.

Furthermore, detention with male prisoners can exacerbate the emotional problems of transgender asylum seekers who suffer from post-traumatic stress disorder (PTSD). Since asylum seekers in general are likely to be survivors of persecution in their home countries, they often suffer from PTSD. Recent studies of PTSD show that asylum seekers are highly susceptible to psychological distress in detention. Being placed in hypermasculine, violent conditions can exacerbate the trauma that transgender asylum seekers have experienced in their home county. One transgender asylum seeker who had been detained, tortured, and raped in her home country said that her detention in the United States triggered flashbacks of these memories. In some cases, detention conditions retraumatized asylum seekers so severely that they chose to return to the violence in their home country rather than remain in detention.

Despite the significance of gender classification to the health and safety of transgender detainees, ICE does not have any written policies that address how to house the detainees. This leaves the determination entirely up to the individual detention centers. Unfortunately, detention facilities are simply not equipped to handle the basic needs of gender variant people. Most facilities employ very rigid gender definitions that classify sex based on the presence of particular genitalia, thus increasing the risk of violence and emotional harm to the detainees.

Harms of Administrative Segregation

Detention administrators commonly respond to the existence of a transgender person or the complaints made by that person with the problematic solution of administrative segregation—the practice of separating the detainee from the general population. In theory, this approach is supposed to be a protective, non-punitive measure, but in practice the conditions are as restrictive as some of the harshest forms of punitive segregation. Many facilities use the same form of segregation to isolate detainees who complain of assault as they do to isolate the most dangerous detainees, or the ones too violent to live with the general population. Administrative segregation often involves completely eliminating contact with other detainees and confining detainees to locked cells for twenty-three hours a day. It also frequently restricts detainees' access to facilities such as religious services, phones, showers, and recreational facilities. Furthermore, facilities often fail to provide educational, rehabilitative, and vocational programs to those segregated.

One transgender detainee who was placed in administrative segregation after she complained of a threat of violence described her experience in this way:

> They moved me to solitary confinement, lockdown for 23 hours a day. 75–80% of the people there are informants and sexual offenders who are at risk in the general population jail. . . . They never let me come out for a break until late when everyone else has gone away. The phones were available from 8 am until 10 pm. They let me out after the phones shut down—midnight, 1 a.m., so I couldn't call anyone, the ombudsman, the warden, a lawyer. They said I was a security risk, and they were short-staffed, so they couldn't let me go to the law library, and so on. Immigration officers don't come to solitary because that's not where immigration cases are.

Like in this example, administrative segregation often takes the form of solitary confinement. Because of the detrimental emotional effects of the confinement, some commentators have suggested that long-term segregation amounts to torture. The effects of solitary confinement are even more extreme on people who have previously experienced mental trauma, namely asylum seekers. Tellingly, many transgender detainees prefer the risks of housing with the general population to the isolation of administrative segregation.

Additionally, administrative segregation does not always provide more protection than placement in the general population. Administrative segregation that takes the form of solitary confinement makes a detainee extremely vulnerable to violence by guards, because there are few others around to witness the guards' misconduct. Because the segregation creates isolation from potential witnesses and cameras, it gives detainees less opportunity to document abuses against them once they occurr.

The story of Esmeralda, a transgender asylum seeker from Mexico, illuminates the many flaws in administrative segregation. Esmeralda came to the United States seeking refuge after being abused in a Mexican jail, but was detained while the final result of her asylum application was pending. The facility automatically placed her in administrative segregation due to her transgender status. She was not allowed to leave her cell to get food or drink, and she was required to go to the bathroom in shackles. Three days after her arrival, a guard forced her to perform oral sex on him while she was shackled. Despite her formal complaint, ICE refused to release her. She became suicidal but was not allowed to see a psychologist. Eventually she opted to return to Mexico rather than to stay in detention any longer.

ICE has a policy addressing administrative segregation, but the policy vests detention facilities with the discretion to determine when and how to implement the practice. The ICE manual defines administrative segregation as a "non-punitive status in which restricted conditions of confinement are required" that may be employed when "the detainee's continued presence in the general population poses a threat to self, staff, [or] other detainees," as well as for "the secure and orderly operation of the facility." According to these regulations, a detainee may initiate the segregation, but an administrator may also place a detainee in segregation against her will when the administration has determined that the segregation is warranted. The ICE policy states that administrative segregation should only be implemented when reasonable alternatives are unavailable, but leaves the determination as to whether reasonable alternatives exist up to each facility. Because of this

leeway, facilities often use the system they already have in place to protect detainees—placing them under the same conditions as they do dangerous prisoners—instead of fashioning more appropriate conditions.

ICE guidelines also do not specify how administrative segregation should be implemented. While the manual sets forth basic guidelines for the proper treatment of segregated detainees, these guidelines are inadequate because they leave implementation of the standards up to individual facilities. The ICE manual mandates that detainees in administrative segregation receive "the same privileges as are available to detainees in the general population," but the ultimate allotment of privileges is varied based on the resources and safety concerns of each facility. Additionally, ICE suggests that detainees in administrative segregation be housed separately from those in disciplinary segregation. Instead of being mandatory, however, adherence to the guidelines is determined by the resources of the individual facilities. Prison and jails are often excused from following the explicit guidelines if they create their own equivalent protocols. This gives each institution the latitude to modify the protocols, potentially reducing the rights of detainees. By giving detention facilities leeway, ICE guidelines have allowed them to create dangerous and restrictive forms of administrative segregation. . . .

Gender Classifications Based on Gender Identity

The National Lawyers Guild and the San Francisco Human Rights Commission created a list of recommended reforms for California prisons that can be used as a guideline for updating detention protocols. They recommend that an individualized assessment for appropriate housing be made for each detainee based on a policy of classifying by gender identity, and that each assessment be reviewed periodically thereafter. According to the recommended classification policy, housing status would be determined by referring to a transgender detainee's official identification only if it matched her gender identity. Otherwise, the detainee would be housed according to the gender by which she identified.

Some fear that a policy classifying transgender women according to their gender identity will encourage men to pose as transgender women to gain access to women's facilities, or will permit transgender women to assault female detainees. While there is no evidence to support these fears, there is little data to refute them because this method of gender classification has not often been employed in the detention context. However, many homeless shelters have integrated transgender women into women's shelters for years without significant problems. In these cases, there have been no documented instances of men dressing as women to gain admittance. Furthermore, these shelters found that transgender women were no more likely to assault other women than were the general female population. In fact, they found that the major concern in the shelters were attacks on transgender women.

One of the greatest challenges to the proposed gender classification will be ensuring the safety of transgender women in women's facilities. While transgender women are less likely to experience violence when housed with other women than with men, they are still likely to be subjected to abuse from other detainees.[1] Furthermore, they are still disproportionately targeted for sexual assault by staff.[2] In order to increase chances of a successful integration of transgender detainees in women's facilities and decrease violence against them both by the staff and the female detainees, administrators should also institute an official policy of respect for transgender people.[3] This includes addressing each detainee by her preferred pronoun and name, even when they conflict with official documents. It also includes providing access to women's clothing and medical hormone treatments. Not only will this policy demonstrate respect to the individual detainee, but it will create an environment where transgender women are seen as women, thus reducing violence directed at transgender women based on their transgender status. Facilities should also provide gender identity training to their guards and healthcare professionals.[4] These trainings can help dispel the gender stereotypes that underlie much of the discrimination. Formal training of detainees on gender identity may be necessary as well, particularly if there are biological women who feel unsafe being housed with transgender women.

Restructuring the gender classification system of detention centers is not a simple solution. It will likely be a complicated and difficult logistical transition for many facilities.[5] When faced with the options provided by the current system, some transgender women may choose to remain in male facilities instead of facing unknown conditions in women's facilities.[6] Until the transition is complete and women's facilities are structured to ensure the safety of transgender detainees, placement in them should be optional.[7]

Protective Custody and Administrative Segregation as a Last Resort

Administrative segregation remains a reasonable method for ensuring the safety of transgender detainees, but it should take a less restrictive form and only be used on a case-by-case basis. The National Lawyers Guild and San Francisco Human Rights Commission's recommendations suggest that transgender detainees be housed in administrative segregation *only* when there is reason to believe the detainees present a heightened risk to themselves or to others, and *only* for that limited period of time during which the heightened risk exists. To guard against indefinite confinement, the facility must prepare a written plan for returning the detainee to less restrictive, but safe, housing. Administrative segregation should be available, but not required, for detainees who express fear of victimization in their current housing. Furthermore, a better form of administrative segregation should be implemented: one which gives detainees access to all of the same services—showers, recreational time, and educational programs—as detainees in the general population, and one that does not isolate them in solitary confinement.

Implementing these new protocols and requiring adherence by detention centers is key to protecting the safety of transgender detainees. Unlike the current ICE protocols, the specificity of these proposed standards will provide each center with clear instructions on how to house and protect transgender detainees, making it more likely that they will receive proper care. In cases where detention centers do not follow the guidelines, harmed detainees can use the protocols to demonstrate a clear violation, force compliance, or gain compensation. . . .

Conclusion

Transgender detainees suffer horrific abuses in immigrant detention when they are housed in men's facilities. The common response to actual or threatened abuse of a detainee is to put the victim in administrative segregation. But segregation is an inadequate solution because it does not properly protect transgender immigrants. In many cases, segregation exposes detainees to further attacks. Thus, there is an urgent need for reform. A policy encouraging the use of alternative measures to detention that ensure an immigrant's presence at removal hearings is the ultimate goal. With many alternative measures demonstrating success rates in the ninetieth percentile, it is illogical that ICE is still using detention as a major form of absconsion prevention.

For those in detention, ICE should change its classification protocol to affirm the gender identities of its detainees instead of relying on genital-based classifications. This is not an easy change to make, but it would protect transgender detainees from conditions that amount to punishment. A change in gender classification procedures should reduce violence against transgender detainees while simultaneously affirming their gender identities. Administrative segregation is inadequate and harmñil; thus, ICE should also end the use of segregation as the primary method of violence prevention. Policies that control the violence instead of isolating a particular victim would make detention safer for all immigrants.

A successful legal challenge to the current ICE policies would force them to make these changes or find other methods of ensuring the safety of transgender detainees. While a due process challenge is not the only way of convincing ICE to change its protocols, a successful case would have a monumental impact. A positive ruling that defines the constitutional protections for detainees and specifies violations within the current system in regards to transgender immigrants would ensure that these protections remain in place regardless of the administration or the political climate. Lobbying ICE through the political process to change its regulations would not have the same guarantee because there is no law preventing ICE from reverting to former policies.

A detainee challenge should incorporate similar cases brought by convicted criminals, but only to illustrate the baseline of protection afforded to detainees. Because current precedent does not afford many protections to convicted criminals, highlighting the distinction between the legal status of the two groups is essential. Linking the vulnerabilities of transgender immigrant detainees with those of juvenile immigrant detainees could bolster a constitutional claim and hopefully provide access to the protections afforded to juveniles. Comprehensive change to ICE protocols geared toward the protection of transgender immigrants could ultimately put an end to the type of violence suffered by Christina Madrazo.

Notes

1. For instance, it is likely that transgender women in women's detention facilities would experience the same type and frequency of abuse as transgender women in homeless shelters. For a brief description of such abuse, see MOTTET & OHLE, *supra* note 111, at 14.
2. Sydney Tarzwell, Note, *The Gender Lines Are Marked with Razor Wire: Addressing State Prison Policies and Practices for the Management of Transgender Prisoners,* 38 COLUM. HUM. RTS. L. REV. 167, 178 (2006).
3. This policy is based on a policy proposed by The National Gay and Lesbian Task Force Policy Institute. *See* MOTTET & OHLE, *supra* note 111, at 11.
4. The Transgender Law Center first provided this suggestion in the context of protecting transgender women in men's prisons, but it is equally necessary to ensure the safety of transgender women in women's facilities. *See* Letter from Christopher Daley, Director, Transgender Law Ctr., to Nat'l Prison Rape Elimination Comm'n, (Aug. 15, 2005), *available at* http://transgenderlawcenter.org/pdf/prisom-ape.pdf.
5. Interview with Alexander Li-Hua Lee, Former Director, Transgender, Gender Variant & Intersex Justice Project (Mar. 16, 2010).
6. *Id.*
7. Allowing transgender individuals to choose their housing during the temporary transitional period would also benefit female to male transgender detainees because they would be at a high risk of violence in male detention centers without protective procedures in place.

LAUREL ANDERSON is a J.D. candidate, 2011, at the University of California, Berkeley, School of Law.

Stephanie Bloyd

 **NO**

'Bathroom Bill' Sparks Accessibility Debate

Boston—An anti-discrimination bill under consideration in Massachusetts could have implications for health club locker room accessibility guidelines.

A Massachusetts state judiciary committee heard testimony last month on House Bill 1728 that supports transgender rights. It would amend the state's nondiscrimination and hate crime laws to make them inclusive for transgendered people.

The Massachusetts Family Institute, a conservative Christian organization, testified against the bill and launched a media campaign that labeled it "the bathroom bill." The group ran a series of radio ads that claimed the legislation would put women and children at risk to male sexual predators, whom they say would be allowed access to public restrooms and locker rooms.

Helen Durkin, executive vice president of public policy for the International Health, Racquet and Sportsclub Association (IHRSA), also testified in opposition to the bill, which the organization says would infringe on the privacy rights of health club members. Durkin asked the judiciary committee to consider exempting health club locker rooms from the bill's language.

"If the proposed legislation becomes law, there would be situations at health clubs where not only adults, but also children, would be in close proximity to an individual with the anatomy of the opposite sex as that individual undressed," Durkin testified.

Some 13 states have passed similar anti-discrimination laws without an increase in restroom-related incidents, according to the Gay and Lesbian Advocates and Defenders (GLAD), a legal rights organization dedicated to ending discrimination based on sexual orientation, HIV status and gender identity and expression.

"A full 37 percent of the American population, in 13 states, live in an area covered by a transgender-inclusive anti-discrimination law, and there have been no reported incidents involving a transgender person threatening the safety of anyone else in a restroom facility," testified Jennifer Levi, attorney and director of GLAD's Transgender Rights Project.

In addition, Levi says privacy concerns can be addressed without discriminating.

"There are very easy ways to address these concerns without jeopardizing passage of the bill," Levi says. "One way people generally address privacy issues is to provide private spaces for anyone who wants to use them."

Levi notes that many health clubs now provide shower curtains and bathroom doors for people who are uncomfortable changing in public.

This is the second time the committee heard testimony on the bill, which needs the judiciary committee's approval before it advances to the state legislature.

STEPHANIE BLOYD is a senior associate editor at *Club Industry*.

EXPLORING THE ISSUE

Should "Transgender" Women Benefit from Gender Equity Policies?

Critical Thinking and Reflection

1. How do we balance the civil freedoms of transgender men and women with their basic human right to safety?
2. How do issues of sex, gender, and identity intersect with and sometimes disrupt our cultural rules for social behavior?
3. Would gender equality translate into a post-gender society? Why or why not?

Is There Common Ground?

During the 2012 elections, the voting rights of some citizens were impacted by what many across the nation characterized as "voter suppression" laws. In particular, newly instituted and recently amended voter identification laws posed challenges for transgender voters. However, barriers at the ballot box were not a phenomenon limited to the 2012 elections. Claire Swinford, a transgender woman, recounted her experience at the polls in 2010. Swinford explained how she was stopped by a poll worker:

> While she had an appropriate ID and her name was on the rolls, Swinford, who was early on in her transition from male to female, hadn't yet changed the gender marker and name on her driver's license to reflect her appearance, because of the cost, which she said was more than $200. Despite the poll worker challenging Swinford's gender, she persisted. "Everyone in the place can overhear the conversation where the person is questioning my identity and calling me sir," she said. The poll worker finally offered her a provisional ballot, and Swinford asked to see a supervisor who could

contact the county elections office. The office said Swinford met the requirements and could vote after all, but "it would have been very easy to walk away from that," she said.

—(Berg, 2012)

Swinford's experience at the polls illustrates how transgender issues transcend the logistics of bathroom parity and impact the most basic of citizenship rights.

Additional Resources

Berg, A. (2012, November 2). "Voter Identification Laws Create Unique Problems for Transgender Voters." *The Daily Beast*. Retrieved from: www.the-dailybeast.com/articles/2012/11/02/voter-identification-laws-create-unique-problems-for-transgender-voters.html

Doan, P. (2009). "Safety and Urban Environments: Transgendered Experiences of the City." *Women & Environments International Magazine*, No. 78/79, 22–25.

Internet References . . .

Canadian Transgender Community Network

http://transcommunity.ca/

The Center: The Lesbian, Gay, Bisexual & Transgender Community Center

http://www.gaycenter.org/

PFLAG

http://community.pflag.org/transgender

Out & Equal: Workplace Advocates

http://outandequal.org/diversity/transgendercommunity

Selected, Edited, and with Issue Framing Material by:
Elizabeth Schroeder, EdD, MSW, *Elizabeth Schroeder Consulting*

ISSUE

Should Public Restrooms Be Gender-Neutral?

YES: The Sylvia Rivera Law Project, from "Talking Points about Gender-Segregated Facilities," *Toilet Training: A Companion Guide for Activists* (2010). http://srlp.org/wp-content/uploads/2012/08/2010-toolkit.pdf

NO: Merritt Kopas, from "The Illogic of Separation: Examining Arguments about Gender-Neutral Public Bathrooms," University of Washington Master's Thesis (2012)

Learning Outcomes

After reading this issue, you will be able to:

- Describe at least one reason why choosing which gendered restroom could be stressful for a transgender person.
- List at least two reasons against creating mixed gender public restrooms.
- Identify at least one alternative to having mixed gender public restrooms that does not place an undue burden on places of business while enabling all people to feel safe and comfortable in the restroom.

ISSUE SUMMARY

YES: The Sylvia Rivera Law Project provides an overview of New York City's anti-discrimination law, passed in 2010, and its impact on previously gender-segregated facilities. Their piece is designed to allay concerns about what the law will mean in practical terms for both cisgender and transgender individuals.

NO: This excerpt from Merritt Kopas discusses some of the most common arguments against creating single-user gender neutral restrooms and multi-user mixed gender restrooms, including the ideas that requiring single-user gender neutral restrooms is not cost effective and that multi-user, mixed gender restrooms are potentially unsafe for children.

Of the many issues and challenges transgender people face as they come out and transition, perhaps the first and most basic is the issue of which public restroom to use. We are a culture of gender binaries—men's rooms and women's rooms; men's locker rooms and women's locker rooms, and so on. Even many toy and party stores will dictate which aisle we should shop in based on the gender of the child for whom we are shopping.

If a transgender person realizes as a child that they are transgender, the easiest and most effective way of making sure that person feels safe and none of the cisgender students feel uncomfortable is by giving that young person the right and access to use the restroom in the nurse's office, which is typically a single-user restroom. In that way, the child is not being forced to choose which restroom to use based on gender. In addition, the child becomes less susceptible to the teasing, bullying, and even violence that can happen in public restrooms. Transgender youth frequently report fear and anxiety about using restrooms and locker rooms at school because they had experienced harassment by other kids—and even by adults—when using them.

As we get older, however, things become more complicated. People who choose to go to college and live in dorms may end up on a floor with students and a restroom all of one sex. A student who is biologically and legally female, but who identifies on the inside as male, will likely feel uncomfortable being part of an all-women's floor or dorm or restroom. At the same time, however, this same student will likely feel uncomfortable living on an all-men's floor, although that may depend on whether he has chosen to transition and if so, where he is in the process. More often than not, this student will not feel safe even if he is perceived by others to be male—were his roommates or others to find out, the risks to his safety could be significant. The stress of keeping such a significant secret, along with the concern about what could happen if the secret were disclosed, can have a significant and negative impact on the student.

Beyond the geographic confines of the college campus is the rest of the world. A transgender person in a shopping mall, movie theater, restaurant, must choose which restroom to use. A trans woman who uses a women's restroom and who is not perceived as female may make other women in the restroom uncomfortable or alarmed. The accompanying experience of being asked by the management to leave the restroom is extremely humiliating to the transgender person.

Some of the discomfort relating to having transgender men and women use the same restrooms as cisgender men and women, respectively, has to do with misunderstandings related to what it means to be transgender. Cisgender people who do not understand what it means to be transgender will mistakenly (and, to the transgender person, offensively) think that they are there to spy on the women or men for whom the bathroom is "intended." Since ignorance breeds fear, even more people mischaracterize transgender people as pedophiles, and are concerned that a transgender woman in a women's restroom is like having a man in the women's room. As a result, they would think younger girls to be at risk—when that is simply untrue. Transgender people go into a restroom for the same reasons cisgender people do—use the facilities, wash up, check themselves out in the mirror, and leave. And if history has taught us anything, a public restroom tends to be far less safe for a transgender person than a cisgender person. What choices, therefore, do transgender people have? One reality expressed by many transgender people is teaching themselves to wait longer than other people would need or be required to wait to use the restroom. Adding that discomfort to the stress of not feeling safe reinforces

why this seemingly minor issue is in actuality quite major in the lives of transgender individuals.

In some socially progressive areas around the United States, organizations, universities, and individuals are working to make their spaces—and, in particular, their restroom spaces—comfortable, safe, and inclusive for people of all genders. The Transgender Law Center in San Francisco created an entire guide for transgender people and their cisgender allies on ensuring public restrooms are comfortable and safe for transgender people. In Washington, DC, the DC Trans Coalition was able to get a policy passed that requires business that have single-stall restroom with a lockable door to label it as a restroom, devoid of gender. Unfortunately, many business are still not in compliance with this rule, but some are. In Ithaca, New York, Out for Health, a program of Planned Parenthood of the Southern Finger Lakes, developed an app that enables people—regardless of gender identity—to find the closest gender neutral, single-stall bathroom to a person's location.

Cisgender people who are opposed to losing gender-specific restrooms have a range of reasons for opposing them. The first has nothing to do with transgender women or men—but with cisgender men. Typically, men's restrooms are far messier than women's, especially when it comes to urine. In addition, some cisgender men have said they don't want single-user, all-gender rest rooms because they're concerned that women will take longer and therefore they will need to wait. While these responses and complaints may feel very stereotypical, they are also very real to those who have them.

The answer is not as simple as it might seem. Requiring businesses and other public entities to add a single-gender restroom places a cost burden on that business that the owners would protest as unfair. Having mixed gender, multi-user restrooms raises the concerns listed above. Regardless of which requirement were placed on business owners, accountability would be challenging to enforce, as the folks in DC have found.

In the following selections, the Sylvia Rivera Law Project emphasizes the need for creating safe restroom spaces for transgender people as part of alleviating the overall stress that comes with their minority status. The excerpt from Merritt Kopas's thesis represents the attitudes from Merritt's sample that were against mixed-gender, multi-use restrooms.

YES

The Sylvia Rivera Law Project

Talking Points about Gender-Segregated Facilities

New York City's Human Rights Law now explicitly protects all New Yorkers from discrimination on the basis of gender identity or expression. This means that, no matter who you are, you should be treated equally and with respect for how you understand your own gender. If you are transgender, transsexual, a feminine man or a masculine woman, or if for any reason you are being denied access to services or accommodations you need on the basis of your gender identity or expression, you are now protected by the law.

One source of curiosity around this law is what happens with gender-segregated facilities like bathrooms, homeless shelters, and locker rooms? The new law means that everyone's gender identity should be respected, and we should all be treated on an equal basis with other people who share our gender identity. No one can be forced to use a facility that does not match their gender identity. If you identify as a woman, you should be allowed access to women's facilities. If you identify as a man, you should similarly be able to access men's facilities.

Frequently Asked Questions:

1. Does this law mean that we have to let men into women's locker rooms or bathrooms?

No. This law does not require that people who identify as men be let into women's facilities, or that women be allowed into men's facilities. Instead, it requires that we respect that some people's gender identity does not perfectly match societal expectations. Some men are more feminine than others, some women are more masculine than others, and some people live in a gender different from what was assigned to them at birth. This law only requires that all people who identify as women be treated as women, and all people who identify as men be treated as men.

2. Will this law endanger women in spaces like locker rooms and bathrooms because it will allow men in who may want to sexually assault women?

No. This law does not invite sexual assault on women in locker rooms and bathrooms. People who enter restrooms or locker rooms with the intent to commit sexual assault are still subject to criminal penalty. However, the people who have often experienced the discrimination and harassment in gender segregated facilities that this law seeks to address, such as women of transgender experience trying to use women's facilities, masculine women trying to use women's facilities, men of transgender experience trying to use men's facilities, and feminine men trying to use men's facilities, are now explicitly protected from discrimination and exclusion. Any notion that these people are sexual predators is based in ignorance and misunderstanding that this new law seeks to remedy. This law does not change the fact that any person who seeks to enter a bathroom or locker room in order to sexually assault another person is punishable under the criminal laws of NY. There is no evidence that allowing transgender people to have safe access to facilities that concord with their gender identities will increase the incidence of sexual assault, however it is clear that the new law will protect them from the harassment and violence they frequently face when trying to access such facilities.

3. Does this law require that new bathrooms be constructed for transgender people?

No. This law does not require any construction. It simply clarifies that all people should be able to access the bathroom that is appropriate for them based on their gender identity, and should not be forced to use a bathroom that is designated for individuals of another gender identity. The Compliance Guidelines do recommend that, because gender segregated bathrooms are often the site of harassment and discrimination for people whose gender expression transgresses societal norms, any single-stall bathrooms be converted into gender-neutral bathrooms. This recommendation comes from our understanding that many people find gender segregated bathrooms inaccessible, including people with disabilities who require attendance in the bathroom and whose attendant is a different gender than they are, parents with children whose gender is different from their own but who wish to accompany their child to the bathroom, and people whose gender expression transgresses societal norms. The Commission on Human Rights set out this recommendation with the safety and convenience of these people in mind, recognizing that all people should be able to safely access bathroom facilities.

4. What about transgender people who have not had surgery? What facilities will they use?

The new law requires that people be allowed to use facilities that accord with their gender identity, not with any particular body part. Just as non-transgender men and women are not asked to prove what body parts they have before entering gender-segregated facilities, transgender people also should not be. All people, regardless of surgical status, are entitled to use facilities which comport with their gender identities regardless of whether their bodies match traditional expectations. Challenging someone's gender identity and/or asking invasive personal questions about their body parts is a form of harassment.

5. What about facilities where people see each other without clothing?

The Commission recognizes that there are still some facilities without privacy, such as totally open showers. The Commission recommends that in circumstances where nudity is unavoidable, basic steps such as the installation of curtains be taken in order to create the minimal amount of privacy needed to maintain the comfort and safety of all people using facilities. Most importantly, this law requires that no person be forced to use facilities that do not comport with his/her gender identity, so employers, housing provider, schools and others maintaining gender segregated

facilities should take the steps necessary to ensure that this requirement is met. Whether by creating private space through curtains, or designating a space as gender neutral, this task should be neither difficult nor expensive. The Commission is available to assist in creating plans to remedy any problems that may arise in the process of making facilities accessible to all people.

Talking Points about Accessible Bathrooms

1. If we had all-gender bathrooms, wouldn't women be less safe?

Many people's first reaction to providing gender non-specific bathrooms is that women's safety will be compromised. However, an analysis of the safety precautions in bathrooms suggests that women are not currently protected by the existence of gender-specific bathrooms. Women's bathrooms do not provide any physical barrier to potential predators, who can just as easily walk through an unlocked door that reads "women" as any other unlocked door. Gender segregation in bathrooms does not prevent sexual assault, and if anything, provides an illusion of safety that is not true. To increase the safety of bathrooms, we would recommend creating single-user bathrooms, providing bathroom doors that go from floor to ceiling without gaps, and eliminating the gender segregation of bathrooms that results in severe access issues for transgender and gender non-conforming people.

2. All-gender bathrooms will make people uncomfortable.

It is true that for people who are used to using gender-specific bathrooms, using gender non-specific bathrooms may feel strange or uncomfortable. Often times, social change that increases access for an excluded group and eliminated discrimination requires a reform of social practices that makes people who have not been negatively affected by the existing arrangements uncomfortable. However, discomfort or modesty, when compared with the inability to engage in basic necessary biological functions at work, school, and in public spaces, cannot be prioritized. As we make changes to increase access and reduce discrimination, we must all commit to adjusting to those changes.

3. The female clients/students/customers at my agency/school/business will not be able to accept using the bathroom with transgender women. Many are survivors of sexual violence, and may be triggered by using the bathroom with someone with masculine body parts.

When we work with populations that have survived violence, it is essential to try to create safe spaces to accommodate their needs. Many of us work with populations that are diverse, with different clients/students/customers having survived different types of oppressions, and sometimes even having misconceptions or biased beliefs about each other. The proper response to a misperception that transwomen are not 'real women' or are sexual predators or a threat to non-trans women is not to exclude transwomen from women's spaces or facilities, but to help educate any people who are concerned about inclusion and dispel myths about trans people. Excluding people because other have biased misconceptions about them only increases oppression and discrimination, and does not work to create safe spaces. . . .

These talking points were drafted by Dean Spade, a member of the committee that drafted the Compliance Guidelines for New York City's gender identity anti-discrimination law. These may be of use for clarifying issues in communities working toward transgender equality.

THE SYLVIA RIVERA LAW PROJECT (SRLP) works to guarantee that all people are free to self-determine their gender identity and expression, regardless of income or race, and without facing harassment, discrimination, or violence. SRLP is a collective organization founded on the understanding that gender self-determination is inextricably intertwined with racial, social, and economic justice, seeking to increase the political voice and visibility of low-income people and people of color who are transgender, intersex, or gender non-conforming.

Merritt Kopas

The Illogic of Separation: Examining Arguments about Gender-Neutral Public Bathrooms

Introduction

Everyday, many of us make use of public and semi-public bathrooms in workplaces, schools, and the myriad other spaces we pass through and occupy while outside our homes.[1] By the time we reach adulthood, many of us have become so familiar with the rules and norms around public bathrooms that we are able to navigate the space as if on autopilot. As a result, we need not speak nor think much about bathrooms nor what goes on behind their doors. This is a tremendous boon in a culture that accords human elimination of waste a taboo status (Cavanagh 2010:4; Chess et al. 2004:220). Evidence of this status can be seen in the range of euphemisms available to spare us the necessity of referring to the acts of urinating and defecating, or to the actual places in which these acts occur (Greed 2010:119; Kira 1976).

As a result of our cultivated inattention to bathrooms, most of us rarely consider the ways in which our cultural norms around public bathrooms represent not natural or inevitable developments, but rather, are the products of historically contingent processes. The separation of public bathrooms by gender is perhaps the most naturalized of these norms. Indeed, people who are not confronted with the problematic aspects of this separation on a daily basis have little cause to remark upon the gendered character of public bathrooms at all.

However, many people encounter gender separation as a barrier to accessing public bathroom spaces. In particular, transgender and gender non-conforming people—including non-transgender feminine men and masculine women—often experience bathrooms as sites of symbolic and physical exclusion and discrimination (Browne 2004; Cavanagh 2010). For this reason, one focus of transgender activism in the United States and elsewhere has been obtaining safe access to public bathrooms—often by advocating for "gender-neutral" options that make no assumptions about the user's gender (Chess et al. 2004; Mateik 2003; Molotch 2010; Safe2Pee 2011; Transgender Law Center 2005).[2] These efforts have occasionally run up against vigorous opposition, but they are more often confronted with apathy or incredulity at the notion that the public bathroom could be a focus of serious political activism. This study builds from this recognition and seeks to understand how people react to the possibilities of organizing public bathrooms in alternative, gender-neutral ways.

This question is of both practical and theoretical significance. Practically, the gendered standard of public bathrooms is unlikely to change without the support of "non-stakeholders," that is, those who do not identify as transgender in a broad sense. Bathroom activists have been quick to note that the benefits of gender-neutral bathrooms would accrue to many diverse populations, but efforts to change the gendered organization of public bathrooms have been most visible as a part of transgender activism. As a relatively small movement and one that is still struggling to gain legitimacy in many parts of the United States, the ability of transgender activists to succeed may depend on the extent to which they are able to create connections with those who do not identify as transgender, and to strive for social changes which will benefit—or more importantly, be clearly *seen* to benefit—those people (Currah, Juang, and Minter 2006:xv).

At least one major study has specifically examined transgender and queer-identified people's experiences with and perceptions of public bathrooms (see Cavanagh 2010). However, little sustained research has examined the ways that non-transgender people talk about and understand the gendered nature of public bathrooms. Indeed, in their review of gender and family issues surrounding public bathrooms, Anthony and Dufresne (2007) call for more research on the practice of and attitudes towards gender segregation. How do men and women react to the notion of gender-neutral or unisex bathrooms? Investigating this question, they argue, might shed light on whether or not gender segregation is still necessary at all (Anthony and Dufresne 2007:289).

Theoretically, the question of how people talk about public bathrooms and gender has relevance to a range of perspectives that see gender as situationally, interactionally, or citationally produced. The public bathroom is a space in which the dominant binary conceptualization of gender is made more concrete than perhaps anywhere else in society (Browne 2004:338). Thus, an examination of arguments about and meanings surrounding the public bathroom has the potential to inform our understandings of the social construction of gender. . . .

Arguments Against Multi-User Mixed-Gender Bathrooms

Unsafe for Children

The argument most vulnerable to critique by others against mixed-gender bathrooms was that they would be unsafe or at least unsuitable for children. These concerns could be classified into two types: first, that children would be at risk of physical harm from adults, and second, that children would be inappropriately exposed to the "other" gender in the bathroom. These concerns were distinctly gendered—in both cases, participants were mainly concerned about the safety and psychological well-being of girls. Both concerns led some participants to argue that mixed-gender bathrooms should have age restrictions.

An arrangement with both "children's" and mixed-gender bathrooms would seem to counter the benefits of mixed-gender bathrooms for families—which arose in discussion fairly frequently. Some participants noted that a mixed-gender bathroom would actually be safer than a gender-segregated bathroom, in that it would eliminate the necessity for parents to send their children into the bathroom alone, a potentially dangerous situation.

> Jacob: [. . .] in a way, a parent may not always be with that child in the bathroom, so if you're sending in the child in a multi-gender bathroom, I think it's opening it up to even more possibility—
>
> Ellen: Well you stay with your child.
>
> Jacob: Well yeah, I know. You want to think as a parent you'd accompany your child, but some parents don't, like there's a bathroom, you can go use it. And if its multi-gender, then if there are going to be problems in single-gender bathrooms, it would be even bigger.

(GROUP 1)

This belief in the danger of mixed-gender bathrooms seems strange if we solely consider physical harm. However, it was clear that participants took a broad view of harm to children when considering mixed-gender bathrooms. Specifically, some participants were concerned that any mixed-gender bathroom with urinals would expose young girls to the sight of adult men urinating, which would be damaging or morally wrong in some way.

> Judy: [. . .] As long as the urinals aren't out in public, I'm not uncomfortable. And also I feel like, if it's going to be a family restroom, then there shouldn't be public urinals if you're bringing children into a bathroom. Even if someone raises their kids in an environment where nudity is totally fine and okay, that's in your house, and the norms of our society are really different.
>
> Michele: Isn't that usually a crime, for an adult to show their—
>
> Judy: To expose themselves? Yeah.
>
> Michele: Yeah, to a minor.
>
> Judy: I think so. I mean, you're not supposed to expose yourself publicly anyway, but you get penalized more if it's to a minor. I don't know exactly, but I would assume that it would be. Because people would have an outrage about you're taking away the innocence of children.
>
> Michele: Yeah, and I have a feeling that these kind of bathrooms will make it more accessible for people who are pedophiles, if this bathroom was available for both adults and families—
>
> Jennifer: Not necessarily even pedophiles, but just voyeurs. People who just want to watch certain things.

(GROUP 7)

A particular view of risk and understanding of who is most likely to harm children lies behind these sorts of arguments. In such an understanding, a mixed-gender bathroom would create a kind of "moral hazard," insofar as it would be attractive to pedophiles who might exploit the space for their own purposes. These fears and beliefs about risk led some respondents to weigh their own sentiments towards mixed-gender bathrooms against the reality of their children using them.

> It's interesting, because I want to be all pro-multi-gendered bathrooms, but I have a 12-year-old

daughter. I would feel mildly uncomfortable peeing in a restroom if I knew a man were in there, but I would worry more about my 12-year-old daughter being in a restroom if I knew men were there.

(Julie, GROUP 3)

Ultimately, however, the argument that mixed-gender bathrooms would be physically unsafe for children was contested by opposing claims that the space would prevent the need for parents to send their children unsupervised into a public bathroom without them. The "visual problem" of young girls being exposed to adult men in the bathroom remained an issue for some participants, but one that would be resolved simply by enclosing urinals within stalls.

Unsafe for Women

By far, one of the most common arguments against multi-user, mixed-gender bathrooms was that the arrangement would be an unsafe one for women. Many participants seemed to consider this configuration as an inherently more dangerous environment than gender-segregated bathrooms. Concerns about safety occasionally led to discussions about the kinds of provisions that would be necessary to make mixed-gender bathrooms acceptable, such as multiple entrances and exits, alarms, panic buttons, and sturdier stall doors. These considerations were premised on two understandings apparently shared among many women participants: that all mixed-gender situations are potentially dangerous, and that the act of using a bathroom necessarily involves placing oneself in a vulnerable position, especially for women.

Judy: [. . .] late at night, if I'm going to the bathroom and some guy walks in, I'm going to fear for my safety and feel uncomfortable. So those are both important things with it.

Jennifer: I try to avoid any situation where I'm solo.

Judy: That's why girls go to the bathroom in pairs.

Jennifer: Yeah, like at night, going to the bathroom and things like that, I totally try to avoid it. And not even going to the bathroom, but just I try to be very aware of my surroundings and try to make sure I'm never in a setting where I'm alone at night. So I think that would definitely be a big factor. And if you're a girl walking into a bathroom at night and you don't know who's in there, it's terrifying.

Daniel: Is it really?

Jennifer: Yeah.

Daniel: Even if you're in a bar and it's a women's bathroom?

Jennifer: I mean, if it were a men/women bathroom. Or even walking into, if I were to go to Qwest Field tonight and there wasn't anywhere there, I would be afraid of walking into a women's bathroom.

Judy: Yeah.

Jennifer: You just don't know, if you're in a big open space, and you don't know who's hiding in any one of those stalls, be it a woman or man, whoever. It's scary putting yourself into—

Judy: I get super freaked out if it's late at night and I have to go anywhere alone. And then going to the bathroom makes me vulnerable. So I just go home. Honestly, I just go home. I wait.

(GROUP 7)

Arguments about women's safety have been common in public discourses about gender-neutral bathrooms. Gershenson (2010:204) notes that the responses to one campus campaign for gender-neutral bathrooms at the University of Massachusetts were characterized by a conviction that the acceptance of alternative bathroom configurations would "unleash male violence and mischief that's already just barely contained." Participants echoed this view when they made statements like:

I'm older, so this doesn't seem as much of a problem, but if I was sending my 18-year-old daughter, or if I was 18, I wouldn't want them to be in a bathroom like this, because I know what 18-year-old boys are thinking about. It just, it might up the odds of rape. But then, who could say that, you know?

(Sarah, GROUP 1)

But these arguments are perhaps so powerful because their intuitive appeal crosses ideological lines—they simultaneously resonate with both feminist concerns for women's safety in public and traditionalist beliefs about men's sexuality as uncontrollable and predatory. Both of these rationales were evinced in participants' claims during the discussions, sometimes by the same participant. Early on in one group, one participant talked about her discomfort at the idea of sharing a bathroom with men:

That's the one I said I would definitely not use. It's just not comfortable. I wouldn't feel even safe.

I wouldn't feel safe going to the bathroom in the same space with a bunch of other boys and girls. Just because, I don't know. Especially with all the muggings and stuff that go around, the bathroom's just one more place that that could happen, if they're joined. So I wouldn't use it at all. . . .

The concerns about women's safety were not limited to the women participants in the discussions. Some male participants also argued that certain kinds of men were untrustworthy and that mixed-gender bathrooms might be attractive to them for the situational opportunities to harass and assault women they would offer.

Ryan: I don't like to think about it, but it might increase crime rates. Especially like we were saying earlier, late-night usage.

Michael: Yeah, because in a gender-segregated bathroom, a guy walks in and it's like automatic, what the hell are you doing? But when it's not gender-segregated, it's kind of a surprise, I guess. So people who are into that type of thing would have kind of easy access.

Ryan: It seems like an ethical problem.

Michael: But I don't think they'd have multi-stalled gendered bathrooms available at late nights.

Ryan: Yeah, they would probably lock them after a certain time.

(GROUP 5)

This language of "moral hazards" was used by many men in the groups, implying a belief that mixed-gender bathrooms would naturally lead to higher rates of victimization and violence, and suggesting that they shared a view of male sexuality as uncontrollable or violent, at least in some cases.

Arguments about women's safety are perhaps the biggest challenge to those advocating for gender-neutral bathrooms. Generally, activists have sought to characterize such arguments as diversionary claims that effectively serve to pit two oppressed groups against each other: non-transgender women and gender-variant people—especially transgender women (Mateik 2003). They have then attempted to defuse these concerns in several ways. First, they have often pointed out that the mere existence of a sign labeled "women" on a bathroom door does not prevent anyone from entering it. On the contrary, gender separation means that somebody looking to assault a woman reliably knows where to look (Transgender Law Center 2005).

Second, activists have pointed out that the image of sexual assault implied by fears about mixed-gender bathrooms draws from the myth that most sexual assaults are committed by strangers rather than relatives or acquaintances. Finally, activists have sought to shift the conversation from the alleged risks to non-transgender women in mixed-gender bathrooms to the harsh realities of violence faced by transgender people in gender-segregated public bathrooms (Feinberg 1996; Mateik 2003).

Some of these counterclaims actually arose during the group discussions. It appeared that some participants recognized that most gendered public bathrooms in the US rely on social, rather than physical barriers, to keep out the "wrong" category of people. The situations in which public bathrooms seemed the least safe to participants—at night, in isolated areas with few other people around—are precisely those in which these social barriers are at their weakest. In such a scenario, then, a mixed-gender bathroom is not necessarily any less safe than a gender-segregated one. And while most participants began and ended the discussion concerned about the potential safety implications of mixed-gender bathrooms, some thus came to see the arrangement as no more dangerous—or in some cases, as less dangerous than gender-segregated bathrooms.

Sarah: Maybe this [multi-user mixed-gender] might be more safe than this [multi-user gender segregated] because if a guy wanted to find a girl, he's going to go in the girls' bathroom. So if it was a unisex bathroom, then what's the chances of him getting a girl? It's 50% either way. So maybe it would be safer to a certain extent.

[. . .]

Steve: I kind of agree with what Sarah was saying. Because if you have strictly a women's and generally you're only going to see women in there, and you might see one guy who thinks hey, only women use this, so I'll go ahead and go in there. Whereas with the multi-sex, there's actually a good chance that if a man were to go in there pursuing a woman, there's a good chance there may be another man in there who could act as her savior, so to speak.

Sarah: Or another girl who's bigger than the dude.

[all laughing]

Steve: Yeah, absolutely, totally.

Amy: That's another thing, the people that are likely to be able to intervene would be people who could come into the multi-gender bathroom. Because just another woman is going to walk in, unless a guy hears her screaming or something.

(GROUP 1)

Julie: [. . .] I think we have this idea that the biggest risk would be sexual assault. But really, if you're a woman, and it's late at night, and you're on campus, and you're in the bathroom by yourself, and there's not really a lot of people in the whole building, anybody could come in. There's nothing to stop them, any more than if it was a co-ed bathroom or not.

Jane: But at the same time, it would be a plain sight. So if a guy walks into a women's bathroom, he's already labeled as a creepster.

Julie: Yeah, but if you're the only one there, and if you're the only one on the whole floor, and a man walks in the bathroom, first you don't know he's a man because he just walked in the bathroom and you're going to the bathroom. There's a bit of safety net because you can say he came in the women's restroom, so clearly this is a bigger issue, whereas if it was a multi-gender bathroom then maybe just the fact he's there isn't obviously a problem. I don't know. . . .

Loss of Bathroom Culture

Case (2010) notes that many people continue to see the ability to be alone with "one's own" (defined by gender) as a benefit of gender-segregated bathrooms. Much like single-user bathrooms, mixed-gender bathrooms were seen by participants as threatening existing "restroom cultures." In this view, these cultures—but especially the culture of the women's restroom—are worth preserving. Both women and men argued that women would lament the loss of this space. Owing to the "mystique" many participants attached to the "other" gender's bathroom and the consequent lack of knowledge of what goes on within, some women thought that men also might regret the loss of spaces for same-sex socializing.

Alexis: It's also kind of a social thing, at least for women, I'm not sure for guys. I don't know how, but, you know, girls going to the bathroom together, there's kind of an unwritten code, that whole aspect of going with your friends. But I feel like even strangers in women's bathrooms will often talk.

Alyssa: Be friendly, yeah. I wouldn't go into a multi-use bathroom and be like, hey Kenny, what's up.

Alexis: Yeah. It's just different. It's a whole camaraderie that happens in the bathroom, and I'm sure it's like that for guys too. And I feel like it wouldn't happen, there wouldn't be that gender bonding if it was both.

[later]

Susan: I just don't like the idea. But I mean, yes, answering the questions on your questionnaire, that was a big part of, one of the reasons why I think some people would oppose single-user bathrooms. Because restrooms are a time for socializing. So maybe if they had stalls around the urinals [. . .]

Tami: I feel like it would restrict the types of things that you talk about in the bathroom. You don't necessarily censor yourself so much when you're around other women. You talk about personal things, but if there's guys there, you probably wouldn't be talking about personal things.

(GROUP 8)

Participants' claims about women's bathrooms—especially those in bars and clubs—point to their status as "sacred spaces" in which women can interact without the intrusion of men (Cooper and Oldenziel 1999; Goffman 1959). Participants noted that the adoption of mixed-gender bathrooms would mean the loss of this space, and would necessitate that both men and women relearn the cultural scripts called upon to navigate interactions in public bathroom.

Some participants perceived the loss of a dedicated space for same-gender interactions as a cost of single-user unisex bathrooms. In the case of multi-user mixed-gender bathrooms, this space is not only taken away, but replaced by something potentially frightening and threatening—the demand that users navigate cross-gendered interactions within a space that is already the source of tensions and anxieties for many. After all, the key difference between single- and multi-user gender-neutral bathrooms is that the latter involves the possibility of (gendered) interaction while the former does not.[3]

Lack of Privacy

The word "privacy" found its way into many participants' initial reactions to the mixed- gender bathroom. Daren's response when asked to explain the reasoning behind his ranking of the bathroom types was typical here: "I just feel there's no privacy anymore involved in that" (Daren, Group 9). But privacy is a complicated concept, and it is worth investigating the complexities concealed by apparently simple and direct statements like Daren's.

One definition of privacy in a public bathroom might be the degree to which one is able to insulate oneself from exposure to an external audience. Using this definition, we might place the multi-user bathrooms on the "less private" end of the continuum, and the single-user bathrooms on the "more private" end. Some participants did explicitly express a preference for this type of privacy, and the sense of ownership of space provided thereby. If most participants had this definition of privacy in mind, and if they held privacy to be one of the most important aspects of a public bathroom, then we would expect them to generally favor single-user bathrooms over multi-user bathrooms.

This was not the case. As the survey data reviewed earlier indicates, the multi-user gender segregated bathroom was the most popular type by far, with the combined total of "most preferred" rankings for both single-user types falling just below the multi-user gender segregated total. This implies one of two things: that contrary to what my participants said, privacy is not really all that important to them; or, that they are operating under a different definition of privacy than that described thus far.

Assuming for the moment that participants really did value privacy, what kind of privacy might they have been thinking of? It seems clear that many participants, when referring to privacy, really meant *gendered* privacy. That is, their conceptions of privacy included two dimensions: the level of exposure to an external audience (analogous to the simple definition above) *and* the gendered composition of that audience. These dimensions were usually not weighted equally. Rather, most participants seemed to consider the gender of their potential audience as much more important in defining a particular situation as private or not. The original dimension of seclusion thus loses its salience—privacy becomes not so much the ability to be *on* one's own as the ability to be *with* one's own.

Here participants discussed the differential socialization of men and women such that women using the bathroom are expected to be silent and odorless, while men are expected to feel no shame or even revel in the "disgusting" nature of excretion. That is, excretory functions were seen by participants as bolstering to performances of masculinity and discrediting to performances of femininity. The discomfort caused by the lack of gendered privacy was primarily seen by participants as centering on women. That is, a mixed-gender bathroom would be uncomfortable for women for their discomfort with a potential male audience, and for men for the direct exposure it would provide them to the reality of female excretion.

Jane: [. . .] I feel like this society makes women feel like they have to uphold this more than men. For example, there are plenty of movies, there is one movie, I can't remember, but I saw a trailer and the two men changed lives, and one of the guys married, and his wife is very hot apparently. But she goes in the bathroom, and she keeps the door open, and she's taking a dump. And the other guy, he switched bodies, so he's not used to that scene, and he's completely turned off.

[all laughing]

Jane: There are a lot of movies like that. And even my boyfriend, he's like, I don't want to know. I don't want to know what you do in the bathroom. Complete denial.

Julie: Yes honey, I shit too. [laughing]

(GROUP 3)

Ursula: Probably females would be more opposed than males.

M: For the safety reasons we talked about?

Ursula: Yeah, and even the privacy.

Lesley: Privacy, yeah.

Ursula: Because we're all brought up to be these dainty things that don't make any, don't have any bodily functions.

[all laughing]

Ursula: So I just feel like females in general are more private about that, and they want to keep it amongst themselves.

Amy: Yeah, I chose C. Because those are the ones I feel most comfortable in when I use them anyway. But it's not practical for high volume. I think once you have a single user, gender segregation doesn't really matter, only one person goes in anyway.

(GROUP 2)

It was often argued that many people already felt a baseline level of discomfort at using multi-stall public bathrooms. For women, this discomfort was related to socialization about femininity as discussed above. Participants had a more difficult time explaining why men might feel uncomfortable about public bathrooms, except by gesturing towards the notion of a general cultural shame about human excretion. Some participants noted that men actually seemed more uncomfortable in public bathrooms than women did, but were generally unable to articulate why. One group was an exception here, suggesting that men's discomfort related to the necessity of sitting on a toilet.

Men are, I feel like they're more, in some ways they're more into the privacy of the bathroom. It's because of the sitting part. I know a lot of guys who cannot take a dump other than their own, they can't sit down. I heard about a guy who moved into one of the dorms, and he couldn't use the bathroom there, so he had to move back home.

[later]

My boyfriend, actually even when we're in Odegaard, there's multi-gender single room bathrooms in the engineering library, fourth floor. My boyfriend likes the fact that it's single user. So no matter where we are on campus, if he has to go, he's going to go there.

(Jane, GROUP 3)

Yet mixed-gender bathrooms, according to many participants, would bring the existing discomfort associated with public bathrooms to new levels. Here it becomes clear that gendered privacy is a (hetero)sexualized concept. The way participants spoke about the potential embarrassment involved in breaches of gendered privacy emphasized the scenario of being in the bathroom with an attractive member of the "opposite" gender.

Elliott: Well I don't think men and women are comfortable going to the bathroom in front of each other. I won't in front of my husband, it was different in the military because I had to, but I don't think most people are comfortable. Like, you've got to take a—

[all laughing]

Elliott: It's on tape. [laughing]

Paul: Two?

Elliott: Yeah. If you're defecating right next to somebody else and then you get out of the stall, and it's some cute guy, and you're like, oh my gosh—

Liz: That would be so terrible.

[all laughing]

Elliott: I think some people would be uncomfortable with that.

Paul: I think it would be uncomfortable, say it's really smelly and you walk out of the stall and there's some cute girl there, and then you're like, oh, that was my smell there.

Nick: If there was like, a group of girls outside.

Paul: Yeah.

Nick: Awkward.

(GROUP 4)

Women participants also talked about the potential discomfort of dealing with menstruation in a bathroom with men. For their part, some male participants agreed that they would rather avoid potential exposure to menstrual pads, tampons, or even conversations about menstruation.

Michele: Also another thing, a lot of public restrooms that are gender-segregated, you could buy your pad or your tampon. I don't think women will feel comfortable buying that when there's a guy standing right there.

Daniel: That is true. I mean—

Judy: Would you want to see a lady buying a tampon?

Jennifer: Guys would rather think that girls don't have periods, girls don't poop. I get that. I totally—

Daniel: No, no no. I don't care, I just don't want to see that stuff. Come on, hide that. It's just the fact that I don't want to deal with that kind of—

Judy: No, exactly. And I don't want guys around when I'm on my period.

(GROUP 7)

These anxieties about exposure to desirable potential sexual partners and to menstruation (culturally coded as "dirty") highlight the continuities between fears around privacy and fears around contamination and boundary-crossing. Mixed-gender bathrooms would dispel the "mystique" many participants associated with the "other" gender's bathroom and expose them to the bodily realities of excretion. That is, the "loss of privacy" participants discussed entails not just being seen and heard by the "other" gender in the bathroom, but being forced to see and hear the "other" gender in turn. As Elliott put it, "we're still a society where some people believe that women do not burp, fart, or poop. Which is totally untrue, but men don't want to see that" (Group 4). Thus, the apparently straightforward arguments made by participants about the lack of privacy mixed-gender bathrooms actually concealed more complex concerns.

Erosion of Gender Boundaries

Rather than argue about the safety or privacy issues involved in mixed-gender bathrooms, some participants expressed a sense of unease stemming from the simple unacceptability of men and women sharing the bathroom space. For the most part, these participants rooted their discomfort in religious beliefs about the naturalness of boundaries between men and women.

> I think that we should work on using this idea of mixing genders and kind of making it all equal in other aspects of society, like the labor force, before we talk about the bathroom, personally. And I'm a Christian, so I'm really conservative, and anything involving a guy on a personal, intimate level like that is unacceptable for me. So a man should not see a woman like that at all. [. . .] If I ever ran across that, I know subconsciously I would probably judge every person that went in there. Because I'd be like, you don't respect yourself, or what is going on, or oh my gosh, you people are weird. So yeah, I would not use one. I would hold it.
>
> (Susan, GROUP 8)

M: Ryan, you said you might use it if you had to, but you'd probably avoid it, right? So what were your reasons for that?

Ryan: I guess they're religious. I don't really feel that it's proper for men and women to be that way, but I couldn't really explain it logically. I guess there's no scientific reason.

M: Doesn't need to be scientific.

Ryan: Yeah, personally I would feel uncomfortable. Whatever the reason.

(GROUP 5)

These participants used terms like "improper," "disrespectful," and "uncomfortable" to describe mixed-gender bathrooms. Here, religious discourses provided ready arguments against the blurring of gender boundaries that mixed-gender bathrooms would apparently entail, insofar as a binary gender system is understood as natural and right in the context of the belief system in question. These arguments, unlike those around more mundane concerns, were challenged much less readily by other participants. This may have been out of a belief that religious claims could or should not be critiqued in the same way as secular ones, stemming as they seem to from deep personal convictions rather than from "rational" argumentation. Another possibility is that religious claims about the naturalness of gender separation resonated with other participants.

Summary

Participants presented a variety of arguments against mixed-gender bathrooms, yet many of them appeared in very similar forms across the focus groups. Arguments about the safety of children and women were the first claims many raised, though these were sometimes discussed and found by other participants to be unjustified concerns. Notions of "privacy" arose repeatedly, and many participants appeared to share concerns about the loss of privacy that mixed-gender bathrooms might entail. Arguments around loss of privacy shaded into concerns that the unique cultures of the women's and men's rooms—but especially the former—would be jeopardized by integrating the two. Finally, some participants argued that mixed-gender bathrooms represented an unnatural or improper mixing of the genders that was unacceptable to them based on their religious beliefs. . . .

Notes

1. I define a "public bathroom" as any toilet facility that is not located in a private dwelling. This is a broad definition that necessarily encompasses a great deal of variation in design and accessibility. Indeed, "public bathroom" is something of a misleading term, a recognition which has led the British Toilet Association to coin the phrase "away from home" toilets (Greed 2010:119). This phrasing more accurately describes the phenomenon in question, but as it is not commonly used in the United States, I will continue to use the familiar construction.

2. Activists have also fought parallel battles for the rights of transgender people to use the gendered bathrooms appropriate to their gender identity rather than their birth-assigned gender. These challenges will not be discussed in detail here, but see Mottet (2003).

3. It is perhaps worth noting that insofar as any actual material benefits of gender segregation do exist, it is likely that they accrue to men, who gain privileged access to a location for informal networking in the workplace (Case 2010:224).

Merritt Kopas is a multimedia artist and game designer interested in play as a utopian project. Merritt writes and speaks frequently about the intersections between play, bodies, sex, and violence, striving to push conversations about media and marginalized populations beyond the question of representational inclusion.

EXPLORING THE ISSUE

Should Public Restrooms Be Gender-Neutral?

Critical Thinking and Reflection

1. Have you ever experienced a co-ed bathroom experience? What was your experience like?
2. Is there another solution you can think of beyond creating mixed gender restrooms or requiring the building of single-sex restrooms that would enable people of all genders to feel safe and comfortable in these spaces?
3. Whose safety and comfort takes precedence here? As a minority group, there are fewer transgender people. Do the needs of the many outweigh the needs of the few? Or should the majority respond to this minority status by being allies and make changes as possible?

Is There Common Ground?

In discussing the restroom issue, there are a number of different possibilities: single-use, unisex restrooms, gender neutral larger restrooms, or keeping restrooms the way they are and people just need to determine for themselves which restroom seems the safest. There are pros and cons to each option—but the deciding factor seems to relate to weighing comfort against safety. Transgender people may feel uncomfortable and unsafe—and cisgender people may feel uncomfortable and unsafe. That is the common ground for stating the problem.

In many cases, situations are problematic due to financial reasons. No business will want to incur the cost of altering or creating new restrooms—so a common ground would be for there to be subsidies or grants available for businesses to apply to fund these changes. If their business would not be negatively affected by this kind of construction, perhaps they would be more likely to want to do it. The added bonus would be the positive regard many people would have for

these businesses for being more inclusive in how they treat their customers.

Additional Resources

Beemyna, G. (2012). The experiences and needs of transgender community college students. *Community College Journal of Research and Practice*, 36(7), 504–510.

Brown, T. (2014). The dangers of overbroad transgender legislation, case law, and policy in education: California's AB 1266 dismisses concerns about student safety and privacy. *Brigham Young University Education and Law Journal*, 2014(2), Article 6.

Transgender Law Center (2005). Peeing in peace: A resource guide for transgender activists and their allies. http://translaw.wpengine.com/wp-content /uploads/2012/05/94930982-PIP-Resource-Guide.pdf.

Internet References . . .

Focus on the Family: Transgenderism

http://www.focusonthefamily.com/socialissues
/social-issues/transgenderism.aspx

Out for Health

http://www.outforhealth.org/

Transparenthood: Experiences Raising a Transgender Child

http://transparenthood.net/